120
DISEASES

120 DISEASES

THE ESSENTIAL GUIDE TO MORE THAN 120 MEDICAL CONDITIONS, SYNDROMES AND DISEASES

amber
BOOKS

Printed and bound in Thailand
Produced by
Amber Books Ltd
74–77 White Lion Street
London
N1 9PF
www.amberbooks.co.uk

Project Editor: James Bennett
General Editor: Jane De Burgh

The pictures contained in this book were originally sourced for the part-work *Inside the
Human Body* produced by Bright Star Publishing plc. For picture credit information
please contact Amber Books at the above address.

Contents

Introduction

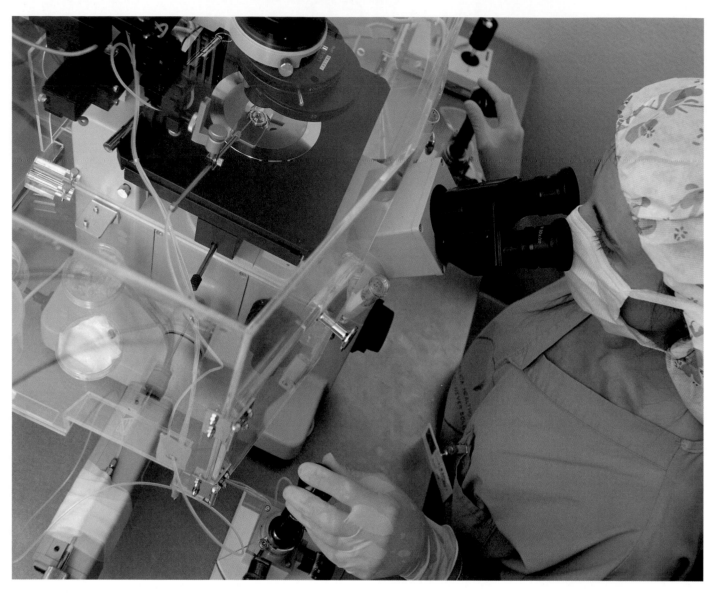

Why do we need another medical encyclopedia? And what does this one offer that others do not? The fact is that there is such an overwhelming array of resources available to us today that sometimes it is difficult to separate out the useful information from the rest. But, when it comes to our health, the most important factor for us as individuals, and for our families, is that the information we receive is comprehensive and reliable, and that we feel reassured by the messages it conveys. Written by experts and presented in an easy-to-read format, with a range of helpful colour illustrations, *The Family Medical Encyclopedia* is a rich source of this information.

CHANGING TIMES
Over the last decade, we have witnessed a growing fascination with the diseases and disorders that cause ill-health, as well as the tests used to identify them and the treatments prescribed to alleviate them. This 'need to know' has been the catalyst for the transition from meek acceptance of a diagnosis to a more questioning attitude. People are demanding more information – they are no longer content to accept what they don't understand and, quite rightly, are asking for the right to be involved in choices about their health care.

Probably as a result of this, there has been a corresponding increase in the provision of information by health services and a growing enthusiasm on all sides to establish productive partnerships between medical professionals and their patients. This change in the cultural climate, coupled with the birth of the internet, has triggered a huge increase in the resources available to the public – what has been termed an 'information explosion'. There are literally thousands of magazines, health books and encyclopedias, CD Roms and websites, providing facts about every conceivable medical condition. In addition, documentaries about medical matters are a regular feature of our evening television viewing. Of course, this vast choice can be daunting, and it's important that we have a sense that we

Modern scientific analysis can discover the cause of many health problems, but early diagnosis and treatment is often essential.

can rely on the information that's provided – that it's up-to-date and accurate, and that it has been provided by professionals with appropriate knowledge and experience.

TAKING CONTROL
On an individual level, this climate of change is extremely beneficial – research clearly shows that people who communicate effectively with their health providers deal with their illness more positively than those who have limited knowledge and involvement.

Additionally, learning about health issues, and being aware of the signs that may indicate the onset of disease, can in the long run mean an earlier diagnosis and a better prognosis. That's not to say that we should become obsessed with our health so that every twinge sends us running to the bookshelf or computer. Rather we should strike a balance between a constructive awareness of the importance of certain symptoms, and a destructive anxiety about our health.

Of course, in a world in which lifestyle factors play such a great role in ill health, it's important to remember that where we have the power to prevent disease, we should make a huge effort to do so. Many serious chronic conditions, such as heart disease, cancer and diabetes, have been shown to be caused largely by factors that are under our control. So, not smoking, drinking alcohol in moderation, eating a balanced and nutritious diet and getting plenty of exercise are all steps that we can take to reduce our risk of

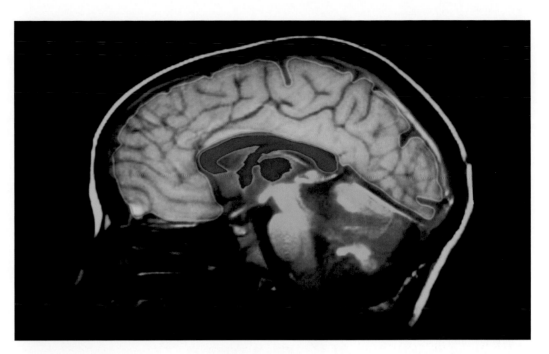

CAT scans (Computed Axial Tomography) can provide a detailed three-dimensional picture of the inner human body, helping doctors to diagnose problems.

those diseases. Genetic factors also play a role in some illnesses, so it is important to know your family history. For example, are there any particular conditions that seem to 'run in the family', and if so, do we have any added risks in terms of our lifestyle that would add to that genetic risk?

Knowing how to prevent illness, then, is the key to good health. This book addresses the important issue of prevention by

providing, wherever relevant, an information box on risk factors for each condition.

The Family Medical Encyclopedia is simple to navigate and the information is laid out in a clear and attractive format. Medical conditions are arranged under body systems, for example 'The Bones, Joints and Tendons' or 'Infectious Diseases'. So, whether you are looking for information about the causes

An MRI (Magnetic Resonance Imaging) scan can penetrate areas surrounded by bone, enabling doctors to find tumours (benign or malignant growths) in the brain.

of a particular disease, its symptoms, or how it is diagnosed and treated, you are certain find the relevant information here.

JANE DE BURGH, GENERAL EDITOR

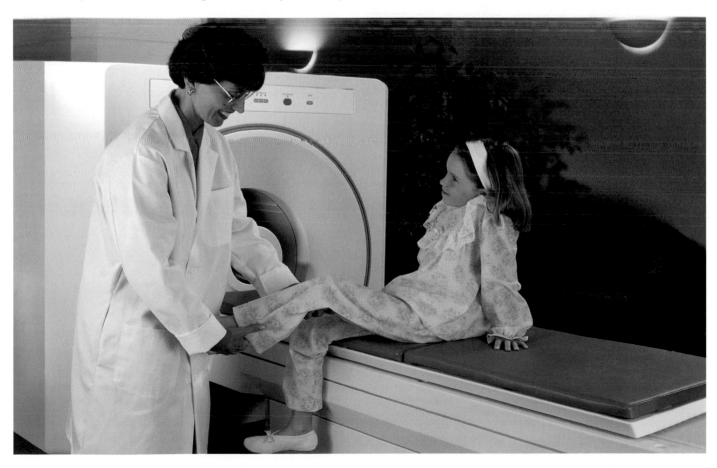

Common cold

Symptoms

The common cold is, as the name suggests, the most common disease caused by infection in the developed world. It is caused by a group of viruses called rhinoviruses, which produce different upper respiratory tract syndromes. Grouped together, these symptoms are known as the common cold, or coryza.

There is an incubation period of one to four days. Symptoms often start in a localized area, for example, the pharynx, but rapidly progress in the following 48 hours when the diagnosis is obvious. The symptoms are due to inflammation and swelling of the nasal mucosa (lining membrane). The symptoms last only for two to four days unless complications develop, and include:
■ Watery nasal discharge
■ Sneezing

■ Blocked nasal passages
■ Congested sinuses causing facial pain
■ Watering eyes
■ Sore throat, dry tickly cough
■ Fever – uncommon in children and rare in adults
■ Purulent nasal secretion (later stage of the disease)
■ Lack of energy.

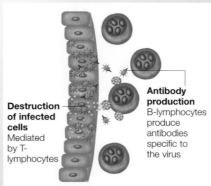

The common cold causes the familiar symptoms of sneezing and runny nose. Both are manifestations of the body's immune response to the virus.

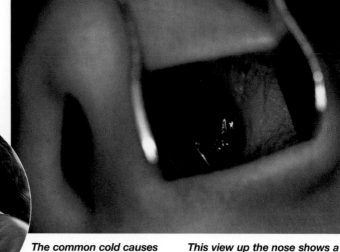

This view up the nose shows a case of chronic rhinitis. This is an inflammation of the nasal lining, and the common cold is often the cause.

Diagnosis

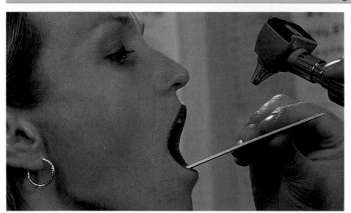

A diagnosis will be made clinically. Colds usually involve infection in the upper respiratory tract, for example, of the nose, eyes (nasolacrimal duct), pharynx and chest, leading to inflamed fauces (the opening from the mouth to the pharynx), sore and painful cough (tracheitis) or bronchitis.

A symptom of the common cold is inflammation of the fauces at the back of the throat. This can be confirmed by visualization using a light source.

Laboratory investigations are not necessary to confirm the diagnosis, but it is known that the nasal secretions will contain rhinoviruses of different types.

Most colds are uncomplicated and self-limiting, resolving spontaneously. However, some cases are complicated by secondary bacterial infections, leading to conditions such as sinusitis, otitis media (middle ear infection) and infections of the lower respiratory tract. In these circumstances, a GP may take a swab sample for analysis.

How the body fights a cold infection

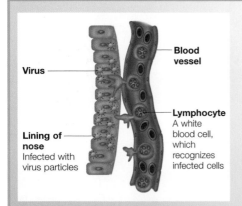

Virus

Blood vessel

Lymphocyte A white blood cell, which recognizes infected cells

Lining of nose Infected with virus particles

The virus is spread as droplets, and enters the lining of the throat and nose, where it replicates. White blood cells are carried by blood vessels, causing swelling and secretion of fluid (a runny nose).

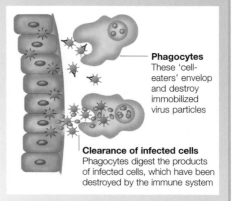

Destruction of infected cells Mediated by T-lymphocytes

Antibody production B-lymphocytes produce antibodies specific to the virus

The immune system has two strategies for dealing with an infection. Antibodies are produced to neutralize the virus particles. Other types of white cell recognize and destroy infected cells.

Phagocytes These 'cell-eaters' envelop and destroy immobilized virus particles

Clearance of infected cells Phagocytes digest the products of infected cells, which have been destroyed by the immune system

Phagocytes, another type of white blood cell, are able to engulf and destroy both virus bound to antibodies and infected cells and their products. The symptoms of the cold soon die down.

Causes

Coryza and febrile colds (colds with fever) may be caused by one of a large group of viruses, such as:
■ Rhinovirus
■ Adenovirus
■ Coronavirus
■ Para-influenza
■ Echovirus
■ Respiratory syncytial virus
■ Coxsackie A
■ Influenza A and B.

The main route of infection is by droplets from the nose and throat, but it may also be spread by contact with skin; for example, fingers infected with nasal secretions coming into contact with the mouth or nose. Thus, coughs and sneezes and direct contact with an infected person will easily transmit the infection.

Immunity following a cold is very short-lived and, because the viruses do not normally enter the bloodstream, there is no common antigen against which the body can build up an immune response.

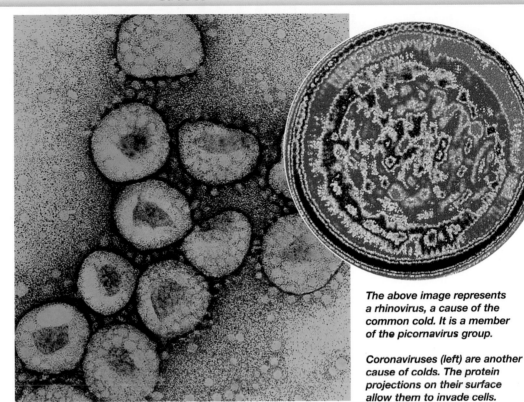

The above image represents a rhinovirus, a cause of the common cold. It is a member of the picornavirus group.

Coronaviruses (left) are another cause of colds. The protein projections on their surface allow them to invade cells.

Prevention

It has been claimed that high-dose vitamin C (ascorbic acid) is effective in preventing colds. However there is no scientific evidence to support this.

Colds are so common that it is difficult to avoid infection. Alternative or complementary medicine approaches to preventing infection exist, but are not validated. High, regular doses of ascorbic acid (vitamin C) used to be recommended, but there is no definitive scientific evidence to confirm that this prevents colds.

The frequency of colds declines with age, and so they are much more frequent in infants and children. There have been various anti-cold vaccines available, but it is not yet possible to immunize or protect people from the common cold.

Prognosis

In children, recurrent colds increase the likelihood of otitis media (middle ear infection). Here, the eardrum has perforated, causing a discharge.

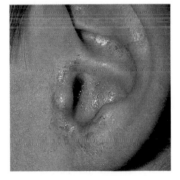

The common cold is a mild illness causing discomfort for two to six days. Only if secondary infection occurs is the illness likely to last longer. The symptoms, including sore throat, coughing and sore chest, usually resolve spontaneously.

Children who suffer six or more infections annually are more likely to suffer secondary infections, such as a middle ear infection (otitis media).

Colds generally resolve with no specific therapy. Antibiotics are only suitable for secondary infection and should not be prescribed prophylactically (as a preventative measure).

Incidence

Coryza is the commonest form of illness in the developed world, and because the cold accounts for a large number of working days lost on account of illness, the social and economic consequences are high.

In an average lifetime of 75 years, a person suffers from more than 200 bouts of common cold, each lasting two to six days. Yet a considerable amount of research worldwide has failed to provide a satisfactory means of preventing the illness or minimizing the severity or prevalence of the illness.

Treatment

Treatment is solely aimed at easing the symptoms. There is no specific antibiotic that works against the common cold virus. General measures include analgesics (such as aspirin), steam inhalation for a blocked nose and hot drinks to soothe a cough. Medicines such as linctuses are of little value. Patients should refrain from smoking and avoid irritating fumes.

No specific therapy or immunization is presently available. Although recent research is believed to have produced a drug likely to shorten or limit the illness, no conclusive data is available.

Drugs with some anti-viral effect used to be prescribed, but they are expensive and because a cold usually only lasted up to four days this practice was discontinued.

Currently, the only methods useful in treatment of the common cold are based on alleviating symptoms. Throat lozenges, for example, are useful in soothing sore throats.

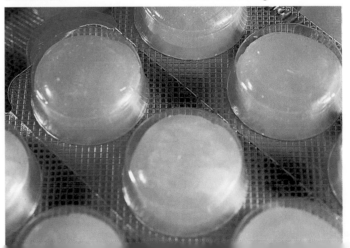

Influenza

Symptoms

Influenza (more commonly known as flu) is a highly contagious viral infection that affects the respiratory system. While some of its symptoms are similar to those of the common cold, it is easily distinguished.

A cold is characterized by a running rose, sore throat and a mild feverish illness with a slow, ill-defined onset. It will usually last from three to five days.

Influenza, on the other hand, has a dramatic and sudden onset. After an incubation period of one to four days, the patient will often complain of headache, backache, myalgia (painful muscles) and shivering. There may also be a stuffy nose, tracheitis (dry throat), husky voice, dry cough, loss of appetite, nausea and insomnia.

Different outbreaks or epidemics are often characterized by different groups of symptoms. For example, apart from the upper respiratory symptoms, there may be a predominance of intestinal symptoms, including abdominal pain, diarrhoea and vomiting (gastric influenza).

MAIN SIGNS
■ Feverish high temperature
■ Loss of appetite
■ Inflamed throat
■ General aches and pains
■ Severe malaise and prostration.

The acute symptoms will usually persist for three to four days. The longer the illness lasts for, the longer the recovery is likely to take.

This electron micrograph shows a group of influenza type A viruses. Both rounded and elongated shaped viruses are visible. Tiny spikes on the coat of the virus are evident – they bind to host cells when the virus invades the body.

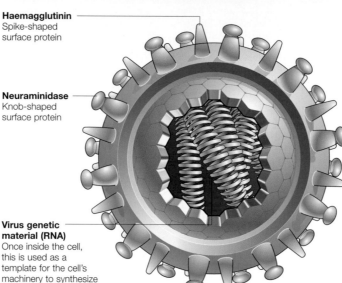

Haemagglutinin
Spike-shaped surface protein

Neuraminidase
Knob-shaped surface protein

Virus genetic material (RNA)
Once inside the cell, this is used as a template for the cell's machinery to synthesize new virus particles

Complications

These are usually associated with secondary bacterial infections.
■ Hyperpyrexia (high fever) with delirium, convulsions and coma – especially in children and the elderly
■ Acute bronchitis – especially in the elderly
■ Neurological changes (Reyes' disease in children)
■ Pneumonia, especially in those with primary chest or cardiac disease. Secondary pneumonia due to *Staphylococcus pyogenes* is very serious
■ Encephalitis (inflammation of the brain)
■ Myocarditis (inflammation of the heart)
■ Exacerbation of diabetes
■ Post-influenzal depression
■ Sudden death especially in the frail elderly

The influenza virus possesses two types of protein spike on its surface, called haemagglutinin and neuraminidase, which allow the virus to enter cells. They are also highly antigenic, triggering the formation of defensive antibodies.

Antigenic shift & drift

It is the unusual structure of the influenza virus that enables it to cause disease and spread within a population.

Two types of protein spike are present on the viral surface. Haemagglutinin allows the virus to bind to epithelial (surface) cells, and is the major structure to which antibodies are formed. Neuraminidase allows viruses to break this bond and spread to other cells. It also elicits antibody formation.

Repeated infections by influenza are due to antigenic shift and antigenic drift. In antigenic drift, small spontaneous mutations in the genes' coding for the surface proteins cause existing antibodies to be less effective. This explains how individuals can be repeatedly susceptible to infection.

Antigenic shift is a far more radical change in protein structure, caused by the exchange of genetic material between different viruses. Existing antibodies to the surface proteins may prove ineffective, and a pandemic (a worldwide epidemic) may result, with high numbers of associated fatalities.

Antigenic drift
Minor genetic changes to viral genes have caused small changes in the structure of viral proteins. This will diminish the effectiveness of any antibodies raised to a previous infection.

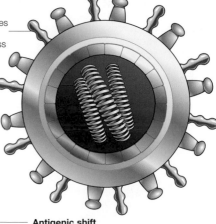

Antigenic shift
Major genetic rearrangements have caused a major change in structure, against which existing antibodies may be ineffective.

Incidence & prevention

Large populations tend to develop immunity over time, but the tendency for influenza type A or B to mutate produces new outbreaks every year – usually during the winter months. The prevalence of a strain tends to peak after two to three years following the discovery of new strains.

There are many different strains of these viruses. Through research, a national epidemic

Influenza vaccines contain dead influenza viruses. When injected, the vaccine stimulates the body's immune system to produce antibodies that protect against future infection.

reference laboratory is able to identify the different strains prevalent at any particular time. Thus, the prediction of a future flu epidemic becomes possible. However, vaccination may only give partial immunity to the current virus.

Influenza vaccines are usually prepared from the two most prevalent epidemic strains of influenza type A, plus the current strain of influenza B each year.

Because of the risk of secondary bacterial infection, annual vaccination in October is recommended for the following

groups of people:
■ Those with chronic heart or chest disease
■ Individuals on immunosuppressive therapy
■ Patients over 65 years of age
■ Persons living in closed communities (retirement homes, residential schools)
■ Diabetics
■ Those with kidney disease.

This graph shows influenza deaths in England and Wales during four epidemics. The 1969–70 peak is the Hong Kong flu outbreak, caused by a shift in the haemagglutinin (H) protein.

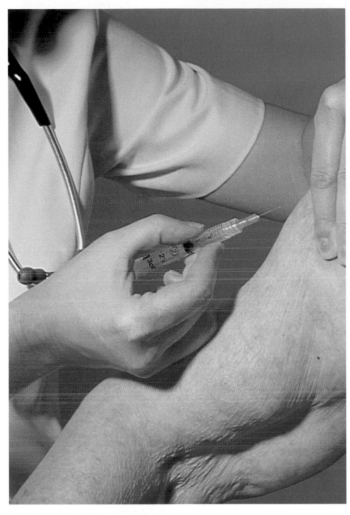

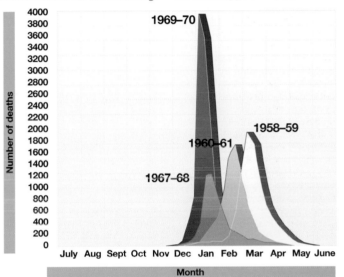

Diagnosis & prognosis

A clinical diagnosis taking account of the patient's history and presentation is usually sufficient.

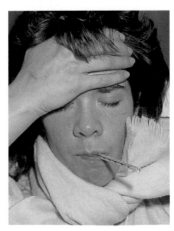

Influenza may be sporadic or may appear in epidemics, so a series of patients with similar symptoms will suggest an influenza outbreak.

It is possible to test the blood serum of affected individuals to identify the virus type responsible, but this is only necessary when a full-blown epidemic occurs.

The prognosis is usually excellent. Children and the elderly require special supervision, however, especially if there are complications due to secondary infection.

The fever symptoms of flu can be self-diagnosed, as fever is characterized by a rise in oral temperature above 37 °C.

Causes & treatment

CAUSES
There are three types of influenza virus – A, B and C. These viruses undergo frequent antigenic changes from year to year, and different strains of virus may occur. Epidemics become known by the area in which the current strain is identified, such as Beijing, Hong Kong or Russian flu.

It is believed that infection is spread by droplet infection from one person to another by coughing, sneezing or direct skin contact with a person incubating the influenza virus.

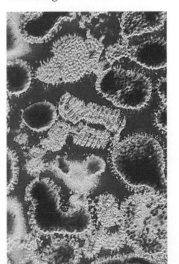

TREATMENT
There is no specific treatment, but the following steps to combat the infection are recommended:
■ Bed rest
■ Adequate fluid intake
■ Paracetamol or aspirin in regular doses to control the pyrexia (fever).

Antibiotics have no place in the treatment of influenza, but they are used to treat secondary infections caused by organisms such as *Haemophilus influenzae* or *Streptococcus pneumoniae* – both are sensitive to certain antibiotics.

There are some antiviral drugs that may be useful, such as amantidine, but these are only prescribed for a very vulnerable or sick patient. Very rarely, full intensive care is necessary in severely affected patients during an epidemic.

The Asian flu virus shows specific characteristics, which are also present in its various virulent strains, such as Beijing or Hong Kong flu.

Glandular fever

Symptoms

Glandular fever, or infectious mononucleosis (IM), is a viral illness, predominantly affecting young adults. It is caused by an infection of B-lymphocytes – the white blood cells which manufacture antibodies – by the Epstein-Barr virus (EBV).

The EBV is carried in saliva and transmitted by close contact. It is most common in early adulthood, particularly in 'closed' environments where there are plenty of opportunities for the virus to be transmitted. EBV is a member of the herpes group of viruses.

Patients with glandular fever may have a range of symptoms, which vary in severity. Generalized symptoms, similar to an influenza infection, include malaise (a feeling of being generally unwell), an extremely sore throat and fever.

SWOLLEN GLANDS
The sufferer may also show cervical adenopathy (enlarged neck glands) and generalized adenopathy (enlarged lymph nodes, particularly in the armpits and groin). The spleen may also become enlarged to such an extent that, in 50 per cent of patients, it can be felt on physical examination. In 20 per cent of cases, periorbital oedema (swelling around the eyes) is apparent. There is often a noticeable 'puffiness' of the face.

Enlarged lymph glands, especially in the neck, are a common feature of glandular fever.

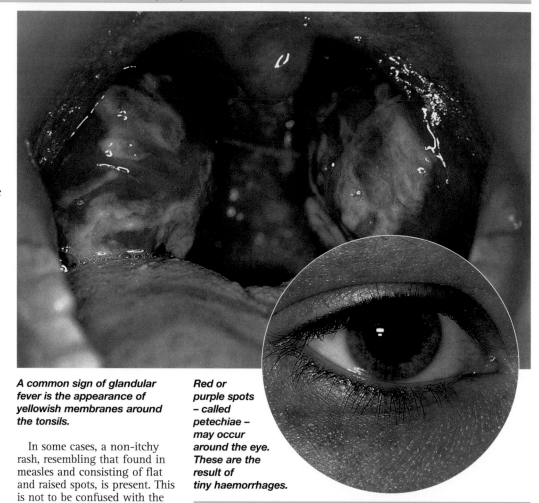

A common sign of glandular fever is the appearance of yellowish membranes around the tonsils.

In some cases, a non-itchy rash, resembling that found in measles and consisting of flat and raised spots, is present. This is not to be confused with the rash induced in glandular fever patients by ampicillin and amoxycillin antibiotics. These antibiotics are sometimes administered to treat the initial symptom of a severe sore throat prior to the patient being diagnosed with glandular fever.

Red or purple spots – called petechiae – may occur around the eye. These are the result of tiny haemorrhages.

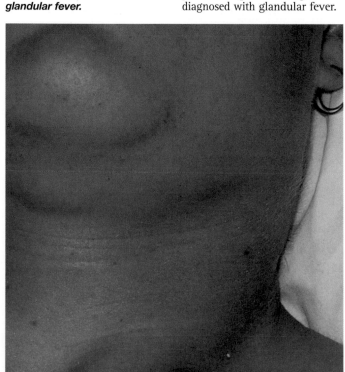

Oral symptoms

A number of signs, indicative of infection with EBV, occur in the mouth. These include:
■ Exudates (membranes) form on the tonsils. These are yellowish-white in colour. If this symptom is present, it is described as the anginose type of glandular fever and can be mistaken for diphtheria.
■ Halitosis (bad breath) – breath smelling sickly sweet and of decay – is common.
■ Palatal petechiae (tiny haemorrhages) appear on the palate and the skin.
■ Vesicular (blister-like) lesions may also be seen on the palate.
■ On examination, the throat may appear very red and sore. One in four patients with glandular fever has a secondary bacterial infection, commonly with ß-haemolytic streptococcus, a group of bacteria responsible for a number of infections.
■ Oedema (swelling) of the fauces – the columns of tissue at the back of the mouth, in front of the tonsils – appears gradually but it may become severe. The mucosa (lining membrane) of the nose, mouth and pharynx may also become swollen, making swallowing very uncomfortable.

Petechiae (tiny haem-orrhages) are seen on the hard palate at the top of the mouth.

Diagnosis

The disease usually affects the young but may rarely occur in patients up to about 70 years of age. Diagnosis depends on:
■ The clinical symptoms
■ Blood investigations – on studying a blood film, there will be an unusually large number of a class of white blood cells, called monocytes. Another class of white blood cell, known as lymphocytes, will also appear abnormal
■ Tests can be conducted to determine whether liver function is abnormal
■ Paul-Bunnell test – a test to detect antibodies to the virus; it is often not positive until the second week of the illness
■ Rapid sheep-cell antibody test
■ Blood tests to reveal the Epstein-Barr virus (EBV) may be necessary in very young patients in whom the Paul-Bunnell test does not appear positive

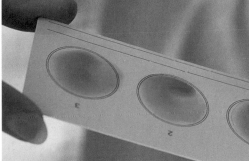

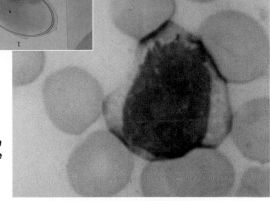

A technician tests a patient's blood sample for the presence of antibodies to the Epstein-Barr virus. Infection produces specific antibodies to the virus, which cause a sample of sheep's red blood cells to clump in a characteristic manner.

Infection can also be detected by studying a blood film – a blood sample is smeared across a microscope slide and stained with specific dyes. Here, an unusual form of a type of white blood cell – called a mononuclear cell – can be seen.

Complications

■ Myocarditis – inflammation of the heart muscle
■ Rupture of the spleen – rare, and usually associated with mild trauma such as coughing; in such cases, surgical intervention would be required
■ Jaundice – mild jaundice is present in about 15 per cent of patients
■ Meningitis – this rarely occurs, but it is benign
■ Pneumonitis – a lung infection

■ Ampicillin and amoxycillin rashes occur commonly when glandular fever patients are treated with these antibiotics, after about 10 days
■ Post-viral fatigue syndrome may follow EBV infection and persist for a number of months
■ Respiratory obstruction due to severe swelling of the throat.

Antibiotic treatment of glandular fever patients often results in a characteristic rash.

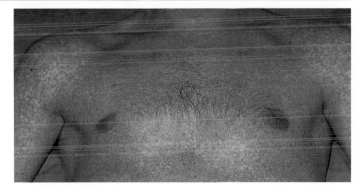

Incidence

The Epstein-Barr virus is a DNA-carrying herpes virus and as such produces latent and active infections. Infection is common in young children and is usually mild or without symptoms, but it normally causes clinical symptoms in the 15–20 age group.

Antibody studies show that about 50 per cent of pre-teens have been exposed to EBV, whilst more than 75 per cent of over 25s have antibodies. By middle age, almost all adults have been infected. Infection tends to occur earlier in developing countries where hygiene is poor.

This coloured electron micrograph shows Epstein-Barr viruses, the agents responsible for glandular fever.

Means of Infection

Glandular fever is caused by the Epstein-Barr virus. The virus enters the body via the epithelial (surface) cells, near the salivary glands, and infection spreads through oral secretions that contain the virus.

The infection is transmitted by close oral contact, such as kissing or sharing utensils, and is sometimes referred to as the 'kissing disease'.

The time from infection to onset of symptoms is approximately seven weeks, by which time large numbers of lymphocyte cells (a type of white blood cell) can be detected in the blood.

Outbreaks may occur in 'closed' communities such as residential schools and universities. Cases are usually isolated and infrequent.

Treatment

Treatment is generally aimed at relieving the symptoms, as there is no anti-viral medication. Antibiotics have no effect on viral infections, such as EBV, and ampicillin-related antibiotics should not be prescribed on account of the risk of producing a severe rash.

Anti-inflammatory drugs or steroids may be prescribed if there is a respiratory obstruction due to swelling at the back of the throat, or if there are any auto-immune manifestations, when the body attacks its own tissue.

Older children and adults can gargle soluble aspirin to relieve a sore throat, and stronger analgesics (painkillers) may be prescribed in severe cases. A small number of patients suffer from post-infectious fatigue and can take up to six months to recover fully.

Chickenpox

Causes

Chickenpox is an illness caused by the varicella-zoster virus. This virus causes two distinct diseases – chickenpox (varicella) and shingles (herpes zoster). It is spread by droplet infection and is considered infectious until all the scabs drop off the skin.

Shingles occurs more often in adult life and is caused by reactivation of the chickenpox virus that has remained dormant in the nerve cells of the spinal cord. It is believed that the dormant viruses may be reactivated by the decrease in immunity in the elderly.

In adults, chickenpox may reach a severe stage. Associated infections (such as pneumonia) may require intensive treatment.

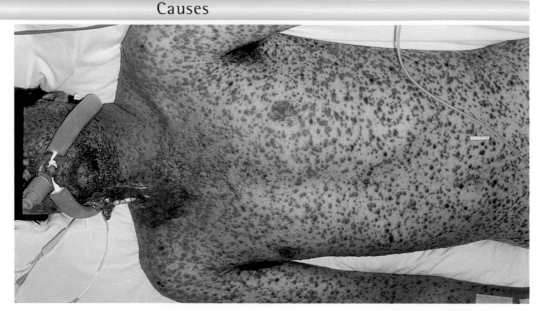

Symptoms

In children, the first sign of infection with chickenpox is often the appearance of a rash. There may be no symptoms of malaise (feeling unwell).

In adults, the illness is often more severe and there are often symptoms during the prodromal period, the time between infection and the appearance of the rash. These symptoms may include fever, malaise, headache and, occasionally, a transient erythematous (blotchy) rash.

The true rash, which is the same in adults and children with chickenpox, is a pink/red rash of small raised spots followed by vesicles (small blisters). The spots are elliptical in shape and erupt in crops at irregular intervals over several days. The spots follow a cycle: pink spot – vesicle – pustule – scab. The scabs ultimately fall off, leaving the skin clear. Fully developed chickenpox will show a combination of all the different stages of the lesion.

The distribution of the rash is typically centripetal (towards the centre of the body) on the trunk, face, scalp and upper limbs. In severe attacks, the spots cover the entire body, although the most dense area of the rash will show centripetal distribution. Blisters also occur on the mucous membranes in the mouth, throat, nose and conjunctivae of the eyes. These may lead to symptoms such as a sore throat, coughing and runny eyes, all of which subside as the lesions heal.

Chickenpox remains infectious until the scabs dry, separate from the skin and drop off.

Despite the rash, chickenpox in childhood is rarely a cause for concern. Fever tends to be mild and recovery is uncomplicated.

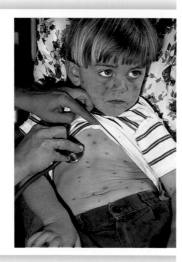

Diagnosis and incidence

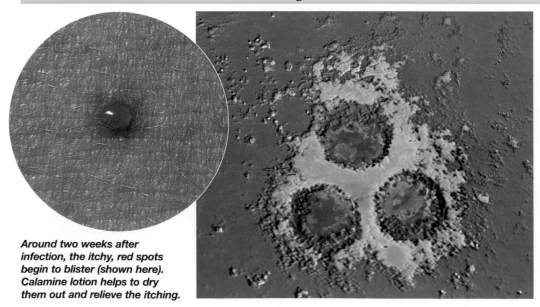

Around two weeks after infection, the itchy, red spots begin to blister (shown here). Calamine lotion helps to dry them out and relieve the itching.

Diagnosis is usually based on clinical symptoms with the appearance of the typical rash. In cases that prove difficult to diagnose, electron microscopy, viral culture and blood tests may be required.

Most children suffer the disease at an early age, and up to 90 per cent of people will have the disease at one stage of their life. It is, however, better to develop chickenpox when young in order to develop resistance to the virus, thus avoiding the threat of a more severe bout of chickenpox in adulthood.

Viruses are too small to be seen with a light microscope, but this electron micrograph enables three varicella-zoster virus particles to be clearly visualized.

Treatment and recovery

There is no specific treatment. Antipruritics (anti-itch remedies), such as calamine lotion or talcum powder, relieve itching and may be all that is required. Antibiotic creams or tablets may be necessary to treat secondary skin infections.

If the disease is severe, as in immunocompromised patients, the antiviral drug aciclovir may be given orally or by injection.

Preventative measures, such as administering varicella-zoster immunoglobulin (antibodies to the virus derived from another patient) may modify or prevent the disease from developing if given within 48 hours of contact with an infected patient. Aciclovir may be used prophylactically (as a preventative measure) for immunocompromised patients exposed to the disease.

Intense skin irritation does occur and it is important to discourage scratching the lesions, as this may leave unsightly scarring. Scratching may also lead to secondary skin infections, often caused by *Streptococcus pyogenes* or *Staphylococcus aureus*.

Recovery is usually complete 14–21 days after the onset of symptoms. Children are advised to stay away from school for two weeks.

Occasionally, lesions can appear on the conjunctiva (surface of the eye). Such ulcers can be treated by a suitable topical cream.

Blisters inside the mouth often cause discomfort for chickenpox sufferers. However, healing will occur without scarring.

Complications

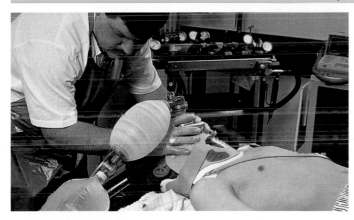

Complications, although rare in children, are more likely in adults and may include any of the following:
◼ Encephalitis (inflammation of the brain)
◼ Secondary skin infections are the commonest complication in children

In severe cases of chickenpox, pneumonitis infection can accompany the rash, leading to respiratory disease. The patient will then require hospitalization and assisted ventilation.

◼ Pneumonia: the development of tachypnoea (rapid breathing) may be an indication of this lung condition. Pneumonia produces opaque nodules in the lungs (characterized by very small nodules or lesions) that calcify when healing, and are apparent on a chest X-ray
◼ Haemorrhagic chickenpox (when the vesicles bleed)
◼ Encephalitis, pneumonia and haemorrhagic complications usually only occur in older or immunocompromised patients.

Prognosis and prevention

As a rule, children make a complete recovery. However, the disease in adults is often a much more severe illness. The development of complications, such as pneumonia, encephalitis, and the haemorrhagic form of the disease, lead to a much more toxic and severe illness, but again full recovery is the norm.

Chickenpox may be life-threatening in the immuno-compromised patient, so other measures are essential. Immunoglobulin and aciclovir help the immunocompromised patient recover from the disease. Recurrent attacks of chickenpox are extremely rare.

Avoiding contact with an infected patient should be sufficient to prevent chickenpox, but it is now considered better to allow children to catch the illness while young, as it is much milder in early life. 'Chickenpox parties' were fashionable at one stage. As soon as one child developed the illness, mothers were encouraged to bring their children into contact with that child to allow them to catch the illness and thus develop lifelong immunity.

A live vaccine has been developed, and this may become useful in treating leukaemia patients and those with weak immune systems, in whom chickenpox could be life-threatening.

This child's rash has reached an advanced stage. The blisters have formed scabs, which will separate from the skin. This normally occurs about 12 days after the appearance of the rash.

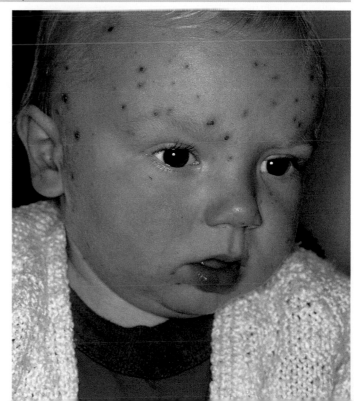

Measles

Causes

Measles is a highly contagious viral disease which tends to occur in epidemics. Incidences have fallen dramatically in countries with immunization programmes, but the condition continues to cause many deaths in developing countries among children aged one to five.

VIRAL CAUSE
In order to survive, the measles virus has become a highly infectious agent. It has no other host besides the human body, cannot survive for long outside its host, and cannot infect those who are immunized or have previously suffered a bout of the disease.

Despite this, the virus continues to thrive due to its ability to spread fast (infecting 90 per cent of those coming into contact with it) and spread remotely through minute air droplets – one sneeze on an aeroplane is enough to infect everyone on board.

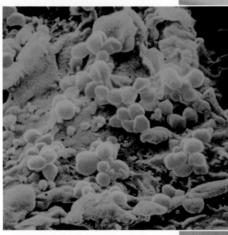

The measles virus (shown in blue) buds off infected cells in the human body. Unable to exist for long outside its host, it spreads quickly in air droplets.

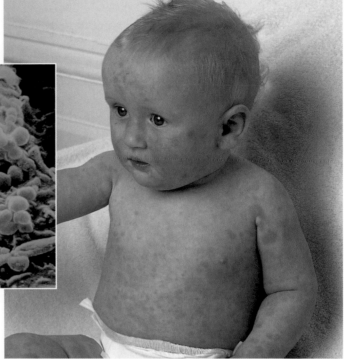

Babies and young children are most at risk of catching measles. Many adults will have had measles as children and developed a lifelong immunity.

Symptoms

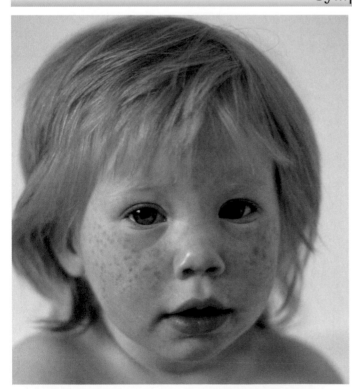

The symptoms of measles usually develop 8–14 days after initial infection.

There are two distinct phases:
■ The infectious pre-eruptive catarrhal stage
■ The non-infectious, exanthematous (rash) stage.

CATARRHAL STAGE
This lasts 1–2 days and is characterized by a cough, runny nose, conjunctivitis and a high fever. Small red spots with white centres known as Koplik's spots develop in the mucous membranes of the mouth.

This young child is exhibiting a typical 3rd-day rash. Beginning on the head and face, the distinctive rash will proceed to spread down the entire body.

EXANTHEMATOUS STAGE.
A rash appears 3–5 days after the onset of symptoms, starting on the head and neck, then spreading down the whole body.

The rash is initially red and flat, occurring in discrete spots. After a week or so these coalesce into larger areas which fade to a brownish colour before finally disappearing completely.

The fever dies down soon after the rash appears and within 4–5 days recovery is generally well established.

COMMON COMPLICATIONS
Common complications of measles include:
■ Acute otitis media – a bacterial infection affecting the middle ear. This occurs in five per cent of cases
■ Bacterial pneumonia – an inflammation of the air sacs in the lungs. This occurs in four per cent of cases
■ Conjunctivitis
■ Bronchitis
■ Gastro-enteritis
■ Croup – an inflammation of the main airway. Children of six

months to three years old are most at risk.

RARE COMPLICATIONS
The following complications are rare but potentially life-threatening:
■ Myocarditis – an inflammation of the heart muscle
■ Hepatitis – an inflammation of the liver
■ Viral encephalitis – an inflammation of the brain. This leads to drowsiness, intense headache, vomiting, speech problems and hearing loss.

Incidence

Measles is potentially a very serious illness, which still affects and kills many children in the developing world. Estimates of around one million deaths each year have been reported.

As recently as the 1980s measles was still responsible for approximately 20 child deaths each year in the United Kingdom. Britain has now been free of measles for a decade or more thanks to an effective and widespread immunization programme using the MMR vaccine.

Diagnosis

The diagnosis is usually made on clinical grounds.

KOPLIK'S SPOTS
A doctor examining a child showing general signs of malaise including flu-like symptoms and a high, swinging temperature would rely on finding signs of Koplik's spots in order to diagnose measles conclusively.

These are small red spots with a greyish-white centre found within the mucous membranes of the mouth.

LATE DIAGNOSIS
Diagnosis is simpler following the onset of the whole-body

Early diagnosis is difficult as the initial symptoms can easily be mistaken for influenza. A high, fluctuating temperature precedes the rash by 1–3 days.

rash. Usually starting behind the ears or sometimes on the forehead, the rash spreads downwards on the body and is maculopapular, combining both flat and raised areas of redness.

If necessary diagnosis can also be made or confirmed by:
■ Immunofluorescence (a technique for observing the amount of antibody or antigen in a sample tissue)
■ Viral isolation
■ Serology (blood tests).

Prognosis

In most cases a complete recovery can be expected in 2–4 weeks. Those most at risk from the disease are people with compromised immune-response systems due to other illnesses, certain treatments (such as chemotherapy) or malnourishment. In these people, the condition can be extremely serious and even life-threatening.

Treatment

Treatment is symptomatic, as there is no cure for measles. The disease runs its course over 2–4 weeks, but symptoms usually disappear within a period of 7–10 days.

CONTROLLING SYMPTOMS
Simple analgesics such as paracetamol can be taken to ease any discomfort and reduce fever. Small children and babies over three months old can safely be given a liquid form of paracetamol such as Calpol. Tepid sponging can also help to reduce the fever.

Conjunctivitis can be eased by eye baths and antibiotic eye drops when appropriate. Any painful crusting, for example around the nose, can be soothed by the application of Vaseline.

SECONDARY INFECTIONS
Measles is a relatively mild disease in a healthy, well-nourished child. However, secondary bacterial infections of the lung and ear can occur, and these can be serious, requiring appropriate antibiotic treatment.

A washcloth moistened with tepid water can be wiped over the child to help reduce fever. Simple analgesics such as paracetamol will also help.

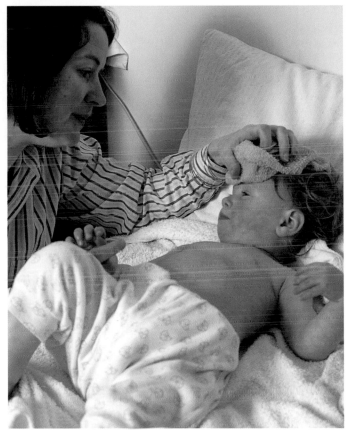

Prevention

The vaccination programme to prevent measles, mumps and rubella (MMR) was successfully introduced in the 1980s.

LIFELONG IMMUNITY
The vaccine is made from weakened strains of the three live viruses. When these are introduced subcutaneously into the body through injection, they prompt the body's immune system to generate antibodies

Children in the UK are offered the MMR vaccination before starting school. High uptake is essential to prevent a return of recurring measles epidemics.

against the diseases, conferring lifelong immunity.

The MMR vaccine is first given at 12–15 months, followed by a booster at 4–6 years. It can also be given to adults considered to be at risk.

VACCINATION RISKS
There is a 1:1000 risk of febrile convulsions after the first dose of MMR, but this should be kept in context – the risk after an attack of the disease itself is 1:200.

Meningitis/encephalitis occurs in one in a million children after MMR and in one in 200–5000 children with measles.

Mumps

Symptoms

The symptoms of mumps are more severe in adults than in children. Common symptoms for all sufferers include:
■ Pain and swelling of the parotid glands, which are found in front of each ear; usually both sides are affected. The pain may be aggravated by chewing and by sour flavours, and the skin over the parotid glands may become swollen, red and warm. The parotid swelling usually subsides in 3–7 days
■ The submandibular and sublingual glands may be affected; in about 10 per cent of cases only one gland is affected. In a similar proportion of cases, the openings of the parotid salivary duct in the lining of the cheek (which allows saliva to enter the mouth from the salivary glands affected) may also become red and swollen
■ Adults are usually more unwell when affected and may experience additional symptoms, such as fever, myalgia (muscle pain), headache, myocarditis (inflammation of the heart muscle), thyroiditis and nephritis (kidney inflammation).

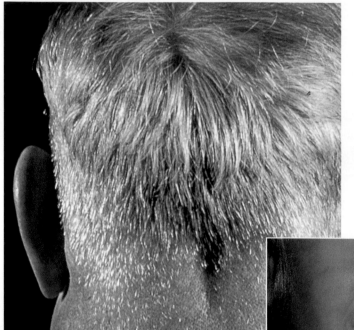

In adults and children, swelling is usually caused by parotid gland enlargement. These are the largest of the three pairs of salivary glands.

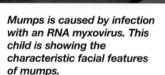

Mumps is caused by infection with an RNA myxovirus. This child is showing the characteristic facial features of mumps.

Causes

Mumps is an acute infectious disease that most commonly affects children up to about 15 years of age. Adults are affected much less frequently.

Mumps is caused by infection with an RNA myxovirus. The illness is most common in the spring and is spread in the saliva and by droplets exhaled or sneezed. Due to vaccination the disease is now uncommon, but if infection does occur, the disease has a rapid onset. The incubation period is 18–21 days; however, about 30 per cent of people exposed to the illness produce no clinical symptoms.

Diagnosis

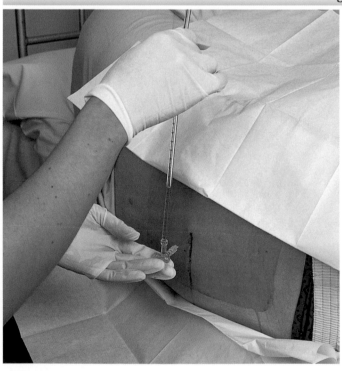

In affected individuals, diagnosis is based on the following signs and symptoms:
■ Swelling and tenderness of the parotid or other salivary glands is the most obvious sign
■ Swelling and tenderness of other glands, such as the pancreas or thyroid
■ Temporary deafness.
   Approximately one third of

In patients with no obvious symptoms, a lumbar puncture may be performed to obtain a sample of cerebrospinal fluid (CSF). The virus – if present – can be identified in this sample.

Mumps infection can be confirmed by rising levels of antibodies detected in the patient's serum. Blood is collected from the patient twice, with an interval of two weeks between samples.

patients have no symptoms to aid diagnosis. In these cases, laboratory tests are needed:
■ Blood tests will reveal a rise in the antibody titre (level) in the serum
■ Serum amylase (a pancreatic enzyme) levels will be raised, especially in pancreatitis
■ The virus may be isolated from the saliva, urine and cerebrospinal (CSF) fluid.

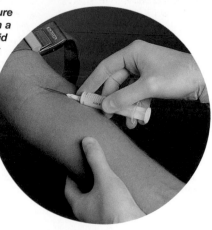

Complications

Complications are more likely in affected adults, but may also occur in children. They include:
■ Meningo-encephalitis (also known as aseptic meningitis) – occurs in approximately 20 per cent of cases. It is characterized by severe headache, neck stiffness and an increase in the number of lymphocytes (white blood cells) in cerebrospinal fluid
■ Orchitis – in adult males, inflammation of the testes may occur; one or both testicles may be painful and enlarged; atrophy of the affected testis may occur, but infertility is rare
■ Oophoritis – inflammation of an ovary may occur in about seven per cent of affected women, producing fever and back pain
■ Pancreatitis – inflammation of the pancreas is rare and characterized by fever, abdominal pain and vomiting
■ Obstructive hydrocephalus – this has been known in the developing fetus due to the mumps virus
■ Other more serious complications include episcleritis (inflammation of the outer covering of the eye), uveitis (inflammation of the iris in the eye), optic neuritis and sensory deafness.

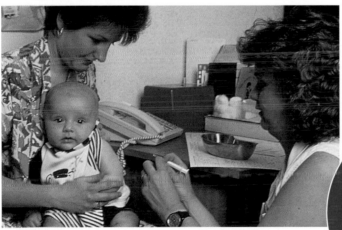

Orchitis – inflammation of the testes – occurs in about one fifth of cases of mumps in adult males. This is generally very painful and accompanied by high fever, but the condition usually subsides within a month.

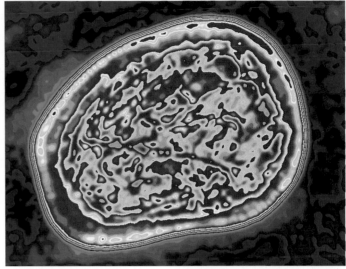

This false-colour electron micrograph shows the mumps virus Rabula inflans. The core contains the genetic material responsible for virus replication.

Pancreatitis, inflammation of the pancreas, is also a rare complication of mumps. It is characterized by severe abdominal pain and occasionally by bruising on both flanks.

Prevention

Mumps has become a relatively rare disease due to the MMR (measles, mumps and rubella) vaccine. This is initially and routinely given to infants at around 12–15 months of age.

The MMR vaccine is a 'live' attenuated (treated to reduce virulence of virus) vaccine. The patient then experiences mild symptoms but produces an effective immune response.

The development of a vaccine has helped the prevention of mumps considerably. The vaccine for mumps is included in the MMR (measles, mumps and rubella) vaccine as part of a routine child immunization programme in the UK. All children between the age of 12 and 15 months are immunized, and a booster dose is given between the age of three and five years.

The vaccine is purely preventative – it cannot help children who have been exposed to the virus without immunity or who are already affected by it. In addition, as the vaccine is 'live' (a small amount of the virus is introduced to the body to help elicit an immune response), it is not suitable for children with a partially or totally impaired immune system.

Recent studies have suggested that the MMR vaccine is linked with incidences of autism and bowel disease, but no firm evidence has been found. Immunization is now considered safe and routine for all children.

Treatment

There is no specific treatment once a person has become infected with the mumps virus. However, painful symptoms can be managed:
■ Pain relief in adults with analgesics, such as aspirin and paracetamol, is beneficial and sometimes necessary
■ An ice bag placed over the tender parotid gland may also help to alleviate pain and swelling
■ Orchitis requires scrotal support; analgesia and corticosteroids may be used to reduce swelling of the testes and pain
■ Avoidance of sexual activity may be wise in adult males during the acute phase of orchitis.

Incidence and prognosis

Mumps has now become uncommon since the introduction of the MMR vaccine. This is highly effective, with more than 95 per cent of recipients developing lifelong immunity. However, a sustained level of immunity of 85 per cent of the population is required to prevent outbreaks. If immunization levels in the population are low, the number of cases occurring will increase, affecting older age groups first.

In a non-immune population, the virus most commonly affects children, but adults and the fetus in a pregnant woman may be affected. Patients develop the disease 18–21 days after contact. Symptoms last about three days.

Rubella

Symptoms

Rubella, or German measles as it is popularly known, has no connection to measles. It is essentially a mild viral infection that causes a rash and fever.

SYMPTOMS
Symptoms of rubella are usually mild and occur two to three weeks after infection. They typically include:
■ A fine pink rash which spreads downwards from the face. This is often the first sign of the illness and occurs in 50 per cent of cases. On the first day it resembles the measles rash but is not accompanied by flu-like symptoms. On the second day it may become confluent (merging into large areas) and bright pink. On the third day it usually disappears
■ Enlarged lymph nodes – typically behind the ears and on the back of the neck.
■ A fever – mild in children, this may develop into a high

fever with headache in adults.
Less commonly, the following symptoms also develop:
■ Arthralgia (aches in the joints) – this affects adults more than children, particularly women
■ Enlarged spleen
■ Conjunctivitis
■ Reddened throat and cough.
Individuals are contagious for about 10 days before and after the appearance of the rash.

CONGENITAL RUBELLA
While usually harmless, rubella has disastrous consequences if experienced during the first four months of pregnancy. The fetus is at risk of developing congenital rubella – a syndrome associated with significant developmental abnormalities.

The first identifiable symptom of rubella is a fine pink rash which merges into larger patches. Its similarity to measles can lead to an incorrect diagnosis.

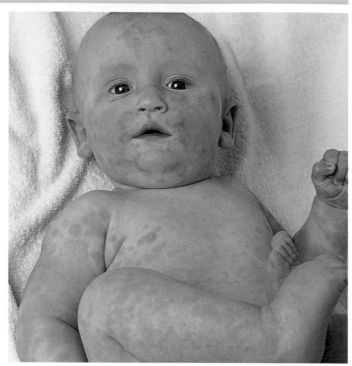

Causes

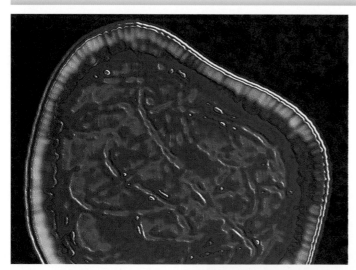

The rubella virus is notable for the following characteristics:
■ It is a single-stranded RNA virus belonging to the togavirus family. RNA (ribonucleic acid) is a type of genetic material that acts as a messenger, in this case delivering the information for replication of the virus
■ Humans are the only host
■ It is passed from one person to another by direct contact and through moisture droplets from the respiratory tract

Rubella is caused by a virus from the togavirus family which contains single-stranded RNA material. The disease is easily spread via minute droplets.

■ It multiplies in the lining of the respiratory tract and is then absorbed into the bloodstream. Once in the blood it is able to spread to different parts of the body including the skin
■ The incubation period from exposure to the appearance of the rash is 14-21 days.

CONTAGION RATE
The chance of a non-immune individual catching the disease is around 60 per cent. However, this can rise to 100 per cent in close-knit communities.
Non-immunized children between the ages of four to 10 are the group most often affected.

Diagnosis

Diagnosing rubella presents the doctor with several problems:
■ The rash can easily be confused with other virus infections such as Coxsackie and glandular fever
■ There are no diagnostic features which are typical. Even occipital lymph node enlargement has no clinical significance
■ Some individuals will not develop a rash at all.
Diagnosis can be confirmed in pregnant women by blood tests for raised antibody levels.

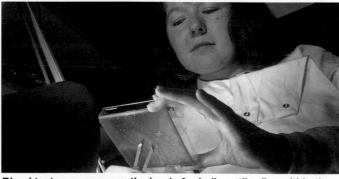

Blood tests can measure the level of rubella antibodies within the bloodstream. This indicates the level of immunity to the disease.

Incidence

Rubella is endemic worldwide. The infection is so common that virtually every susceptible individual will have rubella at some point during their life.
The UK routinely vaccinates children as part of the MMR programme. In countries without immunization rubella occurs as epidemics every seven to nine years.
A general downward trend in outbreaks in the UK was reversed in 1993 when there were several local outbreaks.

Prevention

The rubella vaccine contains live inactivated virus and may produce mild rubella-like symptoms. It is administered as part of the MMR (measles mumps and rubella) vaccine which is routinely offered to babies at 12–15 months.

The vaccine is also offered to all women of child-bearing age who test negative for rubella antibodies. All health care staff in the UK must prove immunity or undergo vaccination.

DURING PREGNANCY
Women are advised to check their rubella immunity before conceiving and to undergo immunization if necessary. Every pregnant woman's rubella status is checked as part of standard antenatal screening.

The following conditions prohibit vaccination:
■ Pregnancy
■ A suppressed immune system
■ An allergy to either of two very uncommon antibiotics, neomycin and polymyxin.

Children in the UK are routinely offered the MMR vaccine at 12–15 months, with a booster at 4–6 years. Epidemics of rubella seem to have been eradicated.

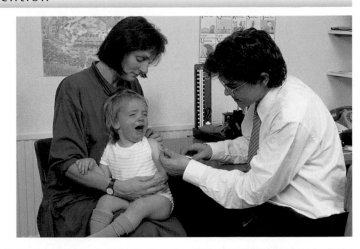

Treatment

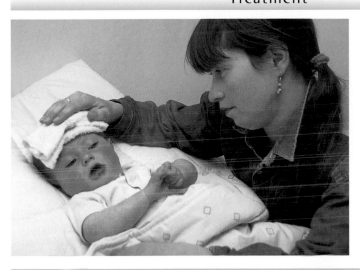

There is no specific treatment for rubella and management is symptomatic.

Fever and general discomfort may be relieved by the following measures:
■ Drinking plenty of fluid
■ Taking simple analgesics such as paracetamol to ease any discomfort and reduce fever
■ Soothing conjunctivitis with eye baths or with antibiotic eyedrops if appropriate.

There is no cure for rubella, so treatment is focused on the alleviation of symptoms. Cool sponge baths can help to reduce fever.

Prognosis

Rubella is a relatively mild illness that rarely causes complications.
Possible complications:
■ Adults and adolescents rarely suffer the complication of arthritis. This usually affects the hands and fingers and can mimic rheumatoid arthritis. It generally resolves within two weeks leaving no permanent damage
■ Encephalitis occurs in approximately 1:6000 cases. This is very rarely fatal, and most people go on to make a complete recovery.

Congenital rubella

Congenital rubella is a syndrome affecting the babies of women who contract rubella when they are in the first trimester of pregnancy.

In congenital rubella, the fetus is at risk of developing a number of serious and potentially fatal conditions. The type of defect depends on the fetus's age at the time of infection.

Fetal defects
Approximately 16 per cent of infants have major defects at birth after maternal infection in the first trimester. These include:
■ Fetal death and stillbirth
■ Growth retardation
■ Eye defects such as retinopathy (retinal disease), micro-ophthalmia (under-developed eyes), cataracts and glaucoma
■ Heart defects such as ventricular septal defect (hole in the heart)
■ Pulmonary stenosis (narrowing of the pulmonary artery)
■ Neuritis (nerve inflammation)
■ Deafness

■ Defects of the nervous system
■ Bone defects
■ Thrombocytopenic purpura (low blood platelet count)
■ Hepatosplenomegaly (enlarged liver and spleen)

■ Hepatitis.

The defects are usually multiple when contagious contact occurs before 10 weeks' gestation, with nine out of 10 babies affected. Between 10 and

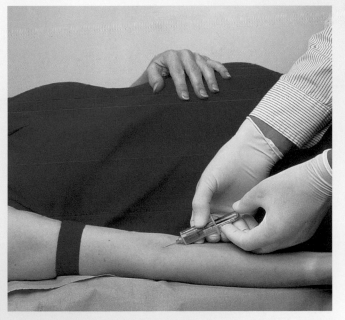

16 weeks' gestation the number affected falls to between 1:5 and 1:10, and contact after 16 weeks rarely results in fetal defects.

Incidence and immunity
Any pregnant woman coming into contact with rubella should check whether the blood test taken routinely in early pregnancy showed immunity. If so, there is no cause for concern even when direct contact is made. Immunity is complete and lifelong.

In the early 1970s there were approximately 1000 rubella-related terminations each year. After the introduction of immunization in 1970 this dropped to 200 per annum.

The incidence of congenital rubella has dropped from 200–300 a year before 1970 to an average of around four per annum by 1995.

All pregnant women in the UK undergo blood tests to test for immunity. If rubella is contracted in early pregnancy, it can have devastating effects.

Tonsillitis

Symptoms

Tonsillitis – inflammation of the tonsils – is usually due to a viral or bacterial infection of the tonsils. It generally lasts for about five days.

CLINICAL FEATURES
Symptoms may be severe in bacterial tonsillitis and the patient will complain of a sore throat often accompanied by:
■ Malaise (a general feeling of being unwell)
■ Pyrexia (fever)
■ Cervical lymphadenopathy (swelling of glands in the neck).

There may be pain referred to the ear – this may be confused with otitis media (middle ear infection) in young children. Very commonly tonsillitis causes halitosis (bad breath).

NECK SWELLINGS
The oropharynx (between the soft palate and the epiglottis) is generally red and congested and there may be exudate over the tonsils. There will always be enlarged lymph nodes in the side of the neck, which will be palpable and often tender.

Gross in the neck and exudate on the tonsil also occurs in glandular fever. Rarely the enlarged tonsils may cause airway obstruction – again this is more likely in glandular fever.

It is necessary to distinguish between the bacterial sore throat of tonsillitis and viral pharyngitis (inflammation of the pharynx).

Bacterial infection will cause redness of the tonsils and fauces (the opening from the mouth into the pharynx), crypts full of pus in the tonsils, bad breath and 'plummy' speech.

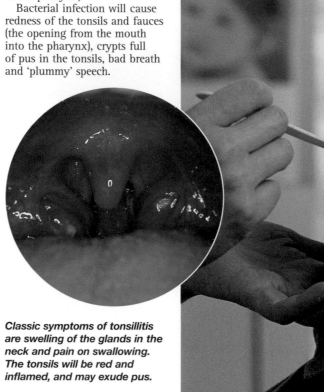

Classic symptoms of tonsillitis are swelling of the glands in the neck and pain on swallowing. The tonsils will be red and inflamed, and may exude pus.

In children the symptoms of tonsillitis may be confused with an inner ear infection, as the pain is often referred to the ear.

Diagnosis

It may not be possible to distinguish between viral infection and bacterial infection initially, and throat swabs may give misleading results.

The diagnosis of tonsillitis must be based on the clinical picture, primarily the swelling in the neck glands and the inflamed tonsils, and the patient's symptoms.

If glandular fever (infectious mononucleosis) is the cause of the inflamed tonsils, a monospot test on a sample of venous blood will confirm this.

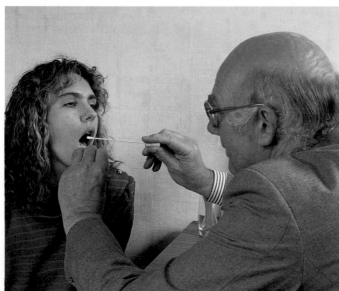

Swollen neck glands are an indication of tonsillitis, and will be tender to the touch. Such swellings rarely cause obstruction of the airways.

A throat swab may be taken to help identify the causative agent in a case of bacterial tonsillitis. However, this is not necessarily an accurate diagnostic test.

Incidence

Sore throat is one of the commonest reasons for a patient going to see the GP, and tonsillitis is probably the cause of up to 30 per cent of all sore throats.

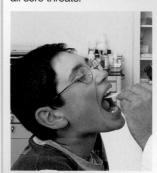

Sore throats are extremely common, although tonsillitis is only responsible for a minority of cases. An oral examination will determine the cause of the discomfort.

Treatment

Bacterial tonsillitis requires antibiotics, preferably oral penicillin or erythromycin if the patient is allergic to penicillin. Amoxicillin is not recommended as this may produce a rash if the case is one of glandular fever.

SURGICAL TREATMENT

Tonsillectomy is now rarely performed as a routine procedure, but is necessary in cases of frequent and recurrent tonsillitis. Sleep apnoea (difficulty in breathing) due to large tonsils, and quinsy (abscess of tonsil) if preceded by recurrent tonsillitis, are other indications for removal of the tonsils.

In adults, gargling with soluble aspirin may help to relieve a sore throat. Paracetamol is the best treatment for pyrexia (fever).

Children under 12 should not be given aspirin, but gargling with cool water may help relieve the symptoms of tonsillitis.

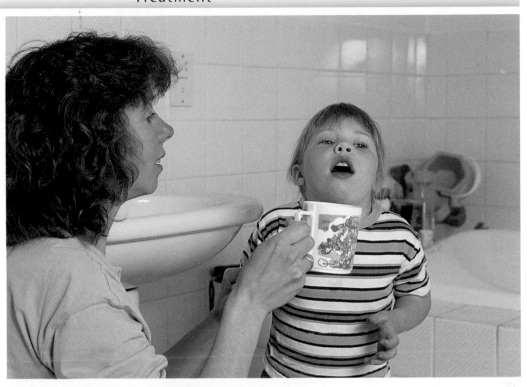

Causes

Often, a white or yellow exudate, consisting of protein and white cells, will form over the tonsils. This is a result of the body's normal defence against infection.

Immunization against diphtheria means that it is now a rare condition in developed countries. It was once a common cause of throat inflammation.

Tonsillitis principally affects children and young adults and is spread by droplet and dust infection. Usually tonsillitis starts as a viral infection, a secondary bacterial infection then developing, usually with the beta-haemolytic streptococcus, which may chronically infect the tonsils.

QUINSY

A quinsy (peritonsillar abscess – collection of pus) is usually unilateral (one-sided) and is due to streptococcal organisms.

Diphtheria used to be a significant cause of a membranous exudate affecting the tonsils and constricting the throat. However, routine immunization has virtually eliminated diphtheria in the UK.

Prognosis

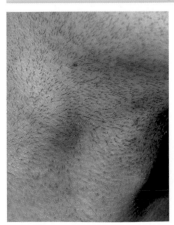

Almost invariably, tonsillitis resolves after about five days. The condition is nearly always self-limiting, although persistently recurring infections may be may be a cause of debility in some patients.

Unilaterally enlarged cervical lymph nodes may be suggestive of neoplasia (formation of a new, abnormal tissue) and should not be ignored.

Enlarged glands on one side may be suggestive of a form of cancer called lymphoma, and should be investigated.

Prevention

Tonsillitis is very common in childhood due to hypertrophy (excessive growth) of the tonsils and repeated infections. Good oral and dental hygiene measures may help to reduce its occurrence. Children with tonsillitis should be excluded from school as the infection is easily spread in crowded classrooms and public places.

Although tonsillitis is rarely serious, affected children should be kept away from contact with other children until the infection passes.

Herpes simplex

Symptoms

Herpes simplex is caused by contact with the herpes simplex virus, of which there are two types (see 'Causes' below).

Symptoms of herpes usually develop within 2 to 10 days of first exposure, although it can take longer. The symptoms may last for several weeks. The first infection may be so mild that it is hardly noticed, but the symptoms can be severe.

After direct contact:
■ The virus starts to multiply within the skin cells
■ The skin becomes red and sensitive and starts to burn, itch and tingle
■ Soon afterwards, one or more little blisters start to appear, which open and shed fluid containing the virus
■ The blisters then form ulcer-like sores; these do not usually leave a scar after healing.

There may be associated systemic flu-like symptoms and the sores may cause pain, especially if they involve the urethra.

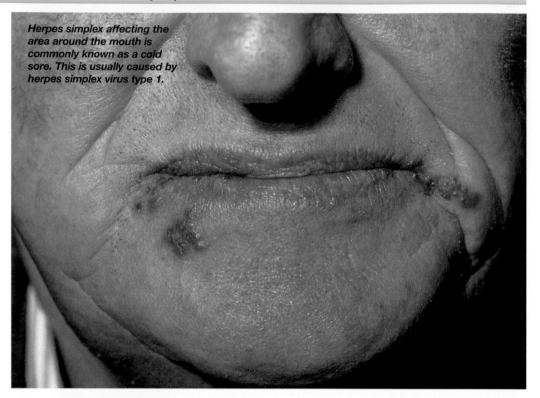

Herpes simplex affecting the area around the mouth is commonly known as a cold sore. This is usually caused by herpes simplex virus type 1.

Causes

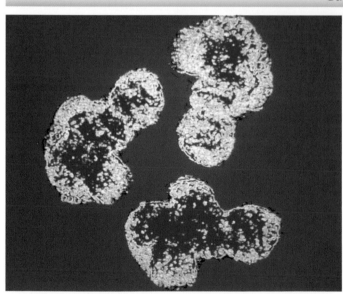

The two types of herpes simplex virus are indistinguishable under the microscope. However, each has different characteristics.

There are two types of herpes simplex virus: type 1 (HSV1) and type 2 (HSV2). HSV1 tends to occur above the waist and HSV2 below. Infection around the mouth is commonly known as herpes simplex and infection of the genitals is known as herpes genitalis.

REACTIVATION
When the acute illness has settled, the virus travels down the sensory nerve that supplies a particular area of skin to reach the nerve cells in the spine. Once there it remains dormant.

The immune system helps to control recurrences, but when it is distracted by other factors such as stress and other infections, relapses can occur. Indeed, the common name 'cold sore' reflects the tendency for the virus to emerge during viral respiratory infections. During reactivation of the virus it travels back along the sensory nerve to the skin.

TRANSMISSION
Herpes is spread by direct skin contact; for example, kissing someone with a cold sore can transfer the infection. Herpes is most easily spread when a sore is present but it can spread at other times if the virus is shed – asymptomatic transmission.

Diagnosis

In most cases a description of the condition and the appearances of the lesions are sufficient for a doctor to make the diagnosis of herpes simplex. However, it should be borne in mind that recurrences can sometimes be atypical.

LABORATORY TESTS
Identification of the virus (type 1 or 2) may be done by taking a swab of the watery fluid from one of the blisters and examining it under an electron microscope to identify the viral particles. If both partners have type 2 virus, precautions during sex are unnecessary as both have the problem.

It is also possible to tell by examination of blood serum whether a person has had an infection with HSV1 or HSV2.

Incidence

Usual sites of herpes simplex infection include the genitals and around the mouth. It is a very common infection and, though rarely serious, it can cause much distress, especially in the genital form.

Genital herpes is the second commonest sexually transmitted infection in the UK, affecting around one in six adults.

About 80 per cent of adults have antibodies in their blood that protect them against HSV1, and approximately 25 per cent have antibodies that protect them against HSV2.

Herpes zoster (or shingles) is caused by varicella, which causes chickenpox. Varicella is also a member of the herpes group of viruses.

Treatment

Genital herpes, in particular, is unpleasant for most people, not least because of overtones of infidelity and the implications for future sexual relationships. Seeing a specialist in sexually transmitted diseases is probably reassuring for most newly diagnosed patients with genital infection.

Bathing the area with Epsom salts in warm water helps to dry the blisters, as does wearing loose-fitting clothes.

DRUG THERAPY

Although there is no cure, medical treatment needs to be started within a few days of the onset of the symptoms if it is to be most effective.

Drugs have proved helpful in reducing the frequency and duration of outbreaks. Antiviral creams containing aciclovir have proved useful for cold sores, and aciclovir tablets can be taken for genital herpes. Aciclovir is also available in cream form over the counter at chemists.

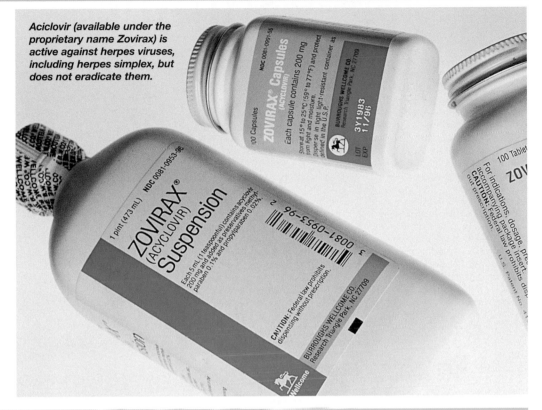

Aciclovir (available under the proprietary name Zovirax) is active against herpes viruses, including herpes simplex, but does not eradicate them.

Prognosis and prevention

RECURRENCE

During a first episode the body develops antibodies which, to an extent, help to modify recurrences, though they do not prevent them. There may, as a result, be fewer sores, which tend to heal faster. A recurrence tends to be less distressing physically. HSV2 is more aggressive and more likely to recur than HSV1.

Genital herpes develops very differently from one person to the next. Some people have frequent attacks and others have very few. The average number of relapses for genital herpes is four attacks per year. Recurrences usually occur near the original site of infection. Outbreaks tend to decline with advancing age.

COMPLICATIONS

Herpes simplex is associated with a number of possible complications:
■ Infection of the eyes – may result in scarring of the cornea
■ Neonatal HSV infection – a baby can contract herpes from its mother during its passage down the birth canal. A Caesarean section may be necessary if the birth coincides with an attack.

Women with genital herpes are statistically around five times more likely to develop cervical cancer, although there is no definite causal link yet known. For this reason, cancer smears should be carried out more frequently for women who have herpes genitalis.

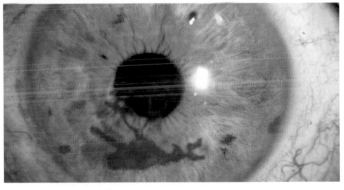

PREVENTION

Infected people need to identify their particular precipitating factors in order to minimize or avoid them. During an attack it is important that patients:

Herpes simplex can affect the cornea. If not treated promptly, it can lead to ulceration and scarring, revealed here by purple dye.

■ Avoid scratching as transmission of the virus to fingers and then other sites including the eyes can occur
■ Wash hands frequently
■ Avoid unprotected sexual activity; condoms offer some protection.

Between attacks patients should look after their general health. Herpes vaccines to prevent first attacks are being developed.

If a pregnant women has herpes, there is a possibility that she may pass it on to her baby at birth. In some cases, a Caesarean delivery is advised.

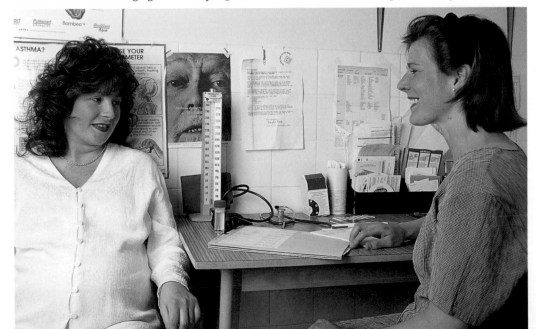

Shingles

Symptoms

The term shingles, medically known as herpes zoster, is derived from the Latin word for 'belt', and describes the pattern of the rash that usually occurs in this viral infection. The shingles rash is often preceded by a painful burning sensation, known as paraesthesia (pins and needles), in the affected dermatome (area of skin served by a specific spinal nerve). This pain, which may be severe and stabbing in character, is often mistaken for a heart attack when apparent in the chest, or the pain of kidney stones, gallstones or even appendicitis, depending on the distribution of the pain.

The chest wall is the most commonly affected part of the body, although the sensory and motor nerves of the face are also often affected. In the face, the ophthalmic division of the fifth cranial nerve (the trigeminal nerve) is particularly affected, perhaps because the forehead is more often exposed to trauma.

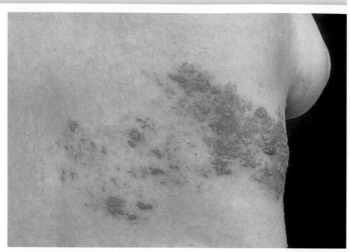

The shingles rash follows a distinctive belt-like pattern across the skin. This woman has a band of lesions running across the back and around the lower chest wall – this is a common site for the rash.

How the shingles rash develops

The shingles rash initially develops as papules (small, raised spots) which then become vesicles (fluid-filled blisters). Three to seven days after the blisters form, they begin to scab. Untouched, the scabs will all separate and drop off within 14 days. They should not be scratched or pulled off, otherwise an unsightly scar will result. Fortunately for the patient, the lesions usually affect only one dermatome (the area of skin supplied by one cutaneous nerve).

Post-herpetic neuralgia (PHN) – pain occurring after the rash has disappeared – may persist for some months, especially in older patients, and is often difficult to control.

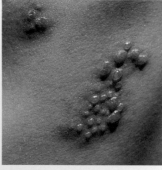

1 *Once the lesions of shingles develop, they soon take the form of fluid-filled vesicles, or blisters. These cluster at the site of cutaneous nerves in the skin.*

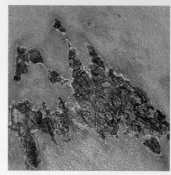

2 *After the blisters have ruptured, they dry out and scabs form, but rarely leave a scar. The rash may be exacerbated by secondary bacterial infection.*

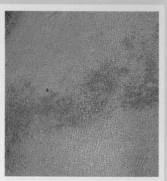

3 *In some cases, the shingles rash resolves, but leaves some pigmentation of the skin. In this case, the underarm area has been affected.*

Diagnosis and prognosis

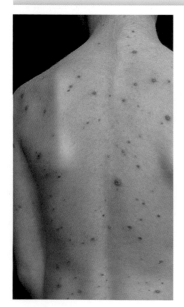

Shingles only occurs in those who have already had chickenpox, shown here. The lesions in each disease are of the same type, but their pattern of distribution is different.

The same virus (varicella zoster) causes chickenpox and shingles. It belongs to the same family of viruses as herpes simplex (HSV).

The diagnosis of shingles is normally straightforward and based on the clinical picture of the patient, including their history, the stabbing pain and the typical rash and distribution of the lesions. Unlike herpes simplex, herpes zoster does not usually recur.

After acute infection with chickenpox, which usually occurs in childhood, the virus remains latent in the nerve cells, only to be re-activated years later as herpes zoster. Although both chickenpox and herpes zoster are caused by the same virus, there may be epidemics of chickenpox but not of zoster. Serology (blood tests) can determine an individual's susceptibility to zoster, and a smear of cells taken from the base of one of the lesions (a Tzanck smear) will show multinucleated giant cells under the microscope.

DURATION
The infection lasts for about two weeks, and full recovery is the norm in the majority of patients. Elderly people are more prone to suffering from post-herpetic neuralgia, and immunocompromised patients may suffer a severe illness with zoster because their immune system is not functioning correctly. In such cases, antiviral chemotherapy is essential. Provided that the patient allows the skin lesions to separate (drop off) spontaneously, no long-term scarring of the skin will occur.

The duration of the illness is very much dependent on the age of the patient. The rash is often barely apparent in children, while in adults it tends to last for five to eight days. In the elderly, the illness and rash may be much more severe, lasting for several weeks, and often with serious effects on the central nervous system – it can cause mental confusion, for example.

Treatment

In order for treatment to be effective, aciclovir – a drug effective against herpes viruses – should be given orally. If prescribed early enough, this should reduce the severity and duration of the attack. Aciclovir or a related drug is essential in the complicated forms of zoster (see below). If the ophthalmic branch of the trigeminal nerve is affected, there may be conjunctivitis, suggesting eye involvement in these cases. Aciclovir eye-drops and antibiotic eye-ointment should be prescribed. Adequate analgesia with suitable painkillers is also necessary.

STEROID TREATMENT
High doses of steroids shorten the duration of pain in acute zoster. However, there is danger of this causing a generalized spread of zoster, and many doctors are reluctant to opt for this method of treatment. Once the acute illness is resolved, steroids may be useful in treating post-herpetic neuralgia.

Carbamazepine (an anticonvulsant drug) may be used in trigeminal nerve zoster

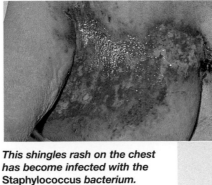

This shingles rash on the chest has become infected with the Staphylococcus bacterium. Such secondary infections will respond to antibiotics.

when hyperaesthesia (a burning sensation in the affected skin) is a problem. Five per cent lignocaine ointment may also give temporary relief for this latter symptom.

Idoxuridine is a topical antiviral agent that may occasionally be prescribed for application to the vesicular (blistered) lesions on the skin.

Many antiviral drugs contain aciclovir (also spelt acyclovir). These are effective in treating herpes zoster infections.

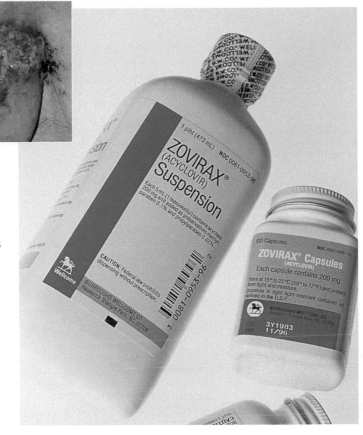

Incidence and complications

At least 20 per cent of adults suffer from zoster at some time in their life, although seldom more than once. The reactivation of the virus is more likely to occur in the elderly and the immunocompromised, such as people with AIDS.

Herpes zoster infection may be more severe or have particular complications:

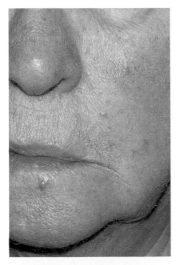

One form of herpes zoster is Ramsay Hunt syndrome, involving the facial nerve. The patient suffers paralysis of one side of the face, as shown by this woman's attempt to smile.

This woman has a facial rash resulting from zoster infection of the trigeminal nerve of the face. As well as the rash on her forehead and nose, the left eye has periorbital swelling.

■ In lymphatic leukaemia and multiple myeloma (malignant disease of the bone marrow), zoster may recur repeatedly and severely.
■ Sacral herpes, in which the nerves of the lower spine are affected, may cause retention of urine.
■ Motor nerves may be affected occasionally, such as in Ramsay Hunt syndrome. This form of herpes zoster involves paralysis of the facial nerve, resulting in a facial palsy, together with lesions in the ear on the affected side.
■ Ophthalmic herpes, which arises only when the trigeminal (fifth cranial) nerve of the face is affected, causes swelling around the eye, conjunctivitis (inflammation of the membrane covering the eye) and, occasionally, severe corneal ulceration.
■ Zoster encephalitis (acute inflammatory disease of the brain) is a rare but serious complication of zoster.

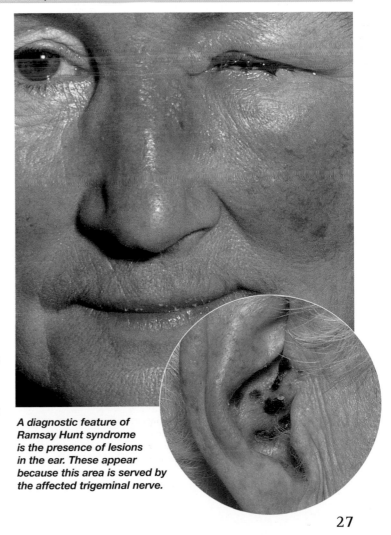

A diagnostic feature of Ramsay Hunt syndrome is the presence of lesions in the ear. These appear because this area is served by the affected trigeminal nerve.

Candidiasis

Symptoms

Candidiasis is a fungal infection that can affect the mouth, alimentary canal, skin, vulva, vagina and anus. It may occur in infants, children or adults, and the symptoms relate to the particular area involved.

Candida organisms are part of the normal flora of the mouth, skin, vagina and alimentary canal. They may, however, proliferate and become pathogenic (disease-causing) under certain conditions, such as in patients with diabetes and in cases of immunosuppression, and after taking certain drugs, particularly antibiotics.

SKIN SYMPTOMS
■ Red, itchy, plaque-like lesions can occur in moist, warm areas, such as under the breasts and in the skin folds of obese people
■ The hands and nails of people who work with their hands in rubber gloves or water (such as washing dishes) can also be affected, causing the skin to thicken around the nail
■ Candidiasis is a common cause of nappy rash in babies, producing a sore, raised, red and irritated rash, sometimes with pimples in the anal cleft and vulval regions.

ORAL SYMPTOMS
■ Soreness and white patches, that often looks like cotton wool, appear on the mucous linings of the oral cavity and pharynx. This is often accompanied by denture stomatitis – a diffuse erythematosus (redness) of the palate and the mucosa
■ Angular cheilitis (cracks and fissures at the corners of the mouth)
■ Dysphagia (difficulty in swallowing) due to oesophageal (gullet) infection, and in some cases a sore tongue.

GENITAL SYMPTOMS
■ Vaginitis occurs if *Candida albicans* colonies proliferate in the vagina. The symptoms include inflammation, accompanied by a thick, white (curd-like) discharge and intense itching. Swelling and soreness of the mucosa (mucous lining) is also common
■ Men may experience penile soreness after sexual contact with an infected female.

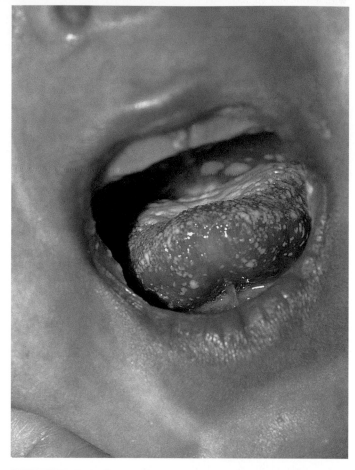

The mouth of an eight-week-old baby shows the white plaque of oral candidiasis. Candida infection is common in infants.

Causes

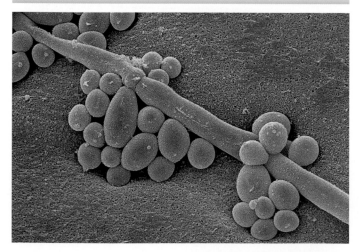

Scanning electron micrograph (SEM) of Candida albicans. The round yeast cells are seen in small colonies.

Candidiasis is usually due to the fungus species *Candida albicans*. The different varieties of *Candida* invade the mucous linings using hyphae (strands), creating superficial infection.

The infection may have an iatrogenic (resulting from treatment) cause, for example, after taking medications. Some medications, such as antibiotics, steroid inhalers and the contraceptive pill, upset the natural balance, allowing the fungus to multiply and cause disease. Some of these infections are associated with endocrine disorders, such as Addison's disease and hypoparathyroidism.

Diagnosis

Diagnosis is usually made on the appearance of the lesions, which is quite typical, particularly when occurring in the mouth or in the vagina. If there is doubt about the diagnosis, microscopic identification can be made of the Gram-positive yeast cells taken from swabs of the infected areas. The fungal hyphae are apparent when seen under a microscope.

Culture using a specific medium is a sensitive test for vaginal secretions when microscopy lacks sensitivity. Endoscopy, along with a culture of the 'brushings' or a biopsy, is used to diagnose *Candida* infections of the oesophagus.

*Candida **fungus thrives in moist areas of the body. Candidiasis is a common cause of painful and itchy nappy rash in babies.***

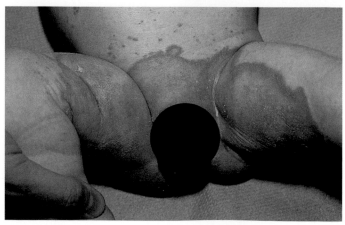

Treatment

Candidiasis is usually treated with antifungal agents applied to the infected surface. Oral candidiasis is effectively treated with a topically applied antifungal liquid, and skin infections respond to creams or nystatin pastilles.

Vaginal infections may be controlled with topical anti-fungal agents that are applied in several ways: creams can be used on the vulva and pessaries or pastilles inserted directly inside the vagina (for example, imidazole pessaries). Intestinal infections may require nystatin tablets.

In patients with severe immunosuppression, such as people with HIV, candidiasis can become systemic and life-threatening. Treatment is with systemic antifungal drugs, such as amphotericin B, fluconazole or itraconazole, although these are not always effective.

Candida septicaemia in an organ transplant patient is very serious, and requires prompt treatment in order for the patient to survive.

Vaginal pessaries contain antifungal drugs, such as clotrimazole. They are widely used to treat cases of candidiasis in the vagina.

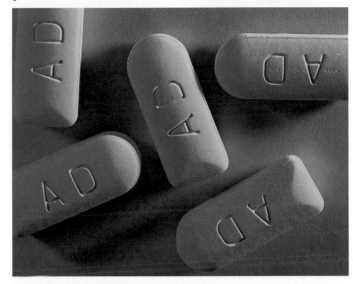

Prognosis

Providing any underlying causes are diagnosed, candidiasis usually resolves with appropriate treatment. The prognosis is largely dependent on that of the underlying condition and the degree to which the patient's immune function can recover.

A light micrograph of the Candida fungus in a urine sample. The fungus has been stained blue.

Prevention

Candidiasis often occurs in bottle-fed infants. The equipment used for feeding should be carefully sterilized.

Steroid (asthma) inhalers can upset the balance of micro-organisms in the mouth. Candida fungus can then multiply, causing oral thrush.

Awareness and management of the predisposing factors reduces the likelihood of recurring candidal infections.
■ Diabetes must be carefully controlled
■ Oral hygiene and dental care is necessary – for example, rinsing the mouth after using oral steroid inhalers; infant dummies, teats and bottles must be carefully sterilized
■ Some medications are known to predispose to candidiasis infections. These include broad spectrum antibiotics and steroid inhalers
■ Patients who are immunosuppressed are susceptible to opportunistic infections, such as candidiasis.

Incidence

Chronic paronychia is an inflammation and swelling of tissue around the nails. Candida albicans is frequently the cause.

Although *Candida* organisms are present in 20–40 per cent of the population, it only multiplies to cause disease under certain conditions.

Hormonal changes, such as during pregnancy or when taking oral contraceptives, predispose women to candidiasis of the groin and vagina and under the breasts. It is also common in diabetes (if it is not controlled) and in 80–90 per cent of immunocompromised patients (such as those suffering from AIDS).

Nappy rash due to candidiasis is usually a superficial infection of the skin. Antifungal drugs, such as nystatin, are effective.

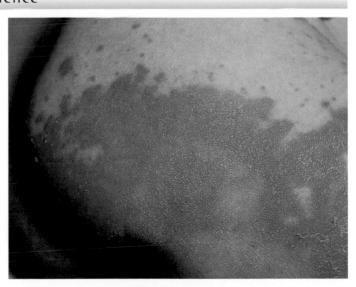

Scarlet fever

Symptoms

In the 19th century, scarlet fever was the commonest cause of death in children, but by 1965 the illness had virtually disappeared, probably due to the widespread use of penicillin.

Known medically as scarlatina, this illness occurs primarily in children of school age. It is highly infectious, but fortunately, nowadays, it is usually a very mild illness. It is often so mild as to escape diagnosis altogether.

EARLY SIGNS
Scarlet fever is a primary infection of the throat – the pharynx and the tonsils. The toxic manifestations include headache, high temperature, rapid pulse, and sometimes vomiting and abdominal pain. The incubation period is two to four days.

In addition to the tonsillitis that is always present, a rash may appear on the palate – this is known as exanthem and it consists of bright red spots on the whole pharynx. The tongue surface becomes white and furred, through which red-tipped papillae appear – the typical 'strawberry tongue'. Later, the furring peels off and leaves a red raw papillate surface known as 'raspberry tongue'.

SWOLLEN GLANDS
The spleen may be palpable and there may be a generalized lymphadenopathy (swollen lymph glands), particularly in the neck and including the tonsillar glands.

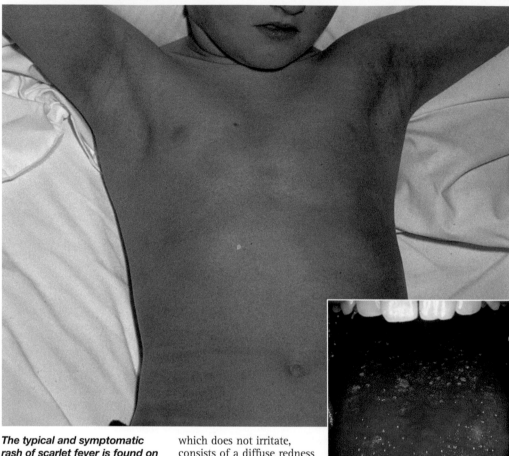

The typical and symptomatic rash of scarlet fever is found on the chest, neck and arms. The rash is red with fine spots and does not cause irritation.

The typical rash appears within 24 hours, first on the chest, neck and arms and then spreading peripherally. It does not usually appear on the hands or feet. The symmetrical rash, which does not irritate, consists of a diffuse redness with superimposed fine spots. The rash becomes intense on the lower abdomen, back, armpit, groin and inner thighs.

Petechiae – tiny blood spots – occur in the skin creases of the front of the elbows, known as Pastia's sign. The face is flushed, hence the name scarlet fever.

A characteristic sign of scarlet fever is the appearance of red-tipped papillae on the tongue. This is commonly described as 'strawberry tongue'.

Diagnosis

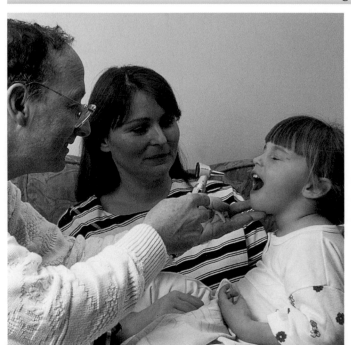

Diagnosis is usually made by assessment of the symptoms and signs alone. The doctor must, however, differentiate scarlet fever from other rashes.

Diagnosis of scarlet fever is made from the characteristic signs and symptoms. As the illness is caused by the erythrogenic toxin of group A streptococci, a tiny amount of filtrate made from cultures of these organisms injected into the skin may reproduce the symptoms. This leads to a local red reaction and is known as the Dick test (this test is rarely used today).

Throat swabs that are cultured to grow *Streptococcus pyogenes* will support the diagnosis of scarlet fever, but this is rarely necessary.

The rash needs to be distinguished from rubella, measles, roseola infantum and drug sensitivity rashes.

Incidence

Although small outbreaks of scarlet fever may occur in closed environments such as boarding schools, the illness is now so mild that it is not diagnosed as frequently today. It is more commonly diagnosed as acute tonsillitis because the rash is so fleeting and transient.

Treatment

The illness is often so mild that no treatment is necessary. But where there is a sore throat and fever it is preferable to treat with oral penicillin for 7–10 days. Intramuscular penicillin may be used in severe cases; erythromycin may be used when the patient has a known sensitivity to penicillin.

Antipyretics (drugs that reduce fever) such as aspirin or paracetamol may be used, but bed rest is only necessary if a child feels ill. Patients should remain at home for a week or so and exclusion from school is necessary while a child is infectious.

In more severe cases of scarlet fever, oral antibiotic therapy alone may not be sufficient. An intramuscular injection of penicillin may also be needed.

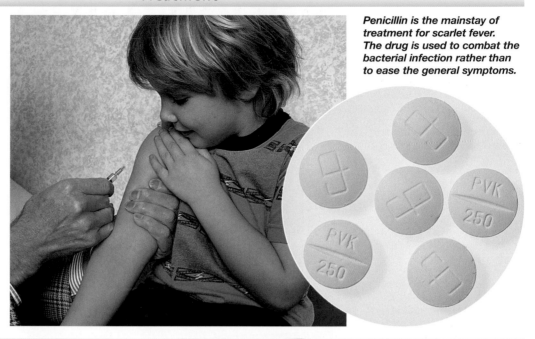

Penicillin is the mainstay of treatment for scarlet fever. The drug is used to combat the bacterial infection rather than to ease the general symptoms.

Causes

Scarlet fever is due to an erythrogenic strain of *Streptococcus* bacteria, 90 per cent of which are Lancefield group A. Entry is usually via the throat, or sometimes via the genital tract, but can follow a wound infection or skin lesion.

Transmission of the bacteria is by droplet infection, but there have been recorded outbreaks where the source of infection has been traced to infected dairy products. When an outbreak occurs in a boarding school or similar closed community, culturing swabs from contacts may be advisable.

In a few cases, outbreaks of scarlet fever have been due to contaminated dairy products. This is an unusual route of infection and rarely occurs.

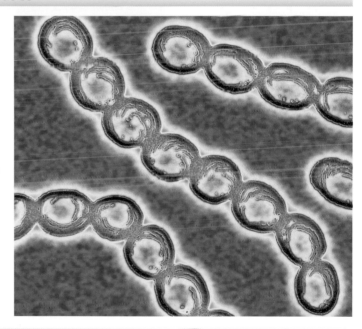

This coloured electron micrograph shows chains of Streptococcus pyogenes. The bacteria are transmitted through droplet infection.

Prognosis

In developed countries, the disease is usually mild, complications are rare and the child is fully recovered after a week. Nephritis (inflammation of the kidneys) may occur as a complication but this is unlikely.

Generally, no treatment is necessary. Complications in the past (before the days of penicillin), included purulent otitis media, rheumatic fever and arthritis, but these are now rarely seen in developed countries.

When the rash persists for several days, there may be peeling of the skin, which may last from two to three days up to about three weeks.

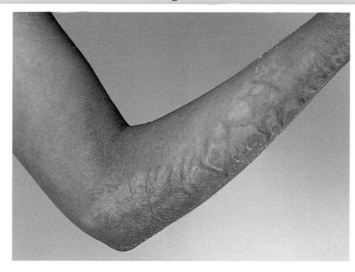

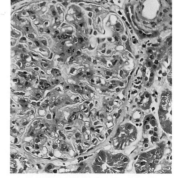

This micrograph shows kidney cells that are indicative of glomerulonephritis. This infection is a rare complication of scarlet fever in some children.

Tapeworms

Symptoms

Tapeworms (cestodes) are flat parasitic worms, of which there are many kinds. Tapeworms have no gastro-intestinal system, so they live in the intestines of humans and other animals (primary hosts) and absorb nutrients through their outer covering. The worms self-fertilize and produce hundreds of eggs, which are passed out in faeces.

WORMS AND LARVAE
Infestation with an adult worm is often symptomless or may cause only minor symptoms, such as mild gastro-intestinal disturbances or tiredness. If larvae (juvenile form) travel to other parts of the body, they can cause serious symptoms, such as:
■ Skin nodules and rashes
■ Seizures
■ Anaemia
■ Chest pain and breathlessness
■ Jaundice
■ Abdominal pain
■ Fever
■ Blood in the urine
■ Visual loss.

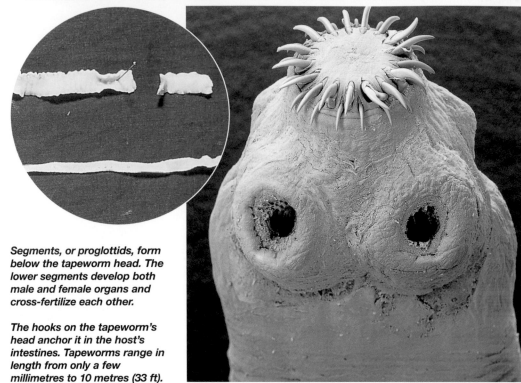

Segments, or proglottids, form below the tapeworm head. The lower segments develop both male and female organs and cross-fertilize each other.

The hooks on the tapeworm's head anchor it in the host's intestines. Tapeworms range in length from only a few millimetres to 10 metres (33 ft).

Causes

Human tapeworm infestations are usually caused by eating raw or undercooked fish or meat infected with tapeworm larvae or food contaminated with faeces containing ova (eggs).

TYPES OF TAPEWORM
There are many varieties of tapeworm, including:

■ **Fish tapeworm**
Diphyllobothrium latum infects humans who eat fish from lakes

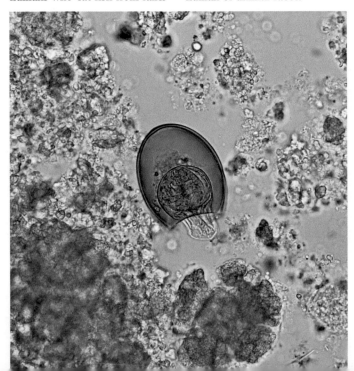

This magnified sample of faeces shows the egg of a fish tapeworm. Humans become infested by eating fish contaminated with these eggs

contaminated with the faeces of infected humans or other fish-eating mammals. The infestation is usually symptomless. About one per cent of infested people become anaemic, as the worm removes vitamin B_{12} (vital for the formation of red blood cells) from the small intestine.

■ **Beef tapeworm**
Taenia saginata infests cattle that eat food contaminated by human or animal faeces

containing ova. The larvae penetrate the intestinal wall and within two months form cysticerci (dormant stage) in the animal's muscle. Humans become infected by eating raw or undercooked beef.

The cysticerci attach themselves to the gut wall and one or two may mature into adult worms and live in the gut for several years. Adult worms can grow to several metres in length, and mature proglottids (segments of tapeworm) may measure 1.3 cm x 1 cm ($\frac{1}{2}$ x $\frac{1}{3}$ in).

Infestation is usually symptomless but may cause anal itching. Proglottids appear in underwear or faeces.

■ **Pork tapeworm**
The life cycle of *Taenia solium* is the same as for *Taenia saginata*, but the pig is the secondary host. Humans become infected by eating undercooked pork containing cysticerci or eating food contaminated with faeces containing ova.

The eggs hatch and cysticerci

migrate into the body tissues. Adult worms are found only in humans and often cause no symptoms, but the cysticerci may cause a serious condition known as human cysticercosis.

■ **Dog tapeworm**
Human infestation with *Echinococcus granulosus* is known as hydatid disease and is caused by the ingestion of dog faeces containing ova from adult worms.

Larvae pass through the gut wall into the bloodstream and from there migrate to the liver and lungs, or less often to the brain or bone. Once there, they gradually form cysts (hydatid cysts), which can eventually contain several litres of highly infectious fluid. If a cyst ruptures, its contents may causes a serious allergic reaction and further infestation elsewhere in the body.

Infestation usually occurs in childhood, but may be symptomless for years unless the cysts affect vital organs. Liver cysts may cause jaundice and abdominal pain, while bone cysts may destroy neighbouring joints. Lung cysts may rupture spontaneously, causing a cough, chest pain and haemoptysis.

Incidence

Tapeworms occur worldwide, but some types are more likely in some areas than others; for example:

■ *Diphyllobothrium latum* – occurs particularly in areas where there are cool lakes, such as Scandinavian countries, but also in Africa and Asia

■ *Taenia saginata* – occurs particularly in cattle in the tropics and subtropics (Africa, Middle East, Mexico and South America) and in Eastern Europe. It is rare in the USA

■ *Taenia solium* – is now rare except in Central Europe, South Africa, South America and parts of Asia

■ *Echinococcus granulosus* – is common in sheep-raising areas of the Mediterranean, the Middle East, Australia, New Zealand, South Africa and South America.

Eating fish caught in a lake contaminated with the faeces of infested humans or fish-eating mammals can cause tapeworm infestation.

Diagnosis

The diagnosis is made from the clinical history, and physical examination may reveal nodules or swellings in body tissues caused by cysticerci.

TECHNIQUES

Microscopic examination of faeces may identify ova and proglottids. Blood tests are available to detect the presence of many tapeworms. Imaging techniques which may detect cysts include: X-rays, ultrasound, CT scans and MRI.

Stool samples help in the diagnosis of infestation. Samples are examined under a microscope to identify tapeworms and their eggs.

Prognosis and prevention

Many tapeworm infestations cause few or no health problems. Fish and beef tapeworm infestation respond well to drug treatment. Cysticercosis is a serious illness, particularly if cysts occur in the brain, but with expert treatment two-thirds of cerebral cysts resolve.

Many tapeworm infestations are preventable by:
■ Cooking all fish and meat thoroughly
■ Attention to hygiene, especially hand-washing before preparing or eating food
■ Worming dogs regularly
■ Preventing dogs from eating sheep carcasses and offal.

Contaminated food is a common source of tapeworm eggs or larvae. Good hygiene helps to reduce the chance of infestation.

Treatment

Treatment will vary according to the type of tapeworm present:
■ Diphyllobothriasis (fish tapeworm) – a single oral dose of praziquantel. Vitamin B$_{12}$ may be needed for anaemia
■ *Taenia saginata* (beef tapeworm) – a single oral dose of praziquantel or niclosamide. Treatment is considered successful when no proglottids

Drug treatments are available for the different types of tapeworm infestation. Often a single oral dose of a particular drug is all that is required.

have been passed for 4 months
■ *Taenia solium* (pork tapeworm) – adult worms are treated as for *Taenia saginata*. Cysticercosis is treated with praziquantel and albendazole. Corticosteroids are also given to reduce the inflammation. Anti-epileptic drugs may be needed if brain cysts occur
■ *Echinococcus granulosus* – mebendazole in high doses or albendazole may be effective with young cysts. Large cysts may be surgically removed, but care is needed to avoid causing further infestation.

Listeriosis

Symptoms

Listeriosis is a potentially serious bacterial infection caused by eating contaminated food. In healthy people, it usually causes only a mild flu-like illness.

However, in vulnerable groups, it may cause serious illness, with destruction of the tissues due to the absorption of bacteria or their toxins into the bloodstream (septicaemia), and inflammation of the brain and its membranes (meningoencephalitis).

HIGH-RISK GROUPS

People at high risk from listeriosis include:
■ Pregnant women – listeriosis is extremely dangerous at any time in pregnancy. It may cause a high fever, headache and pains in the muscles and lower back as well as miscarriages and premature labour
■ Newborn babies – if the fetus becomes infected in the uterus, serious illness may be present from birth. Symptoms may include jaundice, purulent eye infections, pneumonia, and meningitis or encephalitis. A unique feature of the disease is the development of masses of inflammatory tissue

(granulomas), which invade the baby's organs.

Babies infected at a later stage (during birth or cross infected in hospital) are initially healthy, but may develop a life-threatening illness a few days or weeks later
■ Frail elderly people – listeriosis is a known cause of meningitis
■ People whose immune systems are under-active (immunosuppressed) – for example, those with AIDS, inherited disorders and cancer or on steroids and drugs used to prevent transplant rejection.

Listeria monocytogenes causes listeriosis. These rod-shaped bacteria have a thick, protective cell wall covered with fibrous material.

Listeriosis has particular risks for pregnant women. Symptoms include a high fever and headaches, and there is a serious risk to the unborn baby.

Causes

Listeriosis is caused by the bacterium *Listeria monocytogenes*, which infects both humans and animals, causing miscarriages and meningoencephalitis in cattle, sheep and goats.

Listeriosis is contracted through eating contaminated food. Outbreaks of the infection have been associated with soft and blue veined cheeses.

Human infection is acquired by:
■ Contact with infected animals
■ Spread of the bacterium from mother to unborn child
■ Consuming food that has been contaminated.

OUTBREAKS

The exact source of outbreaks of listeriosis often remains unidentified, but they may be associated with eating:
■ Soft cheeses
■ Unpasteurized cheese or milk
■ Ice cream
■ Undercooked meat
■ Raw smoked fish
■ Raw vegetables including coleslaw.

POOR HYGIENE

Person to person infection may occur in conditions of poor hygiene, particularly among people who are immunosuppressed. Close contact in crowded conditions may be important in passing on the disease.

The use of knives to cut contaminated food and then to cut other food products is a

possible cause of an outbreak of the disease.

Using improperly cleaned rectal thermometers in hospital wards may also lead to a spread of the bacterium.

Incidence

Listeria monocytogenes may be present in the intestines of 1–10 per cent of all people without causing symptoms to occur. Listeriosis is rare, with 2–74 cases per million of the population occurring each year.

The number of food-borne cases appears to have increased in recent years, with most reported from industrialized countries.

In the USA, an estimated 2,500 cases of listeriosis occur each year, a relatively small number compared with the number caused by other bacteria that contaminate food, such as salmonella and campylobacter.

Treatment

Treatment aims to eliminate the *Listeria monocytogenes* bacterium with antibiotic drugs.

ANTIBIOTICS
A combination of antibiotics is generally the treatment of choice, including:
■ Ampicillin
■ Gentamicin (this is unsuitable for women who are pregnant).

Other combinations of antibiotics have also been successfully used.

Depending on the severity of the illness and the strength of the patient's immune system, antibiotic treatment may last from between two to six weeks.

PAINKILLERS
To treat symptoms such as headache, muscle pain and high fever, painkillers may be prescribed. However, paracetamol is the only painkiller that should be taken by pregnant women.

HOSPITAL TREATMENT
Patients with listeriosis who become seriously ill should be admitted to hospital, often to a high dependency unit where they receive 24-hour nursing care and round-the-clock monitoring of vital signs.

Newborns with listeriosis will be admitted to a neonatal unit and nursed in an incubator. Babies may need to have artificial ventilation.

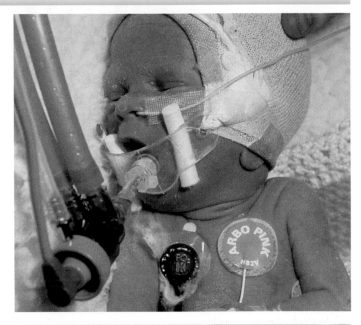

Newborns with listeriosis are at great risk and require hospital treatment in a neonatal unit. Incubators are used to protect babies from further infection.

Prognosis

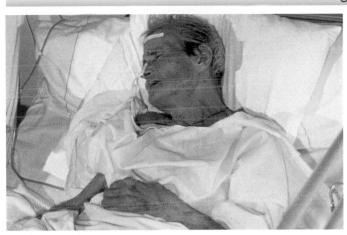

Listeriosis can be serious for certain groups and there is a risk of relapse if treatment is stopped too soon:

■ In pregnancy the mother usually survives but the fetus is at great risk.

■ In newborns with the infection, the outcome is poor,

Patients may develop serious complications, such as septicaemia, as a result of listeriosis. In these cases, the outcome is often poor.

with a death rate of 30 per cent. Later onset of listeriosis in infancy is also associated with a high death rate.

■ In patients with septicaemia and meningoencephalitis, even with antibiotic therapy up to one in two patients die, and survivors often suffer long periods of ill heath.

■ Fit people with a mild attack of listeriosis soon make a full recovery, and there is a very low mortality rate. Severe listeriosis, however, is often fatal.

Prevention

Maintaining good standards of food hygiene in relation to food production, storage and preparation is of prime importance to avoid food becoming contaminated with Listeria.

It is also vital that people in the groups particularly vulnerable to infection avoid high-risk foods.

FOOD TO AVOID
In the UK, the Department of Health advises pregnant women and immunosuppressed people not to eat:
■ Soft, ripe cheeses and blue veined cheeses
■ Meat pâté
■ Chilled meals and ready-to-eat poultry, unless thoroughly reheated, as the bacteria can thrive and multiply in the refrigerator if temperatures are not kept constantly below 4°C (39°F).

Attention to hygiene when preparing and storing food is vital. This can prevent bacteria contaminating food and causing listeriosis.

Diagnosis

The bacteria responsible for listeriosis can be identified from laboratory cultures of specimens taken from:
■ Eyes or nose
■ Blood
■ Urine
■ Cerebrospinal fluid
■ Infected tissues.

Antibodies to the bacteria may also be identified in the patient's blood.

A lumbar puncture is performed to take a specimen of cerebrospinal fluid. The sample is then analysed to diagnose listeriosis.

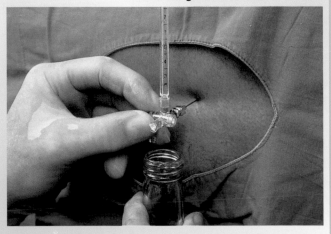

Poliomyelitis

Symptoms

Poliomyelitis is an infectious disease that can affect the nervous system, with symptoms ranging from mild to severe. It mainly affects children who have not been vaccinated, but unimmunized adults can also be affected.

Symptoms include:
■ A high fever with a sore throat
■ Muscular aches and pains
■ Nausea and vomiting
■ Headache and neck stiffness due to meningeal infection.

In most cases, the symptoms subside within one or two weeks.

PARALYTIC POLIOMYELITIS
In paralytic poliomyelitis symptoms differ as follows:

■ The meningitis phase is followed by severe muscle pain, spasms and weakness
■ Lower limbs are more often involved than upper limbs. Activity of any sort during the early pre-paralytic phase may advance the development of paralysis
■ Occasionally, muscles controlling swallowing, talking and breathing are involved (bulbar paralysis) and artificial ventilation is necessary.

Poliomyelitis develops into a paralysing disease in around 10 per cent of cases. While rarely life-threatening, it can be permanently disabling.

Causes

Poliomyelitis is caused by the polio virus (a member of the Enterovirus family). Before the advent of vaccination, the disease caused worldwide epidemics, although the incidence was higher in areas with poor sanitation.

INFECTION
Poliomyelitis is highly infectious:
■ Infection occurs through contact with contaminated

◀ Polio is endemic in Central and West Africa. The disease spreads through the oral-faecal route, generally through contaminated food and water.

▶ The polio virus occurs in three types, each neutralized by different antibodies. The oral vaccine confers complete immunity to the disease.

faeces, food and water
■ The virus multiplies at the back of the throat and in the intestinal tract during a one to three week incubation period before spreading through the circulatory and lymph systems
■ The virus enters through the mouth and the nose and is excreted in the saliva and faeces
■ People are most infectious 7–10 days before and after the onset of symptoms.

Diagnosis

The virus may be identified by:
■ Taking swabs from the nose and throat for five days post-infection
■ Carrying out tests on stool samples for up to five weeks
■ Taking a cerebrospinal fluid sample and culturing it, over the course of about one week.

Blood testing allows different strains to be isolated thereby differentiating wild strains from strains used in vaccines.

Throat swabs taken from children can be cultured to confirm a diagnosis of poliomyelitis. This also allows identification of the virus strain.

Incidence

Prior to the twentieth century, poliomyelitis was endemic (continuously occurring) in many countries. As living conditions improved, the disease tended to occur in epidemics, with large outbreaks in the UK and USA in the 1940s and 1950s. The widespread introduction of vaccination programmes in the 1950s brought the disease under control and outbreaks are now rare in the western hemisphere. Very rarely, a mutated form of the virus causes disease through the live vaccine.

Treatment

There is no specific treatment for polio, but the following applies:
■ Bed rest may limit the severity of paralysis
■ People with severe breathing difficulties will need artificial ventilation
■ People with severe symptoms, such as circulation problems, should be monitored
■ Pain relief, splinting of joints and physiotherapy may be necessary to prevent contractures (permanent shortening of tissue)
■ Patients should be isolated.

Physiotherapy is important for treating paralysis and limb wasting. Exercises can prevent painful and disfiguring muscle contractures from developing.

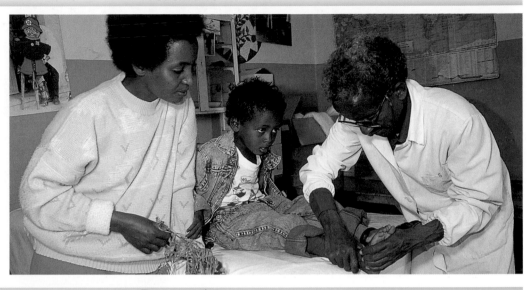

Prognosis

In around 90 per cent of all cases of poliomyelitis, those infected suffer influenza-type symptoms, sometimes developing pharyngitis or mild diarrhoea. This non-paralytic form of the disease is self-limiting and complete recovery can be expected.

The development of secondary complications is common, particularly infections of the chest or bladder. These will need appropriate antibiotic treatment.

PARALYTIC POLIOMYELITIS
Ten per cent of those infected suffer a paralytic form of the

Poliomyelitis occurred in epidemics worldwide prior to the introduction of vaccines. The disease affected children, who were often left disabled.

disease. Studies have shown that within this group around 60 per cent suffer spinal paralysis and mortality can reach 11 per cent.

Within this group:
■ The rate of recovery tends to be slowest in adults and most rapid in young children
■ The most significant recovery takes place in the first 12 months following paralysis
■ Where complete paralysis of a muscle is present six months after the onset of the disease, improvement is unlikely.

POST-POLIO SYNDROME
After a period of prolonged stability many people who have contracted paralytic poliomyelitis develop post-polio syndrome. This causes further impairments in mobility, upper limb function and breathing.

Prevention

An injected form of inactivated polio vaccine was introduced in 1956 and used for routine immunization. It was highly effective and is still recommended for use today in pregnant women, people who are immunosuppressed and unvaccinated individuals over the age of 50.

LIVE VACCINE
The live oral polio vaccine was introduced in 1962. This has many advantages over the non-live form, as it provides intestinal as well as humoral (circulating antibodies in the blood) immunity. Following a live vaccination, vaccine virus is excreted in the faeces for several weeks, allowing the vaccine to spread to close contacts, just as the disease would. This increases

the spread and effectiveness of vaccination considerably.

Children in the UK are immunized as babies, then receive booster doses at five and 15 years of age. The vaccine confers immunity for 10 years.

Adults travelling to South Asia, and Central or West Africa should check their immunity status, as poliomyelitis is still endemic in these countries.

Babies are routinely immunized against poliomyelitis through a course of three doses at two, three and four months. A booster will be given pre-school.

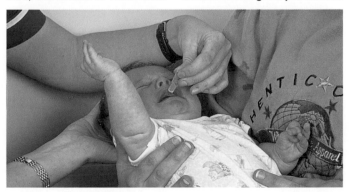

Malaria

Causes

Malaria is caused by a group of closely related protozoan (single-celled) parasites. It is transmitted primarily by the bite of infected female *Anopheles* mosquitoes and can also be transmitted by transfusion of infected blood.

There are four species that cause malaria: *Plasmodium ovale* (Africa), *P. malariae* (Africa), *P. vivax* (Indian subcontinent, southeast Asia, South and Central America) and *P. falciparum* (Africa, Pacific islands, southeast Asia and South America). *P. falciparum*

This Plasmodium *parasite has entered the bloodstream, penetrating and destroying red blood cells. The infected cells are stained purple in this electron micrograph.*

causes the most severe form of the disease, which may be life-threatening. The other species are usually associated with a more benign infections.

Incubation takes 12–28 days but manifestation can occur up to five years later as the parasite can exist for this long in the liver without causing disease.

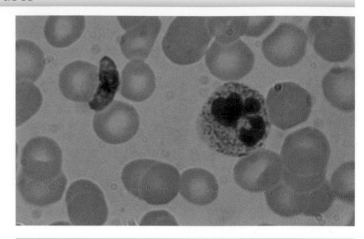

Symptoms

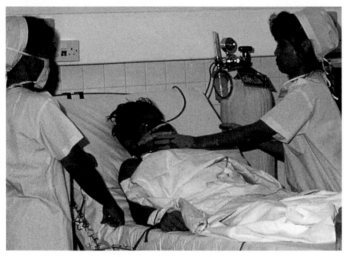

The clinical features of malaria infection are often non-specific, including general malaise, flu-like illness, headache, abdominal pain and dysuria (urination problems).

Symptoms common to all parasite species include abrupt onset of fever which becomes episodic with cold, hot and

In severe cases of malaria, patients need to be hospitalized so that intensive care can be administered. This critically ill patient is being ventilated.

sweating phases over a 6-8 hour period. Enlarged liver and spleen, anaemia and jaundice may also occur.

Diagnosis

Infection with *P. falciparum* causes severe disease that affects all major organs. Complications include cerebral malaria, which may involve fits or loss of consciousness, hypoglycaemia (low blood sugar), renal failure, haemoglobinuria (haemoglobin in the urine) and pulmonary oedema (fluid in the lungs).

The physical examination and the symptoms of malaria are non-specific and cannot be relied upon for diagnosis. A correct diagnosis depends primarily on the identification of the parasite in red blood cells. This can be achieved by using special blood staining techniques. The malaria parasite can be seen within the red blood cells in thin blood films.

Staining techniques are used to identify the species of the

infecting malaria parasite. Often, several films need to be prepared in order to confirm the diagnosis. Other methods include using a dipstick test in which antigens of the parasite are detected by placing a drop of blood on a dipstick.

To detect malaria parasites in red blood cells, a thin blood film is spread on a slide. This is then stained so that the microscopic parasites can be seen.

Life cycle and transmission

The malaria parasite passes through a complicated life cycle with a number of stages:

[1] The saliva of the infected mosquito contains the infective stage, the sporozoite, which is injected into the human following the bite as the mosquito feeds.
[2] Sporozoites enter the liver and its cells, where they mature and multiply, forming schizonts.
[3] The mature schizonts release many merozoites into the bloodstream; each merozoite infects a red blood cell, where it matures and replicates itself.

[4] Within each red cell, the merozoites develop to form either schizonts or gametocytes.
[5] If a schizont is formed, it continues to release merozoites which proceed to infect another generation of red blood cells.
[6] Gametocytes are the sexual stage of the malaria parasite present in the blood stream, and re-infect any mosquitoes that ingest them while feeding.
[7] The gametocytes develop into male and female gametes in the mosquito again, which can subsequently re-infect humans.

The female Anopheles *mosquito is the carrier of malaria. Blood is infected with the* Plasmodium *parasite when a carrier mosquito bites.*

Treatment

The treatment of malaria includes supportive as well as specific therapy. It is essential to lower the body temperature, provide rehydration and monitor kidney function, blood count and glucose levels. Specific treatment includes the use of chloroquine and primaquine for the benign species of malaria (*P. vivax*, *P. ovale* and *P. malariae*).

An increasing problem is chloroquine-resistant *P. falciparum*; in such cases, quinine is used, often in combination with the drug Fansidar. Other treatments include mefloquine and halofantrine.

The mortality rate following infection with *P. falciparum* may be as high as 20 per cent. The response to specific anti-malarial treatment is monitored by both physical examination and repeated blood films. The blood films should be examined until there is no evidence of the malaria parasite present.

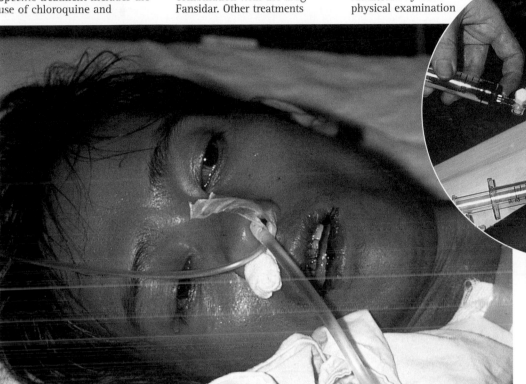

Anaemia is a possible complication of malignant malaria. Blood transfusions may therefore be necessary.

Severe malaria falciparum is often life-threatening. This is because the parasitized red blood cells accumulate, blocking smaller blood vessels.

Prevention

The use of the appropriate antimalarial drugs can reduce the risk of developing malaria. Such drugs include chloroquine and proguanil; mefloquine is recommended for travellers visiting chloroquine-resistant areas such as West, Central and East Africa, and specific areas of Southeast Asia.

Antimalarials do not confer 100 per cent protection, so other methods of prevention must also be followed, including:
■ Preventing or reducing the likelihood of bites by wearing long-sleeved clothing, using insect repellents and sleeping under mosquito nets impregnated with chemical repellents where appropriate
■ Complying fully with antimalarial drug requirements
■ Seeking advice and treatment promptly if unwell.

Travellers are also advised to seek prompt medical attention if they become unwell after visiting a malarial area, even if they have taken antimalarial drugs. Emergency treatment packs are available for travellers who are likely to find it difficult to obtain immediate treatment.

Spray and roll-on repellents, diffusers and chemically impregnated nets can reduce the risk of being bitten by carrier mosquitoes.

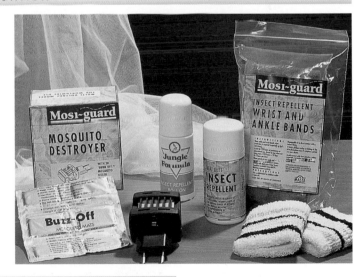

Incidence

Malaria is one of the most prevalent infections worldwide, with 300 million people infected and two million deaths every year.
It remains the single most important disease-hazard facing travellers, with 2,500 cases being reported and approximately 10 deaths per annum in travellers returning to the UK.

Over 50 per cent of UK cases are due to infection with *P. falciparum*, with most of these cases being contracted in Africa (where *P. falciparum* is the most prevalent species resulting in both significant transmission and risk). Malaria is endemic in many parts of Africa, Central and South America, southeast Asia, the Indian subcontinent and the Pacific islands.

The prevention of malaria is therefore of vital importance in at-risk individuals, especially those people who are due to visit endemic areas.

Toxocariasis

Symptoms

There may be no symptoms of toxocaral infection as most infections are mild and go unnoticed. In more serious infections, symptoms include:
■ Fever and abdominal discomfort, sometimes with nausea and vomiting
■ Cough and wheezing
■ Fits, if the brain is involved
■ Visual symptoms as larvae migrate to the eye.

Symptoms of a serious toxocaral infection may include coughing, wheezing and, occasionally, vomiting.

Causes

Toxocara is a roundworm which frequently infects dogs, particularly puppies (*T. canis*), and cats (*T. cati*). It lives in their intestines and lays eggs that are passed out in their faeces. If humans ingest these eggs, they become infected in turn. Most human infections with *Toxocara* (toxocariasis) are caused by the dog roundworm and can range from unnoticed or mild infection to occasionally serious disease and even blindness.

LIFECYCLE IN HUMANS
The adult worm cannot develop inside humans, but the eggs can hatch into larvae inside the intestines. The larvae then migrate, via blood vessels, to the liver, lungs, brain or heart. The larvae may cause inflammation and a form of toxocariasis known as visceral larva migrans (VLM). This disease may pass almost unnoticed or may, in some cases, become serious.

Occasionally, the larvae may migrate to the eye, where even one larva can cause a great deal of damage, leading to the condition of ocular larva migrans (OLM).

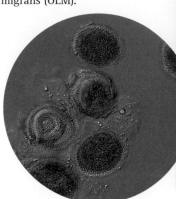

A roundworm embryo is visible within one of the Toxocara canis eggs in this sample. If ingested, they will hatch in the intestines.

The health risks associated with animal faeces are increasingly recognized. People are encouraged to clean up after their pets in public places.

Diagnosis

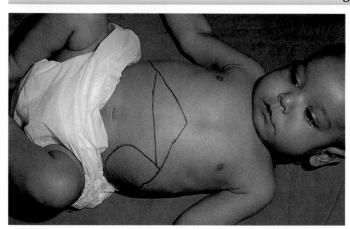

The initial examination by a doctor may reveal:
■ Fever
■ Enlarged liver
■ Altered breath sounds on listening to the chest
■ Enlarged lymph nodes
■ Changes in the eye – seen on examination with an ophthalmoscope (an instrument used for looking inside the eye).

On examination, a doctor may feel an enlarged liver and spleen, which will then be marked on the patient's body. Enlarged liver is a symptom of Toxocara infection.

Blood tests may reveal:
■ Raised levels of white blood cells, especially eosinophilia (white blood cells involved in the defence against parasites)
■ Raised levels of antibodies to the *Toxocara* larvae.

TISSUE BIOPSY
Very occasionally, a piece of affected tissue may be removed for examination under the microscope. The larvae themselves are not visible but there is a characteristic grouping of the defence cells (granuloma), which can aid diagnosis.

Who is at risk?

Toxocara infection is most likely to occur in young children under the age of six who play with puppies or young dogs, or who regularly play on surfaces where dog faeces have been deposited – especially if the child is known to put soil in their mouth. Surveys have shown that up to one in five soil samples taken from gardens, parks and sandpits have been contaminated with *Toxocara* eggs, which can survive in

Infants are particularly prone to infection as they often put their hands and objects into their mouth.

damp conditions for years.

Toxocara infections are found throughout the world. As most of those infected show no symptoms, it is difficult to know

exactly how many people are infected each year, but a survey of blood samples of children in the UK has shown evidence of infection in one in four children.

Sandpits contaminated with dog or cat faeces can harbour Toxocara eggs for years if the conditions remain damp. The eggs hatch after ingestion.

Treatment

Treatment depends on the severity of the infection. In general, most *Toxocara* infections are mild and will resolve naturally within weeks or months without any specific form of treatment. However, the body's immune system is not generally effective against serious worm infestations, and these cases may need drug treatment to kill the parasites or to limit the damage caused to the body by the defence cells. Drugs used to treat worms are called anthelmintics.

If damage to the eye occurs in cases of OLM, the child will need specialized treatment by a skilled ophthalmologist to treat the damaged retina.

DRUG TREATMENT
Drugs that can be used to treat *Toxocara* infections include:

■ **Anti-parasitic drugs**
Severe cases may need to be treated with medicines which act against the worms, such as diethylcarbamazine and thiabendazole

■ **Anti-inflammatory drugs**
These include corticosteroids which may used to reduce the damage caused to the tissues by the body's own defences against migrating larvae.

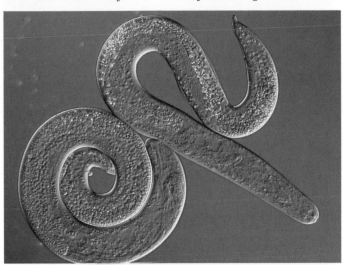

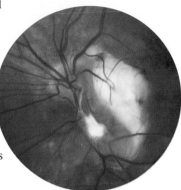

This light micrograph shows two T. canis larvae in their second stage. The larvae invade blood vessels and migrate to the liver, lungs and eye.

A view through an ophthalmoscope shows scarring to the retina due to Toxocara infection. This is called a granuloma.

Prevention

With *Toxocara* infection, prevention is better than cure. Simple steps can greatly reduce the chances of a child becoming infected:

■ All cats, dogs and especially puppies should be wormed regularly so that their faeces do not contain *Toxocara* eggs
■ Dog owners should be responsible for picking up and safely disposing of faeces that their dogs leave behind and be educated as to why this is important
■ Dogs should be completely excluded from children's play areas
■ Sand pits should be covered when not in use to prevent cats using them as a litter tray
■ Children should be taught to wash their hands after playing outside, after touching cats, dogs and puppies and particularly before eating.

Many children become infected with Toxocara every year. Worming pets and encouraging hygienic practices, such as washing hands, are useful.

Toxocara in the eye

Blindness caused by *Toxocara* infection of the eye is an extremely rare occurrence. In the UK, about 50 children a year develop *Toxocara* eye infection and, of these, the majority will keep their sight.

If a child has *Toxocara* eye infection they will complain of a decrease in the vision of the affected eye. In some cases there may be a squint and a condition known as leukocoria, where the pupil of the affected eye appears white instead of the usual black colour. Occasionally there may be pain in the eye. Infected children are usually between the ages of six and 14 years, slightly older than those affected with VLM, the more generalized *Toxocara* infection.

In the most common form of *Toxocara* eye infection, known

If a child complains that their visual field is becoming reduced, a doctor will initially test their eyesight. A further test with an ophthalmoscope can confirm a granuloma.

as posterior pole granuloma, a larva enters a blood vessel in the retina at the back of the eye and the body's own defence cells form a tight cluster around it. The cluster of cells, or granuloma, can be seen when examining the eye with an ophthalmoscope.

Often this needs no specific treatment but the doctor may decide to prescribe anti-parasitic or anti-inflammatory drugs. Rarely, the infection involves the whole eye and does more serious damage. In this case, surgery is ultimately likely to be needed.

Tetanus

Symptoms

Tetanus is an acute, often fatal disease which occurs worldwide, although most commonly in developing countries which have a lower standard of healthcare. It is caused by the bacterium *Clostridium tetani*, which produces a toxin that poisons the central nervous system.

SIGNS OF TETANUS

■ Onset of symptoms is usually about 10 days (but may be 3–21 days) after contamination of a wound previously sustained; shorter incubation periods are associated with heavily contaminated wounds

■ Tetanus causes stiffness and painful muscle spasms which often start in the muscles of the head and neck, and especially

This patient with tetanus shows the fixed 'smile' that occurs when facial muscles spasm. If spasms in the chest occur, breathing may be compromised.

the jaw; inability to open the jaw has given the disease the common name of 'lockjaw'

■ Muscle spasms can occasionally be localized, affecting only one area of the body, but are more commonly generalized, affecting the whole body

■ The diaphragm and intercostal muscles (those between the ribs) are the main muscle groups involved in breathing and spasms affecting them may interfere with breathing to such an extent that artificial ventilation is required

■ Spasms of the facial muscles may cause the face to assume a characteristic expression, such as a fixed 'smile' with raised eyebrows

■ Muscles of the back and abdomen may also become rigid, causing the body to adopt a distorted and painful posture.

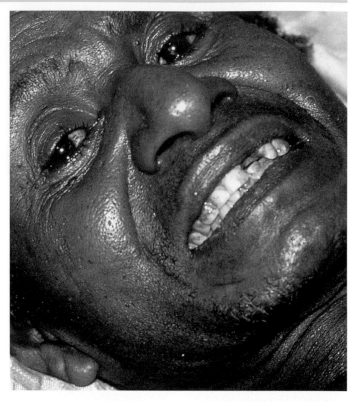

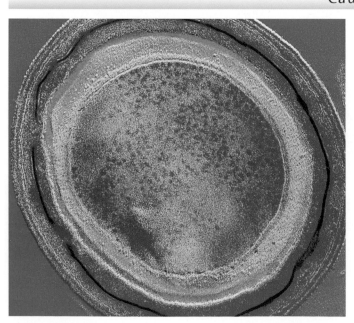

The toxin produced by Clostridium tetani bacteria causes muscle fibres to spasm. This results in deformed and rigid postures and pain.

ASSOCIATED PROBLEMS

Along with the muscular spasms, there may be difficulty swallowing, high blood pressure and abnormal heartbeat, fever, headache and sore throat.

The patient may undergo convulsions as the spasms increase in duration and frequency, and severe injuries may be caused, including fractured bones. Pneumonia

may also develop, caused by the inhalation of fluids from the mouth and stomach.

Death occurs in about 30 per cent of tetanus cases in developed countries; in underdeveloped countries, the death rate may be as high as 50 per cent. Those that survive may be left with residual weakness and stiffness for a prolonged period.

Causes

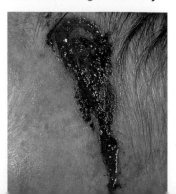

The bacterium *Clostridium tetani* is found in soil and dust almost everywhere in the environment, and particularly in areas contaminated with the manure of horses and other mammals. The bacterium lies dormant in the soil in the form of a strong, heat-resistant spore which enters the body through a wound, often with other material such as soil particles or rust, which help to hide the bacterium from the body's defences.

Within the body, the spores germinate and the growing bacteria start to produce a

This electron micrograph shows a spore of Clostridium tetani. The spores are found in soil and manure and only germinate when introduced into a wound.

potent toxin, which is released into the tissues. This spreads to the nervous system where it has the effect of stimulating excessive activity within various muscle groups, causing them to spasm. If the muscles involved in breathing are affected, death may result.

An open wound, particularly one that has been contaminated with dirt or mud, may harbour Clostridium tetani spores. Careful cleansing is necessary.

Diagnosis and treatment

Diagnosis of tetanus is made clinically by the doctor at the bedside rather than by laboratory tests. As soon as tetanus is suspected, the patient is given an intramuscular injection of 'human tetanus immunoglobulin' (specific antibodies to the tetanus toxin); this neutralizes any toxin which has not yet reached its target.

The wound is opened and cleaned to remove any dead tissue, together with any particles of soil or other foreign matter that may be present.

ANTIBIOTIC TREATMENT

Penicillin is administered to kill any remaining bacteria and the patient may then be admitted to the intensive care ward of a hospital. This allows a high level of supportive care, which can be given until the patient's vital functions are no longer under threat.

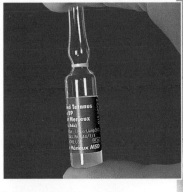

Initial treatment entails an injection of human tetanus immunoglobulin. This counteracts the toxins produced by **Clostridium tetani** *bacteria.*

This baby's muscles have become rigid due to tetanus infection. Admission to an intensive care ward is necessary to treat any life-threatening symptoms.

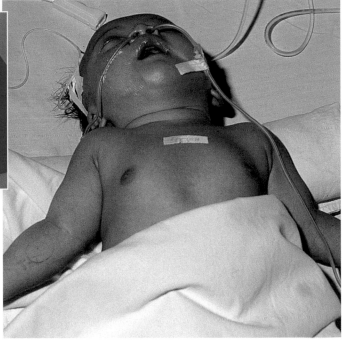

Wound care

All wounds should be cleaned as soon as possible. Simple abrasions can be cleaned adequately by washing them, but more serious wounds, and those which are deep or penetrating, may need to be treated surgically. All dead tissue and foreign material will be removed so that it will not provide a shelter for the bacteria.

Immunization with tetanus toxoid should be given to all those who have not had a booster within the last 10 years.

Antiseptic cream may be applied to smaller cuts or grazes after they have been thoroughly cleaned

Incidence

■ Tetanus is not spread from person to person but is acquired from the environment, most commonly via a puncture wound or a deep scratch
■ In the UK, the disease is rare, but those most frequently affected are unimmunized people who spend a lot of time in contact with the soil, such as gardeners, footballers and agricultural workers; however, as the spores of *Clostridium tetani* are so ubiquitous, any wound could potentially be contaminated
■ In developing countries without adequate immunization, the disease is common and may occur in newborn children due to infection from mud used to seal the cut umbilical cord.

Workers who are frequently exposed to soil and animal manure, such as farm workers, are particularly susceptible to tetanus infection.

Prevention

Tetanus is extremely rare in the UK because of the high level of immunity against the organism within the population thanks to immunization programmes.

Unlike many other diseases, tetanus infection does not leave the body with a lifelong immunity, so previously infected people also need to be immunized. Immunization is routinely given to children and is entirely effective if boosters are maintained every 10 years.

Babies are immunized against tetanus, and booster shots are then given just before starting primary school and again between the ages of 13 and 15.

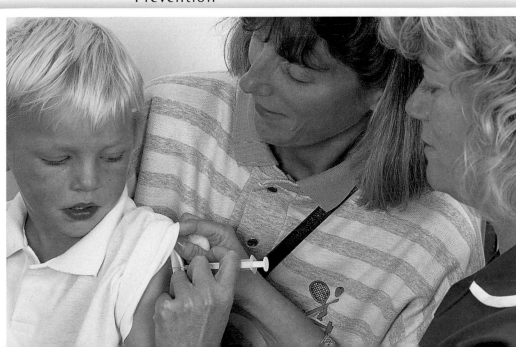

Deep vein thrombosis

Symptoms

A deep vein thrombosis (DVT) is a blood clot (thrombus) that forms in a vein deep in the body, rather than one just beneath the skin. Some thrombi grow large enough to obstruct the blood flow and damage the valves of the vein.

RISK FACTORS
Veins in the legs and pelvis are the most common sites for deep vein thrombosis. Risk factors include conditions that damage vein walls, slow the flow of blood or increase the tendency of the blood to clot.

COMMON SYMPTOMS
Possible symptoms include:
■ Pain – a deep vein thrombosis in the lower leg may cause pain and tenderness in the calf, worse when the foot is flexed, but most cause no symptoms; a thrombosis in the groin or pelvis may cause severe leg pain
■ Swelling of the leg
■ Blue discoloration (cyanosis) of the leg, due to lack of oxygen
■ White leg – from spasm of the neighbouring arteries
■ Feeling of heat in the leg
■ Congested leg veins
■ Slight fever.

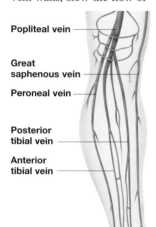

◄*Thrombi usually develop in the deep veins of the leg, shown here. A blood clot forms in a vein deep within the body rather than just under the skin.*

Popliteal vein

Great saphenous vein

Peroneal vein

Posterior tibial vein

Anterior tibial vein

▶ *Swelling of this patient's left leg (right of picture) indicates a deep vein thrombosis. The leg appears red and inflamed and is warm to the touch.*

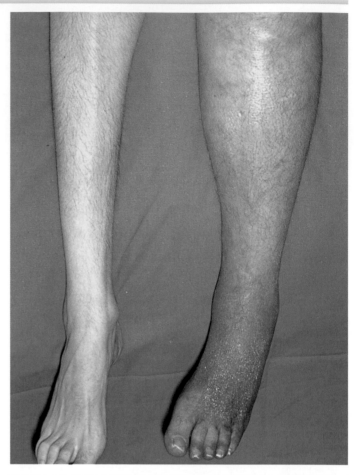

Pulmonary embolism

Pulmonary embolism is a highly dangerous complication of a deep vein thrombosis in the leg or pelvis. It occurs when a thrombus breaks free (forming an embolus) and travels through the bloodstream to the heart.

If an embolus is large enough, it may block the arteries leading from the right side of the heart to the lungs (pulmonary embolism) causing acute heart failure or sudden death. With smaller emboli, sections of the lung tissue may die (infarct), leading to acute pain on inspiration (pleuritic pain) or the coughing up of blood (haemoptysis).

Pulmonary emboli are rare with calf thromboses, which tend to be small. Thrombi formed higher in the leg and in the pelvis are more likely to produce pulmonary emboli.

In this image of lungs affected by pulmonary embolism, the patient's right lung is normal. The left lung (circled) shows infarction caused by an embolus blocking an artery.

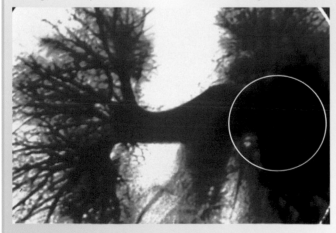

Incidence

Deep vein thromboses are common, with the incidence increasing with age:
■ Each year up to three people per 1,000 aged 65–69 years develop a deep vein thrombosis
■ The figure rises to eight per 1,000 in those aged 85–89 years
■ Deep vein thromboses occur in 50 per cent of patients after prostatectomy and in one third of patients after a myocardial infarct (heart attack)
■ Over 60 per cent of all people dying in hospital and examined post-mortem are found to have a thrombosis in a leg vein.

WOMEN AT RISK
Women are at greater risk of DVT than men as pregnancy, the combined (oestrogen-containing) Pill and hormone replacement therapy (HRT) drugs increase their risk. Each year in the USA, more women die from a pulmonary embolism following a DVT than from breast cancer.

Women are more likely than men to suffer from deep vein thrombosis. Taking hormone replacement therapy (HRT) drugs increases the risk.

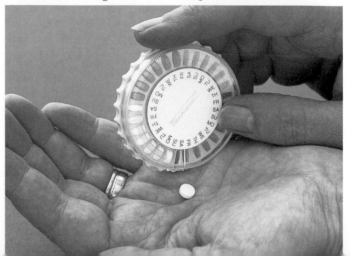

Causes

Deep vein thromboses sometimes occur for no apparent reason, but known risk factors include:

- Age over 40 years
- Obesity
- Immobility, bed rest for more than four days, inactive long-distance travel (particularly if associated with dehydration), recent stroke
- Medication with oestrogens (such as the combined oral contraceptive pill or HRT)
- Pregnancy and the puerperium (the period of up to six weeks after childbirth)
- Trauma – particularly to the pelvis, hips or legs
- Surgical procedures – especially orthopaedic, neurosurgical, urological and gynaecological procedures
- Serious illness, such as heart failure, cancer, myocardial infarct, and inflammatory bowel disease, such as ulcerative colitis

- Personal or family history of deep vein thrombosis or pulmonary embolism
- Severe varicose veins
- Hypercoagulability of the blood; for example, in polycythaemia, the haemoglobin concentration is abnormally high and the blood is thicker than normal; in thrombocythaemia, the number of platelets in the blood increases
- Inherited abnormalities of the blood – the most common is the factor V Leiden mutation, present in about five per cent of the population. This, and similar defects, increase the risk of thrombosis already present in women who are taking the contraceptive pill.

Inactive long-distance travel is a known risk factor. Flying in particular can cause deep vein thrombosis due to the likelihood of dehydration.

Treatment

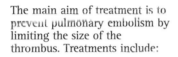
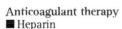

The main aim of treatment is to prevent pulmonary embolism by limiting the size of the thrombus. Treatments include:

Anticoagulant therapy
- Heparin

Intravenous heparin almost immediately reduces blood clotting and should be given as soon as possible. Treatment should continue for at least five days, either intravenously or with subcutaneous injections.

- Warfarin

Oral anticoagulation with warfarin is started on the first day of treatment, but is not effective for up to 72 hours. Once the effect of warfarin is

This venogram shows a large thrombus (dark red, circled) in the calf. A venogram is produced by injecting a radiopaque dye into a vein.

established, heparin can usually be discontinued. The dose of warfarin must be carefully controlled with regular blood tests. It should be avoided in pregnancy because of risk to the fetus.

Thrombolytic therapy
- Clot-dissolving therapy, for example with streptokinase, is occasionally used to dissolve large clots and may be effective in severe pulmonary embolism, although bleeding can occur.

Clot extraction
- Surgical removal of a clot or embolus may be attempted if there is a massive pulmonary embolus or very large thrombus in the groin or pelvis.

General measures
- Mobilization
- Leg elevation
- Compression bandaging.

Diagnosis

The symptoms of deep vein thrombosis are often mild, ill-defined or non-existent. Clinical examination is often an inaccurate way of making the diagnosis. Patients with suspected deep vein thrombosis should be referred urgently to hospital.

Investigations include:
- Doppler ultrasonography – ultrasound waves are used to study blood flow. It is now the investigation of choice as it is reliable and non-invasive
- Venography – radiopaque liquid injected into a vein shows on X-ray as the liquid flows towards the heart. The procedure may be painful and technically difficult. Ultrasonography now usually makes venography unnecessary
- Blood tests – measuring circulating D-dimer concentrations may be used in addition to ultrasonography.

Prognosis

Up to 30 per cent of thromboses in calf veins disappear spontaneously; about 50 per cent remain for long periods; and 20–30 per cent of clots became detached and travel towards the heart, which can be life-threatening

In the long term, about 60 per cent of deep vein thrombosis patients develop a chronic obstruction of the deep veins in the leg, which can give rise to pain and swelling.

Prevention

Exercise and weight control are important, and aspirin may provide some protection. Preventive anticoagulant treatment should be considered for high-risk patients. Intermittent pneumatic leg compression devices offer protection during surgery.

A known risk factor for DVT is obesity. A weight control programme can therefore significantly reduce the risk.

Angina pectoris

Symptoms

Angina pectoris is the name given to the characteristic chest pain that results when the demand for blood by the heart muscle exceeds the supply of the coronary arteries. It is usually associated with atheroma (degeneration due to the formation of fatty plaques) of the coronary arteries.

CLASSIFYING ANGINA
There are several different types of angina:
■ Exertional angina – this typically occurs with ischaemic heart disease (inadequate blood flow to the heart) after physical exertion, particularly in cold weather, after meals, or when the patient is highly emotional. It resolves rapidly with rest
■ Variant angina – this is spontaneous severe angina

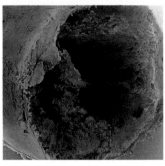

which occurs as a result of spasm of the coronary artery. This type is more common in women and tends to occur in the morning; rarely, it is induced by exercise
■ Crescendo angina – this is angina which occurs when narrowing of the coronary vessel becomes severe, and is sometimes due to a thrombus (blood clot)
■ Unstable angina – this occurs at rest or when the patient is lying down at night. It is due to a thrombus and 30 per cent of sufferers tend to go on to have a myocardial infarction (heart attack).

CLINICAL FEATURES
The typical feature of angina is central chest pain or tightness precipitated by exercise or emotion. The pain may be tight, gripping or crushing in nature, and described as an ache or discomfort behind the breastbone (retrosternally). It may occur after a heavy meal or excessive cold. If the pain is

This micrograph image shows a blood clot (red), caused by a build-up of fatty deposits on the wall of an artery. This can result in angina and/or a heart attack.

brought on by exercise, the pain will disappear at rest.

The pain may radiate to the throat, left arm or both arms, or to the back. The site of the pain may vary and occur in one site only; for example, the left wrist.

ASSOCIATED FINDINGS
The doctor may find symptoms or signs that help diagnosis, including:

Angina is characterized by central chest pain. This can be either crushing or vice-like in nature, and it can extend to the arms, back and neck.

■ Hypertension (high blood pressure)
■ Hypercholesterolaemia (high blood cholesterol levels)
■ Signs of heart failure
■ Xanthelasma (fatty deposits in the skin).

Diagnosis

The clinical diagnosis of angina is usually made on the characteristic history of the type of pain the patient experiences, its distribution and whether it disappears at rest. The following investigations may be necessary:
■ Full blood count to exclude anaemia
■ Thyroid function tests to exclude thyroid disease

A stress test is used to diagnose the effect of exercise on the heart. This is typically used for patients who suffer from angina.

■ Urea and electrolytes to diagnose kidney failure and diabetes
■ Electrocardiography (ECG) – this is often normal between episodes of angina
■ Diagnostic imaging – exercise

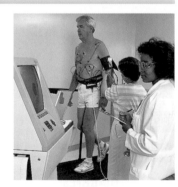

thallium scintigraphy combined with exercise testing (treadmill)
■ Cardiac catheterization and coronary arteriography when the diagnosis is uncertain
■ MGA (multi-gated acquisition scan) and/or stress echocardiography may be needed to identify localized areas of the heart muscle which display abnormal movement.

Angiography is a technique which enables blood vessels to be seen on X-ray. This can be used to diagnose angina.

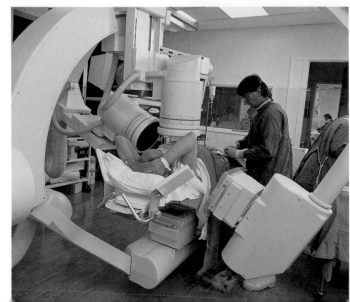

Risk factors

There are a number of factors which predispose to ischaemic heart disease. Some of these are fixed, whereas others (primarily those concerned with lifestyle) can be modified:
Fixed
■ Family history
■ Being male
■ Increasing age
Modifiable
■ Lack of exercise
■ Cigarette smoking
■ Hypertension
■ Poor diet
■ High blood cholesterol.
Patients who seek medical help for angina will be advised on addressing modifiable factors.

Cigarette smoking is a risk factor for angina. Stopping smoking should be a part of treating the condition.

Treatment

The treatment of angina varies according to the underlying cause. Initial management involves modifying lifestyle factors, such as stopping smoking, losing weight, eating a low-fat diet and avoiding stress. Other treatments include:

■ **Drug treatment** – acute attacks may be managed with glyceryl trinitrate. Beta-blockers, calcium antagonists, anti-thrombotic drugs and lipid lowering drugs are all continuous medications.

■ **Surgery** – options include balloon angioplasty, whereby narrowed arteries are enlarged using an inflatable balloon; and coronary artery bypass surgery, when a blood vessel is taken from elsewhere in the body (often the leg) and used to bypass the site of the blockage.

Glyceryl trinitrate is available in patch form which can be worn on the patient's arm. This is useful for patients who suffer from night-time attacks of angina.

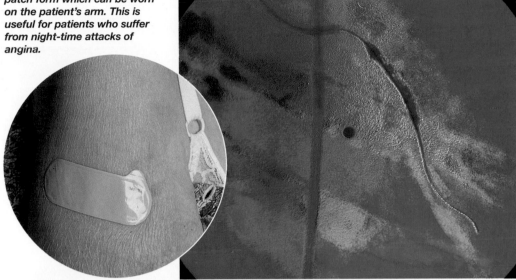

A balloon catheter is used to introduce a balloon to the site of blockage. It is guided into the obstructed vessel using a digital X-ray technique, and inflated.

This arteriogram (above) shows balloon angioplasty. The balloon (orange) has been inflated at the site of a blockage to widen the blood vessel.

Prognosis and incidence

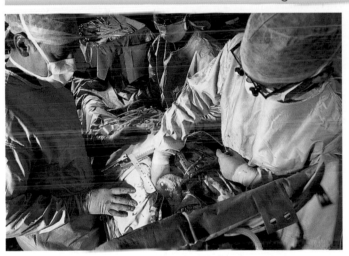

If angina is left untreated, many patients will go on to suffer a heart attack (myocardial infarction). A family history of angina increases the risk in an individual by 20–30 per cent.

Ischaemic heart disease is the main cause of death in developed countries, and it is more common in older men. Premature coronary artery disease is common in men, but in women who have had the

In severe cases of angina, bypass heart surgery may be performed. Blocked blood vessels can be bypassed using veins taken from the patient's leg.

menopause, the incidence increases to that of men of the same age.

SURGICAL PROGNOSIS
There is a 95 per cent initial success rate in balloon angioplasty, but this operation will need to be repeated in 30–40 per cent of patients. Coronary artery bypass surgery, using vein grafts to bypass the blockage, is successful in 95 per cent of patients after one year and 70 per cent after five years.

Internal thoracic (mammary) artery grafts have a success rate of 75 per cent over a 10-year period.

Causes

The pain of angina is caused by a build-up of toxins (waste products) in the heart muscle. Myocardial ischaemia results from an imbalance between oxygen supply and demand. The causes of reduced coronary blood flow are atheroma (a build-up of fatty plaques and scar tissue on the artery walls), spasm of the coronary artery, thrombo-embolism (when a blood clot becomes lodged in an artery) and stenosis (narrowing) of the artery or its branches.

OTHER CAUSES
Chest pain is one of the commonest reasons that people go to see their GP, and there are

many different conditions that can result in such a symptom.

Severe anaemia and thyroid disease can precipitate angina in a patient with minor arterial disease. Chronic chest pain can also be caused by reflux of stomach acid into the oesophagus (often a symptom of hiatus hernia) or due to spasm of the oesophagus.

In cases of angina, however, the pain is often precipitated by exercise or on lying down and characteristically lasts no longer than several minutes.

A blocked coronary artery can be seen in this angiogram (circled). This can cause angina.

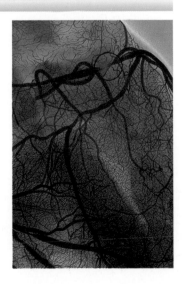

Arrhythmias

Symptoms

An arrhythmia occurs when the heart rate is outside its normal range or when the beat becomes irregular.

In health, the heartbeat is tightly regulated in order to ensure maximum efficiency and optimum performance. The control mechanism involves a wave of electrical activity which spreads through the heart, enabling co-ordinated contraction of the heart muscles, which normally beat between 60 and 90 times each minute.

CLINICAL FEATURES
The symptoms depend on the type of arrhythmia and include:
■ Palpitations
■ Rapid heartbeat
■ Chest discomfort or pain
■ Breathlessness
■ Dizziness and fainting.

Most of us have experienced a 'missed beat' (extra systole). These are usually harmless and require investigation only if they occur frequently.

Arrhythmias can be diagnosed using electrocardiography. The trace produced – the electrocardiogram – shows the electrical activity in the heart and reveals any abnormality.

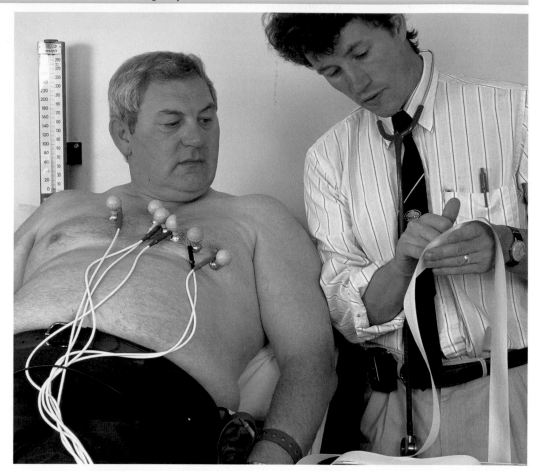

Causes

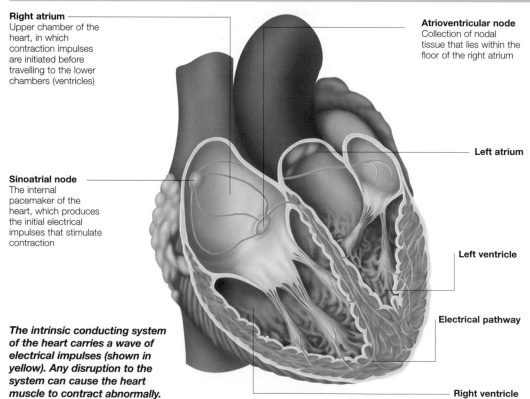

Right atrium
Upper chamber of the heart, in which contraction impulses are initiated before travelling to the lower chambers (ventricles)

Sinoatrial node
The internal pacemaker of the heart, which produces the initial electrical impulses that stimulate contraction

Atrioventricular node
Collection of nodal tissue that lies within the floor of the right atrium

Left atrium

Left ventricle

Electrical pathway

Right ventricle

The intrinsic conducting system of the heart carries a wave of electrical impulses (shown in yellow). Any disruption to the system can cause the heart muscle to contract abnormally.

Abnormal rhythms result when there is an interruption in the normal sequence of heart muscle contraction. This may arise in a number of ways:
■ The heart's inbuilt pacemaker (the sinoatrial node) may fail to trigger the electrical system
■ Abnormal electrical foci of activity may arise in the heart muscle, causing extra contractions
■ The conduction mechanism for the electrical impulse may be damaged.

MEDICAL DISORDERS
A number of medical conditions may cause arrhythmias, such as:
■ High blood pressure
■ Ischaemic heart disease
■ Congestive heart failure
■ Cardiomyopathy, or heart muscle disease
■ Excess alcohol intake
■ Pulmonary embolism
■ Hyperthyroidism.

About one-third of patients with the common arrhythmia, atrial fibrillation, have no obvious primary cause.

Types of arrhythmia

Arrhythmias can affect both the upper chambers (atria) and the lower chambers (ventricles) of the heart. The two main groups of arrhythmias are tachycardias – when the heart rate is too high and bradycardias – when the heart rate is too slow. Specific types of arrhythmias include the following:
■ Atrial fibrillation – the commonest abnormality of heart rhythm in which the heartbeat is very fast and totally irregular. This condition may be constant or paroxysmal and is common in elderly people
■ Supraventricular tachycardia – a rapid but regular heartbeat that occurs more often in young people
■ Ventricular fibrillation – in this arrhythmia, the abnormal stimulus

for a heartbeat originates in the ventricles. The result may be a far more serious form of arrhythmia requiring urgent treatment
■ Complete heart block – the electrical impulses in the atria are prevented from reaching the ventricles, causing the heart to beat extremely slowly
■ Wolff-Parkinson-White syndrome – a rare congenital condition which leads to very rapid heart rhythms
■ Cardiac arrest – a total failure of the heart to pump.

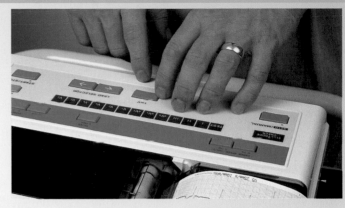

This ECG trace shows supra-ventricular tachycardia, a very rapid but regular heart rate. In this person the rate is about 205 beats per minute.

The heart rate in this ECG trace is very slow, an abnormal rhythm known as bradycardia. In this instance, the rate is about 52 beats per minute.

Modern ECG machines record the heart's electrical impulses automatically at the push of a button. The results help to diagnose an arrhythmia.

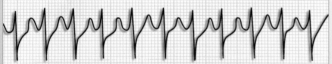

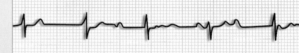

Diagnosis

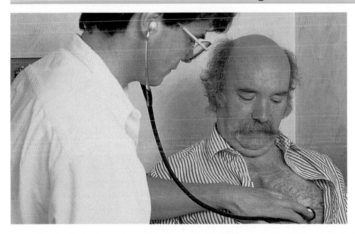

The diagnosis is usually made by taking the pulse at the wrist and then listening to the heart. In some people the diagnosis is then confirmed by carrying out an electrocardiogram (ECG). Since some arrhythmias are intermittent, a 24-hour portable ECG may be arranged.

The doctor may also ask for blood tests for anaemia and a chest X-ray.

An arrhythmia is often initially noted using a stethoscope. Listening to the heart can provide valuable information.

Prognosis

An irregular heart is less efficient. Impaired heart performance may lead to poor blood supply to the heart muscle (ischaemia), pump failure and low blood pressure. The mortality rate with atrial fibrillation is twice that of the general public.

RISK OF STROKE

Pump failure allows blood to remain in the atria, and clots are then more likely to form. These clots may then travel in the vessels to distant organs where they may cause damage; for example, a stroke, as a result of an interruption of blood flow to the brain.

The overall risk of stroke is five per cent every year and it increases with age, high blood pressure, heart failure, diabetes and ischaemic heart disease. Patients under 60 who do not have any of these risk factors have a very low risk of stroke.

Treatment and prevention

Arrhythmias can be treated in different ways depending on the type. Treatments include:
■ Drugs – the most common way of treating tachycardias is by the use of drugs. For instance, the drug of choice in continuous atrial fibrillation is digoxin, which slows the heart rate. Other drugs used are verapramil and beta blockers
■ Cardioversion – this is the administration of electric shocks to the chest under anaesthetic. It can restore normal heart rate in people with severe supra-ventricular tachycardia
■ Radio-frequency ablation of

the AV junction – this destroys the abnormal electrical pathway
■ Pacemaker – if the heart rate is below 60 beats per minute and a person is having black-outs, insertion of an artificial pacemaker may be necessary.

PREVENTION
Arrhythmias can be prevented to some degree by the measures that help to prevent heart disease in general – regular exercise, avoiding smoking and eating a healthy diet.

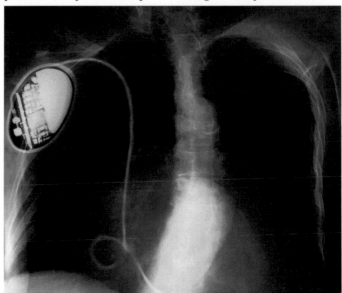

An artificial pacemaker keeps the heart beating regularly. Pacemakers are fitted in patients with a malfunctioning sinoatrial node or a heart block.

Incidence

Most heart arrhythmias are rare in younger people, but become more common with increasing age.

Atrial fibrillation is one exception to this, affecting one per cent of the population between 40–65 and five per cent of people who are 65 and over. About 50 per cent of patients with atrial fibrillation are 75 or over.

Heart failure

Symptoms

Heart failure is a life-threatening condition in which the heart fails to pump blood round the body efficiently. Thus the body's needs for oxygen and nutrition are not met.

The symptoms of heart failure can have an even more profound effect on the quality of life than those of other chronic diseases, such as diabetes and arthritis. The symptoms include:
■ Tiredness – particularly in severe heart failure
■ Breathlessness (dyspnoea) –

at first, this may arise on exertion; later it may occur even when the patient is resting
■ Coughing up white- or pink-stained frothy sputum – this is due to fluid retention and congestion in the lungs
■ Swelling – fluid accumulating in the tissues (oedema) causes swollen ankles in mobile patients and swelling of the lower back and thighs in bed-ridden patients
■ Weight loss – loss of appetite, nausea and vomiting are common
■ Abdominal pain – this may result from liver congestion.

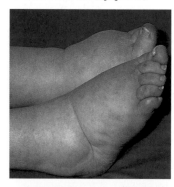

Heart failure commonly causes swollen ankles. The swelling is caused by blood congestion in the veins which results in more fluid being forced into the tissues.

One of the symptoms of heart failure is tiredness. This is often accompanied by breathlessness, even at rest.

Causes

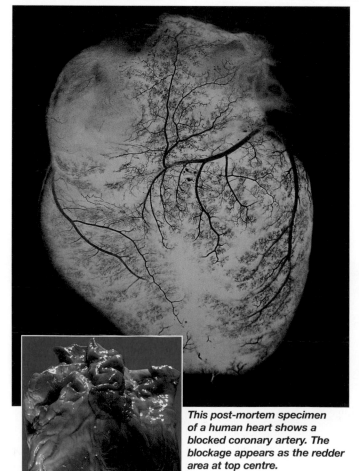

This post-mortem specimen of a human heart shows a blocked coronary artery. The blockage appears as the redder area at top centre.

The arteries and veins in the human heart supply blood to the cardiac muscles. Blockage of the arteries damages the heart muscle.

Heart failure occurs when the heart is damaged or overworked, as in the following conditions:
■ Coronary heart disease – the muscle of the left ventricle is damaged
■ Chronic heart muscle disorders – causes may include viral infections and alcoholism
■ Hypertension – this hardens the arteries, making it difficult for the heart to pump blood
■ Acute or chronic myocarditis (inflammation of the heart muscle) – causes include viral and bacterial infections
■ Valvular disease – the heart valves may be congenitally malformed, deteriorate or become damaged
■ Narrowing of the aorta – a congenital deformity
■ High output demand – when the heart has to work hard to meet the body's oxygen needs
■ Impeded inflow – chronic thickening of the pericardium, for example, will restrict the inflow of blood to the heart so it will have to pump harder to maintain the circulation.

Heart functions

The heart is a muscular organ which pumps blood round the body. The blood, in turn, supplies oxygen and nutrition to the organs and tissues
■ It beats about 100,000 times a day and circulates 25 to 30 litres of blood a minute
■ It is divided into right and left sides, each consisting of an atrium and ventricle
■ Deoxygenated blood from the main veins collects in the right atrium. It is then pumped through the right ventricle to the lungs
■ The left atrium receives oxygenated blood from the lungs and sends it to the left ventricle, which pumps it into the general circulation
■ Valves in the heart prevent back flow
■ The heart muscle has its own blood supply, the coronary arteries. If they are narrowed or blocked, the heart muscle suffers. Complete blockage of a section may lead to the death of part of the heart muscle from lack of oxygen. The left ventricular muscle is most often affected
■ The pericardium is a double-layered membrane that surrounds the heart.

Diagnosis

Heart failure is often diagnosed clinically, but other tests may be needed to determine the underlying cause and best course of treatment. Symptoms such as dyspnoea and oedema suggest heart failure.

INVESTIGATIONS
The following investigations are carried out:
■ Blood tests – for full blood count, for liver, kidney and thyroid functions and for levels of cardiac enzymes, which are raised after a heart attack
■ A chest X-ray – to check for an enlarged heart, fluid in the lungs and hardened arteries
■ Electrocardiography (ECG) – usually abnormal in patients with heart failure
■ Echocardiography – a key investigation; it assesses the left ventricular function, the heart

In heart failure, the heart will sound abnormal when it is heard through a stethoscope. Crackles may be heard from excess fluid in the lungs.

A doctor can use X-rays to check for various signs of heart failure. These include fluid in the lungs and hardened arteries.

valves and the pericardium
■ Colour flow Doppler ultrasonography – used to study the valves and blood flow
■ Cardiac catheterization – gives information about pressures in the heart and coronary arteries
■ Exercise testing – used to check the heart's ability to deliver oxygenated blood.

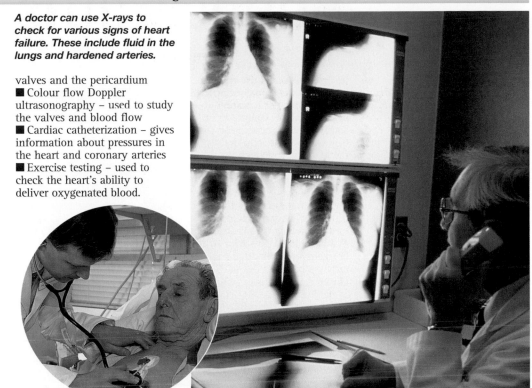

Treatment

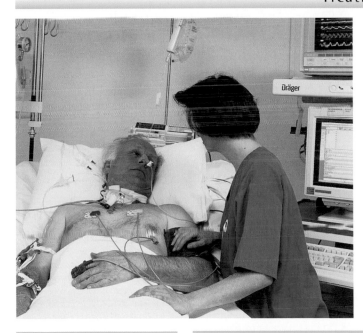

Hospital admission is often advisable for people with heart disease. When possible, any underlying cause, such as anaemia, should be treated.

Rest reduces demands on the heart, but periods of bed rest should be as short as possible to avoid the risk of blood clots (thromboses) forming in the legs

Patients are best nursed sitting rather than lying. Meals should be small and have a low salt content. Alcohol and smoking should be avoided.

Drug treatment includes:
■ Diuretics – these increase urine production and reduce

Hospital admission is usually imperative for treating heart failure. Rest and a combination of drugs are also essential for patients to regain their health.

blood pressure, oedema and dyspnoea
■ Beta-blockers – these help the heart to beat more restfully, but must be started under supervision
■ ACE (angiotensin converting enzyme) inhibitors – these reduce morbidity and mortality rates in chronic heart failure, and also myocardial infarction. The first dose must be supervised
■ Angiotensin-II antagonists – these are similar to ACE inhibitors, but may cause fewer side effects
■ Digoxin – this commonly causes nausea and the dose can be difficult to stabilize. It is chiefly used to steady the heartbeat if the atria beat out of rhythm.

Many patients need a combination of drugs.

Incidence

Heart failure occurs at any age, but it usually affects older people. In Western countries, up to two per cent of the total population, and about 10 per cent of people over 75 years of age, are affected. In the over-65 age group, about 10 per 1,000 people develop heart failure each year.

Since the 1960s, the number of cases of heart failure has approximately doubled, as people are living longer.

Prognosis

Despite advances in treatment, the outlook for patients with heart failure is often poor. Survival rates are worse than for many common forms of cancer. About 50 per cent of patients with severe heart failure die within two years of diagnosis.

Heart patients need to take regular medication. Eighty per cent of patients who have suffered mild to moderate heart failure will survive.

Endocarditis

Symptoms

Endocarditis, formerly known as subacute bacterial endocarditis (SBE), is a condition in which the heart valves or the endocardium (heart lining) become infected. Although usually a chronic illness, it may have a sudden onset. Virulent organisms such as *Staphylococcus aureus* may destroy the heart valves.

DISEASE PROCESS

Clumps of infecting organisms, fibrin and platelets, known collectively as 'vegetations', develop on an affected heart valve. These may destroy the valve cusps (flaps) and lead to regurgitation of blood flow if the valve becomes incompetent. The valve may become stenotic (narrowing of the orifice occurs). Endocarditis should be suspected in any patient with a fever in whom a heart murmur is heard.

CLINICAL FEATURES

Anaemia, flu-like symptoms and weight loss are common and a patient is often diagnosed with influenza or treated with antibiotics before endocarditis is confirmed. As the condition progresses, the following symptoms and signs may occur:
■ Vegetations may break off and circulate in the bloodstream, obstructing blood supply to an organ; this can cause myocardial infarction (death of part of the heart muscle) or a stroke
■ The walls of an artery may become weakened by an infected embolus, causing a haemorrhage
■ Vasculitis (inflammation of small blood vessels) produces small haemorrhages in the skin or mucosa, especially in the throat or the conjunctivae, retina (Roth's spots) or the nail beds (splinter haemorrhages); small red macules (spots) on the hands and painful swellings on the pads of the fingers and toes (known as Osler's nodes) may also occur
■ Haematuria (blood in the urine) is common due to glomerulonephritis or infarction of the kidneys
■ In the late stages of the disease finger-clubbing may occur.

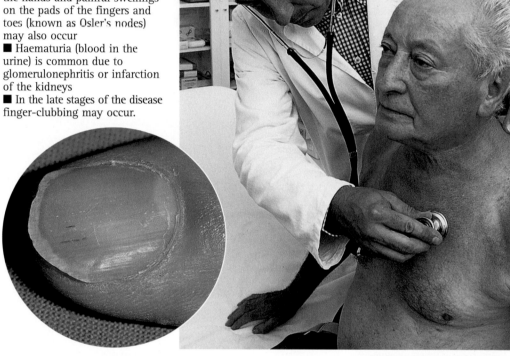

Inflammation of the blood vessels may occur as a result of endocarditis. This may be visible in the form of dark 'splinter haemorrhages' under the nails.

A heart murmur is a sign of an abnormal heart valve. A new murmur or a change in the character of a known murmur may indicate endocarditis.

Incidence

The prevalence is about 5–10 cases per 100,000 of the population in the UK. The incidence increases with age. Endocarditis is much more common in developing countries. It is now more common in older people with degenerative aortic or mitral valve disease.

Causes

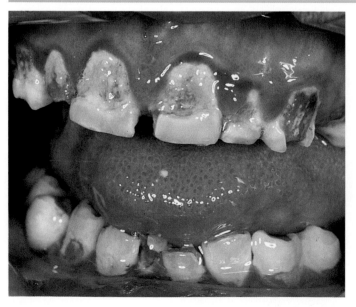

Severe dental decay and gingivitis (gum inflammation) predispose patients to bacteria in the blood, and endocarditis may subsequently develop.

■ Endocarditis usually occurs on abnormal heart valves or on the low-pressure side of shunts such as ventricular septal defects; patients with prosthetic heart valves are vulnerable to infection
■ Patients with an internal pacemaker are susceptible to infective endocarditis
■ Staphylococcal infections from the skin and from conditions such as chronic eczema may cause the disease
■ Endocarditis may occur in patients with severe tooth decay or inflamed gums and after dental procedures or surgery.

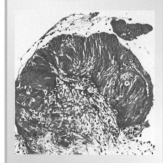

This micrograph shows a mitral valve affected by endocarditis. The red mass is a blood clot on the valve's upper surface.

Diagnosis

Blood cultures are the key to investigating endocarditis. Three samples are usually taken over a 24-hour period before antibiotics are given in order to identify the infecting organism.

A range of blood tests will be performed. These may reveal typical complexes of immune system cells. Certain types of anaemia often develop.

OTHER TESTS
■ Chest X-rays may show evidence of heart failure, pulmonary emboli or abscess
■ Echocardiograms may identify vegetations; however, these need to be at least 2 mm in size to be visualized; trans-oesophageal echocardiography is more sensitive in identifying vegetations
■ ECG readings are usually normal but there may be a characteristic change, which indicates severe infection or possibly an aortic root abscess
■ Antibiotic sensitivities should be performed so that the organism can be targeted.

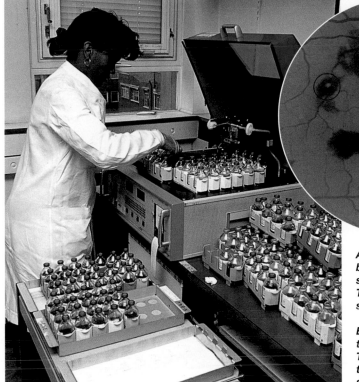

A characteristic finding in bacterial endocarditis are Roth's spots (circled) on the retina. These are white spots surrounded by haemorrhage.

Blood testing is essential for the diagnosis of endocarditis. The clinician will be looking for typical complexes of immune system cells.

Treatment

Any underlying source of infection must be sought. Dental radiographs, for example, may be taken to identify any dental root abscesses.

Antibiotics such as intravenous penicillin and gentamycin are usually started after taking blood cultures. Aminoglycosides will enhance the antibiotic effect. When the *Staphylococcus* bacterium is the

cause, triple therapy using three different antibiotics may be given, as it is a very virulent organism. The drugs are usually administered intravenously for two weeks and then orally.

Surgery may be needed when any of the following are present:
■ Worsening heart failure
■ Uncontrolled infection
■ Prosthetic valves
■ Myocardial abscesses.

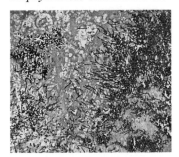

Cardiac surgery is often required when prosthetic heart valves are affected by endocarditis, as the infection is rarely treatable by antibiotics.

This micrograph shows Candida albicans, which has caused fungal endocarditis on the patient's mitral valve. Antibiotics may help to ease the symptoms.

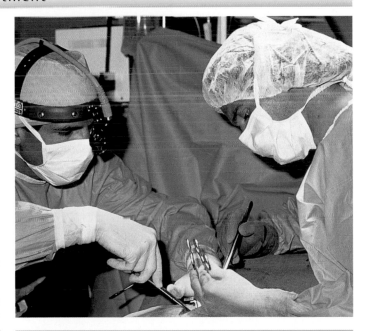

Prognosis

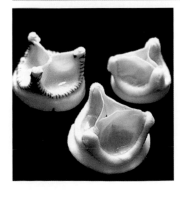

An early fall in the temperature and white blood cell count will accompany the patient's improvement. However, there is a high mortality rate of 20 per cent in the UK due to the high incidence of prosthetic valve endocarditis.

Patients with prosthetic heart valve endocarditis have a poor prognosis. This is because such infection does not respond well to antibiotics.

Prevention

Antibiotics are given prophylactically to dental patients who are known to suffer valvular heart disease or those about to undergo other potentially septic procedures.

For dental treatment, amoxycillin by mouth is given before the start of treatment. Erythromycin may be used for those who are allergic to penicillin. Intravenous vancomycin is advised for those with prosthetic heart valves.

Staphylococcus aureus may cause severe cases of endocarditis. Drug therapy may prevent infection occurring in vulnerable patients.

Pericarditis

Causes

Pericarditis is inflammation of the pericardium (the three-layered membrane that surrounds the heart), which may result in pain in the chest.

The pericardium, or pericardial sac, contains fluid that lubricates the membranes, allowing them to move smoothly as the heart pumps. The pericardium also limits the distension of the heart and acts as a barrier to infection.

Pericarditis may be acute (sudden) or chronic (long-term) and is sometimes accompanied by inflammation of the muscle in the wall of the heart, known as myocarditis.

In the UK, the most common causes of acute pericarditis are:
■ Certain viral infections
■ Myocardial infarction
■ A bacterial infection carried to the pericardium in the bloodstream or directly from the lungs (relatively uncommon).

In developing countries, tuberculosis is a common cause.

Rare causes include:
■ Certain autoimmune disorders such as rheumatoid arthritis
■ Cancer – tumour cells may spread to the pericardium, typically from the lung or breast

■ Chest injury
■ Kidney failure.

In some cases of pericarditis, a cause is never found.

Pericarditis can result as a complication of other conditions. It commonly develops following a myocardial infarction (heart attack).

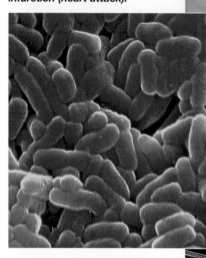

Tuberculosis is one cause of pericarditits. Mycobacterium tuberculosis is a rod-like bacterium that releases toxins which cause inflammation.

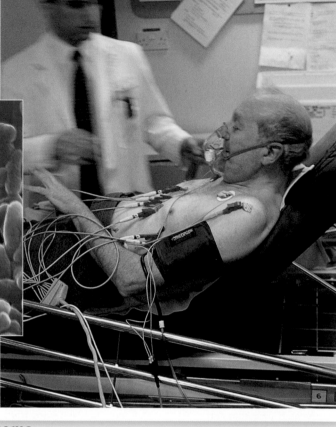

Symptoms

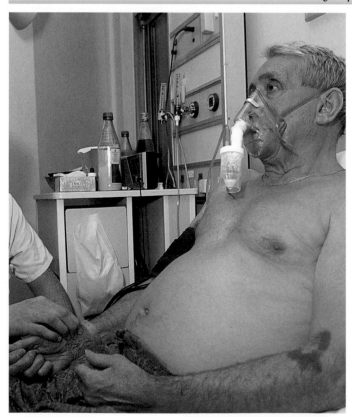

Symptoms can develop rapidly; in viral pericarditis, they can appear within hours.

ACUTE SYMPTOMS
The main symptoms of pericarditis are:
■ Pain in the centre of the chest behind the sternum (breastbone) that may spread to the shoulders and neck. The pain is typically made worse when taking a deep breath, lying down and swallowing, and improves when sitting forwards
■ A mild fever
■ Pericardial effusion, in which fluid accumulates within the pericardium and can stop the heart from pumping effectively. An effusion may cause a sensation of pressure behind the sternum. It can also lead to heart failure, which is typically associated with shortness of breath and ankle swelling.

Chronic pericarditis may develop following an infection. A fast, irregular pulse, known as atrial fibrillation, is an indication of the condition.

CHRONIC SYMPTOMS
In rare cases, persistent pericardial inflammation may follow pericarditis that is due to tuberculosis, a viral or bacterial infection or rheumatoid arthritis. The pericardium becomes thickened and scarred and tightens around the heart, preventing it from filling properly. Symptoms associated with this long-term condition, known as constrictive pericarditis, include:
■ Fatigue
■ Swelling of the ankles
■ Atrial fibrillation (fast and irregular heart beat).

Incidence

Pericarditis can occur at any age. Viral infections are the commonest cause of pericarditis in young adults. In older people the condition is most often the result of a myocardial infarction. About 20 per cent of patients develop pericarditis shortly after a myocardial infarction.

Diagnosis

Suspected acute pericarditis may be investigated using a range of methods:

■ The cardinal sign of acute pericarditis is the 'pericardial rub', a characteristic rustling sound heard through a stethoscope as the inflamed pericardium moves

■ An electrocardiogram (ECG), a recording of the electrical activity in the heart, may show certain changes

■ A chest X-ray may be arranged, possibly followed by an echocardiogram. In echocardiography, an ultrasound scan is used to view the structure and movement of organs. In this case, the investigation is used to assess the thickness of the pericardium and to look for excess fluid around the heart

■ In addition, blood tests may be carried out to check for evidence of an autoimmune disease.

DETECTING AN EFFUSION
A pericardial effusion is often difficult to detect on clinical examination, although sometimes the heart sounds heard with a stethoscope are quieter than usual.

The ECG may show particular changes if an effusion is present, and serial chest X-rays may show rapid enlargement of the heart, occurring over days or even hours. Echocardiography may be used to confirm the diagnosis. Constrictive pericarditis may also be diagnosed by echocardiography.

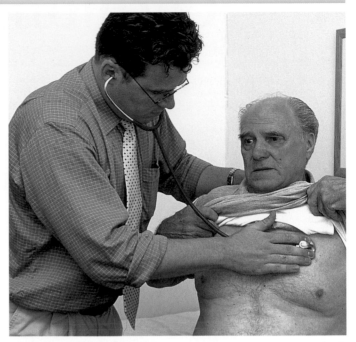

When listening to the heart through a stethoscope a distinctive rustling sound may be heard. This 'pericardial rub' is a classic sign of pericarditis.

Treatment

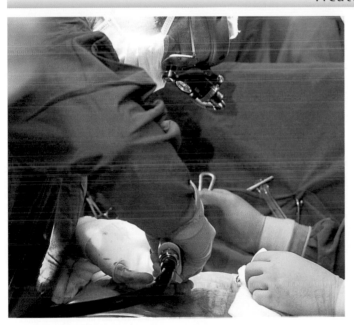

Pericarditis requires admission to hospital. Aspirin or stronger non-steroidal anti-inflammatory drugs may be given to relieve pain. Corticosteroids are sometimes prescribed to help relieve symptoms. In some cases, the underlying cause may require treatment. For example, pericarditis caused by a bacterial infection will require antibiotic therapy. It may also be necessary to drain the infected fluid from around the heart.

If a pericardial effusion is present, the accumulated fluid may be removed using a needle inserted through the chest wall.

A persistent pericardial effusion may be treated with surgery. A small section of the pericardium can be removed to enable the fluid to drain away.

The effusion may be drained completely; alternatively, a small sample of fluid may be withdrawn for diagnosis. If the fluid reaccumulates following drainage, the procedure may be repeated or a small piece of pericardium may be removed to allow continuous drainage.

In constrictive pericarditis, a large section of the pericardium may be surgically removed to restore normal heart function.

Prevention

There are no preventative measures for pericarditis. However, an early diagnosis is vital in order to avoid the occurrence of complications and to prevent the condition becoming life-threatening.

Prognosis

Viral pericarditis usually clears completely within days or weeks. In some people, however, the condition recurs after some months. Pericarditis caused by an autoimmune disorder can also recur.

Some types of pericarditis are particularly serious and, in rare cases, may be fatal. Acute bacterial pericarditis and constrictive pericarditis both fall into this category.

Most people with pericarditis recover fully and are discharged from hospital with no further problems. Patients are followed up on an outpatient basis.

Cardiomyopathy

Symptoms

Cardiomyopathies are a group of rare, chronic disorders that affect the heart muscle. Dilated cardiomyopathy is the most common of these, accounting for four out of five cases, while hypertrophic and restrictive cardiomyopathies are rarer.

DILATED CARDIOMYOPATHY

In dilated cardiomyopathy, one or more of the heart chambers (atria and ventricles) become enlarged (dilated) and contract inefficiently. The condition can occur at any age, but is more common in men over the age of 45. Early disease mildly reduces exercise tolerance, while advanced disease causes:
■ Breathlessness and oedematous swelling related to heart failure
■ Chest pain.

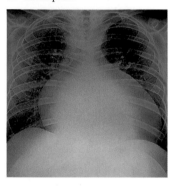

MITRAL VALVE DISEASE

Sometimes, the thickened heart muscle distorts the mitral valve, which lies between the left atrium and ventricle. This prevents the complete closure of the valve when the left ventricle contracts, allowing blood to regurgitate into the left atrium. This leads to breathlessness and heart failure.

HYPERTROPHIC CARDIOMYOPATHY

In this condition, the walls of the heart become thickened and distorted and the heart is unable to beat strongly enough to meet the body's demands for oxygen, particularly during exercise. Many of the heart muscle cells are enlarged (hypertrophied) or misshapen. Symptoms develop in childhood and adolescence when patients may experience:
■ Fainting attacks (syncope)
■ Chest pain on exertion
■ Palpitations
■ Breathlessness.
Most people with hypertrophic cardiomyopathy have only mild symptoms but occasionally an affected person

Cardiomyopathy causes enlargement or distortion of the heart. The ventricles can become abnormally large (enlarged left ventricle shown).

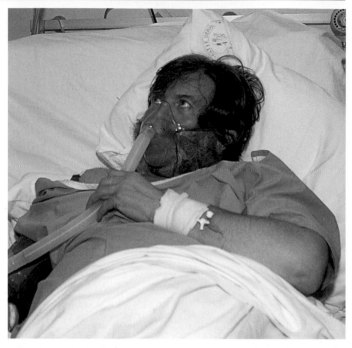

may die suddenly from an abnormal heart rhythm.

RESTRICTIVE CARDIOMYOPATHY

In restrictive cardiomyopathy, the heart muscle walls are infiltrated with abnormal tissue due to an underlying disorder. As a result, they become stiffened and cannot contract normally. The main problem is

Cardiomyopathy may result in emergency admission to hospital as it can lead to heart failure and embolism. Careful medical monitoring is required.

that the heart is unable to cope with increased demand, such as during exertion. Symptoms include shortness of breath, tiredness, and blood clots in the circulation (emboli).

Causes

In dilated cardiomyopathy, the cause is mostly unknown, but there is a possible genetic link as the condition runs in families in at least 25 per cent of cases. In susceptible people, dilated cardiomyopathy is precipitated by factors such as:
■ Excessive intake of alcohol
■ Some chemotherapy drugs
■ Viral infection, particularly

with the Coxsackie virus.
The condition also sometimes develops in people with acquired immunodeficiency syndrome (AIDS).
Hypertrophic cardiomyopathy is a genetic disorder. Some cases occur spontaneously but the disorder usually runs in families, affecting 50 per cent of the offspring of an affected person.

Amyloidosis involves the deposition of abnormal protein in organs (micrograph of the liver shown). In the heart, this can lead to cardiomyopathy.

UNDERLYING DISEASES

In restrictive cardiomyopathies causes may include:
■ Amyloidosis, in which an abnormal protein (amyloid) is deposited in various organs
■ Haemochromatosis, a genetic disease in which the body becomes overloaded with iron
■ Sarcoidosis, a chronic disorder of unknown cause in which masses of granulation tissue (granulomas) consisting of small blood vessels and connective tissue form at various sites of the body.

Alcohol may cause dilated cardiomyopathy to be triggered in susceptible individuals. Other precipitating factors include viral infection and AIDS.

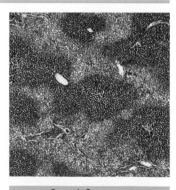

Incidence

Cardiomyopathies affect around 50 to 60 per 100,000 of the population. These conditions can affect all races, but particularly people of African origin. One form of restrictive cardiomyopathy – tropical endomyocardial fibrosis – accounts for 10–20 per cent of deaths from heart disease in Africa.

Diagnosis

Cardiomyopathies must be distinguished from other forms of heart disease, such as those caused by coronary heart disease, hypertension (high blood pressure), congenital abnormalities, diseased heart valves or inflammation of the membrane surrounding the

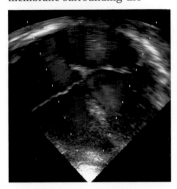

A chest X-ray may help to diagnose cardiomyopathy. The affected individual will also be examined and a medical history taken.

heart (pericarditis). The clinical history and examination may indicate the diagnosis.

Investigations include:
■ Chest X-ray
■ Electrocardiography (ECG)
■ Echocardiography – in which ultrasound waves display the structure of the heart as it beats, indicating irregularities
■ Biopsy of the heart muscle.

Echocardiography uses ultrasound to reveal the structure and function of the heart. The technique helps to reveal cardiac abnormalities.

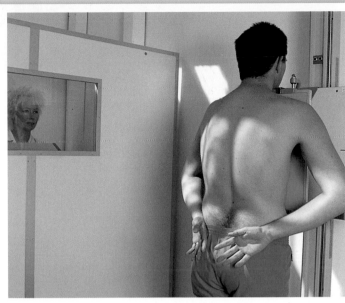

Treatment

Treatment for dilated cardio-myopathy is aimed at relieving the symptoms of heart failure. This may include:
■ Beta-blockers and angiotensin converting enzyme (ACE)

inhibitor drugs
■ Diuretics to reduce fluid retention
■ Anticoagulants to reduce the risk of clots forming in the dilated chambers.

■ Pacemaker if the conduction of the heart has been affected; this involves inserting electrodes into the heart muscle to provide electrical stimuli.

Treatment for hypertrophic cardiomyopathy includes the use of amiodarone, beta blockers such as propranolol or a calcium channel blocker like verapamil to prevent black-outs due to arrhythmias and reduce breathlessness. A pacemaker may be necessary.

If possible, the underlying cause of restrictive cardiomyopathy should be

Drug therapy is the first line of treatment in all types of cardiomyopathy. If medication is unsuccessful, however, surgery may be carried out.

treated. Some of the causative disorders respond to steroids.

SURGERY

There are instances when surgery is carried out to treat cardiomyopathy, particularly if the condition has not responded to medication:
■ Severe dilated cardiomyopathy is the most common indication for heart transplantation, but donor shortage has led to surgery in which the walls of the ventricles are reduced in size or skeletal muscle is wrapped around the heart and electrically stimulated to produce a heartbeat
■ Surgery may be necessary to repair or replace damaged heart valves or to remove very thickened heart muscle.

Prognosis

In dilated cardiomyopathy, 25 per cent of patients develop stable disease or improve. After a transplant, 70 per cent of patients are alive at five years.

Hypertrophic cardiomyopathy is rarely detectable at birth but develops around the age of 10 years, accelerates at puberty and then changes little. It causes few symptoms but a few patients die suddenly. Children and adolescents with recurrent syncope and those with more than two affected siblings who have died

Patients with cardiomyopathy may require a heart transplant. Almost three quarters of patients are still alive after five years.

suddenly are at increased risk. The long-term prognosis for healthy adults carrying genetic abnormalities related to the condition is unknown.

The outlook for advanced restrictive cardiomyopathy is poor – many people die within a year or two of diagnosis.

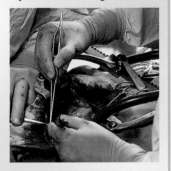

Prevention

Survival in people with cardiomyopathy should improve with the early recognition and treatment of family members who are at risk but as yet have no symptoms, as they can be prescribed medication at an early stage. Patients at genetic risk of cardiomyopathy may be helped by advice to avoid athletic training and jobs involving physical stress.

Once diagnosed, patients with dilated cardiomyopathy should avoid taking vigorous exercise and drinking alcohol.

Prevention of restrictive cardiomyopathy depends on preventing or treating the underlying disease. For example, in haemochromatosis, regular removal of blood can reduce the body's excess iron.

Shock

Symptoms

Shock is a potentially life-threatening condition that sometimes develops in patients suffering from severe trauma, infection, allergy or a heart attack (myocardial infarction). The circulation suddenly collapses and the pressure in the arteries falls below the level needed to maintain an adequate oxygen supply to the tissues.

Patients suffering from shock often have all or some of the following symptoms:
- Pale, cold sweaty appearance
- Nausea and thirst
- Irregular breathing
- Fast heartbeat

- Dry mouth
- Dilated pupils
- Reduced flow of urine
- Confusion or agitation
- Loss of consciousness
- Chest pain
- Warm hands and feet
- Swelling of the face.

Other symptoms relate to the cause; for example a rash and swelling may be due to a severe allergic reaction.

A person suffering from shock will appear pale and sweaty and feel cool. Breathing may be irregular and the pulse may be rapid and uneven.

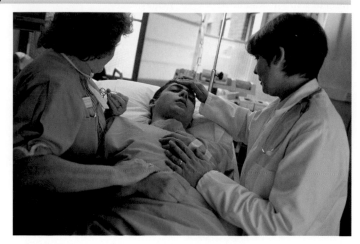

Causes

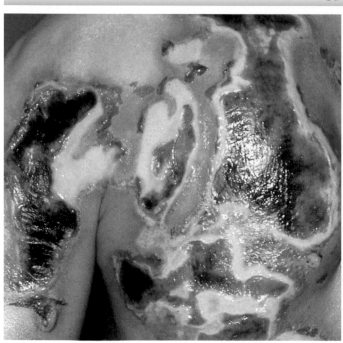

Patients with burns may suffer from dehydration due to loss of fluid through the damaged skin. Shock can develop as a result of low blood volume.

Shock is usually caused by a marked reduction in the volume of the circulation due to:
- Internal or external bleeding
- Dehydration – this occurs because of an inadequate fluid intake or fluid loss from vomiting or diarrhoea. It can also develop due to acute pancreatitis, heat exhaustion, diabetic coma and burns
- Dilated blood vessels – septic or toxic shock caused by bacteria or their toxins in the bloodstream and severe allergic reactions (anaphylaxis) can reduce the volume of circulating blood by dilating the peripheral veins. An increase in permeability of the capillary

walls leads to plasma leaking into the tissues
- Damage to the heart muscle – the heart may not beat strongly enough to circulate the blood after a myocardial infarction
- Loss of the heart's normal rhythm (arrhythmia) – rapid, slow or very irregular heartbeat reduce the heart's effectiveness. Possible causes include a myocardial infarction or severe electric shock
- Pulmonary embolism – a blood clot from a vein elsewhere in the body can lodge in lung tissue and prevent adequate blood flow from the right side of the heart to the lungs
- Cardiac tamponade – excess fluid in pericardium (the sac around the heart) which constricts the muscle and prevents normal filling
- Endocrine conditions such as acute Addison's disease.

Incidence

Anyone exposed to a life-threatening condition, such as a haemorrhage, myocardial infarction, allergic reaction or infection in the bloodstream is at risk of developing shock.

Sepsis is a major cause of shock, particularly in people infected with HIV, whose immune system is suppressed. About 500,000 cases of sepsis occur each year in the USA.

Women using tampons are at increased (but very low) risk of experiencing toxic shock syndrome (TSS). Sixty-five per cent of TSS cases are linked with menstruation, and 99 per cent of these are associated with tampon use.

Toxic shock syndrome (TSS)

TSS is a very rare but potentially fatal condition that has been associated with tampon use during menstruation, but also occurs after insect bites, boils, burns, childbirth and infection acquired in hospital.

The most common cause is a toxin produced by a strain of *Staphylococcus aureus* entering the bloodstream. Other bacteria, such as *Escherichia coli,* are sometimes involved.

Symptoms
TSS typically causes the following symptoms:
- High fever
- Severe headache

- Vomiting
- Diarrhoea
- Muscle aches and pains
- A widespread rash resembling sunburn.

People suffering from toxic shock should be admitted to hospital for emergency treatment with intravenous antibiotics.

Although over half of all incidences of toxic shock involve menstruating women, the rarity of the condition means that advising women to avoid tampon use is not justified.

A synthetic peptide that blocks toxin activity is under development for future treatment of this condition.

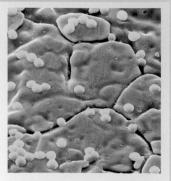

Staphylococcus aureus *is a bacteria that grows in grape-like clusters of small spheres (cocci). It is the most common cause of TSS.*

Diagnosis

The diagnosis of shock is made on the basis of clinical findings, which vary according to cause.

If shock occurs due to a reduction in the volume of circulating blood:
■ The skin is pale and cold and may be blue. If pressed, the skin stays white for a long period after the pressure is released
■ The patient is confused
■ The blood pressure may be normal at first, but then falls
■ The breathing is abnormally fast. The pulse is rapid but weak and may be irregular
■ Little or no urine is passed.

INVESTIGATIONS
Shock and its underlying causes can be investigated with the following blood tests:
■ Full blood count
■ Electrolytes
■ Urea and creatinine (to test for kidney function)
■ Cardiac enzymes (which are raised in cases of myocardial infarction)
■ Culture for bacteria (to test

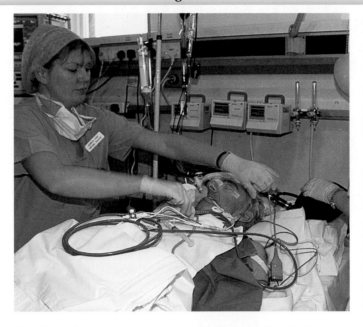

for infection)
■ Arterial gases (to measure the level of oxygen in the blood)
■ Blood sugar.
    Other types of tests to

investigate shock include:
■ Echocardiogram
■ Electrocardiogram
■ Central venous pressure
■ Chest X-ray.

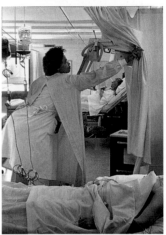

Patients with shock are often cared for on an intensive care unit. Vital signs are monitored and, if necessary, artificial ventilation is commenced.

A chest X-ray can be very helpful to doctors in deciding on the cause of shock. In a very ill patient, a portable X-ray can be carried out on the ward.

Treatment

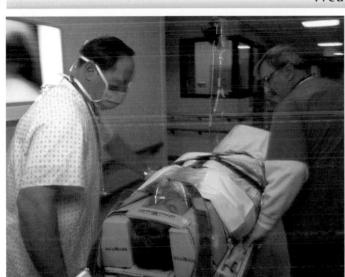

Treatment aims to increase cardiac output, blood pressure and oxygenation of tissues. This can be achieved by treating the cause while also providing supportive measures:
■ Patients should be laid flat
■ Feet should be raised
■ Patients should be kept warm, but not overheated
■ The airway must be maintained
■ Oxygen saturation should be maintained. Oxygen is given via a mask, airway or endotracheal

Immediate treatment for a patient in shock includes ensuring that the circulation is adequate. Intravenous fluids are usually required.

tube. Artificial ventilation may be needed if the patient is unable to breathe independently
■ Intravenous fluids and blood may be given, while being careful not to overload the circulation
■ If kidney failure develops as a result of shock, then dialysis may be required until the organs recover their function
■ The cause of shock must be treated vigorously.

ANAPHYLACTIC SHOCK
In the case of a severe allergic reaction with anaphylactic shock, adrenaline should be administered intramuscularly as soon as possible. If necessary, antihistamine or hydrocortisone may be given intravenously.

Prevention

Patients known to have severe allergies can be provided with adrenaline self-injection kits to use immediately they become aware of any early symptoms, such as difficulty in breathing, abdominal cramps or puffiness.

Early treatment of bleeding, infections and heart attacks is vital in helping to prevent the development of shock.

Shock may also be prevented by: high standards of patient care, gentle handling of internal organs during surgical procedures, the early treatment of severe infections and appropriate pain relief.

People involved in a serious accident are likely to have shock as a result of blood loss. Prompt first aid at the scene can avoid the risk of future complications.

Prognosis

Severe shock is potentially fatal but lives can be saved if the condition is diagnosed and treated promptly. Prognosis also depends on the cause.

Septic shock
Septic shock has a mortality rate of 40–70 per cent. Delayed or inadequate resuscitation increases the risk of the patient developing multi-organ failure (MOF), which is often fatal. MOF occurs if the vital organs are starved of oxygen and become oedematous. The brain, kidneys, liver, heart and lungs

are all vulnerable. MOF can follow any form of severe shock and people infected with HIV are at increased risk.

Other types of shock
Cardiogenic shock from myocardial infarction has a mortality rate of 80–90 per cent. The outcome for shock that occurs from haemorrhage depends on whether the bleeding can be stopped.

Fear and pain can worsen the effects of shock, so confidence on the part of carers and pain relief are important.

Raynaud's phenomenon

Causes

Raynaud's phenomenon is a term used to describe a condition that occurs when the small arteries (arterioles) in the hands and feet suddenly constrict due to spasm in the vessel walls, usually following exposure to cold. As a result, the blood supply is restricted, and the fingers and toes become pale and numb.

The constriction of the vessels in the skin is the body's normal response to cold in order to preserve body heat. In Raynaud's phenomenon, however, this physiological response is sudden, spasmodic, exaggerated and inappropriate.

UNDERLYING DISORDERS
In many people, it is uncertain why these physiological changes occur, and in these individuals the condition is known as primary Raynaud's. In other cases, however, the condition is associated with an underlying condition, usually an autoimmune disease such as systemic sclerosis, lupus or rheumatoid arthritis; this is known as secondary Raynaud's.

RISK FACTORS
In both primary and secondary Raynaud's, the symptoms can be triggered by any of the following factors:
■ Cold weather

Pneumatic drill operators may develop a condition known as vibration white finger. This has similar symptoms to those of Raynaud's phenomenon. ▼

▶ *Spasm in the walls of blood vessels can reduce the blood supply to the fingers or toes. As a result, the digits become pale and sometimes turn blue.*

■ Handling cold or frozen items
■ Emotional stress
■ Drugs, such as anti-hypertensives, nicotine, ergot alkaloids (for migraine)
■ Smoking – nicotine causes blood vessels to constrict.

OCCUPATIONAL CAUSES
'Vibration white finger' is a related condition and can cause similar symptoms to those of Raynaud's phenomenon. People who operate machinery such as pneumatic drills and chain saws may be subjected to constant vibration, which can damage arterioles and set the scene for Raynaud's phenomenon. Typists, pianists and others who subject their fingers to repetitive stress may also be vulnerable.

Symptoms

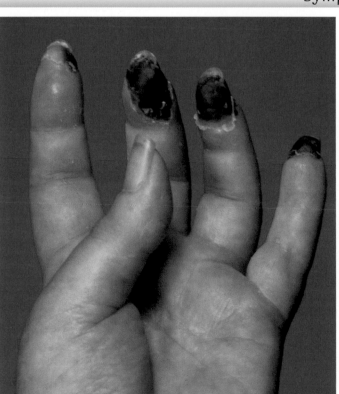

For people with Raynaud's, symptoms range from mild, lasting for less than a minute, to frequent and severe episodes, lasting several hours.

The symptoms of Raynaud's include:
■ Cold, numb, tingling fingers and toes
■ Colour change in the fingers and toes – they turn white or even blue (cyanosis).

Eventually, the episode subsides as measures are taken to treat it, and the digits turn a deeper red and begin to throb. The redness is caused by the return of oxygenated blood to the superficial arterioles.

In rare cases, as a result of

In severe cases of Raynaud's, the constant reduction in blood supply can lead to tissue damage. Ulceration or gangrene can then result.

prolonged interruptions in the circulation, areas of tissue can die. Small ulcers may then appear at the tips of the digits, and gangrene (infection of the nutritionally deprived area) can set in.

Incidence

Raynaud's was first described in 1862 by Maurice Raynaud, a French physician, who believed that this condition was a neurosis.

Between five and 10 per cent of the general population suffer from this disorder, which sometimes runs in families. Raynaud's can occur at any age, but is most common in women between the ages of 15 and 45. Men usually develop the condition later in life.

Treatment

People with secondary Raynaud's are more likely to be prescribed medication than those with primary Raynaud's. If there is an underlying autoimmune disease, immunosuppressant drugs may be prescribed.

Drug therapy may also include vasodilators and drugs known as calcium channel blockers, which dilate (widen) the blood vessels and thus increase blood flow to the extremities. These drugs can help to heal ulcers on the fingers and toes.

SURGERY

Surgery on the nerve that controls constriction of the blood vessels may be required if the symptoms are very severe.

It has been claimed that bio-feedback techniques are helpful and they may well be a useful adjunct to treatment. These involve individuals practising techniques that enable them to keep the extremities warm by increasing blood flow.

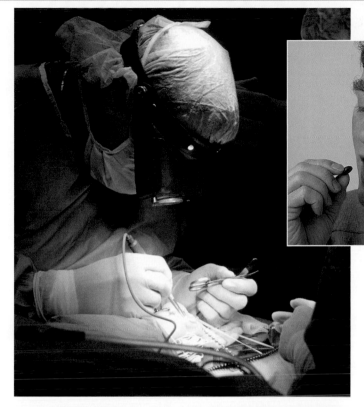

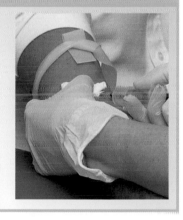

Some cases of secondary Raynaud's are treated with medication. This includes drugs that dilate (widen) the blood vessels, relieving symptoms.

Severe and persistent symptoms may indicate the need for surgery. The nerve that controls constriction of blood vessels can be operated on.

Diagnosis

The diagnosis is based on the patient's history and examination of the affected parts of the body. Characteristically, the patient may describe skin colour changes ranging from white to blue on exposure to cold. An affected person may also admit to experiencing symptoms of emotional stress.

Tests

Investigations such as capillary microscopy and blood tests may help to determine whether an individual has primary Raynaud's or whether there is an underlying cause.

If the doctor suspects that there may be a causative condition, such as rheumatoid arthritis or systemic sclerosis, then investigations into that condition will be carried out.

A blood test is useful in diagnosing Raynaud's. It helps to establish whether there is a specific cause, for example an autoimmune disorder.

Prognosis

It is possible for an individual to prevent permanent tissue damage by avoiding precipitating factors and treating attacks early. However, patients with severe attacks may need surgery.

Raynaud's may be an early symptom of other diseases, such as systemic sclerosis which is characterized by skin thickening. Although many cases of systemic sclerosis start with Raynaud's, only a few patients with Raynaud's develop systemic sclerosis

Prevention

Prevention is based on keeping the extremities warm. This involves common-sense measures, such as wearing several layers of clothes particularly on the hands and feet. Mittens are more effective than gloves because they allow the fingers to warm each other. Specially designed electrically heated gloves and socks and disposable or rechargeable hand warmers are now also available. Some people can avert an attack of Raynaud's by rapidly moving the arms around in a circular fashion, which drives blood to the extremities by centrifugal force.

WARM WATER

Although warm water may be helpful, care must be taken to ensure that it is not too hot because burns can occur, especially if the fingers are numb and cannot accurately assess water temperature.

Individuals with Raynaud's should not smoke.

A GP can offer practical advice as to how to avoid the symptoms of Raynaud's. This includes stopping smoking and wearing gloves in cold weather.

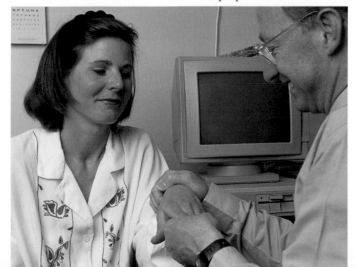

Aneurysms

Symptoms

An aneurysm is a balloon-like swelling in the wall of an artery. This swelling can develop in many of the arteries of the body, the aorta being the commonest site. This large vessel carries oxygen-rich blood away from the heart to supply other areas of the body.

Aortic aneurysms may be:
■ Abdominal – occurring below the diaphragm and especially below the level of the kidneys
■ Thoracic – developing in the part of the aorta within the chest.

ABDOMINAL ANEURYSMS
Large abdominal aneurysms may be associated with:
■ Pain in the upper abdomen, sometimes spreading to the back
■ A pulsatile (throbbing) abdominal swelling
■ A risk of rupture, a serious complication in which the wall of an aneurysm splits allowing blood to leak out of the vessel. This causes acute pain and a dramatic drop in blood pressure.

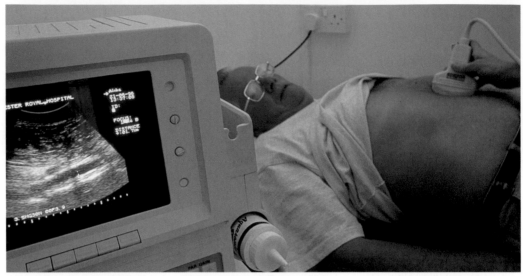

THORACIC ANEURYSMS
In many cases, these aneurysms do not cause symptoms, being detected incidentally on routine examination. However, large swellings may cause:
■ Pain in the chest, and sometimes in the upper back

between the shoulder blades
■ Pressure on nearby structures such as the oesophagus, causing problems in swallowing
■ Rupture – causing severe pain
■ Dissection – usually resulting from a tear in the aortic lining that allows blood to penetrate

Ultrasound scanning of the abdomen shows the blood flow in the aortic artery. This technique can be used to detect the presence of an aneurysm.

the layers of the vessel wall, causing chest pain.

Causes

The major cause of aortic aneurysms is atherosclerosis, a common condition in which fatty deposits accumulate on the inner lining of blood vessels.

RISK FACTORS
Risk factors include:
■ Smoking
■ A high fat diet
■ Excess weight
■ Lack of exercise
■ High blood pressure.

This specimen of an aorta is affected by atherosclerosis, which causes aneurysms. Plaques (yellow and white) build up in the lining of the aorta.

RARE CAUSES
Less commonly, an aneurysm develops:
■ Following an injury involving the aorta that has damaged and weakened an area of the arterial wall
■ In association with an inherited weakness in the wall of the aorta. For example, Marfan's syndrome, a rare inherited disorder of the connective tissue (the tissue that lies between the structures of the body), is characterized by a number of symptoms and complications, including a weakening and swelling of the aorta.

Diagnosis

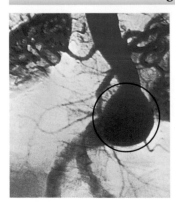

An aneurysm may be diagnosed during a routine examination. Tests to confirm the diagnosis and assess the size of the swelling include:
■ Angiography
■ Ultrasound scanning
■ CT scanning
■ MR imaging.

An aneurysm can be seen on this angiogram as a red swelling (circled). Angiography involves injecting a contrast medium prior to X-raying the arteries.

Other types of aneurysm

As well as occurring in the aorta, aneurysms commonly form in the:
   Iliac arteries
   Femoral arteries
   Popliteal arteries – blood clots can also develop
   Cerebral arteries (known as 'Berry' aneurysms)

Aneurysms can occur in various arteries. The location of the aneurysm determines where pain is felt.

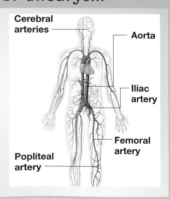

Cerebral arteries
Aorta
Iliac artery
Femoral artery
Popliteal artery

Treatment

Surgery may be recommended to treat an aneurysm. The doctor's recommendation will depend on an individual's age and general health in addition to the size and site of the aneurysm.

SURGICAL INTERVENTION
Large aneurysms and those causing symptoms are more likely to rupture and therefore surgical treatment may be advised. This may involve replacing the weakened area with an artificial graft.

Dissected and ruptured aortic aneurysms usually require emergency surgery.

DRUG THERAPY
Medical treatment may be given in the form of drugs to lower the blood pressure and to control pain.

In those individuals with hypertension (high blood pressure), drugs may be required to lower the raised blood pressure before surgery can be carried out.

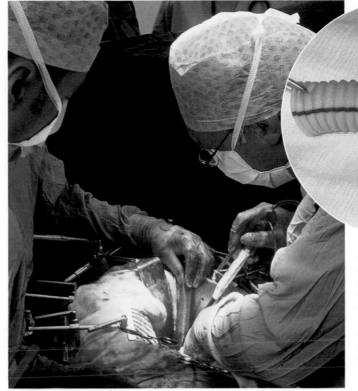

During surgery, a graft is inserted inside the aorta. This graft replaces the weakened section of artery and is made of artificial fibre.

Surgery may be needed to repair an aneurysm of the aorta. If left untreated, there is a risk that the aneurysm will rupture with fatal consequences.

Prognosis

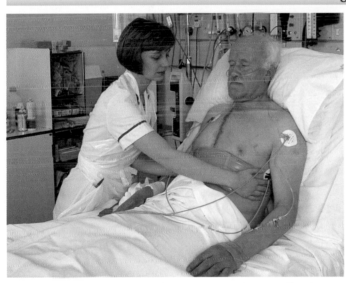

The prognosis depends on the overall health of the individual and the severity of the aneurysm.

NON-URGENT CASES
In general, the prognosis is good for non-urgent surgery performed on abdominal aneurysms that have not ruptured or dissected.

Surgery performed on some parts of the thoracic aorta is more complicated, due to the blood vessels that branch off it.

There is a 15–50 per cent chance of survival in patients with a ruptured or dissected aneurysm. Recovery depends on the site of the aneurysm.

HIGH MORTALITY RATE
In those cases where aneurysms have ruptured or dissected, there is a significant mortality risk, which is partly determined by the site of the aneurysm.

Thoracic aneurysm rupture is particularly associated with a high mortality rate, although surgical intervention can have a successful outcome in some cases.

Incidence

Aneurysms are usually associated with ageing, and tend to occur after the age of 65. Men are affected five times as often as women.

Prevention

Aneurysms can be prevented by undertaking certain lifestyle changes:

■ Smokers should give up cigarettes as chemicals in the smoke damage the lining of the arteries.

■ Low-fat diets reduce the risk of an aneurysm developing. Saturated fat in meat and dairy products should be kept to a minimum as these increase cholesterol levels. A healthy diet should include a high intake of fruit and vegetables as well as products high in fibre, such as pasta, rice and bread.

By reducing the amount of salt in food, blood pressure levels can be reduced.

■ Regular exercise increases the strength of the heart, enabling blood to circulate efficiently.

Exercise helps to maintain a good blood circulation. This can prevent or slow down the progress of atherosclerosis, which causes aneurysms.

Repetitive strain injury

Symptoms

Repetitive strain injury (RSI) is a collective term that covers a range of hand, wrist, forearm, neck, shoulder, back, knee and ankle disorders. The upper limb RSIs are those that are most commonly encountered.

Symptoms may include:
- Sensations of tingling, aching, or burning
- Swelling and/or numbness
- Pins and needles
- Incessant, nagging pain.

There are no characteristic clinical signs in RSI. Due to the ambiguous nature of complaints, RSI is included in the 'chronic fatigue syndrome' category of diseases.

The two main groups of disorders are localized and diffuse RSI.

LOCALIZED RSI
Localized RSIs include:
- Tenosynovitis
- Carpal tunnel syndrome
- Epicondylitis (tennis elbow and golfer's elbow).

These conditions are characterized by clearly defined symptoms and clinical signs; there is little professional disagreement over the existence of such conditions.

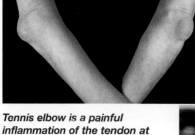

Tennis elbow is a painful inflammation of the tendon at the outer border of the elbow, caused by over-use of the forearm muscles.

Regular use of a keyboard may be associated with upper limb disorders. Tenosynovitis of the wrist is the most frequently encountered injury.

DIFFUSE RSI
Diffuse RSIs include:
- Poorly localized or diffuse patterns of pain
- Tenderness and loss of function in the upper limb.

This grouping, with muscles, nerves, tendons and soft tissues being affected, is a controversial one, with opinions varying over origin (aetiology).

Causes

Repetitive strain injury is common among sportsmen and women. It can result in fatigue and a decline in performance.

There are three main causes:
- Fixed working position
- Repetitive motions
- Psychological stress.

The 'standard' view is that RSIs are musculotendinous injuries of the upper limb, shoulder girdle or neck caused by an overload of particular muscle groups, from repeated use; or by the maintenance of constrained postures, which results in pain, fatigue, and a decline in work performance.

An alternative hypothesis is that RSIs are not organic in nature and are not work-related.

Some experts believe that the condition is due to conversion hysteria, whereby psychological conflict is converted into imaginary pain. Others consider the problem to be a form of compensation neurosis, that is the patients have the symptoms but retain a desire for secondary gain such as compensation payments or time off work.

Repeated use of particular muscle groups can lead to musculotendinous injuries, which are often very painful.

Diagnosis

The diagnosis of RSI may be made by GPs, occupational health physicians, orthopaedic surgeons or rheumatologists. The diagnosis rests largely on reported symptoms, and the nature of the patient's work.

Localized RSIs are more specific than diffuse RSIs and may be more positively identified: for example,

conditions such as carpal tunnel syndrome due to median nerve compression at the wrist, tennis and golfer's elbow and tenosynovitis have more specific diagnostic criteria.

Diffuse RSIs, on the other hand, are more problematic. The diagnosing clinician can only rely on the symptoms, the type of work and its repetitive nature.

Treatment

Treatment of localized RSIs is usually successful with well-documented strategies such as:
■ Steroid injection therapy
■ Rest
■ Splinting
■ Occupational health ergonomics
■ Physiotherapeutic methods.
 In the more diffuse RSIs, treatment is much more difficult and controversial. Many sufferers resort to alternative medicine therapies such as:
■ Acupuncture
■ Manipulation from osteopaths and chiropractors
■ Alexander technique for posture.
 Workplace solutions include:
■ A humane working environment
■ Ergonomically designed workstations
■ Job rotation.

Physiotherapy may be used to treat certain cases of RSI. Techniques include exercise, massage or the application of ultrasound.

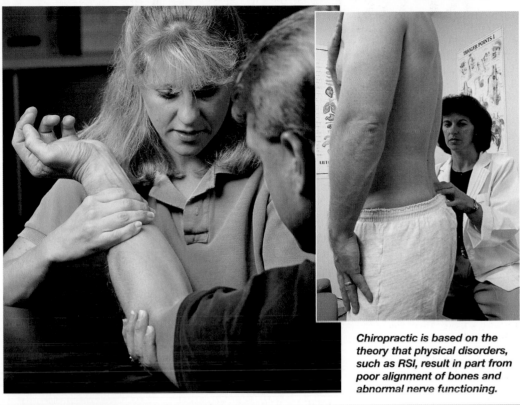

Chiropractic is based on the theory that physical disorders, such as RSI, result in part from poor alignment of bones and abnormal nerve functioning.

Incidence

Most information on incidence comes from Australia, where there was a virtual epidemic of cases between 1980 and 1984. The Australian Public Service, carrying out an RSI audit between 1985 and 1987, found that 2,706 person years had been lost during the two-year period. The prevalence ranged of cases was:
■ One per cent in clerical administrative staff
■ 16 per cent among word processor operators
■ 24 per cent among data processors.
 RSI complainants were

A large percentage of RSI complainants are likely to be female, given that many more women are employed in clerical and data-processing jobs.

more likely to be female - perhaps because of the nature of their work.

UNDERSTANDING RSI
Trade unions are believed to have had considerable influence in protracting the problems, whereas health professionals such as orthopaedic surgeons and rheumatologists have been less sympathetic towards the nature of the disorder. Consequently, the incidence of reporting has lessened markedly since those years.
 The Australian Public Service no longer issued statistics after 1987, and this led to a loss of public interest or awareness. A research project in the USA in 1998 estimated that RSI disorders accounted for 56 per cent of all occupational injuries.

Prognosis

Conditions in the localized group of RSI disorders are amenable to treatment with steroid injections and physiotherapy. Diffuse disorders are far more difficult to treat mainly due to different attitudes of health professionals.
 Often, the disorder will only resolve on change of occupation or satisfactory settlement of compensation. This latter may involve a costly process of litigation.

Physiotherapy helps to restore muscle strength and reduce joint stiffness associated with RSI.

Prevention

Good working practices and the provision of suitable office furniture, for example, may help in the prevention of RSIs. Employment medical services may provide advice, especially with ergonomic design, on providing the optimum work conditions for employees.

Workers in production lines may be particularly susceptible to RSI owing to the repetitive nature of their movements.

Tenosynovitis

Symptoms

Tenosynovitis occurs when the sheath surrounding a tendon becomes inflamed. Tendons (sinews) are tough inelastic cords that attach some of the muscles involved in movements to the skeleton.

Many tendons, particularly those that pass over the shoulder, wrist and ankle joints, are enclosed in double layered sacs (tendon sheaths) that reduce the risk of tendon damage from friction or pressure.

INFLAMMATION

The tendon sheaths are lined with a specialized tissue, synovial membrane, which secretes a lubricating substance (synovial fluid). This normally enables the inner and outer layers of a tendon sheath to glide over each other, allowing the tendon to move freely.

In tenosynovitis, however, inflammation of the tendon sheath prevents this free movement and the inner and outer layers of the sheath rub together making movement restricted and painful.

CHARACTERISTICS

Characteristics of tenosynovitis include:
■ Pain on making a particular movement, such as flexing or extending the wrist or ankle or moving the joint at the base of the thumb
■ The appearance of a longitudinal swelling over the tendon or, in some persistent cases, the formation of a fibrous nodule that can sometimes be seen or felt
■ A feeling of warmth over the affected tendon
■ Creaking in the region of the tendon on movement (crepitus). This may be felt and sometimes heard with a stethoscope or with the naked ear placed on the skin. The sound is like the creaking of new leather.

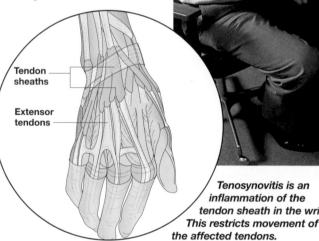

Tendon sheaths

Extensor tendons

Tenosynovitis is an inflammation of the tendon sheath in the wrist. This restricts movement of the affected tendons.

The symptoms of tenosynovitis are restricted movement, pain and swelling. There may also be a creaking sound when an affected person moves his wrist.

Causes

Causes of tenosynovitis include:
■ An acute injury
■ Infection spreading from a nearby part of the body, such as an infection of the finger pulp, or carried in the bloodstream
■ An inflammatory disease involving the synovial membrane, such as rheumatoid arthritis
■ Chronic, repeated, mild trauma or heavy over-use of a particular group of muscles. For example, racquet sports and painting and decorating are particularly likely to affect the tendons that move the thumb. In some cases, tenosynovitis is recognized as an occupational disease.

Harvesting sugar cane can cause severe tenosynovitis affecting the tendons that extend the wrist (cane cutter's disease), and cleaners who repeatedly wring out wet cloths are at risk of developing a chronic fibrous thickening at wrist level in the tendons leading from the forearm to the thumb (de Quervain's disease).

REPETITIVE STRAIN INJURY (RSI)

Workers, such as keyboard operators, who make repetitive movements, sometimes experience pain in their forearms. There are usually no specific signs of tenosynovitis and symptoms can often be relieved by making minor adjustments to work practices.

Tenosynovitis may be caused by repetitive strain injury in office workers. This is due to the over-use of the extensor tendons of the wrists and fingers.

Incidence

Tenosynovitis is a common problem that can affect any age group. The condition causes a significant workload on hospitals and general practice and is a major cause of lost productivity.

Rheumatoid arthritis
Rheumatoid arthritis is a common cause of tenosynovitis and affects:
■ About two per cent of the population worldwide
■ Women three times more than men.

Rheumatoid arthritis is an inflammatory disease of the the joints and typically affects the fingers, wrists and ankles. The condition often develops in people between the ages of 30 and 40 years, but can begin at any age from 10 to 70 years. Rheumatoid arthritis tends to run in families, which suggests that there is a hereditary element.

Diagnosis

The diagnosis is usually made clinically by examining the affected part. The doctor may note that:
■ Movement is limited and painful
■ The tendon sheaths are visibly swollen
■ The overlying skin is red and warm to the touch.

QUESTIONS

To make a diagnosis the doctor will ask questions about the patient's lifestyle, such as whether the individual uses a keyboard at work, or whether the person has been taking unaccustomed exercise.

The doctor may also check for evidence of rheumatic problems in the patient. Blood tests will confirm the presence of a rheumatic disease such as rheumatoid arthritis.

X-RAY

With long-standing tenosynovitis, an X-ray may reveal calcium deposits in the tendon and its sheath.

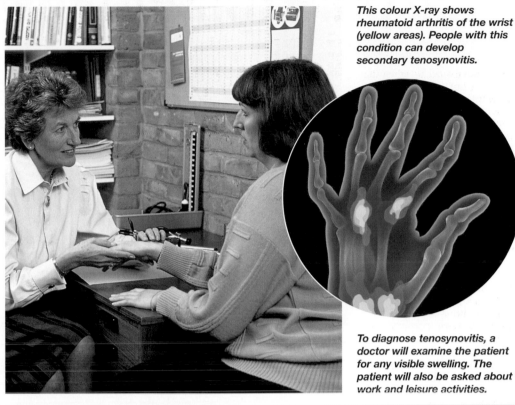

This colour X-ray shows rheumatoid arthritis of the wrist (yellow areas). People with this condition can develop secondary tenosynovitis.

To diagnose tenosynovitis, a doctor will examine the patient for any visible swelling. The patient will also be asked about work and leisure activities.

Treatment

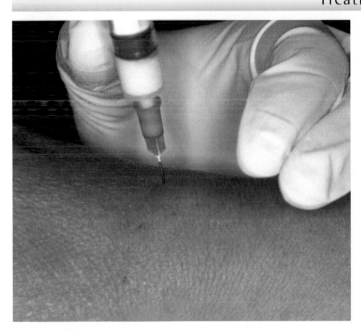

The discomfort of severe tenosynovitis may be relieved by cold compresses, while chronic inflammation may respond to heat.

RESTING

Most cases of tenosynovitis resolve with rest. In severe cases, resting the affected part in a splint or plaster cast for a short period may aid recovery but, once the acute phase has passed, the affected part should be exercised several times a day to prevent the formation of scar tissue that may later cause troublesome stiffness.

Corticosteroids can be injected directly into the tendon sheath to treat tenosynovitis. This acts to reduce the inflammation around the affected tendon.

DRUG THERAPY

Analgesic (painkilling) drugs and non-steroidal anti-inflammatory drugs (NSAIDs) may also be helpful. If there is no sign of infection, injecting a corticosteroid preparation into the tendon sheath sometimes hastens recovery.

In people with rheumatoid arthritis, general measures to treat their disease, such as anti-arthritic drugs, will be necessary as well as local treatment.

Antibiotic treatment will be needed if there are signs of infection.

SURGERY

A minor operation to cut through any fibrous tissue that has developed is sometimes necessary to release the tendon in cases of persistent tenosynovitis.

Prognosis

Most patients recover well from tenosynovitis with rest and treatment.

Recurrence

If a person has had tenosynovitis once, it is likely to recur, especially if the cause is not addressed. It is therefore important to take measures to avoid recurrence by, for example, altering working practices.

Prevention

Tenosynovitis may be prevented by using specially designed equipment, for example in sport, to avoid injury.

People should also avoid sudden, unaccustomed exercise, and instead undertake gradual training.

The design of sports equipment has evolved in recent years. For example tennis racquets are now lighter, which reduces the strain on a person's wrist.

Carpal tunnel syndrome

Symptoms

The carpal tunnel is the space between the bones and the ligaments of the wrist through which the median nerve passes. Carpel tunnel syndrome develops when the nerve becomes compressed. It is a common condition of the hand that affects women more frequently than men.

The symptoms of carpal tunnel syndrome include:
■ Pins and needles or tingling sensations (paraesthesia)
■ Pain or numbness in the hand, typically worse at night
■ Clumsiness and weakness of the hand
■ A weak grip and an impaired ability to bring the thumb across the palm to meet the other fingers
■ Pain in the wrist, forearm or shoulder.

Pregnant women can develop carpal tunnel syndrome due to excess fluid in the tissues. A splint helps by immobilizing the wrist and relieving symptoms.

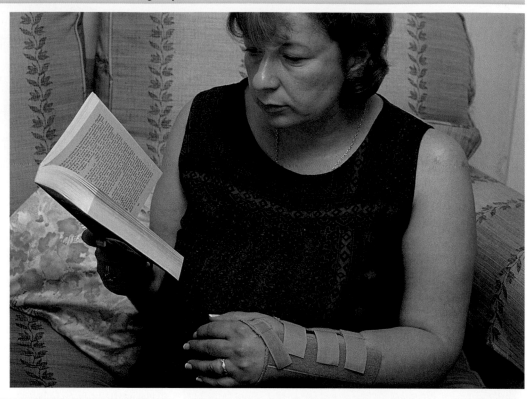

The median nerve

The median nerve is one of the major nerves in the arm. The nerve crosses the front of the wrist in a channel known as the carpal tunnel. This area consists of:
■ The wrist bones which form the base of the tunnel; the roof consists of a tough ligament lying just beneath the skin in the front of the wrist (the flexor retinaculum)
■ The median nerve as well as nine closely packed thumb and finger tendons.

The branches of the median nerve are responsible for the action of some muscles at the base of the thumb and for the sensation on:
■ The thumb side of the palm
■ The palm side of the thumb, index and middle fingers
■ The ring finger (thumb side)
■ The ends of the thumb, index and ring fingers on the back of the hand.

The area inside the dotted line shows the parts of the hand that are innervated by the median nerve.

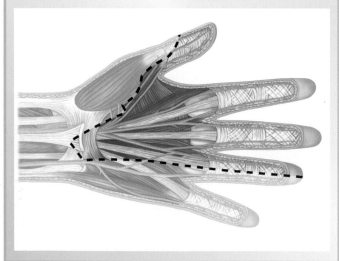

Causes

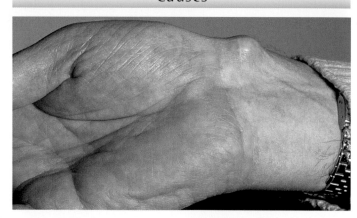

Any condition that narrows the carpal tunnel or produces swelling of or fluid retention by the contents of the tunnel can cause carpal tunnel syndrome. The many possible causes include:
■ Hormonal changes
■ Obesity
■ Diabetes mellitus
■ Rheumatoid arthritis or gout
■ Acromegaly – bone enlargement due to pituitary gland abnormality
■ Underactivity of the thyroid gland (hypothyroidism)
■ Renal failure
■ Alcoholism
■ Amyloidosis – rare condition in which abnormal proteins accumulate in tissues and organs

Conditions such as a ganglion can predispose to carpal tunnel syndrome. The abnormal swelling arising from the joint can compress the nerve.

■ Paget's disease – a chronic bone disease that affects elderly people. The bones become thickened and deformed
■ Tumours – such as lipomas (fatty tumours), ganglions (fluid-filled cysts formed in tendon sheaths), deformities of the wrists after fractures or severe bruising after trauma may also cause pressure on the nerve
■ The use of hand-held vibrating tools – very rarely causes carpal tunnel syndrome.

Diagnosis

The typical history of pain and weakness in the hands usually suggests the diagnosis of carpal tunnel syndrome, but it is important to exclude other conditions that may produce similar symptoms, such as a prolapsed cervical disc or arthritis of the thumb joint.

■ **Physical examination** – this may reveal disturbances in sensation in the area supplied by the median nerve, wasting of the muscles at the base of the thumb and a poor grip

■ **Tinel's sign** – tapping the median nerve at the wrist may reproduce the pain and tingling of carpal tunnel syndrome in an affected person. Flexing the wrist against resistance has a similar effect

■ **Imaging** – an X-ray of the wrist may be used to rule out bony abnormalities, while magnetic resonance imaging (MRI) gives a clear picture of the soft tissues. Electrical tests may be used to assess how effectively the median nerve can conduct impulses.

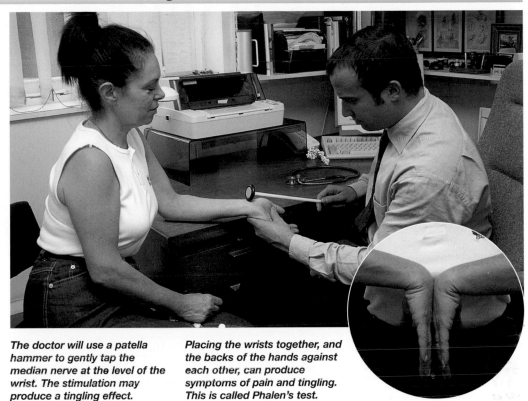

The doctor will use a patella hammer to gently tap the median nerve at the level of the wrist. The stimulation may produce a tingling effect.

Placing the wrists together, and the backs of the hands against each other, can produce symptoms of pain and tingling. This is called Phalen's test.

Treatment

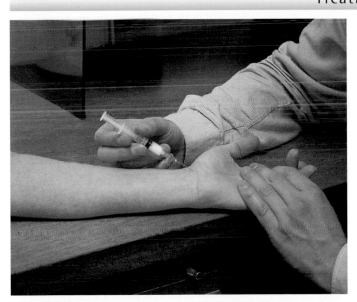

In some cases, an injection of corticosteroids under the ligament that forms the carpal tunnel roof can reduce swelling.

When possible, the underlying cause should be treated. For example, overweight patients should be encouraged to lose some weight and patients with hypothyroidism should receive thyroid hormone replacement therapy.

Some patients recover without treatment, while others respond to rest or simple measures such as the use of a wrist splint for a week or so. In cases where the condition is persistent however, several treatments are available:

■ Anti-Inflammatory drugs may help relieve tendon swelling and pressure on the wrist in rheumatoid arthritis

■ Wearing light splints at night, which hold the wrist slightly forward, may help night pain

■ Diuretics (which increase the volume of urine) are sometimes prescribed to remove excess fluid from the body

■ Steroid injections into the carpal tunnel may provide relief, but must be performed with great care. It is particularly important not to inject the median nerve itself. Any improvement may only be temporary

■ In persistent cases, surgery will be performed in order to reduce pressure on the large median nerve.

Surgery

Surgery is usually advisable for persistent or worsening symptoms to prevent permanent loss of sensation and wasting of the muscles in the hand. In such cases, without surgery, symptoms are likely to persist.

Surgical treatment usually involves dividing the transverse carpal ligament in order to relieve the pressure on the large median nerve. Freeing the nerve enables normal nerve conduction to resume. Traditionally, median nerve decompression was an open surgery procedure, but endoscopic (keyhole) surgery, which allows a faster recovery, is now sometimes possible.

Generally, both open and endoscopic techniques have excellent results, although it may take a few months for grip strength to return to normal.

Using local anaesthetic or a nerve block the surgeon will make an incision over the median nerve. The trapped nerve can then be released.

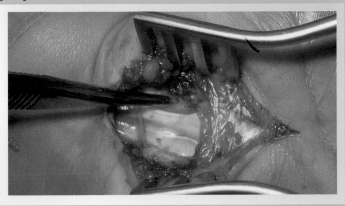

Gout

Symptoms and causes

Gout is the excess accumulation of monosodium urate crystals in body tissues and joints. These crystals are the by-product of the body's purine (nitrogen-containing compound) metabolism.

High levels can result from a high purine intake – such as a protein-rich diet – or from the body's own overproduction of urate. This tendency is inherited and present from birth.

URIC ACID

Uric acid is excreted from the body through the bowel and kidneys. Certain drugs, such as low-dose salicylates (aspirin) and diuretics, interfere with this process and raise urate levels. Crystals of monosodium urate are deposited into the joint causing intense irritation and pain. The joint becomes hot, red and swollen.

Classically, the big-toe joint is affected, but ankles, knees, elbows and the joints of the hands and feet can be involved. Only the large hip and shoulder joints tend to be spared.

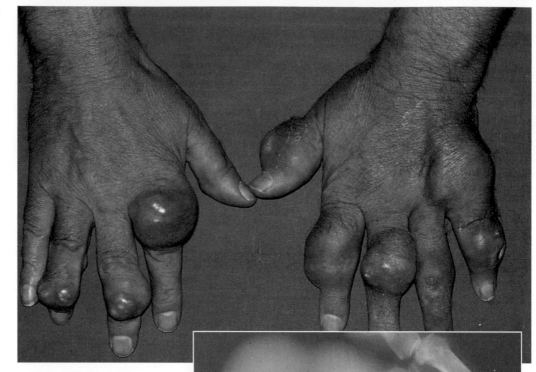

▲ *This man's hands are seriously affected by gout. Uric acid crystals in the blood have been deposited in the tissues, causing swelling and pain.*

▶ *An X-ray reveals the extent of damage to the finger joints. The hard crystals irritate the joint, causing an intense, painful inflammatory reaction.*

◀ *Tophi – hard, crystalline deposits of uric acid in the joints, skin and cartilage – can be seen under a microscope. Tophi are a characteristic feature of gout.*

Predisposing factors

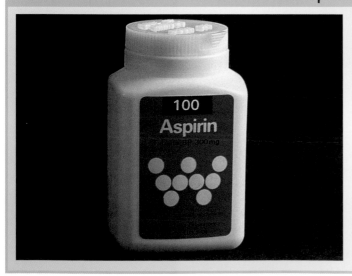

Although aspirin is a non-steroidal anti-inflammatory drug, it is not used to treat gout as it slows excretion of uric acid. This may exacerbate symptoms of a gout attack.

Men are eight times more likely to be affected than women, who are rarely affected before the menopause. The commonest age for a first attack is between 30 and 60. Other risk factors include:
■ A high alcohol intake. In itself, alcohol does not cause gout, but it will provoke attacks in those who are affected
■ A high protein diet
■ Certain races, such as the

Maoris and Polynesians, have higher blood levels of uric acid and are more susceptible to gout
■ Obesity
■ Disorders that cause a high cell turnover, such as polycythaemia (increased red cells), lymphomas and various other cancers
■ A family history of gout
■ Diuretics or low-dose salicylates
■ Kidney disease.

Gout sufferers are more likely to have lipid disorders and high blood pressure. Twenty-five per cent of patients have had an episode of renal colic due to the presence of uric acid crystals before their first attack of gout.

Treatment

In an acute attack, non-steroidal anti-inflammatory drugs (NSAIDs) are very effective at dissolving away the intra-articular crystals. They should be given in high doses early in the attack; most gout sufferers will keep a ready supply in hand. For those who are unable to take NSAIDs, colchicine, one of the oldest known drugs, is also very effective.

DRAWBACKS
The main disadvantage of colchicine is that it has a very narrow therapeutic range, so side effects are common. The salicylates in low dose will aggravate gout; although in high dose they are therapeutic, they are probably best avoided.

Paradoxically, on initial dose, allopurinol, the usual preventative treatment for gout, can actually provoke an attack.

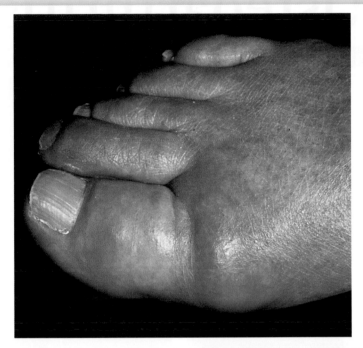

Pus, a fluid containing dead white blood cells, may be found in joints affected by gout that have become infected.

Gout commonly affects the joint of the big toe, causing acute pain. Treatment is with high doses of NSAIDs at the beginning of an attack.

Diagnosis

A classical history in a patient with predisposing factors and an elevated level of uric acid will confirm the diagnosis. If there is doubt then the presence of monosodium urate crystals in a synovial fluid aspirate is diagnostic.

In chronic gout, the joint can be destroyed, and X-rays reveal the typical changes. Similarly, urate is deposited in the tissues in the form of gouty tophi, around the joints, bursae and tendon sheaths and in the cartilaginous helix of the ear.

DIFFERENTIAL DIAGNOSIS
An acute attack can last a few hours to a few weeks. Acute gout can be very similar to septic arthritis and may warrant admission to hospital to exclude this more serious condition. Similarly, inflammatory arthropathies may begin with a mono-arthritis similar to gout.

An acute attack of gout may appear similar to septic arthritis (below). A positive diagnosis may be made after blood testing and X-ray.

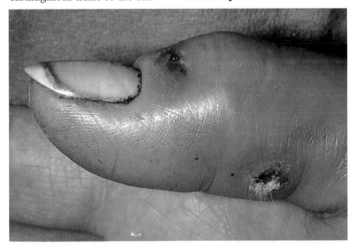

Prevention

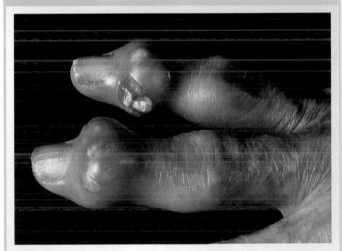

An elevated uric acid level alone is not an indication for drug treatment. The vast majority of patients with raised uric acid will remain asymptomatic throughout their lives. Some will only suffer from intermittent attacks and will benefit most from taking high-dose NSAIDs and following preventative advice, rather than life-long preventative medication.

High-purine foods, dehydration, especially in hot weather, and unaccustomed strenuous exercise should be avoided. Diuretics and low-dose aspirin should only be prescribed with caution.

Drug prevention should be aimed at those at risk of the long-term complications of gout, such as arthritis, and the rare complication of chronic renal disease. Those most at risk are young patients with high

Tophaceous gout is painful and disfiguring. As gout cannot be cured, prevention of the condition is important. This will involve drug treatment and dietary advice.

levels of uric acid, sufferers with evidence of chronic tophaceous gout, those who have frequent attacks of acute gout and people with renal disease.

Allopurinol is one of the commonest preventative drugs. It is very effective and safe even when taken long-term. Some patients suffer from rashes, but these improve when the drug is withdrawn.

The drug inhibits the enzyme xanthine oxidase, which converts xanthine into uric acid. Other preventative drugs are probenecid and sulphinpyrazone, which promote the excretion of uric acid through the kidneys.

Incidence

Gout is a relatively common condition affecting one per cent of the population. It causes excruciating pain in the joints. Historically, it affected the better-off in society (who ate more purine-rich foods), and whose lives were often ruined by the recurrent attacks and destruction of the joints.

Today, the acute pain that the condition may cause can be treated effectively with anti-inflammatory drugs or prevented completely with urate-lowering drugs.

Osteoporosis

Symptoms

Osteoporosis is a common condition that weakens the bones, causing them to fracture easily. This is due to excessive loss of bone mineral and matrix (woven fibres), usually associated with ageing. The condition is often without symptoms until fractures occur.

COMMON FRACTURES

Osteoporotic fractures are particularly common in the:
■ Wrists – fractures typically result from a fall on to an outstretched hand and cause pain and deformity of the lower forearm
■ Vertebrae of the spinal column – fractures often occur suddenly, perhaps when moving the furniture while cleaning, causing acute pain and tenderness. The collapse of several vertebrae causes loss of height and kyphosis, a permanently bent back
■ Hips – fractures are usually caused by a fall and the pain often makes walking impossible.

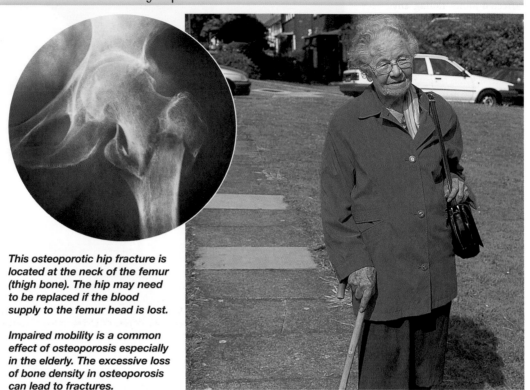

This osteoporotic hip fracture is located at the neck of the femur (thigh bone). The hip may need to be replaced if the blood supply to the femur head is lost.

Impaired mobility is a common effect of osteoporosis especially in the elderly. The excessive loss of bone density in osteoporosis can lead to fractures.

Causes

Bone consists of a framework of collagen fibres (matrix) hardened with calcium salts (mineral). Bone is continually remodelled throughout life by two groups of cells:
■ Osteoblasts, which produce new matrix
■ Osteoclasts, which remove calcified matrix by a process called resorption.

Long-term immobility due to conditions such as paraplegia can cause osteoporosis. This is because bone weakens without regular exercise.

Maximum bone density is reached in an individual's early twenties, when men have naturally denser bones than women. From the late twenties, resorption exceeds rebuilding in both sexes and bone density gradually decreases.

LACK OF OESTROGEN

In osteoporosis, bone loss is much exaggerated, and women become particularly at risk of fractures as their bones thin.

In young women, oestrogen produced by the ovaries normally protects the bone against excessive resorption, but when oestrogen levels fall at the menopause, resorption rapidly increases. In the early years after the menopause, up to five per cent of the total bone mass is lost each year.

RISK FACTORS

There are several known risk factors for osteoporosis:
■ Premature menopause (before the age of 45) occurring naturally or following a hysterectomy, which exposes women to low levels of oestrogen for extra years

■ Previous fragility, such as old fractures
■ Long-term immobility
■ Smoking
■ Alcoholism
■ Genetic factors leading to a small, slim build
■ Medical disorders such as anorexia nervosa, rheumatoid arthritis, testosterone deficiency in young men, over-activity of the thyroid gland or parathyroid gland and coeliac disease
■ Prolonged use of steroids for treating conditions such as asthma, or following an organ transplant.

Incidence

Osteoporosis is a major health problem worldwide. An estimated 3 million people in the UK suffer from osteoporosis.

People at risk

Post-menopausal women are at greatest risk but many men are also affected. Caucasian and Asian women are at much greater risk than black women.

An increasing problem

In the UK, one in three women and one in twelve men develop osteoporosis during their lifetime and the number is expected to double over the next 20 years as the population ages.

Incidence of fractures

About 50,000 wrist fractures, 60,000 hip fractures and probably more than 40,000 vertebral fractures occur in total each year in the UK. Most osteoporotic hip fractures occur in people over the age of 80 years. Hip fractures account for at least 20 per cent of UK orthopaedic bed occupancy.

Diagnosis

Ideally osteoporosis should be diagnosed before a fracture is sustained, as effective treatment approximately halves the risk of symptoms developing. Diagnosis depends on bone mineral density measurements, which give a reliable indication of fracture risks.

DIAGNOSTIC TECHNIQUES
Techniques include:
■ Dual energy X-ray absorptiometry (DEXA)
■ Quantified computed tomography
■ Ultrasound.

Plain X-rays are not sensitive enough to detect osteoporosis until there has been considerable bone loss, and a fracture may have already occurred.

Osteoporosis must be differentiated from other diseases that weaken bone, such as multiple myeloma, secondary deposits from breast, prostate, lung, kidney and thyroid cancer, and osteogenesis imperfecta, a congenital brittle bone disorder.

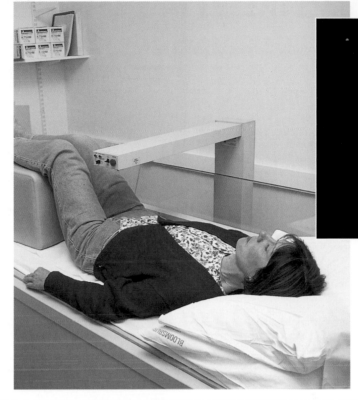

The spine of a woman with osteoporosis is shown in this densitometry scan. The red and yellow areas are the least dense and the green are most dense.

Dual energy X-ray absorptiometry is a technique used to measure bone mineral density. People who are at risk of osteoporosis are screened.

Treatment

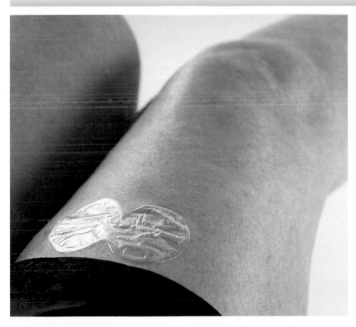

Skin patches are used in hormone replacement therapy (HRT). This is a form of treatment for osteoporosis in post-menopausal women.

Drugs are used to treat osteoporosis, including:
■ Hormone replacement therapy (HRT) – in post-menopausal women HRT with oestrogens reduces the rate of bone loss and risk of fractures. Bone loss is most rapid in the first ten years after the menopause and HRT is most effective during this time, but after 5-10 years, its benefits must be balanced against the risk of breast cancer
■ Oestrogen – given alone this increases the risk of cancer of the lining of the uterus (endometrial cancer), but combined treatment with a

progestogen protects against this risk
■ Biphosphonates – a class of non-hormonal drugs including etidronate, alendronate and risedronate, which inhibit bone resorption and prevent fractures
■ SERMs (selective oestrogen receptor modulators) – have an oestrogen-like effect on bone and prevent vertebral fractures
■ Testosterone replacement helps to slow down bone loss in men with low levels of testosterone
■ Calcium and vitamin D – supplements that benefit frail, elderly people who are housebound. A daily intake of 1500 mg calcium helps to reduce the risk of hip fractures, especially in post-menopausal women not taking hormone replacement therapy.

Prognosis

Osteoporotic fractures may be painful, disabling, and even fatal. An individual who has had one osteoporotic fracture is at increased risk of further fractures.
After a hip fracture:
■ 20 per cent of people die within a year
■ 50 per cent cannot walk without aid
■ 25 per cent need institutional care.

Prevention

Life style measures are important in both the prevention and treatment of osteoporosis.
These include:
■ Regular weight-bearing exercise (such as running, tennis, aerobics)

Regular exercise is an important way of preventing the onset of osteoporosis. Exercise helps to maintain the process of bone remodelling.

■ Adequate intake of calcium and vitamin D
■ Stopping smoking
■ Drinking alcohol only in moderation.

Osteomyelitis

Symptoms

Osteomyelitis is the term used to describe any infection of the bone and may be acute (sudden onset) or chronic (long term). Osteomyelitis is most common in children when it tends to affect the long limb bones. When it does affect adults, the bones of the spine, hip and foot are usually affected.

MODES OF SPREAD
There are two main ways in which bone becomes infected:
■ Direct spread from a nearby infection or following trauma (both accidental and surgical)
■ Via blood-borne bacteria.
  The symptoms vary depending on the bone affected, the age of the individual and the way in which the infection reaches the bone tissue. They include:

■ Nagging bone pain
■ Redness, heat and swelling over the affected bone
■ Restricted movement
■ Fatigue and malaise
■ Raised temperature.
  Osteomyelitis may have a sudden onset, particularly in children, or the condition may take a slower, less noticeable course. Initially, the symptoms may be attributed to the injury or soft-tissue infection that has caused the bone infection. However, if osteomyelitis remains undiagnosed, death of the bone can occur and the infection becomes chronic.
  The first indication of chronic osteomyelitis may be a complication, such as an open sore, a sinus tract that drains pus, wound breakdown, or failure of a fracture to heal.

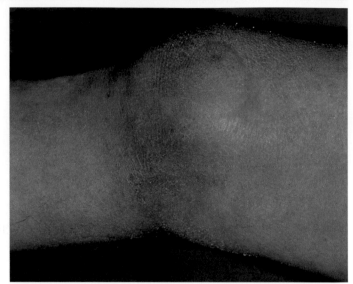

The first sign of osteomyelitis may be redness, swelling and heat over the joint. Here, the knee joint is affected and appears inflamed.

Causes

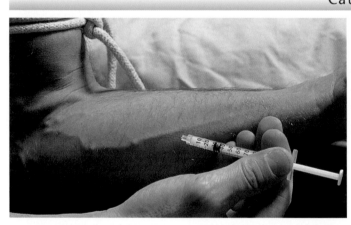

Bacteria spread directly through soft tissues to the bone or they travel in the bloodstream. Sources of infection include:
■ Local infection, such as an infected wound or an abscess.
■ Distant infection – for example, vertebral osteomyelitis can be caused by bacteria that infect the urinary tract

Intravenous drug users are at increased risk of contracting osteomyelitis. Other people at risk are those with a poorly-functioning immune system.

■ Mycobacteria, such as those that cause tuberculosis
■ Indwelling intravenous lines (such as those used for long-term kidney dialysis) or prosthetic implants
■ Intravenous drug use – using contaminated needles and syringes can introduce bacteria into the bloodstream
  Certain groups of people, such as individuals with a suppressed immune system and those with diabetes and sickle-cell disease, have a higher risk of osteomyelitis.

Diagnosis

Early diagnosis of acute osteomyelitis is critical because prompt antibiotic therapy may prevent bone death and chronic osteomyelitis. The first investigation is usually a plain X-ray of the affected bone, but the appearance of obvious abnormalities may be delayed for some time.

Investigative scans
Investigations that do show early changes are MRI, ultrasound, CT, and radionuclide scanning, and a diagnosis is usually made with a combination of these. In 95 per cent of cases, a radionuclide bone scan can provide a positive diagnosis within 24 hours of the onset of symptoms. However, the scan cannot differentiate infection

from other problems such as fractures. Other radionuclide scans, such as white-cell scans, are more specific. MRI can show anatomical changes, and is the investigation of choice for vertebral osteomyelitis.

Taking samples
Once osteomyelitis has been diagnosed using imaging techniques, it is important to determine the cause of infection. Microbiological samples should be taken before antibiotic therapy is started. Culturing a specimen of blood can reveal the identity of the bacteria in some patients. Taking samples of pus and soft tissue or a bone biopsy from the affected bone are alternative ways of making a diagnosis.

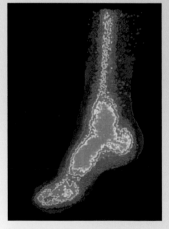

The most effective way of diagnosing osteomyelitis is with a radionuclide scan, shown here. Any infection shows up as a 'hot spot'.

Incidence

In developed countries, most forms of osteomyelitis are uncommon. The incidence is higher in developing countries. UK estimates suggest that acute blood-borne infections causing osteomyelitis in children is increasingly rare with an annual incidence of 2.9 new cases per 100,000 population.
  In the USA, at any one time around 1 in 5,000 children and 1 in 1,000 newborns have osteomyelitis, and every year, around 360 cases of osteomyelitis are diagnosed per 100,000 sickle-cell patients. Osteomyelitis is relatively common following puncture wounds to the foot, and may be as high as 30–40 per cent in diabetics.

Treatment

Osteomyelitis usually requires 4–6 weeks of treatment with antibiotics at doses high enough to penetrate into bone. Ideally, antibiotics are selected based on the identification of the specific bacteria, although best-guess therapy may be started once samples have been taken, then adjusted once the results are known. Initially, the antibiotics are administered intravenously in hospital, although the course may be completed with at-home intravenous therapy or oral antibiotics.

SURGERY

In some cases, surgery may be needed to remove dead tissue, particularly with localized spread of infection or bone abscesses, or to obtain samples for diagnosis. Rest and immobilization of the bone may be recommended. If a large area of bone is removed, a bone graft may be necessary.

Treatment of chronic osteomyelitis can be difficult, so

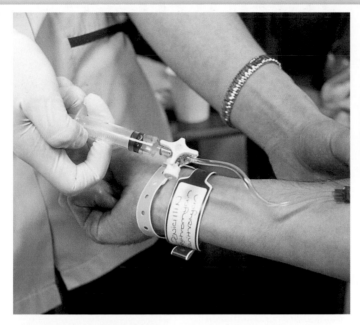

any predisposing factors, such as vascular disease, poor diabetic control, underlying bone disease and inadequate nutrition need to be corrected

first. Newer treatments such as hyperbaric oxygen therapy and antibiotic-impregnated implants are still being researched and are not yet in routine use.

The mainstay of treatment is intravenous antibiotics in hospital or at home. The drugs are given in high doses so that they penetrate the bone.

Rarely, surgery may be necessary to treat osteomyelitis. Dead tissue can be removed from the bone allowing new growth to occur.

Prevention

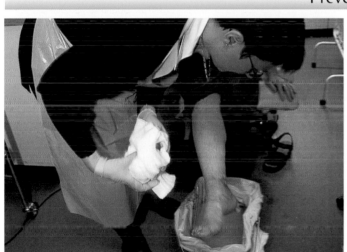

Prevention of osteomyelitis involves appropriate care of wounds and lesions, including:
■ Traumatic injuries
■ Surgical incisions
■ Diabetic foot ulcers.
  Wound care should also be combined with antibiotic prophylaxis as needed.

EARLY TREATMENT
Early and complete treatment of infections is important to

It is essential that leg ulcers are cared for properly to avoid infection travelling to nearby bone. Regular cleaning and dressing changes are vital.

prevent them from spreading to bone, particularly in vulnerable individuals, such as the following groups:
■ Young children
■ The elderly
■ People with weakened immune systems and those with conditions such as sickle-cell disease or diabetes mellitus
■ Individuals who have had their spleens removed.
  People who have had metal and other implants in their bones are at particular risk of contracting osteomyelitis. Consequently, doctors should be especially alert to any signs of infection in these individuals.

Prognosis

The prognosis varies widely between individuals, depending on their age and state of health, but is markedly improved with early diagnosis and aggressive treatment.

COMPLICATIONS
Chronic osteomyelitis may require months or even years of treatment. Complications of osteomyelitis, particularly chronic disease, can cause substantial ill health but death from osteomyelitis is rare. Complications include:
■ Bone abscess
■ Fractures
■ Bacteraemia (the presence of bacteria in the blood)

■ Loosening of a prosthetic implant (such as a hip)
■ Septic arthritis (infection of the joints) can be a serious complication of osteomyelitis. Thankfully this condition is rare, but if it does occur, the infection should be treated immediately with antibiotics.
  In some cases of chronic osteomyelitis, the affected person may need to take antibiotics indefinitely to keep the infection under control.

Chronic osteomyelitis can cause destruction of bone tissue. If this happens, a fracture can occur much more readily than in healthy bone.

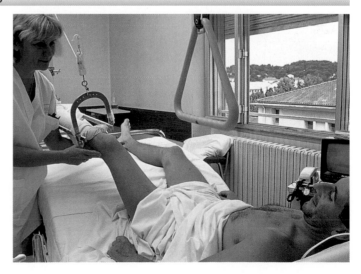

Paget's disease

Symptoms

Paget's disease is a chronic bone disease that occurs most often in the elderly. It is also known as osteitis deformans, and affected bones become brittle and are easily fractured. The most commonly involved bones are femur, pelvis, tibia, humerus, skull and the lumbosacral spine. The disease is identifiable by X-ray in 60–80 per cent of cases, and most patients show no symptoms.

PHYSICAL PROBLEMS
The deformities produced may be crippling, particularly in the limbs. They may also be unsightly when the facial bones are affected, which may further produce problems with:
■ Dental extractions
■ Artificial dentures.
   Marked bossing of the skull leads to problems with:
■ Deafness, due to compression of the auditory nerve
■ Unsightly prominence of the forehead.
   Similarly, compression of the vertebrae may cause lesions of:
■ The spinal cord
■ Nerve roots.
   Around 50 per cent of patients with symptomatic pain develop joint pain in the knee, hip or spine.

ASSOCIATED DISEASES
Increased bloodflow may lead to:
■ Cardiac hypertrophy
■ High output cardiac failure.
   Rarely, osteogenic sarcoma (0.2 per cent of cases) develops in Pagetic bone. The affected bone and overlying skin may

develop increased bloodflow, which may cause hyperthermia. In the skull, this phenomenon may occur at the expense of brain blood supply, affecting the superficial temporal artery, and the patient may become apathetic and withdrawn.

An abnormally prominent forehead (known as bossing) is a feature of Paget's disease. When the skull is involved, nerve damage may occur.

Severe deformity of the leg due to Paget's disease. Affected bones become thickened and deformed by excessive and disorganized bone formation.

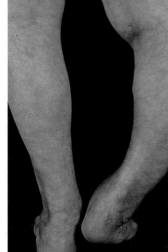

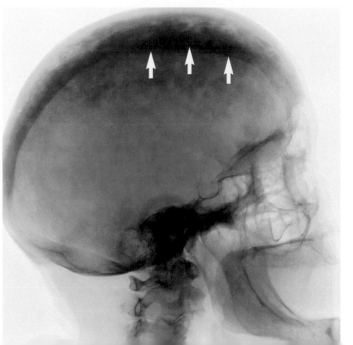

Causes

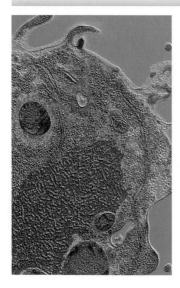

Following experimental research, there is some evidence that possible causative agents of Paget's disease include:
■ Canine distemper (a highly contagious viral disease of dogs)
■ Measles virus
■ Respiratory syncitial disease.
   There is a significant genetic factor for Paget's disease and environmental factors are suggested by the geographic clustering of cases.
   The disease does not spread from one bone to another, and unaffected bones remain normal.

The measles virus, which has infected this human cell, has been suggested as a possible cause for Paget's disease.

Diagnosis

■ X-rays show characteristic changes, with enlargement of bones, osteolytic lesions, sclerosis and thickening of bone trabeculae in the long bones and vertebrae
■ Bone scans show the extent of skeletal involvement; differentiation from metastatic carcinoma is difficult

Coloured X-ray showing a skull in Paget's disease. The skull has a mottled appearance due to its increased porosity, and part of it has become thickened (arrows).

■ Biochemistry – the definitive sign is markedly increased serum alkaline phosphatase (the marker of bone formation) levels, with normal levels of serum calcium and phosphate.
   The degree to which alkaline phosphatase levels are elevated is a useful index of treatment. In the case of a prolonged illness, an immobilized patient may have mild hypercalcaemia (high calcium). Bone reabsorption is measured by testing the ratios of certain urine components.

Treatment

Simple analgesics or non-steroidal anti-inflammatory drugs (NSAIDs) are usually adequate for the pain caused by Paget's disease.

DRUG TREATMENT
Oral bisphosphonates such as alendronate (10–40 mg) should be taken daily for six months. This should be accompanied by the intake of fluids to minimize the possible side effect of oesophagitis. Responses to bisphosphonates are long-lasting, with a 50–70 per cent reduction in alkaline phosphatase activity, and most complications can be prevented.

Intravenous pamidronate as a single or multiple infusion is sometimes used for treatment. Salcatonin (salmon calcitonin) and porcine calcitonin inhibit bone reabsorption, but they are expensive. Calcitonin is also available as a nasal spray, which has fewer side effects.

Surgery is sometimes necessary for joint replacement and osteotomy (cutting of bone).

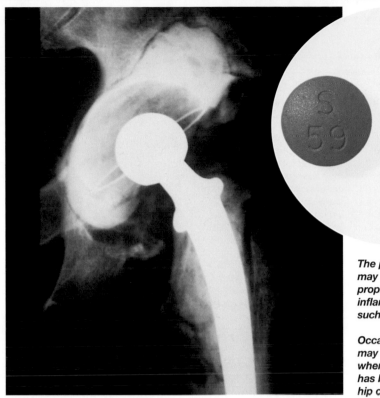

The pain of Paget's disease may be eased by the use of proprietary non-steroidal anti-inflammatory drugs (NSAIDs) such as ibuprofen.

Occasionally, joint replacement may be necessary, particularly when the femur (thigh bone) has been affected. A prosthetic hip can be seen on this X-ray.

Prognosis and prevention

Early diagnosis and appropriate therapy ensures that the symptomatic patient enjoys a normal life. In many patients, the disease is asymptomatic and consequently does not pose a problem. The most devastating complication is the development of osteosarcoma (malignant bone tumour), which has an incidence of 0.2 per cent. In these cases, the prognosis is poor; most affected patients die within 12 months of diagnosis. There is no means to prevent the onset of Paget's disease.

In those patients who do not have symptoms, treatment will not be needed. However, careful monitoring of the condition is important.

This bone densitometry scan of a Paget's disease patient shows the mineral density of bone, ranging from blue (least dense) to red (most dense).

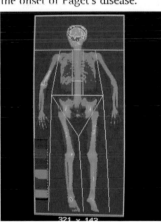

Incidence

The highest prevalence of Paget's disease is probably in the UK (particularly northern England), where 3.6 per cent of the population over 40 years of age and 5.4 per cent of the population over 55 are affected.

GEOGRAPHICAL SPREAD
Paget's disease is also common in much of Europe, but is rare in Scandinavia, India, Japan, the Middle East and Africa.

In the United States, the incidence of disease is greater in the northern part of the country, where it is nearly as high as that in the UK.

The disease seldom occurs in people under the age of 40, but the incidence doubles each decade after the age of 50. Sixty per cent of patients are male.

Some families display a high incidence of the condition, suggesting that there is a familial tendency. The sibling of a patient with Paget's disease is 10 times more likely to develop the condition themselves.

Sagittal MR scan of the lumbar spine of a 43-year-old woman suffering from Paget's disease. The deformation of some of the vertebrae (circled) is clear.

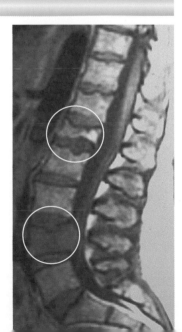

Rheumatoid arthritis

Symptoms

Rheumatoid arthritis (RA) is a chronic inflammatory disease, mainly affecting the small synovial joints of the hands, wrists, feet, elbows and ankles. These are the freely movable joints where the ends of the adjoining bones are covered in a synovial membrane that lubricates the junction. RA may be prolonged, and is typified by periods of exacerbation followed by remission. The commonest physical symptoms are:

■ Aches and pains
■ Stiffness
■ General fatigue
■ Weight loss
■ Tiredness due to anaemia

As other systems in the body – lungs, spleen and kidneys – may also be involved, the condition is sometimes termed rheumatoid disease (RD).

Further effects of RD may include vasculitis (inflammation of the arteries), anaemia, Sjögren's syndrome (dry eyes and lack of saliva), scleritis (inflammation of the white of the eye), pericarditis (inflammation of the heart membrane), peripheral nerve disease, kidney disease and enlargement of the spleen.

Synovial joints are affected progressively in rheumatoid arthritis, although the severity of symptoms varies. (1) The condition begins with acute inflammation of the synovial membrane. (2) This can lead to progressive inflammation, destruction of cartilage and osteoporosis (loss of bone tissue). (3) As inflammation subsides, the pain lessens, but eventually tissue begins to form across the joint space. (4) In the severest cases, the tissue ossifies into bony 'bridges', causing further incapacity.

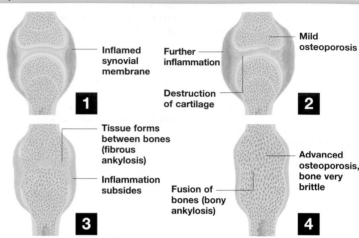

Inflamed synovial membrane — **1**

Further inflammation — Mild osteoporosis — Destruction of cartilage — **2**

Tissue forms between bones (fibrous ankylosis) — Inflammation subsides — **3**

Fusion of bones (bony ankylosis) — Advanced osteoporosis, bone very brittle — **4**

Initial symptoms and signs

RA is characterized by painful swelling of the small joints of the hands, feet, wrists, ankles, knees and cervical spine (neck). Pain occurs less commonly in the shoulders, elbows and hips.

■ Symmetrical distribution of pain is a reliable RA indicator
■ Articular effusion (fluid in the joint) and wasting muscles around the affected joints often accompanies the inflammation

■ Any synovial joint may be affected by swelling, stiffness and 'hot', painful, red joints

As the disease progresses, cartilage, bone and ligament damage occur, producing the deformities typically seen in long-standing, destructive rheumatoid arthritis. Specific deformities include:

■ Carpal tunnel syndrome (numbness and pain in the hand)

■ Swelling of the knuckle and wrist joints
■ Spindling of the fingers (swelling of the interphalangeal joints)
■ Trigger finger (inability to straighten)
■ Tenosynovitis (tendon inflammation)
■ Subcutaneous nodules (tender under-skin swellings of fibrous tissue), commonly on the arm.

Diagnosis

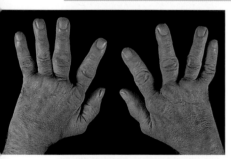

In an advanced case of rheumatoid arthritis, a number of joints will be affected, together with wasting of the small muscles of the hand.

The diagnosis of RA requires careful study of the patient's medical history and a clinical examination. There are several types of test performed to aid accurate diagnosis:

■ Laboratory blood tests will highlight indicators of disease activity
■ Rheumatoid factor
■ Blood counts (for anaemia)
■ X-rays of the hands, wrists, feet and ankles. Characteristic changes reveal synovial destruction and bone erosion. Chest X-rays may indicate heart and lung involvement.

There are commonly agreed criteria for clinically diagnosing RA. Four of the following factors must be present in the patient:

■ Morning stiffness for one hour or more, over a period of at least six weeks
■ Symmetrical arthritis for at least six weeks
■ Arthritis of three or more joint areas for at least six weeks
■ Rheumatoid nodules
■ Bone changes on X-ray
■ Presence of rheumatoid factor in blood serum

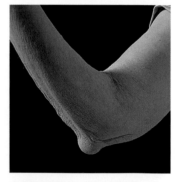

On the elbow of an elderly patient, a characteristic nodule has formed.

Prognosis

After a single episode of RA, 30 per cent of sufferers recover, 65 per cent become chronic cases and 5 per cent develop severe disease and disability.

A severe case of rheumatoid arthritis is shown in this false-colour X-ray. The orange areas are the inflamed and swollen interphalangeal joints.

The clinical course of RA is variable, and regular supervision of patients is required to identify the prognostic factors that are important in planning treatment and management:

■ Failure to respond to non-steroidal anti-inflammatory drugs (NSAID)
■ Poor functional capability

■ Radiological (X-ray) signs, such as bone erosion
■ Development of signs of RD, such as anaemia, vasculitis, nodules, scleritis
■ High levels of rheumatoid factor in blood serum

Careful assessment of these factors will dictate suitable levels of therapy and specific treatments to be formulated.

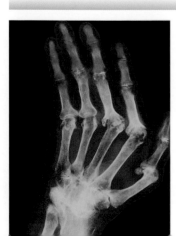

Patient management

The patient and their family need to understand the nature of RA and how it will effect them. They also need to understand the treatment regime and be reassured that the progression of the disease may be slowed or halted with appropriate medication. The available treatments include physical and drug measures.

■ **Physiotherapy** helps to maintain joint integrity and muscle function. Rest, exercise, hydrotherapy and heat treatment all have a part to play in treating patients.

■ **Occupational therapy** is important in maintaining as normal a life as possible. To assist with day-to-day living and activities, patients will be given advice on work, household aids, home appliances and orthotics (surgical supports). All of these are important resources.

■ **Specific therapy** is given to alleviate pain, act on the inflammation and modify the immunological events leading to inflammation. The patient may be treated with varying levels of drug therapy, termed first-, second- and third-line therapy according to the severity of the disease and its

response to treatment.

■ **Surgery** may be used for pain relief, improved function and to correct deformity. This may be by immobilizing a damaged joint, or joint reconstruction in the hands and fingers, often using replacement joints.

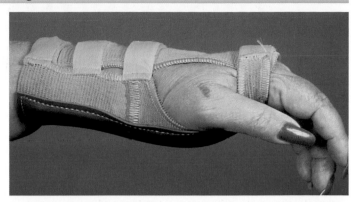

Overuse of an inflamed joint can be aggravating, but supports may provide relief. However, prolonged use of supports can result in marked stiffness.

Drugs and medication

■ Analgesics, such as aspirin, paracetamol and codeine, help to relieve the pain of RA.

■ Corticosteroids, including prednisolone, are potent anti-inflammatory drugs. They are best used to treat complications, such as vasculitis and lung problems.

■ Non steroidal anti-inflammatory drugs (NSAIDs) are widely used in drug therapy, and include benorylate, ibuprofen, naproxen, piroxicam and indomethacin. Care must be taken with them to avoid dyspepsia (indigestion) and gastrointestinal bleeding.

■ Disease modifying anti-rheumatic drugs (DMRDs) are

believed to affect the disease process, although exactly how they work is as yet unclear. They are best started soon after diagnosis under specialist advice. It may take six to twelve weeks before a beneficial response appears.

DMRDs include compounds of gold, by injection or in tablet form, methotrexate, penicillamine and hydroxychloroquine, an antimalarial drug. The latter requires monitoring for visual defects (ocular toxicity). All DMRDs require regular monitoring of urine and blood for signs of toxicity.

Mefenamic acid — available as Ponstan or Meflam – is a non-steroidal anti-inflammatory drug (NSAID) prescribed for the long-term relief of pain and stiffness in rheumatoid arthritis.

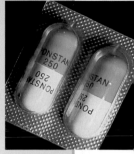

■ Azathioprine, and other immunosuppressants specific against autoimmune disorders, may prove effective against RA, under the correct supervision.

Incidence and care

In the UK, RA affects five per cent of women and two per cent of men. It is more common in females by a ratio of two or three to one. Peak incidence is between the ages of 35 and 55 in women, and 40 and 60 in men. The onset of RA is more common in winter, and there is increased incidence in families.

Patients may require medical

supervision for years by a team of specialists who educate, treat and support. This will include specialist nurses, occupational therapists, physiotherapists, social workers, doctors and orthopaedic surgeons. There is an increasing use of liaison nurses working in primary care together with the hospital rheumatology departments.

The symmetrical nature of rheumatoid arthritis is demonstrated on the X-ray (above) and photograph (right) of an RA patient's severely eroded knee joints.

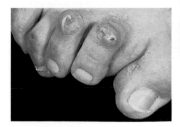

Gross destructive changes in the joints of the feet cause painful deformity and severely limit the patient's mobility.

Causes

Research has suggested a number of potential causes for RA, including infection by microorganisms, autoimmune tissue destruction (in which the body's antibodies attack tissue) and genetic susceptibility. Experimental evidence exists to support all these, but conclusive proof is still awaited.

Prevention

Because of the nature of RA, and the lack of knowledge about its causes, there is no known method for preventing the onset of the disease.

However, much can be done to control RA and alleviate its effects through therapy.

Ankylosing spondylitis

Symptoms

Ankylosing spondylitis is a chronic disorder that typically causes persistent back pain and stiffness, particularly in young men. Women may also be affected, but usually suffer from a much milder form of the disease.

The symptoms of ankylosing spondylitis result from an inflammatory process that often first affects the sacroiliac joints (which connect the pelvic bones to the sacrum). This is usually then followed by the joints that link the vertebrae together (spondylitis), although other joints may also be affected.

FUSION
In some people, new bone develops in the inflamed tissues around the joints, fusing (ankylosing) the joints together

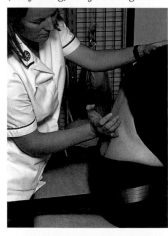

Physiotherapy helps to relieve the pain and stiffness that are common features of ankylosing spondylitis. Regular exercise is vital to maintain flexibility.

Individuals with ankylosing spondylitis may develop inflexibility in the lower back. The upper part of the spine may also become hunched.

and making them inflexible. The inflammatory process also sometimes affects the eyes, lungs, heart and intestine.

The symptoms of ankylosing spondylitis usually appear between the ages of 16 and 40 years, with an average age of onset of 24 years.

SIGNS
Typical symptoms are:
■ Pain and stiffness in the lower back, buttocks and upper posterior part of both thighs. The pain starts insidiously and is typically worse in the morning. It is usually at least partially relieved by moderate exercise but recurs with rest
■ Limitation of spinal movement in all directions and reduced ability to expand the chest
■ Permanent straightening of the curves of the lower back. The upper spine may become hunched (kyphotic) and neck movement may also be limited

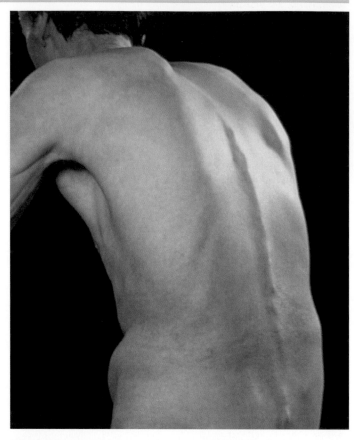

■ Painful, red watery eyes – the iris, choroid (the layer of the eyeball that lies outside the retina) and ciliary body (connects the choroid and iris) are collectively known as the uveal tract. Up to 30 per cent of individuals with ankylosing

spondylitis develop inflammation of the uveal tract (a condition known as uveitis), often on a recurrent basis. Usually, only one eye is affected at any one time, but either eye can be affected during an attack.

Causes

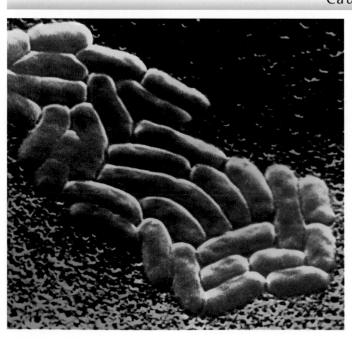

Klebsiella *bacteria have been linked to the development of ankylosing spondylitis. Bacterial infection causes an abnormal reaction in affected people.*

The prime cause of ankylosing spondylitis is unknown, but people with HLA (human leucocyte antigen)-B27 are known to be genetically susceptible to the disease. HLA-B27 occurs in only five per cent of the general Caucasian European population, but in 95 per cent of patients with ankylosing spondylitis.

BACTERIAL INFECTION
It has been suggested that the underlying cause of ankylosing spondylitis is an abnormal response to an infection with strains of bacteria, such as *Klebsiella,* which carry an

antigen that mimics B27, but this has not yet been proved.

Other theories suggest that the disease results from an immune defect or that, since people with ankylosing spondylitis often also suffer from inflammatory bowel disease, the same organisms that inflame the gut may affect the joints.

Incidence

Ankylosing spondylitis normally commences in late adolescence or in early adulthood. It is rare in those individuals who are over the age of 45.

The condition affects four times as many men as women. It can run in families and is more commonly found among Caucasians.

Diagnosis

A clinical history of insidious low back pain with morning stiffness that improves with exercise often suggests the diagnosis of ankylosing spondylitis, especially in a young man. This is usually confirmed by X-ray.

X-RAY CHANGES

Early in the condition, the lumbar spine and pelvis may appear normal, but the sacroiliac joints are often eroded and irregular in shape, and the bone is abnormally dense.

As the disease progresses, newly developed bone may be seen to be fusing the sacroiliac joints together. In the spinal

This coloured X-ray shows the spine of a patient with ankylosing spondylitis. The vertebrae have fused together.

column, the vertebrae become abnormally square in shape and are also fused together by newly formed bone, giving the classic appearance of a 'bamboo spine'.

In advanced cases, the bone of the vertebrae can appear less dense than normal (osteoporotic) and fractures may be seen.

BLOOD TESTS

The erythrocyte sedimentation rate (ESR) and C reactive protein levels may be raised when the disease is most active or severe.

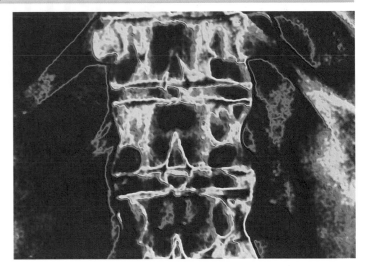

Treatment

There is no cure for ankylosing spondylitis but a combination of daily exercises to mobilize the affected joints and expand the chest, and anti-inflammatory drug therapy, usually helps to keep the spine flexible and relieve pain.

The drug sulphasalazine is sometimes effective in patients who fail to respond to non-steroidal anti-inflammatory drugs.

REGULAR EXERCISE

Physiotherapy and group support can help motivate

Mobilization of the joints can be of great benefit to those with the condition. Back exercises, such as the one shown here, can help strengthen the spine.

patients to continue their exercise programmes in the long term. It is important to avoid the use of corsets and spinal supports, as these will increase immobility.

In severe cases, surgery may be needed to relieve pressure on the spinal cord caused by the spinal curvature. Hip replacement operations are occasionally necessary.

EYE CARE

Prompt treatment is vital to preserve sight. Steroid eye drops are used to reduce the inflammation and the pupil may be dilated to prevent adhesions forming between the iris and the lens. Treatment to lower the pressure within the eye may also be needed.

Prognosis

The outlook for most patients is good. In the long term, about 90 per cent of patients are fully independent or only minimally disabled, even though the spine usually becomes progressively less mobile over the course of a few years.

PROGRESSION

After 10 years of illness, most patients with minimally restricted movements are unlikely to experience any further worsening of their disease. However, one third of manual workers with ankylosing spondylitis are unable to keep working after 25 years.

In women, the disease is

Most people with ankylosing spondylitis have a normal active life. With careful lifestyle adaptations, symptoms rarely disrupt day-to-day living.

usually mild and tends to improve with age. It does not usually cause any restriction of movement or deformity and does not cause problems with childbirth.

Uveitis can potentially cause blindness, but the outlook is excellent with treatment.

A few patients develop inflammation of the aorta (the main artery) or heart muscle.

Prevention

As ankylosing spondylitis is thought to have a genetic origin, it cannot be prevented.

Once diagnosed, however, the condition can be prevented from worsening by seeking early treatment and by taking regular exercise to relieve stiffness and pain in the back.

Chronic bronchitis

Symptoms

Chronic bronchitis is the term used to describe a persistent sputum-producing (productive) cough ('smoker's cough'), associated with a clinical condition referred to as chronic obstructive pulmonary disease (COPD). The cough is often worsened by exposure to cold air, sudden temperature changes, dust and cigarette smoke.

To fit the official medical definition of chronic bronchitis the cough should be present for at least three months of the year for more than one year.

CLINICAL FEATURES
As well as a cough, people with chronic bronchitis may develop:
■ Breathlessness – in the early stages this may occur only on exertion; later it may become so severe that everyday tasks, such as getting dressed, become a major effort or impossible
■ An increased susceptibility to infections – colds and other respiratory infections increasingly tend to affect the chest, along with excessive sputum production, breathlessness and lung damage
■ Lethargy, sleepiness, poor concentration and lack of well-being.

Chronic bronchitis sufferers cough up excessive mucus secreted by enlarged bronchial mucous glands. This is often worsened by air conditions.

Lung tissue is badly damaged by emphysema, a condition that often goes hand in hand with bronchitis. As a result, severe breathlessness develops.

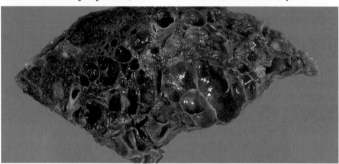

Incidence

Chronic bronchitis usually occurs in older people. It affects 17 per cent of men and 8 per cent of women between 40 and 64 years of age, most commonly those who smoke cigarettes.

Chronic bronchitis is closely associated with smoking. The number of cigarettes smoked a day has an impact on severity.

Causes

The predominant cause of both chronic bronchitis and emphysema (see box) is tobacco smoke. Chronic bronchitis hardly ever occurs in non-smokers, and its severity is related to the number of cigarettes smoked each day. Atmospheric pollution and occupational exposure to dust are lesser causes, but aggravate the condition if it already exists.

In chronic bronchitis, the symptoms are caused by the following sequence of events:
■ Mucus-producing glands in the walls of the bronchi and trachea increase in size
■ These enlarged glands produce excessive amounts of thick, sticky mucus that is expelled as sputum
■ Increased sputum production clogs the airways
■ The bronchial walls become thickened and reduce the airflow further.

In advanced cases, the bronchi become inflamed, full of pus, ulcerated and scarred.

Emphysema

Most patients with COPD have both chronic bronchitis and emphysema.

Emphysema has several characteristics:
■ There is permanent lung damage in which the air sacs (alveoli) of the lungs become enlarged and lose their elasticity
■ The airflow in the lungs becomes increasingly impaired causing breathlessness

■ Emphysema usually, but not always, affects cigarette smokers
■ Some people appear to be genetically predisposed to develop emphysema.

This X-ray of someone with emphysema shows a typical barrel-shaped chest. The ribs are widely spaced due to air trapped in their outer regions.

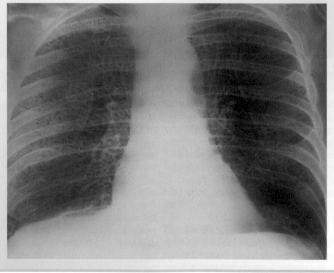

Diagnosis

The clinical picture of a long-term smoker, with a persistent, productive cough, suggests the diagnosis of chronic bronchitis. However, other causes of chronic cough and breathlessness, such as asthma, tuberculosis or lung cancer, must be excluded.

CLINICAL EXAMINATION
In chronic bronchitis, clinical examination may reveal:
■ Wheeziness
■ Crackling sounds or limited air entry to the lungs (through a stethoscope)
■ Rapid breathing
■ Difficulty in breathing – the muscles between the ribs, and the nostrils may be drawn in on inspiration and the lips may be pursed on expiration
■ Poor chest expansion on inspiration
■ Cyanosis – patients' skin may appear blue if they cannot inhale sufficient oxygen or if

lung damage strains the heart (cor pulmonale).

INVESTIGATIONS
Diagnoses are made using different techniques:
■ Chest X-ray – this is not always useful as it may not be abnormal in the early stages of the illness
■ Blood tests – the haemoglobin level and packed red cell volume (PCV) in the blood may be increased, compensating for the low level of oxygen in the lungs
■ Electrocardiogram (ECG) – this may indicate strain on the right side of the heart, which pumps blood to the lungs
■ Lung function tests – these measure the airflow into and out of the lungs and the volume of air in the lungs.

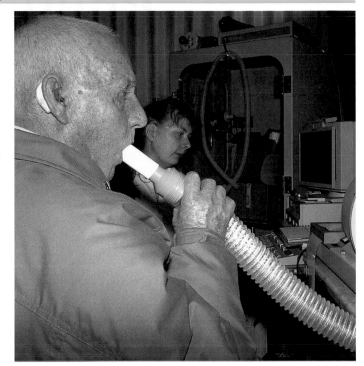

Lung function can be measured using a vitalograph. The patient blows into a mouthpiece and a computer produces the results.

Prevention and treatment

Stopping smoking is of prime importance. Even with severe chronic bronchitis, this will improve the cough. Other aggravating factors, such as pollution and industrial dust, should also be avoided.

DRUG THERAPY
There are several drug therapy options available:
■ Bronchodilators
Drugs that relax the airways, such as salbutamol or ipratropium bromide, help some patients breathe better. They are usually most effective and are best tolerated if inhaled

■ Corticosteroids
These reduce inflammatory changes in the lungs. Not all patients respond to them, but if a trial period of treatment with oral prednisolone for 2-3 weeks decreases breathlessness, long-term treatment with inhaled steroids may be beneficial. The effective dose of inhaled steroids is lower than with oral drugs, so there is less risk of side effects
■ Antibiotics
Acute respiratory infections should be treated promptly with antibiotics to prevent further lung damage. Patients may be given a supply of antibiotics to

keep at home so that they can start treatment if their sputum becomes yellow or green
■ Infection prevention
Yearly immunization against influenza is important for those with bronchitis, who are more vulnerable to infections
■ Oxygen therapy
This may be life-saving for patients suffering from acute worsening of their condition related to an infection. In severe chronic bronchitis, long-term oxygen therapy given virtually continuously, even when asleep, may lessen breathlessness and improve survival.

OTHER TREATMENTS
Other measures may also improve the condition:
■ Physiotherapy manoeuvres – help patients bring up sputum
■ Steam inhalations – thin the sputum, making it easier to cough up
■ Exercise training – patients may feel less breathless and distressed if they are encouraged to take regular mild exercise
■ Assisted ventilation – patients whose condition is temporarily worsened by an acute infection may be helped by the use of a ventilator, if their breathing difficulties have become life-threatening.

A nebulizer is used to deliver drugs directly to the lungs. Nebulizers convert a solution containing the drug into a fine mist which is then inhaled.

Prognosis

At the start of the illness, the symptoms may be relatively minor, with patients coughing and producing a little sputum. If the patient stops smoking, the illness may not progress; the inflammatory changes in the airways may even return to normal.

With more severe chronic bronchitis and continued smoking, infections in the airways are common and may progress to infections in the lung tissue (pneumonia) and respiratory failure.

Smokers are more likely to die of chronic bronchitis and emphysema than non smokers. About 50 per cent of severely breathless patients die within five years, but stopping smoking improves the outlook. The number of deaths increases with heavy atmospheric pollution.

Pleurisy

Symptoms

Pleurisy occurs when inflammation develops in the double membranes that cover the lung and line the chest wall (pleurae). Each pleura forms a closed sac, resembling a plastic bag without an opening. Normally, the inner surfaces of the sac are smooth and moist and glide over each other as the lungs expand and contract.

PAIN

In pleurisy, an area of pleura becomes rough and sticks to the opposite pleural surface, causing a localized sharp pain when breathing in. This pain worsens with deep breathing and coughing and, occasionally, with twisting and bending movements.

The pain is often felt at the site of the inflammation, but is sometimes felt some distance away. Pain in the shoulder tip may result from pleural inflammation in the diaphragm.

PLEURAL EFFUSION

Pleurisy can result in a build-up of fluid in the pleural sac (pleural effusion). If a large volume accumulates, it can cause pressure on the lung and breathlessness.

One symptom of pleurisy is pain when breathing deeply, which is aggravated by coughing. This is caused by an inflammation of the pleural membranes.

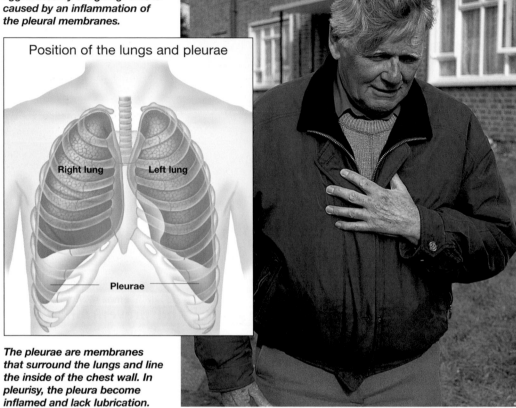

Position of the lungs and pleurae

Right lung   Left lung

Pleurae

The pleurae are membranes that surround the lungs and line the inside of the chest wall. In pleurisy, the pleura become inflamed and lack lubrication.

Causes

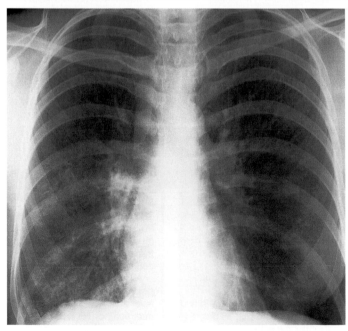

Pleurisy is often associated with an underlying disorder. Causes of pleural inflammation include:
■ Lung infections – ranging from serious pneumonia to milder bacterial and viral respiratory infections that are not evident on an X-ray
■ A lung abscess
■ Cancer of the lung spreading directly to the pleura
■ Secondary cancerous deposits (metastases) from, for example, cancer of the breast or ovary
■ Pulmonary infarct – death of lung tissue due to a blood clot from another part of the body
■ Tuberculosis
■ Trauma
■ Epidemic myalgia (Bornholm disease) – this common cause of pleuritic pain in young adults is due to an infection with the Coxsackie B virus. It causes an upper respiratory tract infection, chest and abdominal pain and muscular tenderness. Recovery usually occurs within a week.

Pleurisy can be caused by many disorders, such as tuberculosis. On this chest X-ray, the red areas show pulmonary tuberculosis in the lungs.

RARER CAUSES

Less usual causes include:
■ Systemic lupus erythematosus (SLE) – a chronic inflammatory disease of connective tissue that affects the skin and various internal organs
■ Rheumatoid arthritis – an autoimmune disease that chiefly affects the lining of the joints
■ Diffuse mesothelioma – a malignant tumour related to asbestos exposure that occurs, on average, 30 years before the pleuritic pain develops
■ Kidney failure – increased waste matter, such as urea, accumulates in the blood and causes inflammation.

Incidence

Pleurisy is the commonest type of chest pain encountered in respiratory disease and is the most common respiratory manifestation of SLE. Every year, around one person in 1,000 visits their GP because of pleurisy or pleural effusion.

Pleural adhesions, thickening of the pleura and pleural effusion often occur in rheumatoid arthritis, particularly in middle-aged men, but rarely in women. The lung problem may precede the development of the arthritis.

Diagnosis

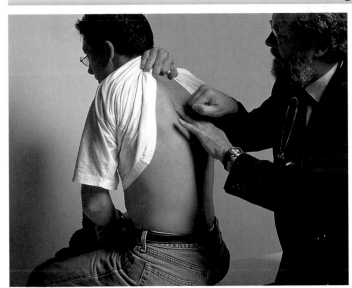

The diagnosis is based on the history of a sharp pain in the chest when breathing in, particularly in patients with a respiratory infection.

A rubbing sound (pleural rub) can sometimes be heard over the inflamed area of pleura when listening to the chest through a stethoscope.

Tapping the chest wall over a pleural effusion produces a stony dull sound, rather than the resonant sound normally produced when percussing the chest wall.

Percussion is a technique used in examining the chest. A doctor taps the chest wall and listens carefully to the sound produced to make an accurate diagnosis.

TESTS
Investigations will determine the underlying cause of the pleurisy. Depending on the duration and severity of the illness, they may include:
■ Blood tests
■ Chest X-ray – in many cases, no change is seen on X-ray. Only pleural effusions of 300 ml or more are detectable on X-ray
■ Ultrasound
■ Aspiration of fluid from a pleural effusion with a needle passed through the chest wall under a local anaesthetic. The fluid will be sent to the laboratory for microscopic examination and culture
■ Sputum examination
■ Respiratory function tests
■ Electrocardiogram (ECG).

Treatment

Treatment aims to relieve pain and distress and treat the underlying cause of the pleurisy. Any of the following treatments may be offered to treat pleurisy:
■ Antibiotics
■ Corticosteroids
■ Chemotherapy
■ Radiotherapy
■ Strong analgesics.

EASING THE PAIN
These treatments may be particularly helpful in helping to ease the pain of this condition:
■ Opiates, such as morphine, may be prescribed, but great care must be taken to ensure that the patient's natural drive to breathe is not dangerously reduced (respiratory depression)

■ Holding a pillow or towel tightly against the chest when breathing or coughing or lying on the side that hurts may help to ease the pain.

PLEURAL EFFUSION
If the patient has a large pleural effusion, draining the fluid will ease breathing, but the fluid must be drained slowly. Rapid drainage may result in a sudden shift in position of the heart and root of the lungs, leading to pain and cardiovascular shock.

Holding a pillow against the chest when coughing can help to relieve the pain of pleurisy. Strong painkillers may also be prescribed by the doctor.

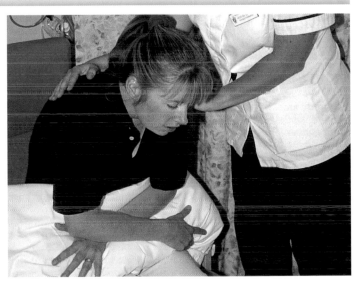

Prevention

Early treatment may reduce the risk of pleurisy associated with respiratory infections. Cancerous deposits on the pleura may be prevented with anti-cancer treatments for lung cancer and cancers likely to spread to the lung, such as ovarian or breast cancers.

Safety measures
Safety measures, such as the wearing of masks and protective clothing, will prevent the inhalation of asbestos fibres and the risk of pleurisy associated with mesothelioma in asbestos workers.

The use of drugs to treat patients with tuberculosis and their close contacts will reduce the risk of pleurisy due to tuberculosis infection.

Protective suits and masks are essential for people who work with asbestos. Inhaling asbestos fibres can cause lung diseases such as mesothelioma.

Prognosis

The outlook depends on the cause. For example, when pleurisy is associated with a respiratory infection, most patients recover rapidly, often without the need for antibiotics. Pleurisy associated with rheumatoid arthritis recovers within a few months. Pleurisy due to TB usually responds to anti-TB drugs, but it is sometimes also necessary to drain pus from the pleural space.

Surgery, chemotherapy and radiotherapy may bring at least temporary relief to patients with cancer-related pleurisy.

Anaemia

Symptoms

Anaemia is a condition in which there is a deficiency of haemoglobin in the blood. There are several different types of anaemia with various underlying causes. Iron-deficiency anaemia is the commonest form of anaemia.

Symptoms may include:
- Tiredness
- Dizziness
- Breathlessness
- Heart palpitations
- Headaches.

A doctor may also note signs such as:
- Angular stomatitis (inflammation and cracking of the mucosa at the side of the mouth)
- Glossitis (sore tongue)
- Atrophic gastritis
- Blood loss
- Koilonychia (brittle, spoon-shaped nails)
- Brittle hair
- Pallor of the skin
- In older patients, swelling of the ankles and chest pain.

Pernicious anaemia is due to vitamin B_{12} or folic acid deficiency. Symptoms include a sore, smooth and inflamed tongue, diarrhoea and tingling fingers and toes. Patients with severe anaemia may have a typical lemon tint to the face.

Patients with sickle-cell anaemia may experience a painful chest, abdomen (girdle syndrome), spleen or bones. Leg ulceration may occur and, more rarely, hemiplegia (paralysis of one side of the body) and convulsions. Kidney damage may occur. The patient will be feverish and feel weak.

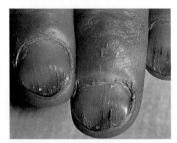

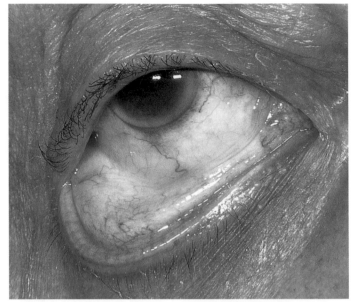

Koilonychia – dish-shaped fingernails – is associated with iron-deficiency anaemia. Prominent ridges are also apparent on these nails.

Patients with anaemia may have signs such as very pale inner eyelids. The patient's skin may also be much paler than normal.

Causes

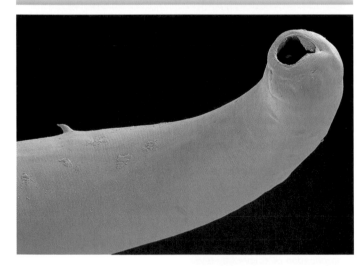

- Red blood cells contain haemoglobin, which transports oxygen around the body; any reduction in the red blood cell count or in the amount of haemoglobin will lead to iron-deficiency anaemia, the commonest type of anaemia
- Thalassaemia is a hereditary condition which leads to the destruction of red blood cells
- Many chronic diseases may cause secondary anaemias; for example, infections, carcinomas, connective tissue disorders and kidney failure
- Anaemia can occur with heavy blood loss during

This micrograph shows the head of a parasitic hookworm. Hookwork infestations cause half of all cases of anaemia in the developing world.

menstruation and when demand for iron is high, such as during pregnancy
- Pernicious anaemia is caused by a lack of intrinsic factor as a result of auto-immune damage to the lining of the stomach
- In developing countries, the commonest cause of anaemia – accounting for 50 per cent of cases – is parasitic infestation with hookworm.

Diagnosis

- **Iron-deficiency anaemia**
A blood film will reveal low levels of haemoglobin, abnormally small red blood cells and low levels of circulating iron. A doctor will check for overt sources of bleeding, such as piles, menorrhagia (heavy periods), gastro-intestinal tumours, diverticular disease of the large bowel and iron-deficiency in pregnancy.
- **Pernicious anaemia**
A full blood count will show abnormally large red blood cells. In anaemia due to alcohol, the blood cells are spherical. Bone marrow aspirate will confirm this type of anaemia. There will also be a low serum B_{12} level.

- **Sickle-cell anaemia**
A full blood count reveals a low haemoglobin level. A blood film will show typical sickle and target cells. A screening test such as 'sickledex' is used to detect the presence of the sickle type of haemoglobin.
- **Thalassaemia**
The blood film will show target cells, Howell Jolly bodies (nuclear remnants of developing red blood cells) and abnormal red blood cells.

This electron micrograph shows typical red blood cells from a patient with sickle-cell anaemia. Tests are conducted to detect these deformed cells.

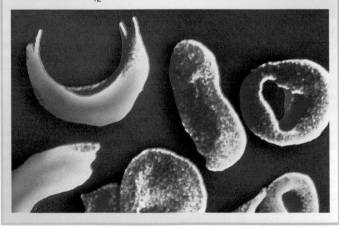

Treatment

Treatment of anaemia depends on the type diagnosed. In iron-deficiency anaemia, the body's iron stores must be replaced by means of iron tablets taken orally, or iron sorbitol by deep intramuscular injection. In very severe anaemia following haemorrhage, a blood transfusion may be necessary.

Specific treatments depend on the type of anaemia:
■ In thalassaemia, regular blood transfusions and iron binding with desferrioxamine infusion and folic acid supplements are necessary
■ Auto-immune haemolytic anaemia responds to prednisolone; removal of the spleen (which breaks down red blood cells) may be necessary
■ Sickle-cell anaemia will require life-long folic acid and penicillin twice daily to prevent infection; a sickle-cell 'crisis' requires rehydration, analgesia and broad-spectrum antibiotics – in a life-threatening crisis, exchange blood transfusion may be required.

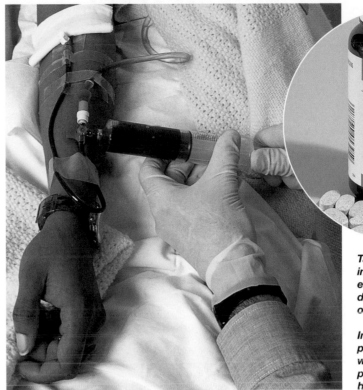

Taking iron tablets and dietary improvements constitute an effective treatment for iron-deficiency anaemia. Injections of iron are rarely used.

In severe cases of anaemia, particularly a 'crisis' in patients with sickle-cell anaemia, a patient may require a life-saving blood transfusion

Prognosis

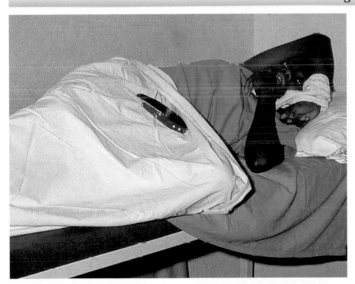

■ In iron deficiency anaemia, replacement of iron by tablets and diet usually solves the problem; the majority of iron-deficiency anaemias respond very well to therapy
■ Pernicious anaemia is a life-long condition but the response to vitamin B_{12} therapy is rapid and complete, providing the condition is diagnosed early enough to prevent the development of complications such as sub-acute combined degeneration of the spinal cord

A sickle-cell 'crisis' can be brought on by a number of factors, including infection or dehydration. A crisis often leads to kidney damage.

■ Aplastic anaemia may be slight or very serious – the diagnosis depends on the platelet counts and blood counts of reticulocytes and neutrophils on examination of the blood; more than 50 per cent of patients with all these features for over three weeks may well die.

SCREENING FOR SICKLE-CELL ANAEMIA
Any patient not of northern European descent requiring anaesthesia should be screened for sickle cells beforehand, as anoxia (lack of oxygen in the tissues) must be avoided in order to prevent a 'crisis'. Antenatal screening is necessary for all sickle-cell disorders.

Incidence

Approximately 5–6 hundred million people are affected by iron-deficiency anaemias worldwide; it is most common in menstruating women. In the UK, 25 per cent of the West African population and 10 per cent of the Afro-Caribbean population have sickle-cell trait; it affects both sexes equally.

Pernicious anaemia accounts for 25 new cases per hundred thousand people over 40 years of age. It is more common in women and affects all racial groups. The average age of patients is 60 years.

Prevention

Attention to diet is essential in deprived people as iron-containing foods, together with vitamin C, should prevent nutritional iron-deficiency anaemias from occurring.

Any source of persistent or recurrent bleeding or 'hidden' bleeding must be investigated to prevent chronic loss of blood.

Folate and B_{12} deficiency can be prevented and supplements may be required in pregnancy. Poor diet in pregnancy, together with the increased physiological requirement for iron, may also lead to anaemia.

Iron-deficiency anaemia can be prevented by eating a balanced diet and taking iron supplement tablets. Other causes of anaemia should be addressed.

Haemophilia

Symptoms

In a healthy person, small wounds stop bleeding in minutes with the help of effective blood-clotting mechanisms. In the rare condition known as haemophilia, a vital clotting factor is deficient, resulting in excessive bleeding. There are two types of haemophilia:
■ Haemophilia A
■ Haemophilia B, also known as Christmas disease.

NORMAL CLOTTING
The clotting process requires a number of blood protein constituents or factors. Altogether there are 12 different clotting factors (I–XII).
■ In haemophilia A there is a deficiency of factor VIII
■ In Christmas disease there is a lack of factor IX.
   These deficient factors may be simply low in concentration or entirely absent. Consequently haemophilia may be mild, moderate or severe.

CLINICAL FEATURES
The symptoms of haemophilia depend on existing levels of clotting factors:
■ Mild haemophilia often remains undiagnosed until bleeding problems develop after trauma or surgery
■ Moderate disease occasionally leads to spontaneous bleeding into joints and, rarely, internal

bleeds. There may also be problems with excessive bleeding after surgery or trauma.
■ Skin is easily bruised
■ In severe haemophilia, internal bleeding may occur without any obvious cause.
   There is a high risk of bleeding after dental work and surgery and following trauma. Joint bleeds are a major problem and can lead not only to pain but to permanent damage and loss of movement.
   Some female carriers have no symptoms. Others have low factor levels and may suffer menstrual problems, bruising, and other bleeding disorders.

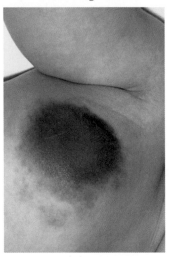

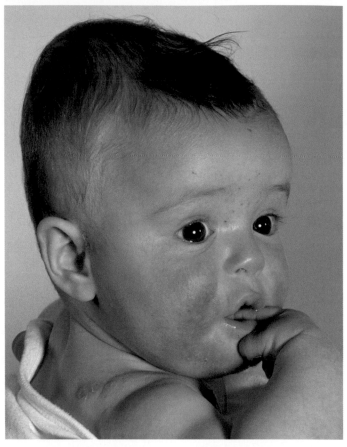

Abnormal bruising is a common sign of haemophilia. Minor bumps can lead to large, sore bruises that are usually out of proportion to the injury.

Bleeding underneath the skull – a cephalohaematoma – can affect babies with haemophilia. This baby has a marked swelling on the top of the head.

Causes

Haemophilia is an inherited recessive disorder, meaning that it is passed from mother to child. In haemophilia A and Christmas disease, it is almost always males who are affected.

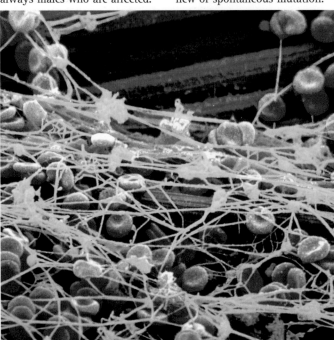

The normal blood clotting mechanism, shown on this micrograph, is absent in haemophilia. This is a result of a genetic defect, passed from parent to child.

This is because the faulty gene is carried by the female on one of her two X chromosomes.
   In about a third of cases the problem occurs as a result of a new or spontaneous mutation.

PATTERNS OF INHERITANCE
The pattern of inheritance of haemophilia is linked to which parent carries the disease. Males have an X and a Y chromosome. Females can have one normal X chromosome (since they have two X chromosomes). In such a case, there is a 50 per cent chance that:
■ A female carrier can pass the defective gene on to her male offspring
■ A female carrier can pass the gene on to her female offspring – meaning that there is a 50 per cent chance that each of her daughters will be carriers.
   Boys born to a father who has haemophilia and a mother who

is not a carrier will not have the disease. This is because boys get their X chromosome from their mother and their Y chromosome from their father.
   All daughters born to men with haemophilia will inherit the gene. This is because they get one X chromosome from their father and one from their mother.

Incidence

All forms of haemophilia are relatively rare. Haemophilia affects all racial groups and is found worldwide:
■ There are about 10,000 people with haemophilia in the UK
■ Haemophilia A affects 1 in 5,000 to 10,000 males
■ Haemophilia B, or Christmas disease, affects 1 in 30,000 males.

Diagnosis

Most children regularly acquire cuts and bruises, and these minor injuries are considered part of growing up. However, children with haemophilia often show signs of bleeding that are not entirely normal and this may arouse the doctor's suspicions

SUSPICIOUS SIGNS
Indications of a more serious problem include:
- Bleeding from the gums
- A nose bleed or a minor injury that continues to bleed even after applying pressure for 20 minutes or more
- Severe bruising (haematoma) in the absence of a fall
- Swollen and tender joints.

All these symptoms require medical attention.

DIAGNOSTIC TESTS
The diagnosis is best made at a hospital with a haemophilia centre. Tests to assess how long blood takes to clot and to measure levels of clotting factors will confirm diagnosis.

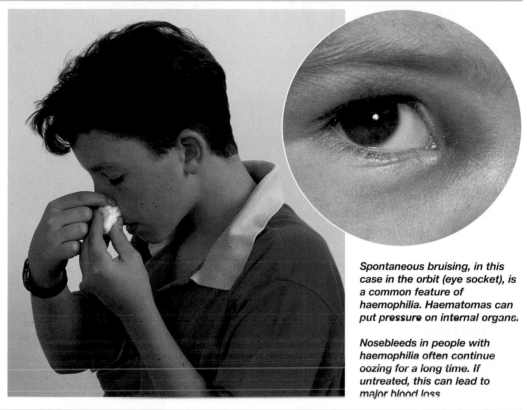

Spontaneous bruising, in this case in the orbit (eye socket), is a common feature of haemophilia. Haematomas can put pressure on internal organs.

Nosebleeds in people with haemophilia often continue oozing for a long time. If untreated, this can lead to major blood loss

Treatment

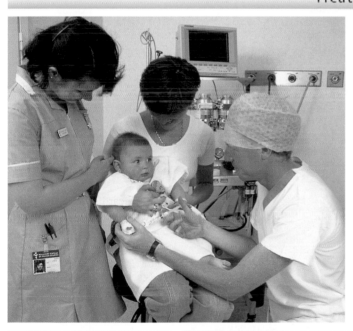

Haemophilia is usually treated by replacing the missing clotting factor. Lifelong regular injections are given routinely two or three times a week to people with severe haemophilia. These help the blood to clot and prevent permanent joint damage. Extra doses are required during active bleeding.

CLOTTING FACTORS
Clotting factors are derived from donated blood. Nowadays all blood products undergo heat and chemical treatment to kill viruses, but before 1986 much of the clotting factor derived

The aim of treatment is to correct the clotting defect. This involves regular intravenous injection of concentrated preparations of factor VIII or IX.

from donated blood had been contaminated with HIV and hepatitis virus. Sadly, many people with haemophilia were infected by these viruses.

More recently, recombinant clotting factor or synthetically produced clotting factor has become available. It is limited in supply, however, mainly due to its high cost.

IMMUNE TOLERANCE THERAPY
About 10 per cent of people with haemophilia, more commonly those with a severe form of the disorder, develop antibodies to replacement products which make them less effective. These people need to receive immune tolerance therapy to destroy the antibodies.

Prognosis

The main complication of haemophilia is chronic joint disease, or arthropathy, caused by uncontrolled bleeding into the joints. Severe and life-threatening haemorrhage is a constant risk for people with severe haemophilia.

Interest is being shown in the possibility of gene therapy, in which normal genes are transferred to a patient's body so that they will produce the missing clotting factor.

Prevention

For couples who already have a child with haemophilia, genetic counselling will be advised if they plan to on have another child. Prenatal diagnosis is possible by chorionic villus sampling the placenta at 10 to 12 weeks of pregnancy.

Prenatal diagnosis allows parents to discover whether a baby has haemophilia. Other options include pre-implantation genetic diagnosis.

Thalassaemia

Symptoms

Thalassaemia, also known as Mediterranean anaemia, is a hereditary blood disorder. Affected individuals have low levels of haemoglobin (the oxygen-carrying pigment in red blood cells), the body tissues thus being deprived of oxygen. It is one of a group of blood disorders known as the haemaglobinopathies.

The disorder is usually detected in childhood and may be mild or severe.

TYPES OF THALASSAEMIA
There are two types of thalassaemia:
■ Beta-thalassaemia – nearly 200 variants of this genetic defect have been identified. Children with a severe form (thalassaemia major) require life-long treatment. Children with beta-thalassaemia minor are carriers but may be symptom free themselves
■ Alpha-thalassaemia – depending on the number of abnormal genes, this can be mild or fatal before birth.

EARLY SYMPTOMS
Children with mild disorder often have no symptoms at all, or only very minor ones. Those children with severe disorder, however, develop symptoms usually in the first year of life, including:
■ Pale skin
■ Jaundice
■ Inability to feed properly
■ Failure to thrive
■ Intermittent bouts of fever
■ Recurrent persistent infections
■ Bouts of abdominal pain
■ Shortness of breath.

ADVANCED DISEASE
As the illness progresses, the bone marrow, liver and spleen increase their activity in an attempt to produce more red blood cells to replace the deficient ones.

The following signs are a direct result of this increased activity:
■ Thickened bones in the skull and face due to expanding bone marrow. Affected children may have overgrowth of the jawbone

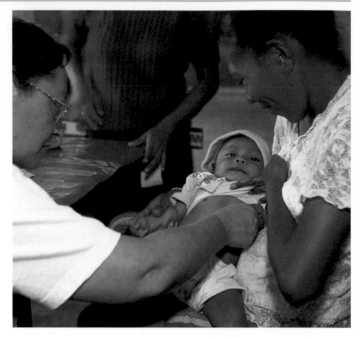

■ Broadened and thickened bones in the hands
■ Enlarged spleen (splenomegaly)
■ Enlarged liver (hepatomegaly).

Thalassaemia is a hereditary blood disease in which there are abnormal haemoglobin levels. The disease is normally diagnosed in childhood.

Causes

Haemoglobin consists of four protein chains (globins), two alpha and two beta. Normally these are produced in balanced quantities. Various genes are responsible for the formation of the different globins.

GENETIC DEFECT
In thalassaemia there is a genetic defect that causes failure to produce enough alpha or beta chains. This leads to deficiency in one globin with an excess in the other.

Thalassaemia is caused by a genetic defect. This affected child is drawing up the inheritance pattern of one of the thalassaemia genes.

BETA-THALASSAEMIA
A child with beta-thalassaemia who inherits the defective gene from one parent only, has a mild form of the disorder. If the faulty gene is inherited from both parents the symptoms are more severe.

ALPHA-THALASSAEMIA
Alpha-thalassaemia is caused by the deletion (absence) of a gene rather than a mutation. There are normally four genes for alpha globins.

The severity of the disorder depends on the number of missing genes. Absence of all four genes is incompatible with life, and the fetus will die before birth.

Incidence

Incidence differs according to the type of thalassaemia:

■ Beta-thalassaemia is common in a broad belt of land that spreads across Mediterranean areas, parts of North and West Africa, the Middle East, the Indian subcontinent and South-East Asia. In some areas, up to 30 per cent of the population carry the defective gene

■ Alpha-thalassaemia has a similar distribution to beta-thalassaemia, but serious forms occur mostly in people living on Mediterranean islands and in South-East Asia.

The high number of thalassaemia carriers in these areas is due in part to the fact that carriers are protected against a severe and often fatal form of malaria.

MIGRATION
In recent years, thalassaemia has become increasingly widespread through migration and marriages between people of different ethnic groups.

Thalassaemia is one of the most common inherited disorders worldwide. Both beta- and alpha-thalassaemia occur in South-East Asia.

Diagnosis

The diagnosis of thalassaemia depends on the clinical history and examination and is confirmed by blood tests.

CLINICAL EXAMINATION
On examination, the child may appear very pale. If the spleen is greatly enlarged, the abdomen may be swollen. If the illness is not treated, the skull bones may become enlarged due to an increased amount of bone marrow in the bones.

BLOOD TESTS
Blood tests reveal:
■ Haemoglobin levels – these may be as low as 2–8 gram/litre (normal values are 12–16 g/l in females and 14–17 g/l in males). Beta-thalassaemia carriers may be mildly anaemic (haemoglobin 9–11 g/l) or may become anaemic at stressful times, such as in pregnancy or during an infection. They are unlikely to have an enlarged spleen
■ White cell and platelet count – these may also be low if the spleen is enlarged.

BONE MARROW SAMPLE
Bone marrow aspiration and examination may show over-production of immature red cells – the body's attempt to combat the effects of anaemia.

ELECTROPHORESIS
Electrophoresis, a technique used to separate proteins by passing a current through a solution, is used to reveal the exact haemoglobin abnormality.

POST-MORTEM
Post-mortems of stillborn babies and neonates may reveal thalassaemia. Infants are usually stillborn at about 28–40 weeks of pregnancy or die shortly after birth. They are very pale, have generalized oedema (fluid swelling) and massive swelling of the abdomen due an enlarged liver and spleen. The afterbirth (placenta) is often large and unusually fragile.

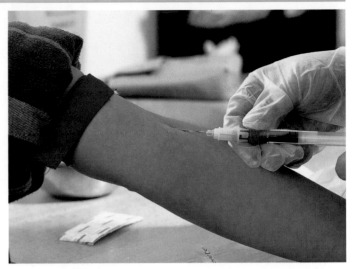

One method of diagnosing thalassaemia is a blood test to determine haemoglobin levels. Anaemia can be severe and requires urgent treatment with blood transfusion.

Treatment

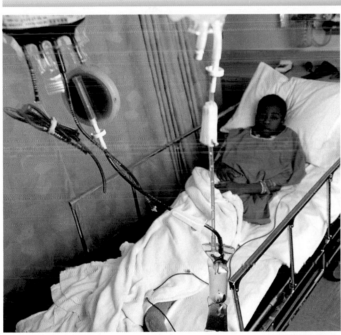

Children with thalassaemia major need regular blood transfusions. These help to raise their abnormally low haemoglobin levels.

Treatment varies depending on the type of thalassaemia in question:
■ Alpha-thalassaemia patients often need no treatment
■ Patients with beta-thalassaemia minor either need no specific treatment or an occasional blood transfusion.

SEVERE DISEASE
Patients with the most severe form, thalassaemia major, need:
■ Blood transfusions – these are needed every four to six weeks to raise the haemoglobin level to normal
■ Regular use of a drug called desferrioxamine – this reduces the levels of iron in the tissues that has accumulated from repeated blood transfusions. Excess iron can damage the liver, endocrine glands and heart. The drug is given by subcutaneous infusion over 8–12 hours several times a week. Ascorbic acid may be prescribed at the same time to increase the output of iron in the urine
■ Bone marrow transplantation – this is most effective if carried out in early life. The procedure is only possible if a suitable donor is available
■ Surgical removal of the spleen (splenectomy) – if the spleen is enlarged. Anti pneumococcal and anti-*Haemophilus influenzae* vaccines and penicillin V are given to protect the patient against infection
■ Gene therapy – may be an option in the future.

Prevention

Symptomless carriers of the thalassaemia gene can be identified by a simple blood test.

SCREENING
Pregnant women should be screened to see if they are thalassaemia carriers (have the thalassaemia trait) at their first visit to the antenatal clinic.

If the trait is present, the father should also be screened. If both parents have the trait, the fetus is at risk of thalassaemia major and prenatal diagnosis can be offered after a full discussion of the implications of the disorder and ethical issues.

Prenatal diagnosis is made by the study of DNA material from the fetal membranes (chorionic villus sampling) from 10 to 12 weeks of pregnancy or, a little later, from fetal blood. Some women may choose to have a termination.

REDUCED NUMBERS
The use of screening and counselling has greatly reduced the number of children born with thalassaemia in areas where many affected children were once born.

Prognosis

Beta-thalassaemia major is fatal if untreated. However, many children who once would have died in early life are now receiving treatment. Blood transfusions allow the child to lead a relatively normal life, but iron overload due to the regular blood transfusions must be controlled.

Too high a dose of regular desferrioxamine can cause:
■ Cataracts
■ Nerve deafness
■ Stunted growth
■ Failure to mature sexually
■ Heart disease in adolescence.

Pernicious anaemia

Causes

Pernicious anaemia is caused by vitamin B_{12} deficiency. It is a relatively common autoimmune condition, in which the body produces antibodies that attack the stomach lining and cause a deficiency in a protein called intrinsic factor. This protein is vital to the absorption of vitamin B_{12}, and so without it no absorption takes place.

RED CELL PRODUCTION
Lack of vitamin B_{12} interferes with the production of red blood cells. This means that the blood is unable to transport sufficient amounts of oxygen to the tissues in the body.

OTHER CAUSES
Vitamin B_{12} deficiency has causes other than lack of intrinsic factor including:
■ Surgical removal of the stomach (gastrectomy)
■ Malabsorption, due to inflammatory bowel disease or pancreatic failure
■ Certain drugs.

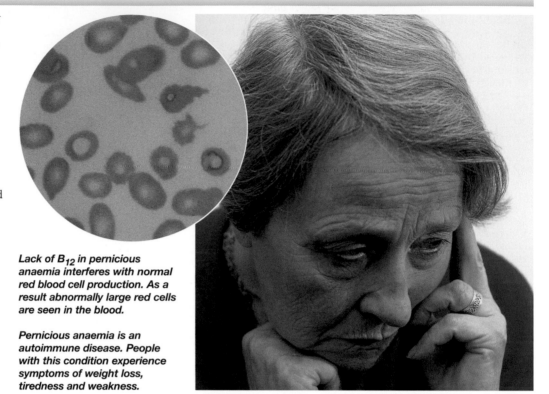

Lack of B_{12} in pernicious anaemia interferes with normal red blood cell production. As a result abnormally large red cells are seen in the blood.

Pernicious anaemia is an autoimmune disease. People with this condition experience symptoms of weight loss, tiredness and weakness.

Symptoms

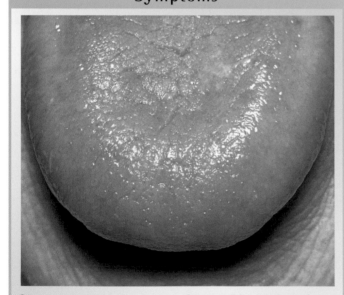

Common symptoms of pernicious anaemia include:
■ Tiredness and weakness
■ Headache
■ Weight loss
■ Chest pain
■ Breathlessness
■ Dizziness
■ Tingling sensations
■ Reduced sense of touch and vibration
■ A sore red tongue and reduced sense of taste
■ Diarrhoea

One possible symptom of pernicious anaemia is a sore, inflamed and smooth tongue. This is associated with a loss of the sense of taste.

■ Depression and poor brain function (occur sometimes)
■ Visual disturbances (in rare cases)
■ A lemon-yellow tinge to the the skin
■ Angular cheilosis (lines at the corners of the mouth).

Diagnosis

If anaemia is suspected a blood sample is taken and sent to the laboratory to establish the precise type of anaemia.

APPEARANCE OF BLOOD
Blood affected by pernicious anaemia shows the following characteristics:
■ Low haemoglobin levels
■ Abnormally large, fragile red blood cells
■ Immature forms of red cells in the bone marrow that are larger than normal.

BLOOD TESTS
Diagnosis relies on blood tests, which include:
■ A full blood count – this shows low haemoglobin and increased red cell volume
■ A blood film – this shows oval enlarged red cells and white cells with excessively segmented nuclei
■ Serum B_{12} level – this is low
■ Serum bilirubin level – this is raised
■ Test for antibodies to intrinsic factor (not present in all cases)
    A Schilling test may also be performed – this measures the body's ability to absorb vitamin B_{12} from the bowel.

OTHER DISEASES
Pernicious anaemia should not be diagnosed in people under 40 unless other causes of malabsorption have been ruled out, such as Crohn's disease.

If pernicious anaemia is suspected in a patient, blood samples are taken. The samples are then sent to a laboratory and subjected to many tests.

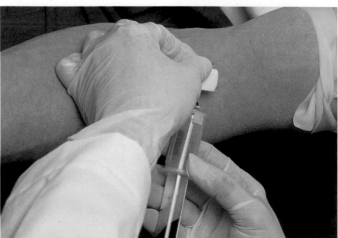

Treatment

Since in pernicious anaemia the problem is not the amount of vitamin B_{12} in the diet but the inability to absorb the vitamin in the stomach, treatment has to be given by injection.

■ **Intramuscular injection**
Hydroxocobalamin (synthetic B_{12}) is given by intramuscular injection. Initially regular doses are given every two or three days to replenish body stores. A maintenance dose is then given every three months.

■ **Oral supplements**
Once blood abnormalities have returned to normal, it is sometimes possible to replace

Pernicious anaemia is treated with hydroxocobalamin injections. At the start of treatment, injections are given every two or three days.

intramuscular therapy with oral supplements. In a person lacking intrinsic factor, only about one per cent of the vitamin B_{12} ingested will be absorbed but this is more than enough to prevent future deficiency.

MALABSORPTION
If deficiency is due to a different malabsorption problem, the treatment depends on the cause. If the cause is a deficient dietary intake, for example in vegans, an initial injection of vitamin B_{12} may be given followed by oral supplements until symptoms subside. A daily maintenance dose prevents a recurrence. In these cases, advice from a qualified dietitian may be advisable.

Oral supplements of vitamin B_{12} can be taken to prevent B_{12} deficiency. Vegans, for example, often take these vitamins to supplement their diet.

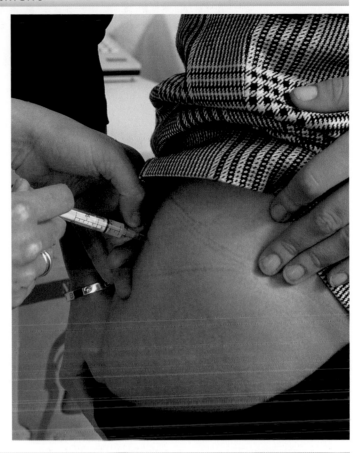

Prevention

Pernicious anaemia cannot be prevented as it is an autoimmune disease. However it is possible to prevent the onset of vitamin B_{12} deficiency due to other causes:
■ Older people with low stomach acid may benefit from the small amounts of B_{12} found in B complex and multivitamin tablets
■ Doctors recommend that strict vegans add some B_{12} supplements to their diet. There are vegetable sources of B_{12} such as tempeh, which is a

Excessive alcohol intake can cause gastritis – inflammation of the stomach lining. In turn, this can lead to poor absorption of vitamins and nutrients.

fermented soya bean product and seaweed but B_{12} content is variable and insufficient to prevent deficiency
■ Alcohol abuse should be treated as it can cause gastritis which may lead to poor absorption of vitamin B_{12}
■ People with B_{12} deficiency must not take large amounts (greater than 800 mcg) of folic acid without the supervision of a doctor. At high levels folic acid can mask the signs of B_{12} deficiency with the potential consequence of serious and irreversible nerve damage
■ It is recommended that affected people undergo endoscopy to screen for stomach cancer developing in damaged stomach lining.

Incidence

Pernicious anaemia is most common in northern Europeans although it occurs worldwide. There are 6,000 cases a year in the UK. Women are affected more than men and the peak age of onset is 60. It is associated with blue eyes, early greying of the hair and the blood group A. There is a family history in 3 out of ten cases.

Prognosis

With the correct treatment, people with B_{12} deficiency anaemias do very well. There is, however, a risk of certain complications developing:
■ Risk of cancer – about two to three per cent of patients with pernicious anaemia develop cancer of the stomach
■ Autoimmune diseases – thyroid disease, vitiligo, and Addison's disease are associated with pernicious anaemia

■ Nervous system damage – there is a risk of permanent damage to the nervous system if the disease is not treated early enough. This was the cause of death before the source of the disease was identified.

In people with pernicious anaemia, there is a small risk that stomach cancer may develop. Patients are screened for this risk using endoscopy.

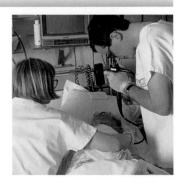

Sickle cell disease

Symptoms

In sickle cell disease, abnormal forms of haemoglobin (oxygen-carrying protein) in red blood cells cause them to become or sickle (crescent) shaped. This makes the cells inflexible, and thus they are more likely to block small blood vessels. The cells are also fragile and do not survive for as long as they should. Although sickle cell disease is inherited and present at birth, symptoms do not usually occur until after four months of age.

LONG-TERM SYMPTOMS
Most people with sickle cell disease suffer some degree of chronic anaemia, which results in pale skin, fatigue and shortness of breath. Other long-term symptoms may include:
■ Jaundice (yellowing of the skin and eyes) – this may develop because red blood cells break down too quickly
■ Skin ulcers, particularly on the legs – these arise due to poor oxygen supply (the sickle cells are unable to carry adequate oxygen)
■ Enlargement and deterioration of the spleen – this can compromise the immune system and increase vulnerability to infection, especially

pneumococcal and blood-cell-damaging viral infections
■ Delayed growth and late onset of puberty
■ Gallstones, caused by high concentrations of red blood cell breakdown products
■ Impaired kidney function, and an enlarged liver and heart
■ Narrowing of blood vessels and thus increased risk of stroke
■ Deterioration of retina – can lead to blindness.

HAND AND FOOT SYNDROME
Hand and foot syndrome is common in children with sickle cell disease. The blockage of small blood vessels causes painful swelling of the hands and feet, due to death of areas of bone. This may be the first sign of sickle cell disease in infants.

CRISIS EPISODES
Some sickle cells are present at all times, but under certain conditions many more cells are affected. Infection, dehydration or decreased levels of oxygen in the blood can trigger a sickle cell crisis, in which the following symptoms occur:
■ Pain, particularly in the abdomen or long bones

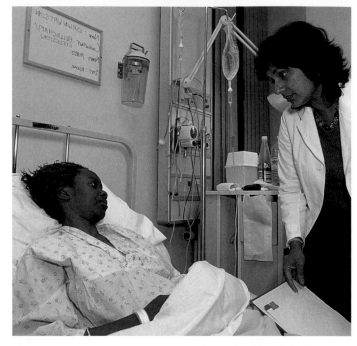

■ Chest pain
■ Convulsions
■ Fever
■ Priapism (a prolonged and painful erection). This is a common problem, affecting 10–40 per cent of young men.
　Crises tend to occur in 70 per cent of cases and can last for hours or several days. The

Factors such as infection or dehydration can bring on a sickle cell crisis. Hospital admission is then necessary for pain control and rehydration.

frequency of crises varies – sufferers can have 15 or more episodes a year or only one every few years.

Causes

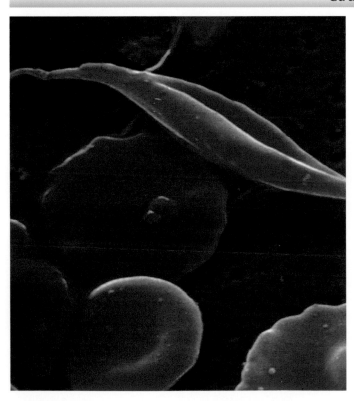

Sickle cell disease occurs when abnormal haemoglobin is produced. This causes red blood cells to become sickle shaped (shown here, top of image).

Sickle cell disease is caused by a defective form of haemoglobin, called haemoglobin S. Haemoglobin S proteins have a tendency to link up into rod-like chains when they are deprived of oxygen, warping red blood cells into a sickle shape.

When the cells become sickle-shaped, they lose their flexibility and cannot pass through narrow blood vessels, and have a shortened lifespan of 10-20 days as opposed to 120 days for a normal red blood cell.

PATTERN OF INHERITANCE
The gene for haemoglobin S is recessive; therefore a child must inherit two copies – one from each parent. A person who has only one copy of the gene is a carrier, and said to have sickle

cell trait. Carriers rarely exhibit any symptoms of the disease, but their children could also be carriers. If two carriers have a child, then there is a 25 per cent chance that the child will have sickle cell disease and a 50 per cent chance that he or she will have sickle cell trait.

Incidence

The gene for haemoglobin S evolved as a defence against forms of malaria in Africa, and spread through the population of sub-Saharan Africa and parts of the Middle East and Mediterranean. In the West, the disease mainly occurs in people of African descent although people of Middle Eastern or Mediterranean extraction are also affected.
　The number of people in the UK who have sickle cell disease is rising and there were an estimated 10,000 sufferers in the year 2000.

Diagnosis

Severe joint pain associated with the symptoms of anaemia and jaundice in someone of African or Mediterranean extraction are obvious signs of sickle cell disease. In infants, hand and foot syndrome may alert doctors to the diagnosis. The condition can be confirmed by taking blood samples for investigation.

ELECTROPHORESIS

Sickle-shaped cells are visible under the microscope, while haemoglobin S is detected by using electrophoresis. This is a simple test in which passing a current through a gel or solution containing samples of haemoglobin causes different types to move at different rates. The patient's haemoglobin can then be compared with controls.

BIRTH AND GENETIC SCREENING

In some parts of the world, haemoglobin electrophoresis is done routinely on samples taken from newborns to detect infants at risk of the condition before they develop the disease.

Another type of screening is genetic screening, in which prospective parents who may have sickle cell trait are tested for the presence of the sickle cell gene. They can then make decisions about having children and use fetal genetic screening, which can be done through amniocentesis.

Education is important so that people at risk understand the genetics. This boy with sickle cell disease is outlining the pattern of inheritance.

Treatment

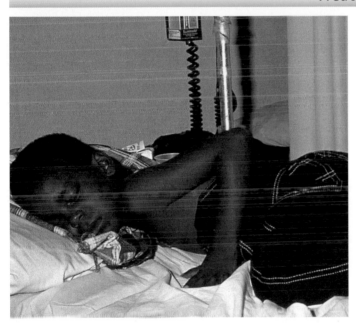

There is no cure for sickle cell disease, but management of the condition and treatment of complications have advanced considerably, such that life expectancy for affected individuals has increased by about 25 years.

INFECTION

Bacterial infections used to be the main cause of infant mortality from sickle cell disease because of a damaged spleen and consequent reduced immunity. Nowadays, children with the disease are given oral penicillin from the age of two

Some sickle cell patients may require a blood transfusion. Such treatment may be required for patients who experience frequent sickle cell crises.

months until at least the age of five to prevent infections developing. Affected children should also be vaccinated against certain infections.

SICKLE CELL CRISIS

Episodes of sickle cell crisis are extremely painful, and usually require hospital admission. Treatment then involves strong painkillers (often opioids), rehydration with intravenous fluids, and oxygen therapy. Antibiotics are given if the crisis has been triggered by an infection.

If anaemia is severe, or if a patient is having frequent crises, a blood transfusion may be necessary to boost the numbers of healthy red blood cells in the circulation and to relieve symptoms.

Prevention

The incidence of sickle cell disease can only be reduced by genetic counselling in people who are potential carriers of the faulty gene. Affected people may then consider whether to start a family.

REDUCING CRISES

People with sickle cell disease need to maintain good health in order to avoid infections. Poor hydration and low blood oxygen levels can also increase the risk of crises, so affected individuals should drink plenty of fluids and take care when travelling by aeroplane, scuba-diving and when they are in other situations that involve low oxygen levels.

Current research

Treatments currently under investigation include:
■ Hydroxyurea – this anticancer drug reduces the frequency of crises and avoids the need for transfusions. It is thought to work by boosting production of fetal haemoglobin, a protein normally made only by fetuses and newborns. The drug is still being monitored for side effects
■ Bone marrow transplant – this can help, but chances of finding a match are low
■ Gene therapy – one approach is to engineer haemopoietic stem cells and implant them into the marrow; another is to turn off the defective gene while switching on the gene for fetal haemoglobin.

It is hoped that gene therapy will find a cure for sickle cell disease. Two genetic approaches are currently being studied by scientists.

Septicaemia

Symptoms

Septicaemia is a condition in which the presence of bacteria in the blood causes destruction of tissues. It is associated with shock and patients will usually be extremely ill.

Symptoms include:
■ Rigors (sensation of heat with shivering)
■ Nausea and confusion
■ Tachycardia (rapid heart beat) and vasodilatation with warm hands and feet ('warm shock')
■ Hypotension (low blood pressure) with clammy cold peripheries ('cold shock')
■ Disorders of body temperature, either well above normal (severe pyrexia) or below normal (37 °C/98.6 °F); the latter is hypothermia, and is associated with a worse prognosis.

During this state, the patient may develop kidney failure and respiratory distress syndrome. There may be headache, neck stiffness and confusion. Meningococcal septicaemia is suggested by a characteristic skin rash.

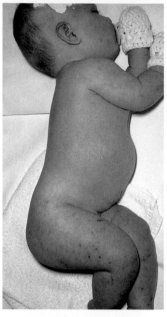

Meningococcal septicaemia may be characterized by a high fever and typical 'flea-bite' rash (seen on the legs of this baby). It must be rapidly treated.

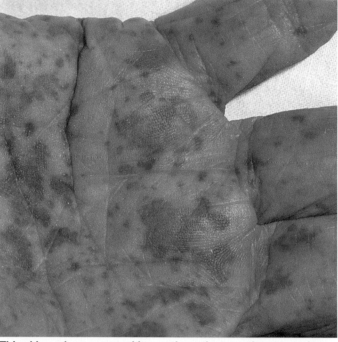

This skin rash was caused by septicaemia secondary to a urinary tract infection. The rash indicates destruction of tissues by bacterial toxins.

Causes

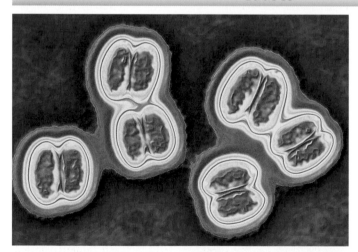

Bacterial endotoxins – poisons released from Gram-negative bacteria when they die – and other bacterial products initiate an 'inflammatory cascade' of reactions leading to widespread cell damage, low blood pressure (hypotension), shock, multi-organ failure and death.

BACTERIAL INFECTIONS
Community-acquired primary septicaemia may be due to gonorrhoea, staphylococcus, *Streptococcus pneumoniae*, *Strep. pyogenes*, salmonella, *Strep. faecalis*, *Neisseria meningitides*, listeria, *E. coli*

and pseudomonas infection. All of these organisms are capable of causing severe infections and warrant careful measures to limit further contamination.

HOSPITAL-ACQUIRED INFECTIONS
In hospital, the most common cause of septicaemia is probably the systemic spread of E. Coli from a urinary tract infection

The raw skin exposed by a burn is readily infected by bacteria in a hospital. This can lead to septicaemia if the infection is widespread.

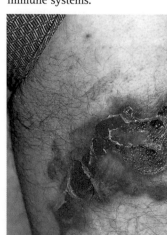

Neisseria meningitides bacteria may cause meningitis. The infection leads to inflammation of the lining of the brain and spinal cord and septicaemia.

caused by indwelling catheter use. Other primary sources of bacteria include chest, obstetric and gynaecological infections.

Infection following a pregnancy termination is now uncommon but infections due to intra-uterine devices (IUDs) are quite frequent, as are post-partum infections with retained products of conception and pelvic infections. Young women may acquire septicaemia due to pelvic inflammatory disease.

Other patients at increased risk include burns patients and those with compromised immune systems.

Prevention

There is no control over cases arising in the community but most of the cases arising in hospital are preventable. Isolation of infected patients, hygiene measures, washing hands between patients and wearing sterile gloves when changing dressings and catheters, and care during surgery, are all measures aimed at prevention of infections in hospital.

Toxic shock syndrome caused by staphylococcus enterotoxin F. was originally described in association with the use of tampons.

Preventative measures are based on scrupulous hygiene practices, such as cleaning hands thoroughly before contact with patients.

Diagnosis

Investigations must be directed towards identifying the infective organism and the site of the infection, the severity of the illness and complications of Gram-negative sepsis.

Other causes of shock, and other infections, must be excluded as more than one factor may contribute to shock in an individual patient. Other infections (for example, Gram-positive bacteria, fungi, malaria, staphylococcus or streptococcus) may be implicated in toxic shock syndrome.

LABORATORY TESTS

Blood, urine, pus and body fluids must be cultured to ascertain the causative organisms. Chest X-rays, blood tests (including white blood counts, platelet counts and coagulation studies) are performed in order to find evidence of blood clots. Arterial blood gas analysis is performed to determine respiratory function, metabolic acid levels and possibly hypoxia.

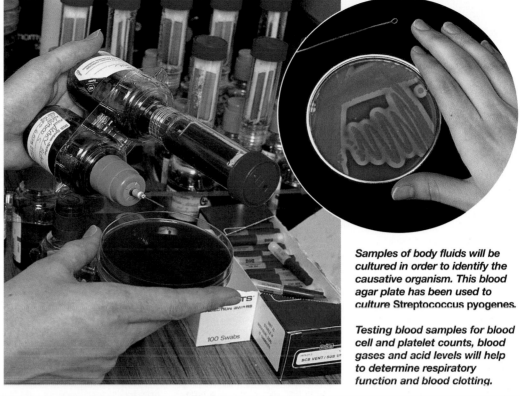

Samples of body fluids will be cultured in order to identify the causative organism. This blood agar plate has been used to culture Streptococcus pyogenes.

Testing blood samples for blood cell and platelet counts, blood gases and acid levels will help to determine respiratory function and blood clotting.

Treatment

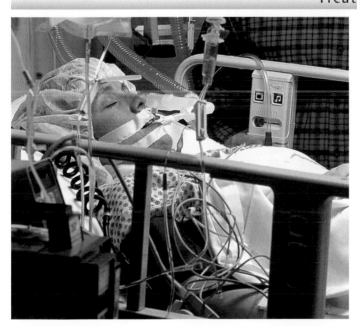

Intensive care is often necessary for patients with septicaemia. Treatment aims to maintain essential bodily functions and kill the bacteria using antibiotics.

The aim of treatment is to control infection, maintain the perfusion of organs with essential nutrients and the delivery of oxygen to tissues, and ensure drainage of pus and the surgical removal of dead or infected body tissue.

DRUG TREATMENT

The choice of antibiotic depends on the site of the infection. For example:
■ Urinary tract – co-amoxiclav or cepatoxamine
■ Pneumonia – ceftazidime, or piperacillin with gentamycin
■ Intra-abdominal infections –

will require cefotaxime with metronidazole, or piperacillin with gentamycin
■ Biliary tract infections – piparicillin with gentamycin.

INTENSIVE CARE

Severe cases are treated in the intensive care unit especially for the management of Gram-negative bacterial shock. This treatment will include:
■ Monitoring blood pressure, central venous pressure and oxygen saturation
■ Cardiac output
■ Catheterization measurement of urinary output.

Treatment may require blood transfusion, pressor drugs (for raising or maintaining blood pressure), drugs to maintain renal perfusion, inspired oxygen and nutritional support.

Prognosis

The prognosis will depend on the severity of the illness and the presence of complications, such as:

■ Kidney failure
■ Disseminated intravascular coagulation (overstimulation of the blood clotting mechanism) – a very serious complication
■ Liver failure
■ Respiratory distress syndrome – this occurs in 15–40 per cent of adult patients.

Gram-negative septicaemia plus shock has been increasing in the past 30 years. Bacteraemia is found in seven in every 1,000 hospital admissions. Septic shock complicates 20 per cent of all bacterial infections. The mortality rate is high, even in otherwise healthy individuals.

Septicaemia is a risk for many patients who are hospitalized, especially if their immune system is already weak.

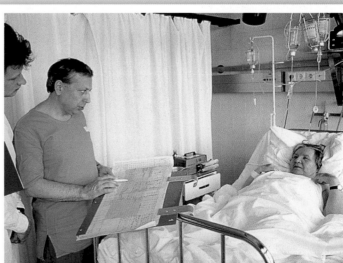

Leukaemia

Causes

Leukaemia is a form of bone marrow cancer that develops as a result of disrupted blood cell production. The main abnormality in leukaemia is the excessive, uncontrolled production of cancerous white cells that prevent normal blood cell development.

The development of blood cells is genetically controlled and some genetic abnormalities are thought to lead to leukaemia. The abnormal Philadelphia chromosome is associated with 95 per cent of cases of chronic myeloid leukaemia. Usually, however, there is no obvious specific cause, although certain factors increase the risk. These include:
■ Some viruses
■ Certain chemicals and drugs
■ Radiation.

BLOOD CELL PRODUCTION
All blood cells are manufactured in the bone marrow. The cells develop from primitive stem cells, which grow into mature functional cells of different types. About 2.5 million red

cells are produced every second; red blood cells outnumber white cells by 700 to one.

TYPES OF LEUKAEMIA
Leukaemia is classified according to the speed at which it develops (acute or chronic), and the type of cell affected (myeloid or lymphatic). Four main types of leukaemia exist:
■ Acute myeloid leukaemia
■ Acute lymphoblastic leukaemia
■ Chronic myeloid leukaemia
■ Chronic lymphocytic leukaemia.

People with leukaemia often have reduced numbers of red blood cells in the circulation. A blood transfusion may be necessary to correct this.

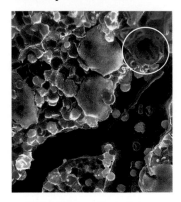

Bone marrow contains red blood cells (red spheres), white blood cells (blue) and platelets (top left, circled). In leukaemia, too many white cells are produced.

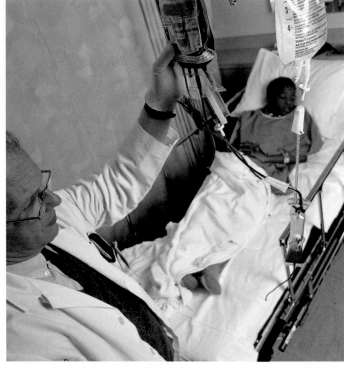

Diagnosis

A physical examination of the patient may reveal an enlarged spleen; there may also be a history of fatigue or malaise (feeling of being unwell).

BLOOD TESTS
A blood sample will provide an accurate count of the blood cells. A person with leukaemia is often anaemic, with a low level of platelets (the cells responsible for clotting) and a high white cell count. In this instance a bone marrow aspiration is undertaken.

MARROW ASPIRATION
In this procedure, a needle is inserted under local anaesthesia into the hip bone.

Two types of tissue are removed for examination:
■ Bone marrow cells are aspirated with a syringe
■ A core of bone, including marrow, is also taken.

Normally, the spleen cannot be felt during a physical examination. In leukaemia, the organ enlarges dramatically, as shown by the shaded area.

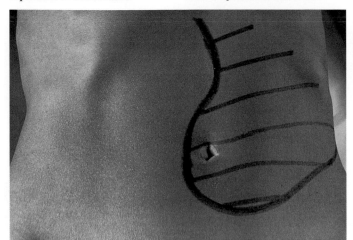

Symptoms

All kinds of leukaemia have common symptoms, although the severity of these depends on the type. Symptoms include:
■ Excessive tiredness
■ Breathlessness and pale skin
■ Easy bruising and unusual bleeding
■ Recurrent infections
■ Pain in bones and joints
■ Persistent fevers and night sweats.
Some patients with a very slow progress of the disease may have few symptoms.

PHYSICAL SIGNS
On examination, enlarged lymph glands are often found in the neck, armpits and groin. The abdomen may be distended due to an enlarged spleen.

Bruising – bleeding under the skin – occurs more easily in leukaemia. This is due to the low levels of platelets (cells responsible for clotting).

Incidence

Leukaemia has an overall incidence of five per 100,000.
■ Acute lymphoblastic leukaemia is commonest between the ages of two and 10, with a peak between the ages of three and four. It is the commonest malignant disease in childhood and accounts for 85 per cent of childhood leukaemia cases
■ Acute myeloid leukaemia is the commonest leukaemia in adults
■ Chronic myeloid leukaemia is more common in 40–60 year olds. About 700 new cases occur annually in the UK

Treatment

Treatment is usually provided at specialist centres. The primary aim is to induce a full or partial remission. In full remission, there are no symptoms and there is no evidence of the disease on blood testing. Not all leukaemias, however, require aggressive treatment initially.

DRUG THERAPY
The mainstay of treatment is the use of chemotherapy drugs, which act by killing cancer cells. A combination of the disease itself and the chemotherapy drugs reduce the body's ability to fight infection. Prophylactic antibiotics and antifungal drugs may therefore be prescribed.

More recently, new drugs, called growth factors, have been introduced. These can be used to stimulate bone marrow before or after chemotherapy. Interferon – a natural substance which fights viruses – is now manufactured, which helps with some forms of cancer.

STEM CELL TRANSPLANT
When the bone marrow is so damaged that it no longer functions, a bone marrow transplant may be necessary. Bone marrow is taken from a donor or is obtained from the patient's own marrow, saved for that purpose during a remission.

The marrow, containing normal stem cells, is then transfused into the patient's bloodstream. The new stem cells are absorbed into the patient's own marrow, where they begin to produce normal blood cells.

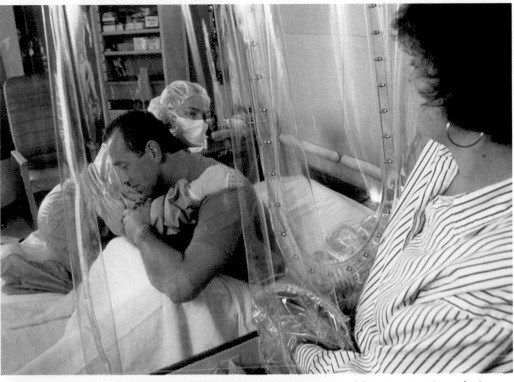

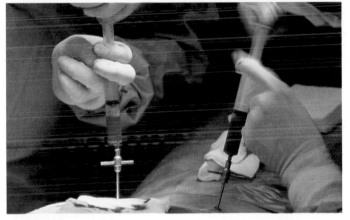

A bone marrow transplant replaces diseased tissue with healthy tissue. This man is being nursed in protective isolation following a transplant.

Bone marrow for a transplant is taken from a suitable donor. Under general anaesthetic, marrow is aspirated from various points on the hip bones.

Prognosis

The different types of leukaemias vary in the course they take. Some are rapidly fatal if not treated, while others progress more slowly.

It should be noted that, even if treatment is successful, relapses may occur over time. A relapse can indicate resistance to the drugs used or it can occur while the patient is not receiving treatment. In the latter case, treatment will be recommenced.

IMPROVEMENTS
In the past 40 years, advances in the treatment of acute leukaemia have improved the chance of cure from virtually zero to 20–75 per cent, depending on the age of the affected person and the type of leukaemia.

■ In acute lymphoblastic leukaemia, 65–75 per cent of children will be alive five years after diagnosis. In adults, this figure will be 20–30 per cent

■ In acute myeloid leukaemia, 40–60 per cent of patients under the age of 55 will be alive five years after diagnosis; over age 55, this falls to 20 per cent.

MONITORING
Follow-up is important, especially in children, not least because of growth and hormonal function, which requires specialist monitoring.

Treatment advances have improved the chances of a leukaemia patient being cured. Follow-up care is important, especially for affected children.

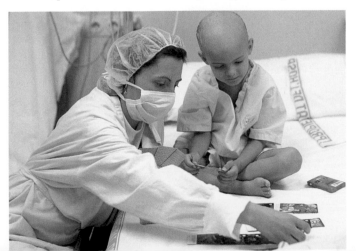

Lymphomas

Symptoms

Lymphomas are malignant (cancerous) growths of the lymphatic system and spleen and are medically classified as either Hodgkin's disease or non-Hodgkin's lymphomas.

LYMPHATIC SYSTEM
The system consists of:
■ A network of vessels that carry fluid called lymph from the tissues to the bloodstream
■ Glands (lymph nodes) which occur at various points along the course of the lymphatic vessels, such as in the groin, armpit and neck. These filter lymph and produce lymphocytes, a variety of white blood cells that are involved in immune reactions
■ Bone marrow

HODGKIN'S DISEASE
The first symptom of Hodgkin's disease is usually a group of enlarged lymph nodes in one area of the body, for example the neck or armpit. The nodes feel rubbery and are painless,

except in rare cases when they become painful if the patient drinks alcohol. The disease spreads through the lymph system and, as it progresses, neighbouring groups of lymph nodes enlarge.
Some patients also have:
■ A fever
■ Drenching night sweats
■ Intense itching
■ Weight loss
■ Bone pain, breathlessness and abdominal swelling, from the involvement of other organs.

NON-HODGKIN'S LYMPHOMAS
In non-Hodgkins lymphomas, nodes are also enlarged, but symptoms may relate to other affected organs and the spread of disease is less predictable.
Primary tumours sometimes develop in:
■ The gastro-intestinal tract
■ The brain
■ The thyroid
■ Bone
■ The testis.

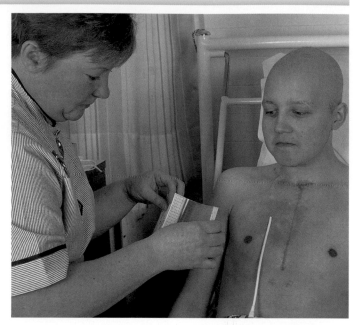

Malignant cells often infiltrate the bone marrow, leading to tiredness (from anaemia), abnormal bleeding and recurrent infections.

In a patient with lymphoma, a special catheter is used to administer drugs or draw blood. The tip of the catheter is positioned in a vein in the chest.

Causes

The cause of Hodgkin's disease is unknown but the condition may be related to some form of infection. The Epstein-Barr virus – the virus that causes glandular fever (infectious mononucleosis) – is sometimes involved; people with Burkitt's lymphoma, which

is common in equatorial Africa and New Guinea, have been found to have high levels of antibodies to the Epstein Barr virus. Burkitt's lymphoma occurs mostly in 4-7 year olds and typically causes large jaw tumours.

GENETICS
Most non-Hodgkin's lymphomas arise from clones of a single genetically abnormal (mutant) cell. The malignant cells resemble B-lymphocytes (white blood cells that produce antibodies), but they

occasionally resemble T-lymphocytes (which are primarily involved in cell-mediated immunity). Some stomach lymphomas are associated with *Helicobacter pylori* infection.

RISK FACTORS
People with suppressed immune systems are likely to be affected by lymphomas; for example, those infected with HIV.

▶ *Burkitt's lymphoma causes large destructive tumours in the jaw. It is common in children in a wide equatorial belt of Africa and New Guinea.*

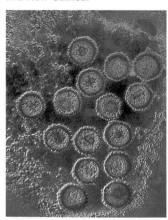

▲ *The EB virus is shown magnified as small, red and gold circles. This virus may lead to Burkitt's lymphoma, a condition associated with malaria.*

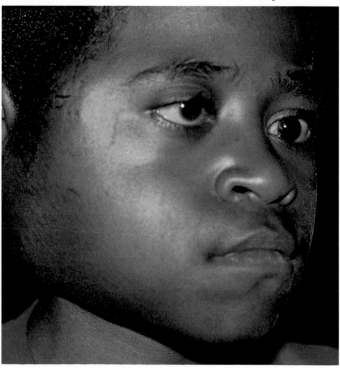

Incidence

Hodgkin's disease
This affects about 2.4 per 100,000 of the UK population. The disease is twice as common in men as in women and most cases tend to occur in early adult life or between the ages of 55 and 70 years.

Non-Hodgkin's lymphomas
The annual incidence in the UK is about 8.2 per 100,000 of the population. Most cases occur in people over the age of 50, but a few cases occur around the time of adolescence. The disease is also seen in adults with HIV infection that has progressed to an advanced stage.

Diagnosis

Lymph node biopsy – the removal of a lymph node for examination under the microscope – is essential to confirm the diagnosis. Findings include:
■ The presence of abnormal cells with two or more nuclei (Reed-Sternberg cells) in Hodgkin's disease
■ Sheets of tumour cells replacing normal cells in non-Hodgkin's lymphoma.

ASSESSMENT
Investigations to assess the extent of the disease include:
■ Chest X-ray
■ CT scan of chest, abdomen and pelvis
■ Full blood count
■ Blood tests for liver and kidney function
■ Bone marrow sampling.
   Lymphomas are graded according to their microscopic appearance:
■ 'High-grade' lymphomas consist of rapidly dividing cells
■ 'Low-grade' lymphomas contain slowly dividing cells.

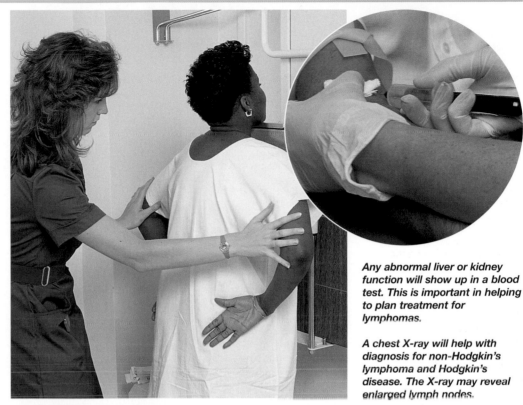

Any abnormal liver or kidney function will show up in a blood test. This is important in helping to plan treatment for lymphomas.

A chest X-ray will help with diagnosis for non-Hodgkin's lymphoma and Hodgkin's disease. The X-ray may reveal enlarged lymph nodes.

Treatment

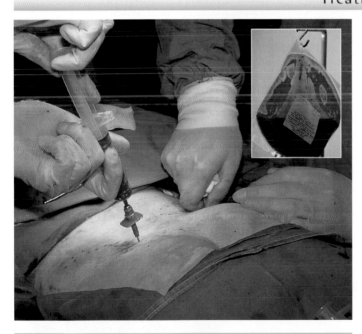

Treatment for lymphomas is usually given with the hope of curing the disease.

HODGKIN'S DISEASE
Treatment for Hodgkin's disease is likely to include:
■ Radiotherapy and chemotherapy – this extends over about six months. People can often receive this treatment on an outpatient basis rather than be admitted to hospital
■ A bone marrow or stem cell transplant may be considered for patients who fail to respond to treatment or who relapse some time later.

In a bone marrow transplant, marrow is taken from a compatible donor. The marrow (inset) is then infused into the patient's bloodstream.

NON-HODGKIN'S LYMPHOMAS
Treatment for non-Hodgkin's lymphomas may include:
■ Localized disease – radiotherapy may be the treatment of choice
■ Generalized disease – chemotherapy and corticosteroids are sometimes combined with radiotherapy
■ Relapses – a drug called alpha-interferon has been used to prolong remission, and high dose chemotherapy/radiotherapy linked with stem cell transplantation may be effective.

STOMACH LYMPHOMAS
Lymphomas that are linked to the bacterium *Helicobacter pylori* sometimes resolve with antibiotic therapy.

Prognosis

Many patients are cured or maintain a reasonable quality of life for a considerable period.
■ Hodgkin's disease – between 70 and 80 per cent of patients survive for five years and most are cured. The outlook depends on the extent of the disease at the time of diagnosis, the presence or absence of symptoms other than enlarged glands, the microscopic appearance of lymph nodes, the initial response to treatment and

whether an early relapse occurs.
■ Non-Hodgkin's lymphomas – most patients with localized disease can be cured but the disease is usually widespread before diagnosis. However, even then, a cure is possible.
   Patients with high-grade lymphomas are more likely to be cured, but patients with low-grade lymphomas may still live for a number of years and make several temporary responses to treatment.

Prevention

Prevention of lymphomas is very difficult. Relatives of patients with *H. pylori* related lymphoma may carry the bacterium. The infection can be diagnosed with a breath test and treated if necessary.
   The Epstein-Barr virus is difficult to avoid as it is the cause of glandular fever, and most children have been exposed to this virus by the time they reach adolescence.

AIDS

Causes

AIDS (Acquired Immune Deficiency Syndrome) is not a single disease but a combination of signs and symptoms resulting from damage to the immune system. It is caused by the human immunodeficiency virus (HIV).

HIV was first identified in 1983, and it belongs to a group of viruses known as retroviruses. These contain RNA, the genetic material of HIV. The virus infects and destroys cells (CD4 lymphocytes) which are critical to the body's immune response, thereby suppressing the patient's ability to fight infections.

The outer layer of the HIV virus cell is covered in coat proteins, which can bind to certain white blood cells. This allows the virus to enter the cell, where it then corrupts the DNA.

These patients in a hospital AIDS ward receive combination drug therapy to slow the damage that HIV causes to their immune system. Although the symptoms can be treated, the condition can not yet be cured.

Diagnosis

There is no specific test for AIDS. The blood test that is often mistakenly called an 'AIDS test' only shows whether a person has developed antibodies to the virus, which is a sign of infection. Antibodies to HIV take two or three months, sometimes longer, to develop after initial infection, so HIV testing should be delayed for at least three months after possible exposure to the virus. A positive result confirms infection. False positive results occasionally occur, so a positive result must be rechecked and those tested should receive counselling.

If HIV antibodies are found in a blood sample, the AIDS test returns a positive result. HIV is the causative agent of AIDS.

IMMUNE SYSTEM

The immune system defends the body against infection and cancers and one of its main weapons are CD4 cells, a specialized type of white blood cell (lymphocyte). HIV infection leads to a fall in the number of CD4 cells which is associated with the onset of AIDS. In the USA, a diagnosis of AIDS is made if a patient suffering from specific clinical conditions related to immune deficiency has a CD4 cell count of less than 200 per ml. In Europe, the definition of AIDS is based on the clinical picture.

Micro-organisms that are usually harmless can cause severe or fatal illnesses in AIDS patients. These are called 'opportunistic infections'.

00000070
Anti HIV 1/2

Incidence

About 42 million people worldwide have been infected with HIV to date, and AIDS has caused millions of deaths. Only conditions typical of old age, such as heart disease, stroke and acute lower respiratory infections cause more fatalities worldwide.

In Africa, HIV has reached epidemic proportions and AIDS is now the most common cause of death overall; it was responsible for one in five deaths in 1998.

In the UK, at the end of March 1999, 37,820 individuals were known to be HIV positive.

Transmission

HIV is transmitted from person to person in several ways:
■ Through unprotected sexual intercourse (anal or vaginal) with an infected person. The use of condoms is of vital importance in prevention
■ By the use of contaminated equipment for injections (by drug users or as a result of medical treatment in developing countries)
■ From an infected mother to her baby before or during birth, or by breast-feeding.

The use of blood transfusion equipment and blood contaminated with HIV has caused infections in the past, but stringent testing and new manufacturing techniques mean that there is now a minimal risk of this occurring in developed countries.

In the UK in 1998, 22 per cent of the 37,820 HIV infected

Intravenous drug use, especially where needles are shared, is a known route of HIV transmission. It accounts for nine per cent of cases in the UK.

individuals acquired their infection by heterosexual intercourse; 60 per cent through homosexual intercourse between men; and nine per cent by injecting drugs.

Symptoms

As the CD4 cell count falls, patients with AIDS become increasingly susceptible to infections such as tuberculosis, candida and herpes. They often suffer from several infections at once, but may not develop typical symptoms as their immune response is impaired. Illnesses can be difficult to diagnose, leading to dangerous delays in starting the correct treatment.

Patients often experience weariness, weight loss, night sweats and diarrhoea early in their illness. Rashes, skin infections and soreness of the mouth are common, as are tingling, pain or weakness of the legs. Intellectual function may become impaired and depression may follow.

INITIAL INFECTION
Usually a person will have no symptoms when they are first infected with HIV, although

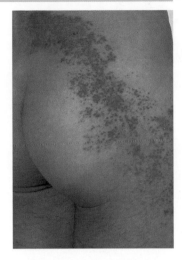

Herpes zoster infection is often the first sign of a compromised immune system. Here, the zoster virus is apparent as shingles.

about 10 per cent of AIDS patients suffer from a short flu-like illness and some develop persistently swollen glands. Once infected, however, a person remains infected for life and poses a risk of infection to others. HIV infection almost always leads to AIDS, but AIDS may not develop for up to 10 years or more after the initial infection with HIV.

EFFECTS OF HIV
The virus damages an infected person's immune system. This damage increases over the years, even though the infected person may feel healthy for a long time. Eventually, they become susceptible to many types of infections and some cancers, and are said to have developed AIDS.

Kaposi's sarcoma is a malignant tumour arising from blood vessels in the skin. It is normally rare, except in AIDS patients.

Treatment

As yet, there is no cure for HIV infection, but several drugs reduce the number of virus particles in the blood, slowing damage to the immune system. However, patients may have to take large numbers of tablets, which carry side effects. They also require treatment for infections or tumours.

When first developed, anti-retroviral drugs were prescribed once patients developed AIDS, but they are now used before symptoms develop. Evidence suggests that early treatment may delay the onset of AIDS.

Three types of drug are used:
■ Nucleoside analogues – zidovudine (AZT), didanosine (ddl, DDI), lamivudine (3TC), stavudine and zalcitabine
■ Protease inhibitors – indinavir, nelfinavir, ritinovir

and saquinavir
■ Newly introduced non-nucleoside reverse transcriptase inhibitor – nevirapine.

Combinations of drugs are sometimes used to increase the effectiveness of drug regimes.

DRUG THERAPY
Advances in modern medicine now mean that many infections and cancers in AIDS can be effectively treated.

Anti-retroviral drugs weaken the virus and, although they cannot eliminate it, they may delay the onset of AIDS or prolong reasonable health.

Treatment for AIDS depends on the circumstances of individual patients. Specialists will determine the most suitable drug combination.

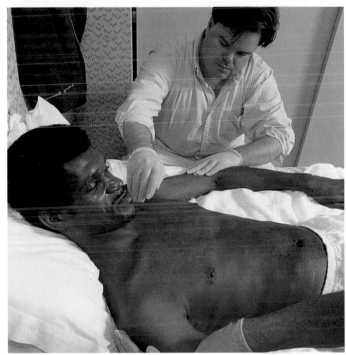

Common opportunistic infections in AIDS

Type	Causative agent	Condition
Protozoal	*Pneumocystis carinii*	Pneumonia
	Toxoplasma	Brain inflammation and abscesses
	Cryptosporidium	Severe diarrhoea
	Microspor	Diarrhoea
Fungal	*Cryptococcus*	Meningitis, lung problems
	Candida	Infections of mouth, pharynx, and vulva/vagina
Viral	Cytomegalovirus	Blindness, inflammation of colon, oesophagus, brain and lungs
	Herpes virus	Severe oral and genital ulceration
	Papovavirus	Progressive neurological disease
Bacterial	General	Recurrent bacterial infections
	M.tuberculosis	Affects lungs
Tumours	Kaposi's sarcoma	Usually affects the lower extremities
	Lymphoma	Cancer of lymph cells

This AIDS patient has seborrhoeic dermatitis. An extensive attack, in an HIV positive patient, is clinically indicative of full-blown AIDS.

Headaches

Symptoms

Headaches are common – surveys suggest that 80 per cent of the population suffer from headaches in any one year. Although usually harmless, they are frequently a source of nuisance.

OCCURRENCE
About 15 per cent of women and six per cent of men suffer from migraine, a condition resulting from spasm and overdilation of certain arteries in the brain, which results in a throbbing headache affecting one side of the head. On average, each migraine sufferer loses six to nine working days every year. This adds up to 18 million working days lost each year from this disorder alone.

Symptoms associated with a migraine include nausea. Before the onset of a headache, a warning sensation may occur in the form of visual disturbance.

Causes and diagnosis

There are many different causes and types of headaches. For example, any virus infection can be associated with headache.

DIAGNOSIS
In order to make a diagnosis a doctor will need to find out certain details regarding the headache, such as the time of occurrence, the exact location, the intensity, the duration and the general effect.

CLASSIFICATION
The most significant types of headache can be classified under the following headings:
■ Tension headaches. These are by far the most common type of headache; they are mild to moderate and are felt on both sides of the head. They often feel like a tight band of pressure around the head. They can last for days and can worsen during the day.

Men seem to suffer from cluster headaches more than women. This type of headache can cause severe pain and last for up to 60 minutes.

■ Cluster headaches. These are more common in men. The pain is severe and usually one-sided. They last for 20–60 minutes and may wake the sufferer several times at night. The headaches come in clusters and may be seasonal. There may be watering and reddening of the eyes and the nose may feel blocked
■ Chronic daily headaches. These occur more than two weeks in every month. Tension or migraine headaches may also occur. They can be associated with taking too many opiate-based tablets
■ Migraines. These come in attacks lasting 4–72 hours. They may be preceded by an aura and are described as moderate to severe. The sufferer feels a throbbing pain on one side and may experience nausea and vomiting. Migraines may be made worse by light, noise or simple daily activities.

Migraine often causes a one-sided throbbing headache: the red-shaded area shows a typical pattern of pain distribution.

SERIOUS CONDITIONS
People with persistent headaches worry that there may be a serious cause such as a brain haemorrhage or tumour. Possible warning signs of these serious conditions are:
■ Vomiting which does not relieve the headache
■ Neurological disturbances (including seizures).
Other signs that may provide a cause for concern are:
■ Persistent headaches in children
■ Pain on touching the temple area, which is a feature of temporal arteritis (an inflamed blood vessel at the side of the head above the ear). This invariably responds to steroid treatment.

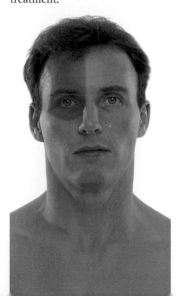

Treatment

Most headache sufferers manage themselves. They know what causes them and how to make the appropriate lifestyle changes which help to avoid them. They usually have a headache remedy that works for them and rarely visit the doctor.

The most popular remedies include aspirin, paracetamol and ibuprofen. Combination remedies such as those containing codeine, are more expensive and, when abused, are known to be associated with chronic daily headaches. Appropriate lifestyle changes may include:
■ Diet
■ Regular meals
■ Regular sleep patterns
■ Reducing stress factors.

PAIN-REDUCING DRUGS
Headaches may be difficult to control with the use of normal painkillers, such as paracetamol, especially if the pattern of attacks keeps changing. There are certain drugs that doctors can prescribe such as:
■ Domperidone – which will diminish nausea
■ Amitryptyline – an antidepressant particularly used in tension headaches
■ Sodium valproate – an anti-epileptic drug which is also used in tension headaches.

There are certain migraine-specific drugs such as:
■ Ergotamine – this is a 5HT agonist, and should not be taken by patients with ischaemic heart disease or uncontrolled blood pressure.

Cluster headaches can be treated by:
■ A 5HT agonist nasal spray or injection
■ Oral steroids (60 mg) – taken daily for two weeks, these will abort a cluster headache.

Stress can often be an important factor in headaches. Lifestyle measures to reduce stress may help headache sufferers.

OTHER THERAPIES
Complementary therapies, such as osteopathy, acupuncture, aromatherapy, massage and homeopathy, have all been tried by headache sufferers.

Hormone replacement therapy (HRT) can also be useful in cases of migraine associated with the menstrual cycle (14 per cent of women with migraine have attacks only around the time of menstruation).

However, hormone-based therapies such as the oral contraceptive pill or HRT are used cautiously in migraine sufferers as they are three times more likely to develop a stroke, especially if there is a family history of the condition.

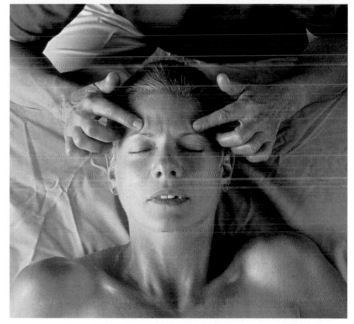

Alternative therapies, such as head massage, have been known to help headache sufferers. Massage aids relaxation and relieves pain.

Prognosis

The outlook for people with chronic headache is difficult to predict. The good news is that they can almost always be helped by treatment, but the headaches may flare up again. For instance, migraine can be active for up to 20 years during a person's life. Women seem to be particularly vulnerable to headaches at certain stages of their lives, namely puberty, pregnancy and the menopause.

Girls going through puberty may be particularly susceptible to headaches. This may be due to hormones which are released during the menstrual cycle.

Prevention

If attacks of migraine are occurring frequently, not responding well to treatment or interfering with quality of life, tablets may be taken regularly to reduce the frequency of these attacks. Propranolol, atenolol and pizotifen are commonly used. About half of all patients taking such drugs respond significantly. Cluster headaches can be reduced in frequency by verapamil, a calcium-channel blocker.

Regular headaches can have an impact on a person's quality of life. Certain types of medication can reduce the frequency of attacks.

Temporal arteritis

Symptoms

Temporal arteritis is a condition that causes inflammation of the medium-sized blood vessels that supply the scalp, especially those in the temples. If the condition is widespread, it is known as giant-cell arteritis or cranial arteritis.

CLINICAL FEATURES
Symptoms of temporal arteritis include:
■ Headache
■ Intermittent impaired vision, such as double vision
■ Sudden vision loss in one eye
■ Jaw claudication (cramp) – affects 50 per cent of patients
■ Tenderness on the scalp.

A quarter of patients also suffer from polymyalgia rheumatica (PMR), a condition which causes symmetrical pain and stiffness in the shoulders and hips.

Sometimes, patients with giant-cell arteritis have vague symptoms, such as tiredness, depression, prolonged fever, weight loss and reduced appetite

Temporal arteritis causes headache and tenderness on one side of the scalp above the ear, in the region of the temporal artery.

Diagnosis

It is essential to diagnose temporal arteritis as promptly as possible in order to reduce the risk of blindness. A medical history, an examination of the patient and a simple blood test are usually used to help diagnose temporal arteritis.

During the examination the physician will check whether there is any tenderness over the superficial artery in the temple, and whether there is any loss of pulsation in the artery.

FURTHER TESTS
■ An eye examination
■ Blood tests – these will show mild anaemia and a raised platelet count if the disease is present. The most important indicator of temporal arteritis is a raised ESR (erythrocyte sedimentation rate). The ESR is markedly raised – above 50 mm/hr – in temporal arteritis. However, in around 10 per cent of affected patients, the ESR may be normal; this complicates the diagnosis.

ARTERY BIOPSY
It is useful to perform a temporal artery biopsy to confirm the diagnosis. This procedure entails the removal of a segment of the artery, which lies just under the skin. It is performed under a local anaesthetic.

The biopsy will be analysed to see whether there is an inflammatory arteritis along with the presence of multinucleated giant cells (hence the name giant-cell arteritis). The biopsies of the temporal

arteries of up to 20 per cent of patients with polymyalgia rheumatica are similar to those of patients with temporal arteritis.

Sometimes, biopsies are falsely negative in temporal arteritis due to 'skip lesions' with areas of normal artery or because steroid treatment is already well established.

Swelling of the optic disc at the back of the eye may indicate temporal arteritis. This is detected by examination utilizing an ophthalmoscope.

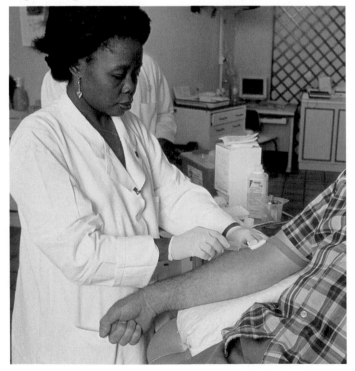

Blood tests may be used to confirm the diagnosis of temporal arteritis. Affected patients will have mild anaemia.

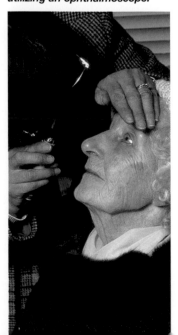

Causes

The cause of temporal arteritis is unknown, but the disease is thought to be due to an abnormal immune response within the wall of arteries. The same pathology is thought to cause polymyalgia rheumatica.

The loss of vision in temporal arteritis is caused by thrombosis (solidification) of the blood vessels that supply the retina at the back of the eye.

Intermittent symptoms of visual impairment or jaw pain are caused by partial blockage of blood vessels. There is no evidence to suggest that the condition is infectious.

Temporal arteritis is not a directly inherited condition, but variations in its incidence between different races suggests that genetic predisposition may play a part in the aetiology (origin) of the condition.

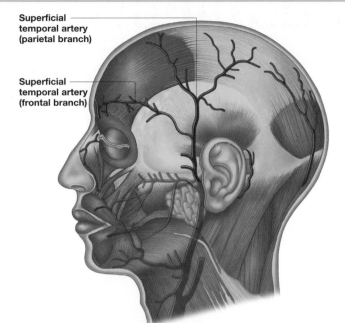

Superficial temporal artery (parietal branch)

Superficial temporal artery (frontal branch)

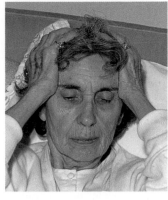

Temporal arteritis is rare in people under the age of 50. The headaches are a result of inflammation of the arterial walls.

The arteries most often affected are the two main branches of the superficial temporal artery, which supply the scalp.

Treatment

Giant-cell arteritis responds within two to three days to treatment with large doses of steroids. Some physicians advocate initially administrating it intravenously (directly into the vein) if they believe that vision may be threatened.

If there are visual symptoms, then oral doses of at least 60 mg of prednisolone a day are recommended.

It is important that treatment is not delayed until a temporal artery biopsy has been carried out. The biopsy should be organized as soon as possible. It may still be positive for more than a week after starting steroids.

The progress of patients diagnosed with temporal arteritis is monitored by regular checks on their erythrocyte sedimentation rate (ESR).

LONG-TERM CONTROL
Once the disease has come under control, the physician will gradually reduce the intake of steroid tablets to a lower maintenance dose – 7.5 mg to 10 mg a day. The lowest possible dose is used to minimize the risk of the side effects of steroids, such as osteoporosis and infection.

Immunosuppressant drugs – such as azathioprine and methotrexate – are occasionally used as a substitute for steroids in patients who have difficulty coming off steroids.

Treatment needs to be continued for around two years in order to prevent relapse.

The progress of patients is monitored by:
▪ Checking how much the patient's symptoms have come under control
▪ Monitoring the patient's ESR.

Prognosis and incidence

The prognosis for temporal arteritis depends on the promptness of treatment. If sight is already severely affected, it is unlikely to completely return to normal. However, there may be partial improvement, and the disease is unlikely to get worse once the patient is on steroid treatment.

Lowering the dose of the steroid administered may trigger a relapse, but this is less likely after the first 18 months of treatment or over a year after stopping treatment. Typically, complete remission occurs after about two years.

INCIDENCE
Temporal arteritis almost always affects people over 50 years of age, with the average age of onset around 70 years. It is at least twice as common in women than in men. The incidence of temporal arteritis varies in different areas of the world. In northern Europe, the incidence of the condition is up to 20 cases per 100,000 in people aged over 50.

If temporal arteritis remains untreated, 50 per cent of patients may experience vision loss in one eye.

Epilepsy

Symptoms

Epilepsy is a relatively common brain disorder that has a complex collection of symptoms. People with epilepsy have a continuing tendency to have seizures in which there is a sudden electrical discharge from some brain cells. The seizures cause disturbances in mental function, consciousness, sensory perception and body movements.

A person has to have had more than one seizure to be classified as having epilepsy.

CLASSIFYING EPILEPSY

Classification of epilepsy depends on what form the seizure takes, whether an electroencephalogram (EEG) reveals any changes in the brain, where in the brain the seizures originate, if there is any trigger or cause and the patient's age.

The electrical activity of the brain is recorded using electro-encephalography. It is important for diagnosing epilepsy.

Types of seizure

Epileptic seizures can be divided into generalized seizures and partial seizures.

Generalized seizures (primary epilepsy)
These affect the whole brain, although there is no detectable abnormality. They include:
■ Tonic-clonic seizures (formerly called *grand mal*) – patients suffering from these seizures lose consciousness completely. They also become stiff and then jerk rhythmically. They may also lose bowel or bladder control
■ Absence seizures (formerly called *petit mal*) – abrupt lapses of consciousness that may only last a few seconds and might go unnoticed. They occur mainly in children, who may

appear to be daydreaming
■ Atonic seizures – usually occur in children, who fall suddenly to the ground
■ Status epilepticus – seizures occur successively with no intervals of consciousness, and can be fatal.

Partial seizures (secondary epilepsy)
These affect only one part of the brain and are due to a structural abnormality. They sometimes progress to generalized seizures. They may be:
■ Simple seizures – patients experience unusual sensations with no loss of consciousness
■ Complex seizures – the same as above, but patients lose consciousness.

Diagnosis

An EEG can be taken as one way of diagnosing epilepsy. Electrodes placed over the patient's scalp record electrical impulses generated by part of the brain called the cerebral

This EEG shows the electrical activity in a healthy person's brain. An EEG of a patient with epilepsy may reveal an abnormal rhythm of brainwaves.

cortex. This will show the functional behaviour of the cells. Abnormalities in the brain tend to occur when cells fail to work together.

A routine EEG lasts about 15 minutes but can often miss characteristic changes associated with epilepsy. For this reason several EEG tests may be needed before conclusive results are obtained.

The symptoms of epilepsy range from headaches to convulsions. Observation of symptoms by a friend or relative may help in diagnosing the disease.

MEDICAL HISTORY

A full medical history should be taken, along with a description of the seizure characteristics and frequency. The exact nature of a seizure will help to identify the type of epilepsy and where the electrical discharge arises.

In some types of seizure a warning 'aura' may precede a seizure and afterwards the individual may be confused, have a headache and/or have sore muscles. A reliable eyewitness account is invaluable.

FURTHER INVESTIGATION

Further investigation may be needed to ensure that there has been a seizure, to clarify what

kind of seizure it was, and to find what (if anything) caused the seizure. Such investigation may include:
■ Blood tests – to identify any abnormal levels of chemicals in the blood
■ Magnetic resonance imaging (MRI) – this is a useful tool for identifying any structural problems within the brain.

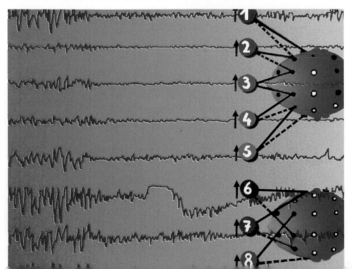

Treatment

Once a diagnosis has been made, the patient is started on an anticonvulsant medication. There are many anticonvulsants available – including carbamazepine and sodium valproate – but no single one is suitable for all forms of epilepsy. Which one is used will depend on the type of epilepsy, the patient's age and whether there are any other limiting factors, such as pregnancy.

A low dose is given initially, and then increased until control is achieved. If too high a dose is used, the patient is likely to experience unwanted side-effects, ranging from drowsiness to excess body hair. Repeated testing to find the correct level of drug is sometimes necessary, since the same dose can lead to different effects in different people.

SURGERY

Surgical treatment is today reserved for rare cases when drugs fail and a specific identifiable point in the brain is causing the stimulus.

A person who has lost consciousness during a seizure but is still breathing, should be placed in the recovery position. This will prevent the patient from choking.

First aid

The first-aid procedure for an tonic-clonic epileptic seizure is as follows:
■ The area around the patient is made safe for both the first-aider and the patient
■ Any tight clothing on the patient is loosened
■ The patient's head is cushioned
■ Artificial respiration is given if the patient stops breathing
■ When the limbs have stopped jerking, the patient is put in the recovery position.

Nothing should be put in the patient's mouth, and an ambulance needs to be called only if the seizure is the patient's first, if there is any injury or if the seizure has lasted over three minutes.

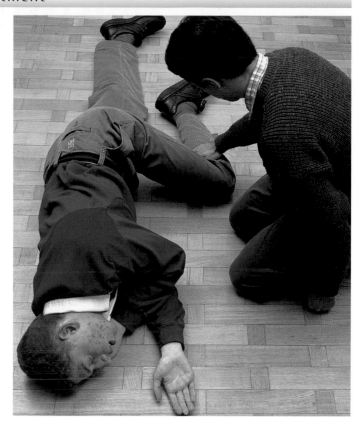

Prognosis

Most people with epilepsy are able to live a normal life. It is important that possible trigger factors, such as strobe lights and loud music, are avoided.

The prognosis for children with epilepsy is generally good. As a precaution, children who have epilepsy should always bathe or swim under adult supervision.

Most patients who experience a seizure will have a second one within two years. This usually occurs in the first few weeks after the initial attack.

The decision to opt for treatment before the second seizure takes place will depend on whether it is thought that recurrent seizures are likely to seriously affect a patient's life and work.

DRUG TREATMENT

Drug treatment completely controls seizures in a third of patients with epilepsy and greatly reduces their frequency in another third.

About two-thirds of people with epilepsy whose seizures are controlled will eventually be able to discontinue treatment. However, this will need to be carried out very slowly as seizures can recur as the drug levels fall.

SOCIAL ASPECTS

Epilepsy still has a certain stigma. In fact, some patients do not tell their friends, work-mates or even employers of their condition for fear of negative consequences.

RESTRICTIONS

A seizure-free period of one year is required before a driving licence can be granted in the UK. This restriction also applies to people with epilepsy who are on drug treatment.

Children should not bathe or ride a bicycle unsupervised.

With the correct diagnosis, treatment, and commonsense precautions, most patients will be able to control their condition.

Meningitis

Symptoms

Meningitis – inflammation of the meninges, membranes in the skull and spine – is often a childhood disease. There are two forms: viral and the more serious bacterial. The clearest sign of the illness is the appearance of bruise-like rashes, caused by bleeding from the small blood vessels (capillaries) in the skin.

The meningitis rash may appear suddenly and spread rapidly to cover the limbs and whole body. In extreme cases, the child may collapse within hours of this rash appearing, so treatment should be rapid.

The fontanelle (the soft spot on top of a baby's head) may be bulging and firm to the touch.

The appearance of blotchy rashes (known as petechiae) is the most ominous sign of meningitis. These rashes do not pale when pressure is applied, so test for this by pressing on the rash with a tumbler.

■ A baby that is irritable, vomiting repeatedly and has a high-pitched cry should be seen by a GP or A&E department without delay.

■ Older children will show sensitivity to light (photophobia) by closing or covering the eyes.

■ Headache will be present, as will vomiting and an inability to bend the head forward or, when sitting, to place the lips on the knees. This is due to back and neck stiffness.

Diagnosis

A lumbar puncture is performed to confirm the diagnosis of meningitis. In this procedure, a needle is inserted in the back into the spinal canal, and cerebro-spinal fluid (CSF) is extracted. This fluid, which surrounds the spine and brain and contains the meningitis bacteria or viruses, is then sent for detailed examination.

If the fluid is cloudy to the naked eye, it suggests infection due to meningitis. Microscopic examination, however, will reveal the number and type of cells present, and the type of 'bug' causing the infection. The organisms that cause meningitis are either bacterial or viral, and identification of these determines the correct therapy. Antibiotics, for instance, are only used for bacterial meningitis.

The most dangerous type of infection is from meningococcus bacteria, which enter the bloodstream and cause severe septicaemia (blood poisoning). Other bacteria that commonly cause meningitis are *Haemophilus influenzae* type B (Hib) and *Streptococcus pneumoniae*.

In a lumbar puncture, spinal fluid (CSF) is taken from the spinal canal, using a puncture needle with an added tap. Cloudy cerebro-spinal fluid suggests the presence of meningitis, and this may be confirmed after microscopic examination.

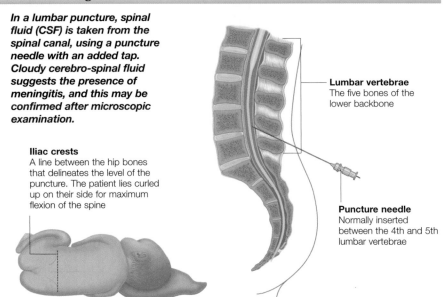

Iliac crests
A line between the hip bones that delineates the level of the puncture. The patient lies curled up on their side for maximum flexion of the spine

Lumbar vertebrae
The five bones of the lower backbone

Puncture needle
Normally inserted between the 4th and 5th lumbar vertebrae

Prognosis

The course of the infection depends on the organism responsible. Viral meningitis is usually self-limiting. In cases due to bacteria, early diagnosis and treatment are the keys to survival. Late diagnosis may lead to complications and death. Prognoses include:

■ Paralysis of cranial nerves, leading to squints, deafness and limb paralysis

■ Unconsciousness due to fluid build-up in the brain

■ Mental and behavioural problems; finally death

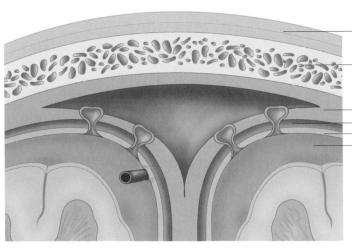

Scalp

Skull

MENINGES
- Dura mater
- Arachnoid
- Pia mater

Brain

This skull cross-section shows the meninges, the three membranes that surround the brain and the spinal cord. Meningitis causes an inflammation of the layers, which, if not treated in time, can kill.

Causes

The bacterium that causes meningitis enters the bloodstream via the nose and throat, causing blood poisoning (septicaemia), which in turn infects the meninges.

The principle types of bacteria that cause meningitis are:
■ Meningococcus
■ Pneumococcus
■ Haemophilus influenzae
■ Streptococcus
■ Staphylococcus

Sometimes other causes may be involved:
■ In tiny babies, meningitis can be caused by *E. coli*, the source of infection being the umbilicus.

■ Viral and fungal infections can be other causes of meningitis.

NOTIFIABLE

Because it is such a serious illness, meningitis is 'notifiable'. This means that any case must be immediately reported to the relevant Health Authority.

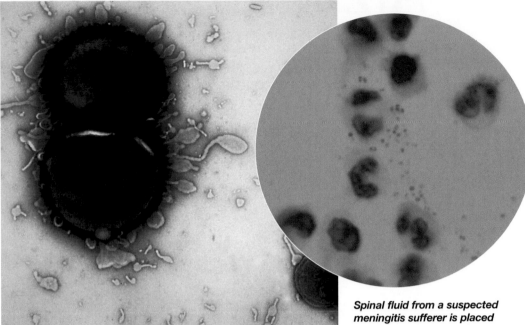

This micrograph shows a meningococcus bacterium, Neisseria meningitidis. It is one of the micro-organisms that causes meningitis. The bacterial infection spreads rapidly and results in meningococcal septicaemia, characterized by a haemorrhagic rash (one caused by blood loss) that spreads over the body.

Spinal fluid from a suspected meningitis sufferer is placed under the microscope for analysis. Meningitis is confirmed by the presence of bacteria (small dark-red spots) on the white blood cells that appear here as large red patches.

Incidence

Two-thirds of all meningitis cases occur in children under 15 years of age. Of these, 80 per cent occur before the age of five. Neonates (babies up to three months) and children between six and nine months are most at risk. In the neonatal period, infection is primarily due to the *E. coli* organism that lives in the gut and arises from umbilical infection.

■ Most cases of bacterial meningitis begin as septicaemia; the germ enters the bloodstream from the nose.

■ Ear infections may be responsible for introducing meningitis.

■ In rare cases, meningitis will result from infection from a compound (open) fracture of the skull.

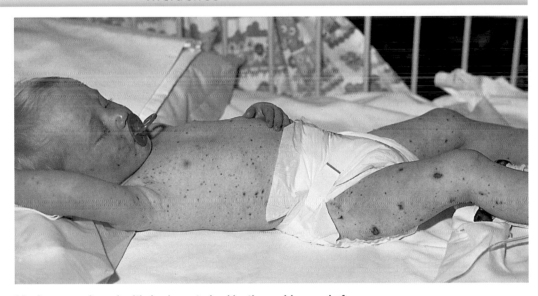

Meningococcal meningitis is characterized by the rapid spread of bruise-like haemorrhagic rashes over the patient's body. If the sufferer goes undiagnosed or untreated, the meningitis can prove fatal to a young child.

Treatment

If bacterial meningitis or septicaemia is suspected, penicillin (benzylpenicillin, or Crystapen) should be given as soon as possible, preferably by injection into muscle tissue. A single injection may be life-saving: fatality rates range from 7 to 20 per cent, depending on the type of infection.

Once the analysis has established the type of organism causing the meningitis, the appropriate antibiotic may then be prescribed. Treatment usually lasts for at least 10–14 days.

Viral meningitis will usually only require treatment with rest and painkillers; antibiotics are not effective against viruses.

Prevention

Hib vaccine now protects against *Haemophilus* meningitis and is routinely given at two, three and four months. Meningitis is infectious, so suspected cases should be isolated immediately. Local outbreaks can occur, so anyone in contact with sufferers should be immunized.

Alzheimer's disease

Symptoms

Alzheimer's disease is a form of dementia, a chronic disorder of the mental processes due to progressive brain disease. It is most common in older people, particularly over the age of 80, but occasionally occurs in younger people.

People with Alzheimer's disease become increasingly forgetful and eventually develop severe memory loss, particularly of recent events. Their ability to concentrate, cope with numbers and verbally communicate declines, and they often become anxious and depressed. Sudden mood swings and personality changes are common, as is socially unacceptable behaviour.

With advanced disease, patients are often disorientated, especially at night, and may neglect personal hygiene and become incontinent. Some people become docile and helpless; others are aggressive and difficult to care for.

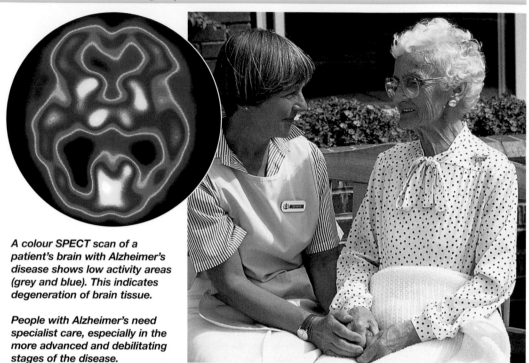

A colour SPECT scan of a patient's brain with Alzheimer's disease shows low activity areas (grey and blue). This indicates degeneration of brain tissue.

People with Alzheimer's need specialist care, especially in the more advanced and debilitating stages of the disease.

Causes

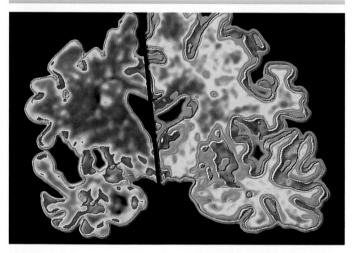

Many people have a genetic predisposition to Alzheimer's disease, but most are unlikely to develop the disease unless other factors come into play. Only 15 per cent of people with Alzheimer's disease have a family history of the condition, so the disease is not usually directly inherited.

CHROMOSOME MUTATIONS
The first gene to be linked to Alzheimer's disease was found on chromosome 21. This chromosome is abnormal in people with Down's syndrome who, as a group, are at high risk of developing Alzheimer's disease. Genes increasing the

A computer-enhanced image contrasts the brain of an Alzheimer's patient (left) with a normal brain (right). The Alzheimer's brain has lost volume due to cell death.

risk for developing Alzheimer's disease have been identified on other chromosomes. The mutation of a single gene causes about five per cent of cases of Alzheimer's disease and three genes have been identified that, if mutated, can cause severe disease under the age of 65.

Attempts are being made to identify the factors that lead to Alzheimer's disease in genetically predisposed people.

Diagnosis

There is no single diagnostic test for Alzheimer's disease, and the diagnosis is usually made by eliminating other potential causes of dementia. Tests include blood and urine checks, electrocardiography and electro-encephalography. Scans may provide a clue to the diagnosis by showing cerebral atrophy (shrinking of the brain). Mental status tests may be important.

A definite diagnosis can only be made by examining brain tissue at post-mortem. Brain cells are destroyed by a build-up of disordered protein strands (neurofibrillary tangles), particularly in the areas of the brain that deal with memory. Clusters of degenerating nerve cells containing a protein core (amyloid plaques) are also characteristic.

A striking change is the loss of acetylcholine, a chemical neurotransmitter in the brain. Patients with the most severe dementia have the lowest levels of acetylcholine.

This coloured CT scan shows the atrophy of the brain that occurs in Alzheimer's disease. The arrows highlight areas of reduced brain volume.

A CT scan may help confirm a diagnosis of Alzheimer's disease. Changes in brain structure may be visible.

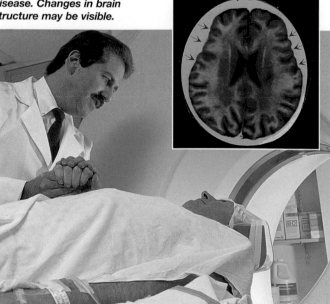

Treatment

No currently available drug can reverse memory loss that has already occurred, and patients often need an immense amount of supportive care as their mental and physical state declines. With severe dementia, drugs may be needed to control anxiety, restlessness, paranoia and hallucinations.

DRUG THERAPIES

Two drugs, donepezil (Aricept) and rivastigmine (Exelon) are now available in the UK. These drugs can slow the rate of deterioration in some patients, but not all, and they do have side effects. They act by increasing the level of acetylcholine in the brain.

Drugs that mimic the action of acetylcholine stimulate the regrowth of nerves, or inhibit the formation of amyloid or neurofibrillary tangles may become available. Trials are under way to see whether vitamin E or selegiline, a drug used in Parkinson's disease, or anti-inflammatory drugs have a place in Alzheimer's treatment.

This coloured TEM shows beta protein filaments, which occur in Alzheimer's brain tissue. Senile plaques are produced that consist of tangled masses of filaments, as shown here.

This researcher is testing a man for signs of Alzheimer's; this timed test involves fitting wooden shapes into a template while wearing a blindfold.

Prognosis and prevention

Currently, there is no cure for Alzheimer's disease. Affected people inevitably deteriorate with time, but the rate of decline is variable.

There is no known way of preventing the disease, but a healthy lifestyle, education and a stimulating environment may help. Trials are underway to see whether supplementing the diet with folic acid and vitamin B_{12}, or taking low-dose aspirin or cholesterol-lowering drugs reduces the risk of being affected.

Specialists are looking at the possibility of transplanting nerve cells into the brain to help restore normal function in people with Alzheimer's disease.

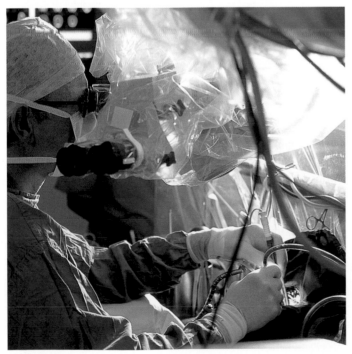

Incidence

Alzheimer's disease was first described in 1906 by Alois Alzheimer, a German psychiatrist and pathologist. He reported, following pathological examination, that the brain of a 56-year-old woman who had died after suffering from progressive dementia for many years contained neurofibrillary tangles and amyloid plaques in the cerebral cortex – the area of the brain responsible for memory and reasoning. Alzheimer deduced that these changes were the cause of her illness.

Dementia currently affects about 20 million people worldwide, and this number may double by the year 2025 if the expected increase in the world's population of people over 65 takes place. In the UK, about 750,000 people suffer from dementia and about 50 per cent of these people have Alzheimer's disease.

Alzheimer's disease affects 5–10 per cent of people aged 65–74 and 20–50 per cent of those aged 75 and over. Men and women are equally likely to be affected.

The financial cost of caring for these patients is immense and the disease also extracts a physical and emotional toll from carers.

Although much research into the treatment of Alzheimer's disease is being done, as yet, the deterioration of the cerebral cortex (a section of which is shown here) is irreversible.

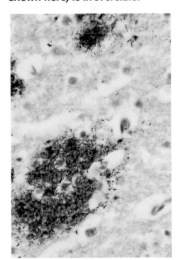

Parkinson's disease

Symptoms and signs

Parkinson's disease is a degenerative brain disorder associated with ageing. A distinction is often made between Parkinson's disease and parkinsonism, in which the same symptoms are produced by causes other than age.

A typical first sign is a slow tremor (shake) on resting, often initially on one side of the body. This is typically 'pill rolling' in form and diminishes on voluntary movement. It affects both sides involving the arms, legs and the jaw. Slowness of movement is often first noticed by the family rather than by the patient.

Rigidity ('cogwheel type') of the muscles occurs, which adds the general slowness and leads to a stooping posture and 'shuffling' gait. There is a noticeable loss of arm swing on walking. The patient develops monotonous speech, a mask-like expressionless face and dribbles saliva because of difficulty in swallowing. Muscle aches and cramps occur, fatigue is often present and constipation is common. Writing becomes small, tremulous and untidy on account of the rigidity.

As the disease progresses, there may be major disability when the patient becomes immobile and chair-bound. The latter may lead to complications such as pneumonia, bedsores and urinary tract infections. Most patients have normal intellectual function but, with time, a proportion develop structural mental changes.

The most common initial sign of Parkinson's disease is a coarse, rhythmical slow tremor of the hands. It diminishes during conscious movement.

Diagnosis

Diagnosis is made entirely on the clinical picture, which is usually characteristic. Careful history and examination are required to exclude causes of parkinsonism. These include:

■ Drugs – phenothiazines, reserpine, methyldopa
■ Infections – following brain swelling (encephalitis)

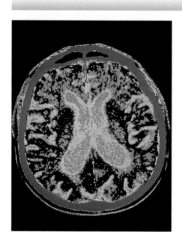

This coloured CT scan is from a Parkinson's patient. Loss of density in the brain tissue has caused the ventricles (blue) to increase in size.

■ Toxins – including carbon monoxide and manganese
■ Hypothyroidism
■ Vascular – cerebrovascular disease
■ Trauma to the head – particularly in boxers
■ In combination with other conditions, for example Alzheimer's disease or Huntington's chorea.

There are no diagnostic tests for Parkinson's disease but CT and MR scans, and biochemical tests may be necessary to exclude other causes.

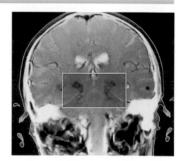

The boxed area in this MR scan is the basal ganglia of the brain. This area contains dopamine-producing cells, which are lacking in Parkinson's disease.

Causes and prognosis

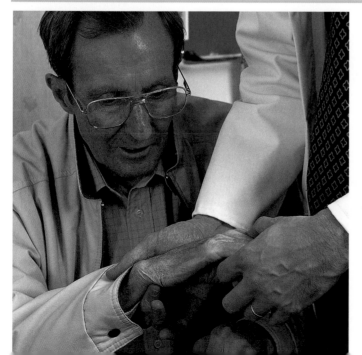

Extensive microbiological studies have failed to find an infective cause. Degeneration of the brainstem, presence of large bodies within brain cells, and loss of neurones in important regions of the brain, causing severe loss of dopamine, are the main pathological changes. These important discoveries have led to treatment with L-dopa to replace the lost dopamine in the body.

A Parkinson's patient undergoes a medical examination. The doctor is testing the rigidity of the wrist and the slow finger movement (bradykinesia); both are symptomatic of the disease.

The disease is usually progressive and patients may become increasingly bedridden or chairbound on account of immobility. However, many patients remain reasonably active and the rate of progression is very variable.

Since the introduction of L-dopa therapy, life expectancy in Parkinson's patients has significantly increased. Studies have shown that with present day treatment, a person with Parkinson's disease is likely, on average, to live as long as an unaffected person of the same age. The average duration of the disease is 15 years, from diagnosis to death.

Treatment

DRUG TREATMENT
Specific treatment involves the use of anti-parkinsonian drugs. It is usual to start treatment when the symptoms become severe enough to interfere with the activities of daily living.

Treatment with L-dopa tablets begins with a small dose of L-dopa and a peripheral dopa decarboxylase inhibitor. Selegiline (MOA oxidase type B inhibitor) was thought to delay the progression of the disease, but this is now doubtful.

Dopamine agonists (stimulators such as pergolide, lysuride, bromocriptine and apomorphine) generally cause fewer side effects, but not all patients respond. Apomorphine is given by subcutaneous injection and is used for the troublesome 'on-off' phenomenon. This occurs when the effect of a drug wears off quickly, requiring increasingly frequent doses of medication.

Anticholinergic drugs, such as benzhexol and orphenadrine, are useful for prominent tremors. These drugs may cause increased confusion, blurred vision and a dry mouth, especially in the elderly.

Patients who respond well to L-dopa may find the duration of therapeutic effect from each tablet becomes shorter leading to marked fluctuation of symptoms – this is the 'on-off' effect described above.

Dopa
The chemical that begins the pathway (the substrate); L-dopa boosts the level of substrate

Dopamine
Dopa is converted into neurotransmitter dopamine; facilitates communication between cells

Dopamine re-uptake
Dopamine binds to dopamine receptors and is then recovered; amantadine blocks re-uptake

Dopamine receptor
Binding of dopamine to the receptor results in signal transmission along the adjoining cell; induced by dopamine agonists (pergolide, apomorphine)

Breakdown of signal
An enzyme called monoamine oxidase breaks down the nerve signal; inhibited by the drug selegiline

Nerve cell
The synaptic bulb at the end of the nerve cell releases neurotransmitter into the synapse

Synapse
Physical gap between two nerve cells

Nerve cell
Neurotransmitter binds to specific receptors

Parkinson's disease affects groups of nerve cells involved in movement, where the neurotransmitter dopamine facilitates signals across nerve junctions (synapses). Various drugs can partially restore this system.

Other treatment

Supportive treatment
Occupational therapists and physiotherapists are important in helping to maintain independence in everyday activities for as long as possible.

In the later stages of the disease, when mobility is limited, family support and day care are very important.

Symptomatic treatment
Treatment may be required for constipation, depression or musculo-skeletal pain.

Surgery to the thalamus of the brain was popular in the 1950s and 1960s. Surgery is now only considered for patients resistant to drug therapy and whose tremor is severe.

Incidence and prevention

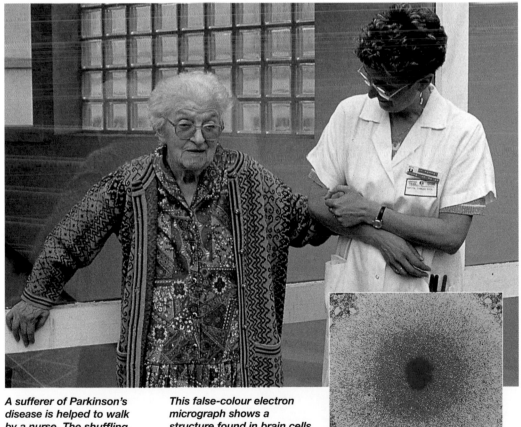

A sufferer of Parkinson's disease is helped to walk by a nurse. The shuffling, unbalanced walk and slow trembling are typical of the disease.

This false-colour electron micrograph shows a structure found in brain cells called a Lewy body. This is a pathological feature of Parkinson's disease.

Parkinson's disease affects about 1 in 10,000 of the population. After the age of 50, the prevalence is about 1 in 200. It is slightly more common in men than in women and does not seem to run in families. Interestingly, patients with Parkinson's disease are less likely to die from lung cancer than the rest of the population.

As the cause of Parkinson's disease is currently unknown, prevention is not possible. The use of embryonic brain cell implants has been mentioned, but their use raises serious ethical issues, as their source would be aborted fetuses.

Parkinsonism occurring following the administration of antipsychotic drugs will usually resolve following cessation of the drug treatment.

Stroke

Symptoms

The term stroke is used to describe an event during which the blood supply to a part of the brain is suddenly interrupted. The symptoms start abruptly and may slowly worsen over a few hours or days. Symptoms always last more than 24 hours and depend on which cerebral blood vessels and which part of the brain are affected.

TYPICAL SYMPTOMS
Typical symptoms are:
■ Weakness or paralysis of one side of the body (hemiparesis or hemiplegia)
■ Speech difficulties
■ Sudden severe giddiness
■ Nausea and vomiting
■ Loss of sensation, for example, numbness of the face
■ Difficulty in swallowing (dysphagia)
■ Double vision (diplopia)
■ Loss of vision in one eye
■ Drooping of one upper eyelid

(ptosis) with a small pupil and lack of sweating on that side of the face (Horner's syndrome)
■ Sudden severe headache
■ Confusion
■ Coma.

A WARNING SIGN
Transient ischaemic attacks (TIAs) are sometimes known as 'mini strokes'. They occur when the blood supply to part of the brain is temporarily interrupted, for example by a small blood clot or vascular spasm. Symptoms disappear within 24 hours, or even sooner. In the five years following a TIA, one in six patients has a stroke and one in four dies, usually from a stroke or heart disease.

Mobility may be considerably reduced after a stroke. When recovering from a stroke, patients may need to use a walking aid.

Causes

About 80 per cent of strokes are due to a blood clot blocking an artery in the brain (ischaemic), while the remainder are due to bleeding into brain tissue from a ruptured blood vessel (haemorrhagic). Either event causes the death of an area of brain tissue (cerebral infarct) and the permanent loss of cells.

The underlying cause of a stroke is usually atherosclerosis (hardening of the arteries). In

Atheroma is the build-up of fatty plaques in the walls of the arteries. This blocks the blood supply and may lead to strokes and heart attacks.

The brain has a rich supply of blood provided by a network of arteries. A stroke occurs when one of these vessels becomes blocked or ruptures.

atherosclerosis, fatty plaques and scar tissue form in artery walls, restricting the blood flow; blood clots (thrombi) often form on the plaques, further blocking the arteries. Fragments of clot may detach and circulate in the bloodstream (emboli). If a fragment lodges in a smaller blood vessel in the brain, it may block it and cause a stroke.

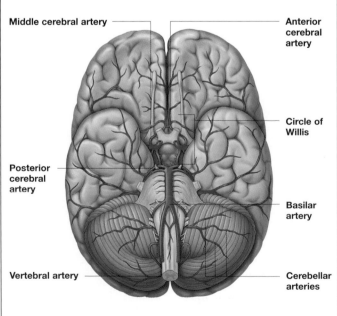
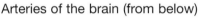

Arteries of the brain (from below)

Middle cerebral artery

Anterior cerebral artery

Circle of Willis

Posterior cerebral artery

Basilar artery

Vertebral artery

Cerebellar arteries

RISK FACTORS
Risk factors for stroke include:
■ Hypertension (high blood pressure)
■ Heart disease – abnormal heart valves, damage to the heart muscle from a myocardial infarct (heart attack) and abnormal heart rhythms may lead to the formation of emboli
■ Weaknesses in blood vessel

walls in the brain (aneurysms) – ruptured micro-aneurysms cause bleeding in the brain tissue (intracerebral haemorrhage). Intracerebral haemorrhage occurs in 10 per cent of strokes and usually affects patients with hypertension. In five per cent of strokes, bleeding into the space around the brain (subarachnoid haemorrhage) from a ruptured aneurysm occurs
■ Blood diseases – haemophilia and sickle cell disease can cause increased bleeding or clotting
■ Drugs – some anticancer drugs, anticoagulant drugs and phenylpropanolamine (used in 'cold cures'), if taken in large doses or with a monoamine-oxidase inhibitor (antidepressant).

Incidence

Stroke is rare below the age of 40 years but is a major cause of illness and death in older people. It is the third most common cause of death in the UK, following heart disease and cancer.

Each year, up to three people per thousand of the general population in Europe and the USA have a stroke. Black people are at higher risk than white, and men tend to be at slightly higher risk than women.

Diagnosis

The history and examination of the patient are important to confirm the diagnosis and exclude other diagnoses such as a brain tumour or abscess, subdural haematoma (an accumulation of blood beneath the outer covering of the brain, often occurring after trauma), acute migraine or meningitis.

INVESTIGATIONS
Investigations may include:
■ CT scanning – this confirms the presence of a cerebral infarct. In the first few days after a stroke, it can differentiate between brain damage caused by bleeding and damage caused by an embolus
■ An MRI scan – this usually shows up an abnormality within a few hours of the stroke
■ Lumbar puncture – blood in the cerebrospinal fluid that bathes the spinal cord, suggests a diagnosis of subarachnoid haemorrhage
■ Carotid Doppler and duplex scanning – this specialized form of ultrasound scanning is used to detect narrowing of the carotid arteries, the arteries that supply the brain
■ Angiography – this also detects narrowed blood vessels
■ Blood tests – for example, full blood count, erythrocyte sedimentation rate, blood electrolyte and glucose levels
■ Chest X-ray
■ Electrocardiogram (ECG).

This angiogram shows narrowing of a branch of the carotid artery (circled). This type of imaging enables visualization of the blood vessel's structure.

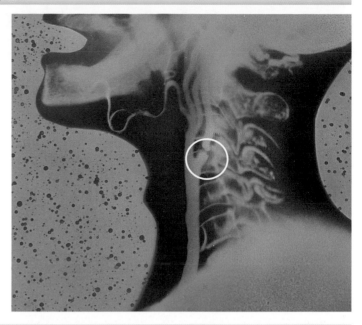

Treatment

Most patients are admitted to hospital for investigation and treatment. Treatment includes:
■ Anticoagulant drugs – these may be prescribed if the stroke is caused by a blood clot
■ Surgery
■ Rehabilitation.

Nursing care is essential as many patients are immobile following a stroke and are at risk of developing pressure sores and deep vein thromboses.

Difficulty with swallowing is another problem as choking can occur and fluid or food may accidentally be inhaled into the airways.

In some patients, a stroke can cause speech difficulties. In such cases, a speech therapist can work with a patient to help improve speech quality.

Blood pressure control is vital for patients with hypertension, and readings are closely monitored

SURGERY
In severe continued bleeding, surgery may be carried out to clip a bleeding vessel. Surgical unblocking (endarterectomy) of the internal carotid arteries may be considered for patients with stroke symptoms whose arteries are severely narrowed by atheroma.

MEDICAL SUPPORT
Physiotherapy, speech therapy and an assessment of the patient's need for modifications in their home are important. Psychological support is vital for patients who cannot resume their previous jobs or lifestyle.

Prognosis

Complete or partial recovery may occur, but the rate and extent of recovery is variable. Most recovery occurs within the first three months, but improvement may continue for up to two years.

Six months after a stroke, 60 per cent of sufferers have either died or depend on other people for their care.

Factors suggesting a good outlook include mild stroke with no mental disturbance, young age, urinary continence and rapid immediate improvement. Death within hours of the onset of symptoms is rare, except in subarachnoid haemorrhage.

Prevention

Hypertension is a major risk factor associated with strokes. It is therefore important to treat high blood pressure at an early stage. As well as lifestyle changes, such as stopping smoking, people with high blood pressure may be prescribed antihypertensives.

TIAs should be investigated in order to treat the underlying cause. If the cause is thought to be small blood clots, a small dose of aspirin each day reduces the risk of stroke after a TIA.

One low-dose aspirin a day is thought to reduce the risk of stroke in people suffering from TIAs. Aspirin acts on platelets and effectively 'thins' the blood.

Cerebral palsy

Symptoms

Cerebral palsy (CP) is a leading cause of physical disability, and around one child in 400 is affected. It is defined as 'a disorder of posture and movement caused by a discrete non-progressive lesion of the developing motor pathways of the brain'. The main associated disabilities include:

■ Hypotonia – loss of normal muscle tone
■ Spasticity – limbs resistant to passive movement
■ Ataxia – shaky movements
■ Athetosis – involuntary movement.

Although the extent of the brain damage does not progress with time, the manifestations of CP develop as the brain matures.

Newborns may show a variety of symptoms, including:

Children with CP may also have defective sight and hearing. The nature of CP means that the brain damage does not worsen.

■ Poor sucking ability
■ Abnormal muscle tone
■ Abnormal reflexes
■ Convulsions or drowsiness.

CP may not be suspected for several months until motor development is abnormal or delayed. Signs of this include:

■ Normal head control not showing by three months
■ Unable to sit unsupported at 10 months
■ Baby stiff on handling
■ Persistence of primitive reflexes
■ Characteristic involuntary movements at one year
■ Ataxic CP children are hypotonic (have diminished muscle tone) and may later show intention tremor.

The distribution of neurological involvement leads to the classification of the spasticity of CP: quadriplegia – all limbs involved; diplegia – arms or legs involved; hemiplegia – arm and leg on one side only involved; atonic or ataxic CP – depending on the area of the brain involved.

The main symptoms associated with CP are concerned with movement. The severity of the disability varies a great deal.

Other features

CP may be complicated by other neurological and mental problems. Intellectual impairment varies, so speech development is important in predicting a prognosis.

■ Visio-spatial and auditory perceptual disabilities can lead to learning difficulties. Speech and feeding difficulties affect up to 50 per cent of the patients, such as difficulty swallowing and dysarthria (speech disturbance).
■ Orthopaedic complications associated with CP can include contractions of muscles due to spasticity, leading to contractures within the joints. Discrepancies in growth can occur, with conditions such as pelvic tilt and curvature of the spine resulting. Convulsions affect 25–30 per cent of people with CP.
■ Behavioural and emotional problems can occur. Parental over-protection and community attitudes often prevent CP children attaining their full physical potential.

Diagnosis

CP may be diagnosed at birth but this is frequently delayed, particularly in mildly affected children. In these cases, CP is generally recognized during the second year of life due to abnormalities in the child's gait (posture and walking).

As there are several different causes of CP, diagnosis may not be straightforward. If CP is suspected in the early weeks of life, monitoring developmental milestones at regular intervals may make diagnosis possible before two years of age. Careful attention to the mother's concerns often reveal the diagnosis at the earliest possible time.

This baby is displaying the abnormal muscle tone and posture that is a typical presentation of CP in newborns.

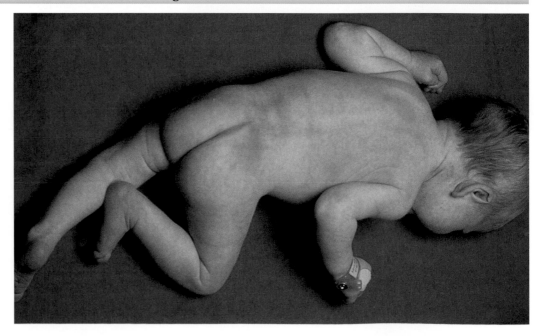

Causes

Prenatally, CP can be caused by cerebral malformations due to disturbances of brain development, intra-uterine vascular accidents (interrupted placental blood flow, haemorrhage), trauma, infection – including inflammation of the brain, for example, due to toxoplasmosis, cytomegalovirus, or hypoxia (lack of oxygen reaching the tissues).

Prematurity and low birth weight, prolonged labour, traumatic delivery, asphyxia and intra-uterine growth retardation are all important factors in spastic CP. Complications of jaundice in the newborn may also cause CP, although this has diminished in frequency because of improved postnatal care of neonates.

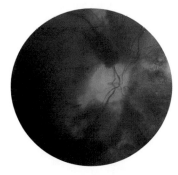

Infection with cytomegalovirus, shown here, has been identified as a possible cause of cerebral palsy in the antenatal period.

Another cause of CP is cerebral malformation. This may result from haemorrhaging (circled) within the brain before birth.

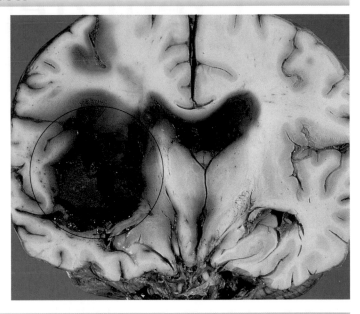

Treatment and management

Physicians, therapists and educators all play an important part in the multi-disciplinary team involved in the frequent assessment of people with CP and the structured treatment programmes designed for them.

Physiotherapy helps normal motor development and prevents contractures. Intellectual disability is managed by specially trained doctors and personnel. Visual impairment, squints, deafness and orthopaedic deformities are treated by specialists in each particular field, and epilepsy is controlled with

Using a special control, this boy can operate a computer. Such equipment can play an important role in the lives of people with CP.

appropriate medication.

Specialist schools and units for physically disabled people provide speech therapy, physiotherapy and hydrotherapy. Facilities for the children's physical needs are provided, including special furniture and mobility aids, physiotherapy equipment and hydrotherapy pools, together with provision for their educational needs.

More and more children are now being cared for in the community. As many children with CP as possible are encouraged to attend normal schools to help avoid the social stigma of physical handicap. Employment is also a special consideration, and support is available for people with CP when seeking employment.

Prognosis

The degree of disability will determine the seriousness of the prognosis. Many children with less severe forms of CP lead normal lives. Remedial physiotherapy is helpful for many children with CP and some will attend special units.

Speech disorders are common, as are behavioural disorders, mainly due to frustration. Contractures of the limbs may need future surgery to improve mobility as neglect of these deformities can lead to osteoarthritis.

Sixty per cent of people with CP will have some degree of intellectual handicap; 20 per cent are affected by visual impairment and hearing loss; and about 30 per cent will have epilepsy.

Special equipment can help to ease some of the postural problems of CP. This girl is using a physiotherapy table and chair.

Prevention

Increased testing during pregnancy to diagnose congenital disorders and better obstetric care has reduced the incidence of CP caused by trauma. Early and adequate treatment of haemolytic diseases of the newborn – where the mother develops antibodies which destroy the baby's red blood cells – by exchange transfusion reduce the incidence of brain damage.

The early treatment of intra-cerebral infections with antibiotics also reduces the incidence of CP. Infections occurring in the first three months of pregnancy – for example, pertussis and rubella – are now preventable by immunization.

Cerebral and cerebellar tumours

Symptoms

The brain is protected by the bony skull, and brain tumours therefore have little room to expand without pressing on other parts of the brain, damaging the nervous system and threatening life.

Possible symptoms include:
■ Headache – particularly in the forehead (frontal) region
■ Nausea
■ Intellectual impairment with loss of memory, impaired judgement, confusion, drowsiness or dementia
■ Difficulty formulating or understanding speech (aphasia)
■ Personality and behaviour changes
■ Eye problems (double vision, visual impairment or blindness)
■ Hearing loss
■ Fits (seizures)
■ Disturbances of balance and limb movements.

Persistent frontal headaches made worse by bending over may alert a doctor to look for signs of brain disease.

Causes

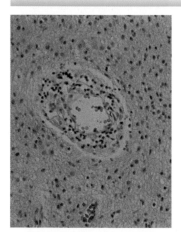

Eighty per cent of brain tumours arise from the substance of the brain (primary tumours), while 20 per cent result from the spread of cancer elsewhere in the body (secondary tumours). Cancers of the lung, breast, kidney, colon, stomach and thyroid are particularly liable to cause secondary tumours, and 40 per cent of melanomas (skin cancers) will reach the brain.

The microvascular cell proliferation seen surrounding this blood vessel is a hallmark of malignancy in astrocytomas.

The cause of most primary brain tumours is unknown. They almost always arise from cells in the supporting tissues or membranes of the brain or lining of the ventricles, and almost never from neurones. They may be benign or malignant, but they do not metastasize (spread) to other sites. The outcome of a tumour is determined by the affected region.

Cancer of the breast (circled) is associated with a risk of metastatic (secondary) spread to the brain.

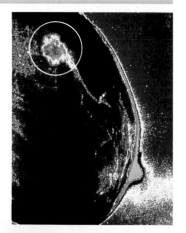

Structure of the brain

The brain consists of right and left cerebral hemispheres. Each hemisphere consists of:
■ An outer layer of 'grey matter', the cerebral cortex; these cells almost never form tumours
■ A core of 'white matter' composed of nerve fibres, which connect the neurones to the rest of the body
■ Support cells for the neurones, a common source of brain tumours; they include oligodendrocytes, which produce insulating myelin sheaths for nerve fibres, and astrocytes,

which nourish the neurones and may help store information.

The brain is covered by membranes – the meninges – from which benign tumours called meningiomas may arise. Other possible sites are the cerebellum, which controls balance, and the brainstem, which regulates respiration and the heartbeat.

The three membranes that line the brain – the meninges – are sites for tumours. These are called meningiomas.

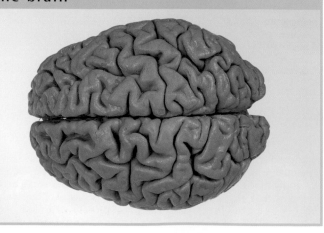

Diagnosis

Diagnosing a brain tumour is difficult as the symptoms are often insidious and the signs can be difficult to detect. It is important to search for signs of raised intracranial pressure: headache, vomiting and papilloedema (fluid accumulation in the optic nerve, causing it to swell).

Other signs of damage to the nervous system may be evident, but their absence does not exclude the presence of a tumour.

IMAGING TECHNIQUES
■ Magnetic resonance imaging (MRI) is the most effective tool for diagnosing brain tumours
■ Conventional X-rays are no longer used, having been replaced by CT scanning
■ Angiography (X-ray examination of the blood vessels) may reveal a tumour.

Since many tumours are secondary to other cancers, a general medical examination and routine tests, such as a chest X-ray, are very important.

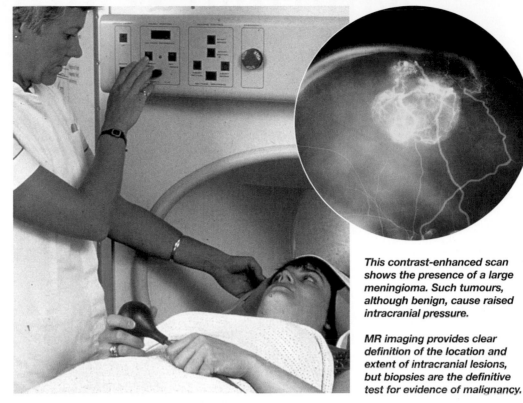

This contrast-enhanced scan shows the presence of a large meningioma. Such tumours, although benign, cause raised intracranial pressure.

MR imaging provides clear definition of the location and extent of intracranial lesions, but biopsies are the definitive test for evidence of malignancy.

Treatment

Brain tumours are often treated using surgery. The tumour may be removed whole or in part. If there is no cure, surgery will alleviate symptoms.

Surgery plays a major part in the treatment of many brain tumours. Surgeons often remove a small portion of the tumour for microscopic examination (biopsy) to identify its type and plan future treatment.

Some benign tumours can be completely removed, curing the patient. If a cure is not possible, surgery may still be used to reduce the bulk of the tumour, reducing the pressure on the brain and relieving symptoms. Some benign tumours that cannot be removed completely re-grow only very slowly, so surgery may well be an option.

Patients with incurable malignant tumours may benefit if the bulk of the tumour is reduced. Stereotactic surgery, using a CT-guided scan, helps surgeons operate on deep tumours.

OTHER TREATMENTS
■ Radiotherapy – sometimes effective, but can cause unpleasant side effects
■ Chemotherapy – not often effective, although much research is being done
■ Analgesics – may be needed to control pain
■ Corticosteroids – patients with raised intracranial pressure and cerebral oedema may gain rapid relief from corticosteroids; this may be injected in an emergency
■ Anticonvulsants
■ Anti-emetics.

Prognosis

Prognosis varies according to the type of tumour. The outlook is good for some benign tumours, but very poor for malignant tumours – less than 50 per cent of patients survive for one year after diagnosis.

Gliomas (primary tumours originating from the supporting tissues of the brain) almost never spread outside the central nervous system. This type of tumour is common in children.

Types of glioma include astrocytomas and oligodendrocytomas:
■ Astrocytomas are the commonest primary malignant brain tumours; some grow slowly over many years while others cause death within a few months – they are usually relatively benign in childhood
■ Oligodendrogliomas grow slowly over many years; they usually occur in adults and have a relatively good prognosis.

Other tumours include medulloblastomas and ependymomas, which arise from cells lining the ventricles (fluid-filled cavities) in the brain:
■ Medulloblastomas are the most common brain tumours in children; 60 per cent respond well to chemotherapy or radiotherapy
■ Ependymomas often occur in childhood and adolescence and grow at a variable rate; less than 30 per cent of affected children survive long-term.

Multiple sclerosis

Symptoms

Multiple sclerosis (usually referred to as MS) is a chronic disease of the central nervous system (CNS), primarily affecting young and middle-aged adults. The illness causes damage to the myelin sheaths which surround and insulate the nerve cells in the brain and spinal column. The patches of inflammation are called lesions or plaques, and they affect the function of the nerves involved. This means that symptoms are variable, depending on which part or parts of the CNS are affected.

Typical symptoms that might be displayed are as follows.

White matter of the brain:
- memory and concentration difficulty
- dementia
- depression
- confusion

Optic nerve:
- retrobulbar (optic) neuritis: inflammation of the optic nerve resulting in blurred vision and pain on moving the eyeball, sometimes loss of vision in one eye

Brain stem:
- lack of hand co-ordination
- facial weakness
- difficulty in swallowing
- dysarthria (slurred speech)
- double vision
- nystagmus (rapid involuntary eye movements)
- unsteady gait

Spinal cord:
- weakness
- heaviness in the limbs
- loss of sphincter control (incontinence of urine or faeces)
- urinary problems, such as increased frequency, bladder irritability
- paraesthesiae (pins and needles) in limbs, face or trunk

Paroxysmal symptoms:
- trigeminal neuralgia, brief spasms of searing pain in the trigeminal nerve of the face
- 'useless hands' – loss of joint and position sense
- Lhermitte's sign – 'electric shock' sensation down the trunk or arms on flexing the neck

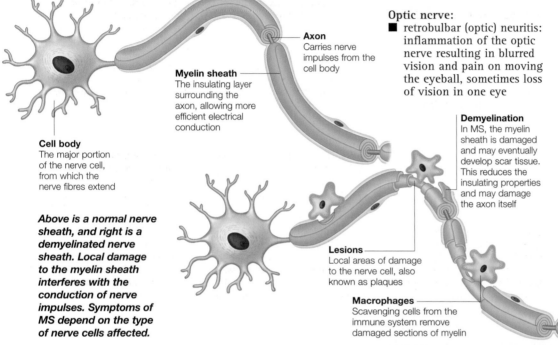

Axon
Carries nerve impulses from the cell body

Myelin sheath
The insulating layer surrounding the axon, allowing more efficient electrical conduction

Cell body
The major portion of the nerve cell, from which the nerve fibres extend

Above is a normal nerve sheath, and right is a demyelinated nerve sheath. Local damage to the myelin sheath interferes with the conduction of nerve impulses. Symptoms of MS depend on the type of nerve cells affected.

Demyelination
In MS, the myelin sheath is damaged and may eventually develop scar tissue. This reduces the insulating properties and may damage the axon itself

Lesions
Local areas of damage to the nerve cell, also known as plaques

Macrophages
Scavenging cells from the immune system remove damaged sections of myelin

Diagnosis

Diagnosis of MS by a doctor is difficult at the outset, because of the very nature of the illness: symptoms are often short-lived and may disappear in a few weeks. The diagnosis must therefore be clinical, confirming the presence of plaques in at least two areas of the CNS at two or more separate times.

The episodes must last for a minimum of 24 hours and be at least a month apart. Furthermore, other conditions which show similar symptoms must be excluded, such as AIDS, lymphoma (tumour of the lymph nodes), Friedreich's ataxia (an inherited disorder of the nervous system), or spinal damage.

A lumbar puncture needle is inserted into the lower back under local anaesthetic, and a small sample of cerebrospinal fluid is collected. This sample can then be tested for particular antibodies.

A specific diagnosis of MS has to be supported by results from several investigations, which may include:
- **Lumbar puncture** – the cerebrospinal fluid (the fluid enveloping the brain and the spinal cord) can demonstrate abnormalities of the immune system not seen in blood serum.

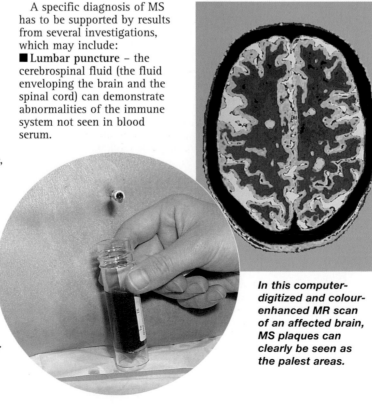

In this computer-digitized and colour-enhanced MR scan of an affected brain, MS plaques can clearly be seen as the palest areas.

- **Electrophysiological tests** – visual and brain stem responses will typically be slowed in MS.
- **MRI** (Magnetic Resonance Imaging) of the spinal cord or brain will reveal affected areas. The location of the first symptom will dictate the area to be scanned.
- **Cystoscopy** (looking into the bladder), **urodynamics** (recording of bladder pressures), and **renal and bladder ultrasound**, for assessing patients with urinary symptoms.

Because no test can be 100 per cent conclusive it may take months or even years for a diagnosis to be confirmed. A doctor will often not make a diagnosis known to the patient until there is reliable confirmation of the disease.

Prognosis

MS is an unpredictable illness. The typical pattern is of relapses lasting a few weeks, followed by remissions which may last for months or even years. Less often, the illness takes a progressively worsening course from the start. The physical disability that may occur during the course of the illness is unpredictable, and may result from incomplete recovery, slow progression, or a combination of the two.

Early age of onset, occurrence of optic neuritis or sensory disturbance (pins and needles) often indicate a better prognosis. A poor prognosis is associated with paralysis and bladder or cerebral dysfunction.

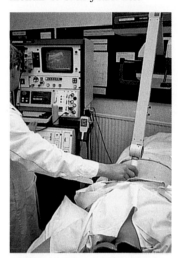

A doctor performs a renal and bladder ultrasound on a patient who has shown some of the characteristic signs of MS. The results of the scan will contribute towards the diagnostic picture for confirming the condition.

A high degree of remission from the first attack and a long-lasting first remission may indicate a better outcome. Frequent relapses may be associated with increased disability. The more lesions that are apparent in a scan, the higher the chance of increased disability.

Types of multiple sclerosis

There are four main types of multiple sclerosis:

Benign MS (around 20 per cent of cases) starts with a number of mild attacks followed by a complete recovery, with no worsening over time, and no permanent disability.

Relapsing-remitting MS (25 per cent) involves attacks which can last from hours to months, during which symptoms may recur or new ones appear, followed by periods of recovery of any length of time, even some years.

Secondary progressive MS (about 40 per cent develop this form) starts in the same way as relapsing-remitting MS, but remissions stop and the MS moves into the progressive stage.

Primary progressive MS (15 per cent), also known as chronic progressive, involves steadily worsening symptoms, and progressive disability. There is no clear cycle of attack and remission. The illness may continue to worsen, or may stabilize at any time.

Incidence

In the UK, about five new cases per 100,000 people are diagnosed every year. The typical age is 20-40 years and 67 per cent of cases are female. The disease primarily affects Caucasians in northern Europe and North America, as it is more common in temperate zones and rarer in the tropics. Some 15 per cent of cases in the UK have an affected first-degree relative, although it is not an inherited condition. In general, if a parent has MS, the child has a 20 to 40 times greater chance of becoming affected. It should be remembered, however, that the overall likelihood even in these instances is still lower than that of suffering from cancer or heart problems.

Causes

So far, no definite cause for MS has been identified, but there is a large amount of research taking place. It has been suggested that an immunological response to an outside infection is a factor behind MS. Recent research has shown that injections of beta-interferon (a substance which interferes with the growth of certain viruses) produce a favourable response, slowing the progress of the disease by reducing the severity of relapses.

Some researchers believe that MS is an autoimmune disorder, where tissue is destroyed by the body's own immune system. In either case, certain cells of the immune system are associated with the MS lesions.

There is as yet no known means of preventing MS.

Treatment and management

The symptoms of MS are often individual to the sufferer and vary in their severity. Drug treatment, lifestyle and dietary modifications, and counselling can all make the disease more manageable and extend periods of remission.

Physiotherapy, occupational therapy, goal-orientated rehabilitation and psycho-social counselling can all help a patient cope with MS. Making the most of a patient's own potential will allow them to live as independently as possible. A doctor should assess mobility, such as whether or not the toilet and the bath can be used independently, and should regularly review these functions to ensure maximum benefit. Although there is no cure for MS, medical treatment with steroids can speed recovery from an acute relapse and can lengthen the interval between relapses.

Specific drug treatment to alleviate certain symptoms is of benefit as follows:

- carbamazepine tablets for trigeminal neuralgia
- baclofen, tizanidine for spasticity (baclofen may be injected into the cerebrospinal fluid through a lumbar puncture)
- anticholinergenic drugs for bladder instability
- laxatives for constipation
- beta-blockers, clonazepam or isoniazid for tremor
- methyl prednisolone in short courses and oral steroids suppress disease activity
- amantadine (also used in Parkinsonism) for fatigue
- a diet rich in linoleic acid (a chemical found in corn and soyabean oil) is believed by some to be beneficial.

Spina bifida

Symptoms

Spina bifida is a birth defect of the central nervous system. The defect occurs in the neural tube, a fetal structure that develops in early pregnancy and later becomes the brain and spinal cord and their coverings (meninges). The several types of spina bifida vary in severity.

SPINA BIFIDA OCCULTA
In spina bifida occulta the defect is hidden and rarely causes disability. There may be:
■ A skin dimple or a tuft of hair at the site of the vertebral defect
■ Tethered cord syndrome – in this instance the spinal cord becomes attached to the vertebral defect, causing mobility and bladder difficulties.

SPINA BIFIDA CYSTICA
Spina bifida cystica is characterized by a visible sac on the back over the lower spine. Two types of this defect exist:
■ Meningocele – this is the mild form in which the sac contains the meninges and cerebrospinal fluid (CSF). People with a meningocele usually have little disability if the spinal cord is not damaged and if the spinal nerves function normally

■ Myelomeningocele – the sac contains the meninges, CSF and the spinal cord. Affected people usually have a damaged spinal cord. There is a degree of paralysis and loss of sensation below the level of damage. Loss of bowel and bladder control is also a feature.

CRANIUM BIFIDA
In cranium bifida the bones of the skull do not develop fully. This may be characterized by:
■ Encephalocele – a sac containing connective tissue, CSF and sometimes brain tissue
■ Anencephaly – missing brain tissue; the baby may be stillborn or die shortly after birth.

HYDROCEPHALUS
Most babies with spina bifida also have hydrocephalus, in which there is excess CSF in the brain. This may cause:
■ The head to enlarge
■ Damage to the brain – resulting in learning problems.

The spinal cord is often damaged in children with spina bifida. Despite impaired mobility, however, many are able to lead an independent and active life.

Diagnosis

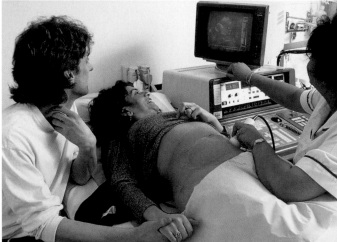

Ultrasound scans are performed before the fetus is 20 weeks old. This scan can detect fetal abnormalities, such as a failure of the neural tube to develop.

is swelling of the optic discs at the back of the eyes, a condition known as papilloedema
■ X-rays – in people with spina bifida occulta there may be no visible signs and the defect may be detected by chance later in life, when investigating other conditions such as back pain.

Spina bifida can be diagnosed at different stages using various methods:
■ Blood tests – can be carried out in pregnant women. A high level of alpha-fetoprotein may be associated with this defect
■ Ultrasound scans – are routinely performed 11 to 20 weeks into pregnancy and can confirm the diagnosis
■ CT or MR scans – will be

performed after the birth of an affected baby to assess the severity of the defect
■ Clinical examination of the eyes – one effect of raised pressure in the brain

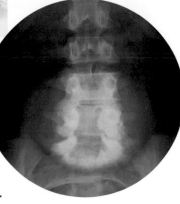

A large myelomeningocele in a patient with spina bifida is shown on this X-ray. The defect is around the lower lumbar vertebrae (orange area).

Causes

The cause of spina bifida is unknown, but it is thought to be associated with:
■ **Environmental factors**
Low folic acid intake in women before conception and in the first months of pregnancy is a factor. Folic acid is a B-group vitamin which is particularly important for fetal growth
■ **Genetic factors**
The defect is thought to have a hereditary element. If one parent has spina bifida the chances of offspring being affected are between one and five per cent. This increases to 15 per cent if both parents are affected.

Incidence

About one per 1,000 babies are born with spina bifida.

■ Between five per cent and 10 per cent of people have spina bifida occulta.

■ Only about one per cent of people with spina bifida occulta have any problems.

Treatment

The suitability of treatment depends upon the type and severity of spina bifida.

MANAGING INCONTINENCE
Children with bowel and bladder complications may need:
■ Training in learning to manage these functions
■ Insertion of catheters (tubes) to allow urine to be drained.

IMPROVING MOBILITY
Children with impaired mobility may require:
■ Physiotherapy – to develop mobility skills and achieve as much independence as possible
■ Mobility aids, such as crutches, braces or a wheelchair.

EDUCATIONAL NEEDS
Affected children who also have a history of hydrocephalus may have learning problems. Early specialist intervention can help to prepare children for school.

People with spina bifida may also have psychological difficulties associated with low self-esteem due to their disability. These feelings will need to be addressed.

NEUROSURGERY
Neurosurgery may be necessary for patients with:
■ **Spina bifida cystica**
In cases where a baby is born with a spinal protrusion which

is at risk of becoming infected, surgery may be required in the first 24 hours of life to close the affected area of the spinal cord.
■ **Spina bifida occulta**
In patients who have developed complications due to tethered spinal cord syndrome, an

operation may be performed to detach the spinal cord tissue from the backbone.
■ **Hydrocephalus**
Surgical intervention aims to control pressure inside the skull. This involves placing the upper end of a shunt (drainage tube)

into the ventricle of the brain and the lower end into the abdomen; the whole tube lies inside the body. The shunt allows excess CSF to drain from the brain into the abdominal cavity, where it is absorbed into the bloodstream.

Shunt in ventricle of the brain

Shunt leads to the abdomen

To treat hydrocephalus, a shunt (tube) is inserted into a ventricle of the brain. It drains CSF from the brain to the abdomen, where the fluid is absorbed.

Children with spina bifida may have specific educational needs. Most schools are able to adapt equipment, such as computers, to affected pupils' requirements.

Prognosis

The majority of infants with spina bifida survive into adulthood, although posture problems increase the risk of developing osteoarthritis later in life.
■ If the defects are only mild, children born with spina bifida have a normal life expectancy
■ Children with myelomeningocele and hydrocephalus have a good chance of survival due to neurosurgery.

Mainstream schooling is often very helpful for children with spina bifida. It enables affected pupils to interact with children of their own age.

Mainstream education
Most children with spina bifida are able to attend mainstream schools. Teachers and parents should encourage affected children to take a full part in school activities with their classmates.

Prevention

There are some measures that can reduce the risk of babies being born with spina bifida:
■ Taking folic acid supplement before conception and in the early weeks of a pregnancy reduces the risk by between 50 to 75 per cent.
■ It is generally recommended that women with spina bifida or a family history of the condition should receive higher

prescription doses of folic acid before they plan to become pregnant. This reduces the risk of babies having spina bifida.

GENETIC COUNSELLING
Genetic counselling is available for people who have an affected baby or who have had a termination because of the existence of this condition.

Women are advised to take folic acid tablets before conceiving and in early pregnancy. Folic acid reduces the risk of babies being born with spina bifida.

Muscular dystrophy

Symptoms

Muscular dystrophy refers to a number of inherited disorders characterized by progressive degeneration of different groups of muscles without involvement of the nervous system. Several major types of muscular dystrophy have been classified, but in each form of the condition, different muscles are selectively affected.

DUCHENNE MUSCULAR DYSTROPHY (DMD)

Duchenne muscular dystrophy is one of the most common types of the condition and it occurs only in boys; the disease becomes evident by about two years of age. It is due to an X-linked recessive gene. The common symptoms of DMD include:

■ Weakness of the muscles. This may be noticed when a child experiences difficulty in walking or using a limb. A child may start to 'waddle', be unable to climb stairs properly or only be able rise to their feet by using their hands to 'climb up the legs'. This is called Gower's sign, and occurs because of weakening of the pelvic muscles

■ Although there is no pain or tenderness of the muscles, certain actions become difficult. Affected muscles are weak, but often appear enlarged – this is known as pseudo-hypertrophy

■ Contractures. These are a common feature in the later stages of DMD. Often, where some muscles are weak, their opposing muscles remain strong and so affected children begin to walk on their tip-toes. Posture becomes difficult to maintain and patients may need to use a wheelchair

■ Progressive deformity and skeletal distortion and wasting occur, until by the age of 10 most patients are unable to walk. Death usually results from lung infection associated with wasting of the respiratory muscles, or cardiac failure towards the end of the second decade.

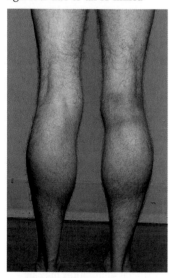

A distinctive feature of Duchenne muscular dystrophy is prominence of the calf muscles. This is due to increased bulk of the muscle fibres (hypertrophy), although the muscles are weak.

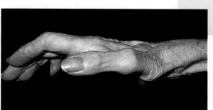

Contractures – when muscles stiffen and shorten, resulting in joint deformity – often affect the wrist and hand in DMD.

Duchenne muscular dystrophy only affects males. It is an X-linked recessive condition, which means that the defective gene is carried on the X chromosome.

Less common forms of muscular dystrophy

There are a number of other types of muscular dystrophy.

■ Becker type is a more benign X-linked disorder, with milder symptoms than Duchenne muscular dystrophy, which has an onset at 5–25 years of age. People with this type tend to have a longer life-expectancy.

■ Limb girdle dystrophy occurs equally in both sexes and usually appears at 20–30 years of age. In about 50 per cent of people with this type of muscular dystrophy, the weakness begins in the shoulder girdle and may not spread to the pelvic girdle, whereas in the remaining 50 per cent the pelvic girdle muscles are affected and weakness affects the shoulders within about 10 years. The course of the disease is generally more benign in those in whom the upper limbs are affected.

■ Facioscapulohumeral muscular dystrophy is inherited by an autosomal dominant mechanism, occurs equally in the sexes and can begin at any age from childhood until adult life, but is usually first recognized in adolescence. 'Winging' of the scapulae (shoulder blades) is common in this type. In some people, a severe lumbar lordosis (curvature) of the spine occurs.

Facial weakness may cause an inability to whistle, pout the lips or close the eyes. Weakness of the grip and fine finger movements or 'foot-drop' may occur, depending on which groups of muscles are affected.

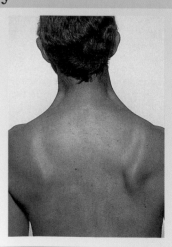

Winging of the shoulder blades is a sign of facioscapulohumeral muscular dystrophy. It is caused by atrophy of the muscles of the neck and shoulders.

Treatment and prognosis

There is no drug treatment for muscular dystrophy; however, complications such as respiratory and urinary infections require antibiotics.

Management includes:
■ Physical exercise – this may delay the onset of weakness and contractures; a programme of activity supervised by a physiotherapist will help
■ Passive stretching of tendons that show a tendency to shorten will also help
■ Light spinal supports when there is spinal deformity and calipers are valuable
■ Surgical lengthening of the shortening tendons may be appropriate
■ Psychological management is of great importance; family support and home care are vital.

The Muscular Dystrophy Campaign has family care officers to offer support and advice to people with neuromuscular conditions.

Research into congenital muscular dystrophy is ongoing at centres such as Hammersmith Hospital's Neuromuscular Unit.

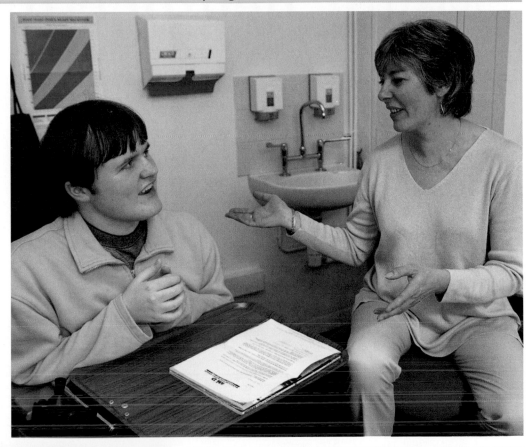

Prognosis and incidence

In some cases of muscular dystrophy, the prognosis is not good, particularly in people with the Duchenne type. The extent of the disability may be considerable and walking may eventually become impossible. Most sufferers of limb girdle type can be helped to lead a fulfiling life, though modified, for 20–40 years or even longer. People who develop muscular dystrophy in their late teens tend to have a better prognosis.

Prevention of muscular dystrophy is not yet possible, although the identification of the defective gene has raised the possibility of gene therapy.

Incidence
Muscular dystrophy is a relatively rare condition, but it occurs worldwide and affects people of all races.

There are probably 5–6,000 cases in the UK at any one time. Approximately one in 3,500 boys is born with Duchenne muscular dystrophy.

Causes

All forms of muscular dystrophy are genetically determined, yet the precise nature of the cause of the muscle wasting is as yet unknown. It is possible that the primary abnormality is in the plasma membrane of the muscle cell allowing uncontrolled entry of calcium, which activates proteases (enzymes) that digest muscle fibre contents.

Antenatal diagnosis by examining the amniotic fluid before birth is possible. Genetic counselling, however, is important for parents and people affected by muscular dystrophy.

Diagnosis

The typical slowly progressive case is often self-evident clinically. Patients will have a high serum creatine kinase, especially in the Duchenne type. Electromyography may be necessary to distinguish muscular dystrophy from other muscle disorders. Biopsy will usually confirm the diagnosis; histochemical studies will distinguish a dystrophy from other types of primary myopathy.

On testing, the blood serum of patients with DMD is found to have very high levels of the enzyme creatine kinase.

Motor neurone disease

Symptoms

Motor neurone disease (MND) is the generic term used for a number of illnesses resulting from degeneration of neurones that make up the pathway carrying information from the brain and spinal cord to the muscles.

CLASSIFYING MND
There are four main types of motor neurone disease. These classifications are based on the anatomical position of the motor neurones that are affected. Broadly speaking, there are two types of motor neurone. Upper motor neurones have their cell body in the brain and an axon that projects into the spinal cord. Lower motor neurones have their cell body in the brainstem or spinal cord and an axon that projects into a muscle.

The four main types of motor neurone disease are:
■ Amyotrophic lateral sclerosis (ALS). This is the most common type of MND and results from the degeneration of both upper and lower motor neurones. It is characterized by symptoms of muscle weakness, muscle twitching (fasciculations) and stiffness
■ Progressive bulbar palsy (PBP). This is also the result of degeneration of upper and lower motor neurones, though in this disorder only the muscles involved in speech and swallowing are affected

■ Primary lateral sclerosis (PLS). A less common form of MND in which only the upper motor neurones degenerate
■ Progressive muscular atrophy (PMA). This occurs when lower motor neurones degenerate.

SIGNS
Jaw weakness, facial weakness and fasciculation (involuntary twitching) in the tongue and face may occur, although twitching tends to lessen as the condition progresses. Eventually, wasting of the muscles becomes profound and the hands become flexed. The respiratory muscles also become involved, and there may be orthopnoea (breathlessness on lying flat). Intellect is not affected, but dementia occurs in five per cent of cases.

With progressive muscular atrophy, the tendons of the hands become more prominent as the muscles waste. Eventually, the hands become flexed.

The symptoms of MND vary significantly, depending on which motor nerves are affected. However, even when movement is restricted, people with MND can lead a full life.

Diagnosis

Extensive investigations are seldom necessary for MND, except to exclude other disorders that may mimic the condition.

A blood sample may be taken in order to conduct a full blood count and ESR to exclude underlying malignancy. Blood glucose levels will be checked to rule out diabetic amyotrophy (loss of muscle bulk). Thyroid function tests may also be done to exclude thyroid disease.

The patient may be tested for syphilis to exclude tabes dorsalis. This condition involves degeneration of sensory nerve columns in the spinal cord caused by untreated syphilis.

IMAGING
CT and MR scanning may be used to to exclude brain tumours. MR imaging or myelogram (specialized X-ray of the spinal cord) may also be taken of the cervical and thoracic spine to rule out cervical spondylosis.

In some patients, a biopsy of muscle tissue may be necessary to exclude polymyositis (an autoimmune muscular disease).

Nerve conduction studies will exclude motor neuropathy, and an electromyogram (EMG) will show widespread denervation.

CT scanning may be used to rule out other possible causes of the patient's symptoms, such as a brain tumour.

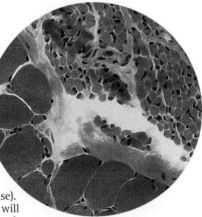

This micrograph shows muscular atrophy. The muscle fibres supplied by damaged neurones become small and atrophic (wasted), appearing in distinct groups (right of image), compared with normal fibres.

Treatment

The treatment of MND is aimed at relieving the symptoms:
■ When there is a difficulty with swallowing (dysphagia), the patient's diet may be modified and, in extreme cases, liquid food may be given via a nasogastric tube or by gastrostomy (an opening made directly into the stomach)
■ Excessive salivation is managed using portable suction and anticholinergic drugs
■ Muscle cramps can be treated using quinine, which acts as a muscle relaxant
■ Patients with speech disorders affecting pronunciation (dysarthria) require speech therapy and, in some cases, communication aids
■ Spasticity is treated with drugs which relieve muscle spasms and rigidity. This also enables physiotherapy to take place
■ Respiratory failure may be helped with physiotherapy
■ Depression is treated with drugs

This woman is using a communication device which she can 'speak' through. The keyboard is activated by a pointer attached to her head.

■ Difficulties with the activities of daily living can be addressed by occupational therapy, as well as aids such as wheelchairs and stair lifts
■ Limb weakness may require splints and collars or more advanced control systems.

Simple, practical measures – such as the provision of a lifting chair – help to make life easier for people with MND.

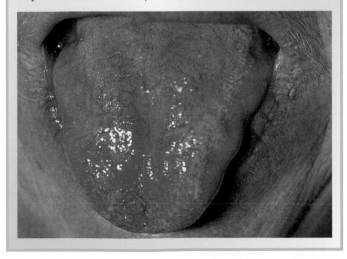

Managing MND

■ Psychological support by a neurologist and other practitioners throughout the illness is recommended
■ A multi-disciplinary team is required to meet the changing physical and psycho-social needs of patients and their carers
■ Drug therapies are limited. Riluzole is the only drug that may extend survival (though only for about three months)

after 18 months' administration. Gabapentin may slow the progression of the disease, but is used only in a few centres. In some cases, vitamin E may be taken in an attempt to lessen the effects of nerve damage.

The tongue may appear wasted in patients with progressive bulbar palsy. This is because the nerves in the motor cranial nuclei are affected.

Causes

About 90 per cent of MND patients have no family history of the disease. This form of the disease, known as sporadic MND, has no known cause. In the remaining 10 per cent, the disease is thought to have an inherited component (familial MND).

In 1993, researchers located a mutated gene, called SOD1, responsible for around one fifth of the cases of familial MND. As a result of this mutation, a defective protein is produced. In healthy people, this protein protects motor neurones by clearing away toxic waste products called free radicals.

Incidence

Six in 100,000 people are affected by motor neurone disease. Incidence (the number of new cases a year) is two cases per 100,000 of the population per year.

The incidence rises with age and MND is rare in patients under 50; the peak incidence is between 60 and 70 years of age. The condition is familial (inherited) in about 10 per cent of all cases. Men are affected more often than women.

Prognosis

Prevention of MND is not yet possible. Degeneration of the motor neurones leads to progressive signs of upper and lower motor neurone dysfunction. The average expected survival for patients with motor neurone disease is between three and five years from first symptoms. A small proportion of patients – about 10 per cent – live for more than 10 years.

Early involvement of the medulla oblongata (one of the brain centres responsible for respiration) worsens the prognosis.

Huntington's disease

Symptoms

Huntington's disease (often known as Huntington's chorea) is a rare hereditary condition, affecting about one in 10,000 people worldwide. The disease causes progressive damage to the nervous system.

Nerve cell damage is greatest in two distinct masses of nerve cells located deep in the substance of the brain – the caudate nucleus and putamen. These areas are involved in the subconscious regulation of voluntary movements.

Symptoms of the disease usually start in early middle age and include:
■ Disturbances of movement
■ Progressive deterioration of mental function, leading to dementia
■ Other symptoms related to damage to the nervous system.

MOVEMENT
Involuntary jerky movements (chorea) affect about 90 per cent of patients and are often the first obvious symptom. Other movement disturbances include:
■ Loss of normal muscle tone or increased rigidity
■ Difficulties in posture and movement

■ Dysarthria (inability to pronounce words clearly, despite knowing their meaning)
■ Dysphagia (difficulty in swallowing)
■ Abnormal eye movements.

MENTAL DETERIORATION
Affected people invariably experience a gradual deterioration in mental ability and may develop psychiatric disorders. Symptoms include:
■ Impaired intellectual ability
■ Loss of concentration
■ Loss of short- and long-term memory
■ Loss of problem-solving ability
■ Dementia.

Some people may suffer psychiatric disorders, such as:
■ Personality changes, including irritability, apathy, aggression, changed sexual behaviour
■ Depression
■ Psychoses (illnesses in which the patient loses contact with reality, such as schizophrenia).

Huntington's disease is a rare genetic disorder that damages the nervous system. Symptoms include disturbed movement and impaired mental ability.

Causes

Huntington's disease occurs in individuals who inherit an abnormal gene on chromosome 4. This leads to the formation of abnormal proteins that invade and destroy nerve cell nuclei.

The defective gene is dominant (anyone who inherits the faulty gene will, at some stage, develop the disease). Children of an affected individual have a one in two risk of inheriting the gene.

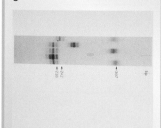

Huntington's disease is caused by an abnormal dominant gene. This gene can be detected using gel electrophoresis.

Diagnosis

A family history of Huntington's disease will suggest the diagnosis if an individual develops typical symptoms of the disease. However, an accurate family history may not always be available.

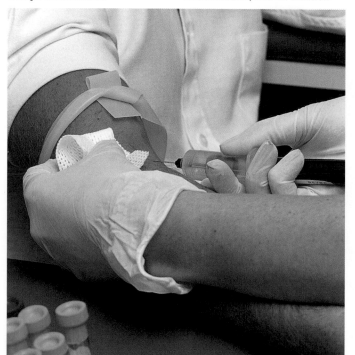

TESTS
In individuals carrying the Huntington gene, expert examination of the nervous system may identify subtle changes in speed and control of movement, and in reaction time long before chorea becomes very obvious.

GENETIC TESTING
Tests using blood DNA samples can now be used to identify the abnormal gene in the following groups:
■ Individuals who have symptoms
■ People who carry the abnormal gene but have as yet no symptoms
■ Unborn babies.

Genetic testing can, however, cause severe psychological distress and raises a number of issues, including ethical issues about abortion.

OTHER CAUSES
Other causes of chorea, such as a stroke, certain drugs or long-term alcohol abuse, must be excluded during diagnosis.

The diagnosis of Huntington's disease can be confirmed by taking a blood sample. The sample is then tested for the presence of the abnormal gene.

Treatment

Huntington's disease is, at present, incurable. Treatment therefore aims to reduce the effects of the disease as much as possible and to provide psychological support.

DRUG THERAPY
Some medications can minimize the unpleasant symptoms of the disease:
■ Treatments are available to relieve depression, anxiety, apathy, aggression and irritability
■ Phenothiazines, including pimozide and/or haloperidol, may be used to control the chorea if it is seriously incapacitating. Treatment should be carefully tailored to the patient's needs as side effects may be a problem
■ Dopamine agonists may be used to control rigidity. However, they are generally less effective in Huntington's disease than in Parkinson's disease.

SUPPORT
Patients and their families are likely to need a great deal of skilled psychological and social support. Patients frequently become extremely depressed as they often retain a considerable amount of insight into their condition throughout a large part of their illness.

Speech therapy is sometimes helpful if a person has dysarthria and an occupational therapist can enable a person to lead as normal a life as possible. As the condition progresses, nursing care may be necessary.

FUTURE TREATMENT
Future therapies for the treatment of Huntington's disease which are currently being tested include:
■ Neuroprotective drugs, which may delay the disease onset
■ Neurotransplantation (the transplantation of fetal cells into the brain of a Huntington's disease patient)
■ Gene therapy.

There is, at present, no treatment for Huntington's disease. However, medication can be used to control some of the unpleasant symptoms.

People with the condition may benefit from occupational therapy. This patient is receiving therapy to improve her co-ordination and muscle control.

Prognosis

Once symptoms begin to develop, Huntington's disease pursues a relentless course and most patients eventually require full-time nursing and residential care.

The average time of survival from the time of diagnosis is about 16 years, but patients may live for much longer or shorter periods.

Many patients die from pneumonia caused by food and liquid entering their lungs as they lose their ability to swallow correctly.

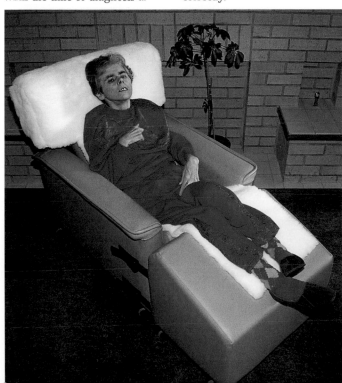

Prevention

Prospective parents at risk of having a child with the disease may choose to have prenatal genetic testing to determine whether the fetus is carrying the abnormal gene. If tests prove positive, they may consider termination of the pregnancy.

GENETICS
As the symptoms of Huntington's disease usually do not appear until early middle age, an affected person will often have had children by the time the disease is diagnosed. This partly explains why the disease continues from generation to generation.

ETHICS
Ethical issues arise over the question of whether the offspring of affected individuals decide to remain in ignorance of their condition, or whether they choose to be tested for the presence of the abnormal gene before they decide to have children of their own.

People with Huntington's chorea often become less mobile as the disease progresses. Adapted furniture can help to maintain comfort.

Gastro-oesophageal reflux disease

Symptoms

Gastro-oesophageal reflux disease (GORD) is the persistent regurgitation of acid, bile and food from the stomach, which causes inflammation of the lower end of the oesophagus.

Symptoms of GORD typically occur after meals and when bending forward, lifting, straining, or lying flat. The severity of the symptoms is often unrelated to the degree of reflux.

COMMON SYMPTOMS
Common symptoms include:
■ Heartburn – a burning discomfort or pain felt behind the sternum (breastbone), often starting in the upper abdomen and spreading up towards the throat. It is sometimes severe enough to be mistaken for angina (pain from heart disease)
■ The appearance of acid fluid (brash) in the mouth.

LESS COMMON SYMPTOMS
In some cases, people experience:
■ Vomiting
■ Toothache resulting from the destruction of tooth enamel by acid
■ Hoarseness due to inflammation of the larynx
■ Recurrent pneumonia or wheeziness due to the inhalation of stomach contents.

Inflammation of the lower end of the oesophagus can cause severe discomfort. The condition is sometimes experienced during pregnancy.

Causes

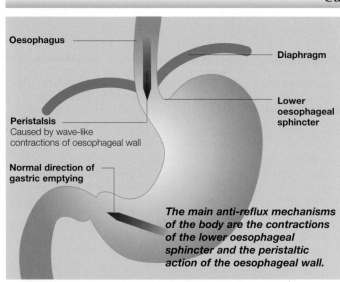

Oesophagus

Diaphragm

Lower oesophageal sphincter

Peristalsis
Caused by wave-like contractions of oesophageal wall

Normal direction of gastric emptying

The main anti-reflux mechanisms of the body are the contractions of the lower oesophageal sphincter and the peristaltic action of the oesophageal wall.

GORD is caused by a failure of anti-reflux mechanisms. However, certain behaviours, such as eating fatty foods, can trigger an attack.

GORD occurs when the mechanisms that normally prevent regurgitation fail to act efficiently, either because:
■ They have become abnormally weak, or
■ The pressure in the abdomen has become abnormally high.

REFLUX MECHANISMS
The reflux of the stomach contents into the oesophagus is primarily prevented by the contraction of a specialized ring of muscle at the lower end of the oesophagus (the lower oesophageal sphincter), which seals off the entrance to the stomach. Other mechanisms that counteract regurgitation include wave-like contractions of muscles in the wall of the oesophagus (peristalsis). These, together with the pinching action of the diaphragm, propel food down towards the stomach.

If the muscle tone of the sphincter is decreased through dietary factors, medication or pregnancy, some of the stomach contents are able to pass back into the oesophagus after meals and GORD may develop.

RISK FACTORS
The following conditions may cause an attack of GORD:

■ Obesity
■ Pregnancy – hormones relax the sphincter muscle while abdominal pressure increases
■ Medications such as calcium antagonists (used for heart disease) and beta 2 agonists, (used to treat asthma)
■ Smoking
■ Drinking coffee, tea or alcohol
■ Eating fried or fatty foods.

HIATUS HERNIA
People with GORD may also have a hiatus hernia, a condition in which part of the stomach passes into the chest cavity through the hole in the diaphragm for the oesophagus.

This often causes no symptoms and most people with a hiatus hernia do not have GORD. However, most patients with oesophagitis (inflammation of the oesophagus) do have a hiatus hernia.

Incidence

GORD is an extremely common condition, and the incidence appears to be rising worldwide. Many people with the condition treat themselves and never consult their doctors, so it is impossible to know exactly how many people suffer from GORD. However, it is estimated that in Western countries around 5–8 per cent of adults have the condition.

Diagnosis

In young patients, it is often possible to diagnose GORD on the basis of the typical clinical history alone: heartburn after meals and changes of posture, such as bending or lying down.

People over the age of 45 who develop symptoms for the first time and those with unusual symptoms, such as bleeding from the gastrointestinal tract or difficulty in swallowing, need further investigation. This is particularly to exclude the possibility of cancer.

INVESTIGATIONS
The most useful investigations are as follows:

■ Endoscopy – here a viewing instrument is passed down the person's throat to directly visualize the lining of the oesophagus and stomach. Biopsies (samples of tissue) can be taken from the walls of the stomach and oesophagus and examined microscopically
■ Barium swallow – a radio-opaque substance is swallowed and a series of X-rays are taken allowing reflux to be seen as it actually occurs.

A barium swallow will reveal any problems relating to the oesophagus. Here a hiatus hernia is seen to be contributing to the problem.

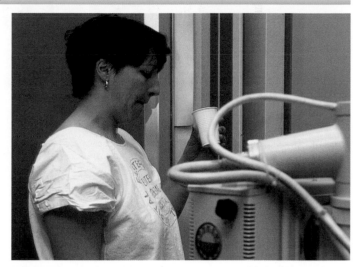

Treatment

Many people with GORD respond well to:
■ Losing weight
■ Avoiding large meals
■ Avoiding onions, spicy or fatty foods, tea, coffee, fruit juices and citrus fruits
■ Avoiding tight-fitting clothes
■ Raising the head of the bed on 15 cm (6 in) blocks at night
■ Reducing alcohol intake
■ Stopping smoking
■ Adjusting any medication to avoid drugs that affect the oesophageal sphincter.

MEDICATION
Antacids are drugs that neutralize stomach acids, and can be very effective for short-term relief. When combined with a substance called alginate

Changing lifestyle factors can play a large part in treatment. Losing weight, especially by cutting out fried foods, may help to cut down GORD attacks.

(a type of seaweed), they form a 'foam raft' on top of the stomach contents, which acts as a barrier to reflux.

Drugs that suppress the production of acid in the stomach may be prescribed. There are two main classes of these:
■ H_2 receptor antagonists – such as ranitidine or cimetidine. Short, intermittent courses can be very effective
■ Proton pump inhibitors – such as omeprazole. These drugs are indicated for patients with severe or resistant disease.

Maintenance treatment is often needed as GORD usually relapses when treatment stops.

SURGERY
An operation to prevent reflux is sometimes indicated for otherwise fit patients with persistent disease. This involves surgery to wrap the upper part of the stomach around the lower end of the oesophagus.

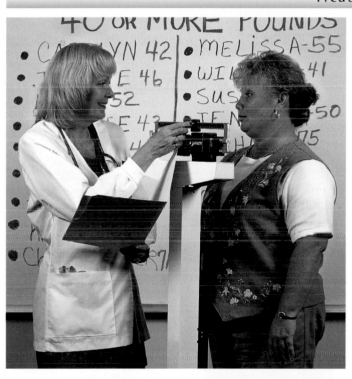

GORD in infancy

GORD is very common in infancy. Most cases resolve naturally between 12 and 18 months of age, but medical advice should be sought in all but the mildest cases.

Regurgitating milk is the chief symptom. Occasional complications are:
■ Failure to gain weight
■ Temporary cessation of breathing (apnoea)
■ Pneumonia caused by fluid spilling into the lungs.

Treatment involves changing the baby's position, thickening feeds and the use of an alginate-containing compound with low sodium and aluminium levels designed for infants.

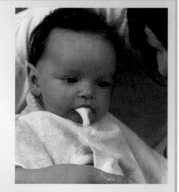

Many children suffer from a form of gastro-oesophageal reflux disease during infancy. The main symptom in these babies is regurgitation of milk.

Prognosis

GORD typically runs a chronic relapsing course. About two-thirds of patients need to take drugs continuously or intermittently for many years to control their symptoms.

The major long-term complication of GORD is scarring and consequent narrowing (stricture) of the lower end of the oesophagus. This usually affects people over the age of 60 years and causes difficulty in swallowing over a prolonged period.

In a few cases, long-standing oesophagitis may lead to pre-cancerous changes in the oesophagus (Barrett's oesophagus), but these can be reversed with drug therapy.

Gastric and duodenal ulcers

Symptoms

Gastric and duodenal ulcers occur in the walls of the stomach and duodenum (the first part of the small intestine) respectively. Most such ulcers result from the corrosive effect of an imbalance of acid and pepsin, which are produced in the stomach; these are known as peptic ulcers. They are often symptomless, but may cause:
■ Recurrent attacks of upper abdominal pain
■ Indigestion
■ Loss of appetite, weight loss
■ Vomiting of blood (haematemesis) and/or passing stools containing partly digested blood, which often makes them appear black and tarry
■ Bleeding – occurs when the ulcer penetrates a blood vessel; it is sometimes the first sign of an ulcer
■ Back pain – may occur if a duodenal ulcer extends into the pancreas
■ Severe abdominal pain, shock and collapse – can occur if the ulcer makes holes in the wall of the intestine. Escaped intestinal contents may cause acute peritonitis (inflammation of the abdomen's lining) or abscesses
■ Vomiting of food eaten hours before.

Vomiting is one of the symptoms of ulcers. However, the pain caused by gastric ulcers is sometimes made worse by food and relieved by vomiting.

The role of acid

Glands in the stomach wall produce gastric juice containing hydrochloric acid (HCL) and pepsin (an enzyme). Although an excess of HCL can cause peptic ulcers, it plays a key role in:
■ Killing potentially harmful micro-organisms
■ Providing the necessary pH for pepsin to start protein digestion
■ Stimulating the flow of bile and pancreatic juice.

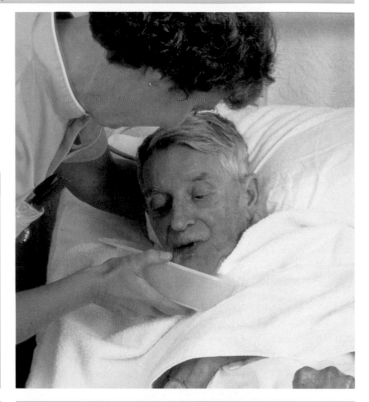

Causes

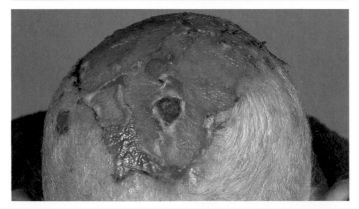

Most peptic ulcers are known to be associated with chronic inflammation of the stomach lining (gastritis). Gastritis is caused by infection with the bacterium *Helicobacter pylori* (see box).

Gastritis causes an imbalance between acid and pepsin production and substances that protect the gut wall, such as mucus and prostaglandins (hormone-like substances involved in the process of inflammation). Other risk factors for peptic ulcers include:

Severe head injuries and burns are associated with the development of acute gastric ulcers. This is due to the stress caused by the injury or burn.

■ Taking drugs such as aspirin or other non-steroidal anti-inflammatory drugs (NSAIDs) and corticosteroids. These may create holes in the intestine and cause bleeding
■ Smoking
■ Hereditary factors – duodenal ulcers run in families, especially in those with blood group O.

Bacterial causes

Infection with the bacterium *Helicobacter pylori* increases the risk of developing duodenal and gastric ulcers.

H. pylori infection is one of the world's most common infections, affecting a very high percentage of adults. Many remain symptom-free, but a significant number develop gastro-intestinal disease.

The bacterium probably spreads from mouth to mouth and faeces to mouth. Childhood infection is very common in crowded living conditions.

H. pylori from the human stomach was first cultured in 1982. A junior doctor in Australia was the first to prove that *H. pylori* caused gastritis. He did this by swallowing a culture of *H. pylori*.

A Helicobacter pylori bacterium has thin, whip-like threads (flagella). These help it to move around the intestine.

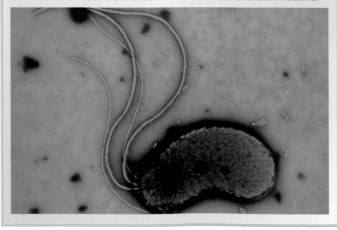

Diagnosis

It is not possible to diagnose a gastric or duodenal ulcer definitely by clinical examination. The symptoms do not always pinpoint the site of the ulcer, and can also be caused by gallstones, inflammation of the gullet and pancreas (oesophagitis and pancreatitis) and gastric cancer.

ENDOSCOPY

Endoscopy is the most reliable means of diagnosis, giving better results than X-rays. In an endoscopy of the stomach and duodenum, an instrument with a light and camera attached is passed through the mouth. The instrument relays pictures of the organs to a monitor. A small sample of tissue is collected, which can be analysed for *H. pylori*. Blood and breath tests are also used to detect *H. pylori*.

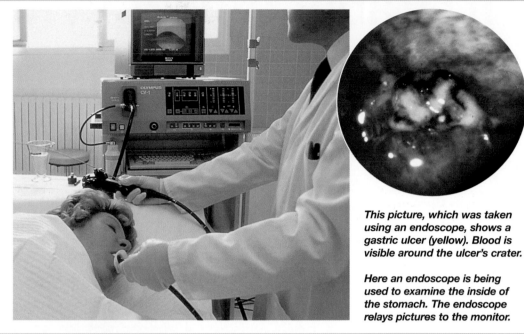

This picture, which was taken using an endoscope, shows a gastric ulcer (yellow). Blood is visible around the ulcer's crater.

Here an endoscope is being used to examine the inside of the stomach. The endoscope relays pictures to the monitor.

Treatment

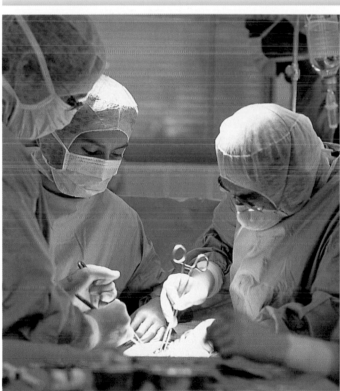

In severe cases of gastric ulcer, a part of the stomach can be removed. This reduces the production of gastric acid and pepsin, helping to cure the ulcer.

Treatment for gastric and duodenal ulcers can be divided into medical and surgical categories.

MEDICAL

■ Stopping smoking and minimizing alcohol intake are very important.

■ Drugs that contain aluminium or magnesium compounds and neutralize acid (antacids), and drugs that suppress acid production, such as omeprazole, may provide temporary relief.

Long-term healing is most likely to be achieved by eradicating *H. pylori* from the stomach. This usually involves a week-long course of ranitidine or omeprazole, combined with two antibiotics, such as clarithromycin and amoxicillin (triple therapy). Triple therapy eradicates *H. pylori* in over 90 per cent of patients.

Patients with gastric ulcers may be advised to have a repeat endoscopy six weeks after triple therapy. If the ulcer has not healed, a repeat biopsy may be needed to exclude a cancerous tumour. This follow-up is less important in the case of duodenal ulcers as they are less likely to be related to cancer.

SURGICAL

With efficient medical therapy, surgery is rarely used, but it still has a place when there is:

■ Severe haemorrhage or perforation

■ Gastric outflow obstruction due to scarring from a duodenal ulcer or inflammation that fails to respond to medical treatment

■ Repeated relapses despite medical treatment.

Partial gastrectomy is used to remove the part of the stomach that produces gastrin, a substance that stimulates the production of gastric acid.

Incidence

Duodenal ulcers are about four times more common than gastric ulcers. Gastric ulcers occur more frequently in women, those aged over 60 and those on non-steroidal inflammatory drugs (NSAIDs). They are also more prevalent in areas of social deprivation.

About 5–10 per cent of the population have a peptic ulcer at some time in their life. The annual incidence is 1–3 people per 1,000.

Prognosis

Medical treatment for gastric and duodenal ulcers is very effective. If *H. pylori* is eradicated, recurrence is rare, and there is no need for prolonged, and often very expensive, acid-suppressant therapy. Eradication of *H. pylori* eliminates the risk of complications, and may reduce risks of cancer and lymphoma.

Surgical treatment is usually successful, but recurrence may occur in about 10 per cent of patients. After gastric surgery, the stomach sometimes empties very quickly and patients may experience sweating, palpitations, faintness, a feeling of abdominal fullness after a meal, diarrhoea, anaemia and thinning bones.

Duodenal ulcers tend to heal spontaneously with age as the stomach produces less acid. However, gastric ulcers become increasingly common with age.

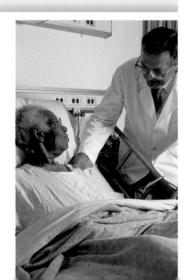

Irritable bowel syndrome

Symptoms

Irritable bowel syndrome (IBS) is a very common bowel disorder which probably accounts for about 50 per cent of referrals to gastro-enterological clinics in the UK. There is, however, no simple explanation for the symptoms of abdominal pain and disordered bowel habit. The disorder causes a great deal of anxiety and stress, which probably exacerbate the symptoms. Firm reassurance by experienced gastro-enterologists is usually necessary to allay the natural anxiety that the symptoms may be due to more serious organic disease, such as cancer of the large bowel.

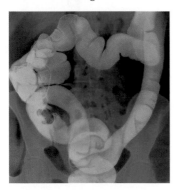

Contrast X-ray, in which barium appears opaque, is used to investigate problems in the stomach and intestines.

Common gastro-intestinal symptoms include:
- Abdominal pain anywhere in the abdomen, but most commonly below the navel
- Constipation with ribbon-like or pellety faeces, or diarrhoea
- Passage of mucus rectally
- Rectal dissatisfaction – incomplete evacuation after defecation
- Abdominal distension, borborygmi (noisy bowel sounds) relieved by passing intestinal wind
- Excess flatulence
- Other symptoms may include nausea, vomiting, heartburn, dyspepsia, dysphagia (difficulty in swallowing), and stabbing rectal pain.

Other IBS-related symptoms can include:
- Psychological symptoms – anxiety, depression and pre-occupation with bowel habit
- Gynaecological symptoms in women – dyspareunia (pain during sexual intercourse), dysmenorrhoea (painful menstruation) and bowel symptoms related to the menstrual cycle
- Urinary symptoms – increases in frequency and urgency of urination
- Tiredness and headache.

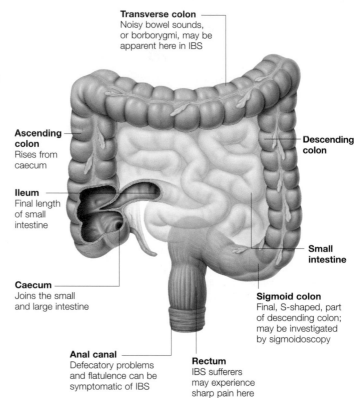

Transverse colon
Noisy bowel sounds, or borborygmi, may be apparent here in IBS

Ascending colon
Rises from caecum

Descending colon

Ileum
Final length of small intestine

Small intestine

Caecum
Joins the small and large intestine

Sigmoid colon
Final, S-shaped, part of descending colon; may be investigated by sigmoidoscopy

Anal canal
Defecatory problems and flatulence can be symptomatic of IBS

Rectum
IBS sufferers may experience sharp pain here

The varied physical symptoms of IBS manifest within the structures of the large intestine. Psychological factors may also contribute to the problem.

Diagnosis

A detailed physical examination may reveal widespread or local tenderness of the abdomen, a tender and palpable descending colon and/or a 'squelchy' caecum. Loud gurgles of fluid and gas in the intestine may also be detected. Sometimes these flatulence symptoms can be replicated in the patient by the blowing of air into the colon during examination with a sigmoidoscope (see right).

The doctor will examine the patient's abdomen to locate any tenderness. This can be one of the symptoms of IBS.

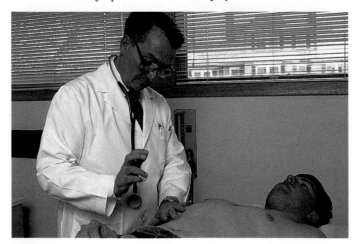

Investigations

If IBS is suspected, a doctor will initially request a number of tests. These usually include:
- Full blood count
- Normal erythrocyte sedimentation rate (ESR), a test to see how quickly blood cells settle in a column; this is a non-specific indicator of disease
- Sigmoidoscopy – a sigmoidoscope is an instrument used for investigating the sigmoid colon and rectum
- Rectal biopsy.

If there is doubt about the diagnosis it may be necessary to perform:
- Examination of faeces for pathogens such as bacteria, viruses and parasites
- Further sigmoidoscopy
- Barium meal and follow-through to visualize the digestive tract on X-ray
- Endoscopy of the upper gastro-intestinal tract
- Abdominal ultrasound.

Microscopic examination of faeces samples may be necessary to exclude a microbiological cause of IBS.

Causes

The causes of IBS are not known, but other possible diseases must be excluded. Personality disorder may be considered, as IBS sufferers often seem anxious or depressed. Food intolerance is not confirmed as a cause, but if a patient suspects that certain foods exacerbate the condition those foods should be excluded from the diet. Episodes of infective gastro-enteritis may precede the condition.

It is sometimes necessary to exclude diseases and infections. These may include:

■ Malabsorption syndromes such as coeliac disease (an intolerance of gluten, a constituent of wheat) and lactase deficiency in young adults
■ Giardiasis disease caused by infection with the parasite protozoa *Giardia*
■ Pelvic inflammatory disease
■ Thyrotoxicosis (a syndrome caused by excess levels of thyroid hormones in the blood)
■ Colorectal cancer, diverticulosis, peptic ulcer, and gallstones must be excluded in older patients.

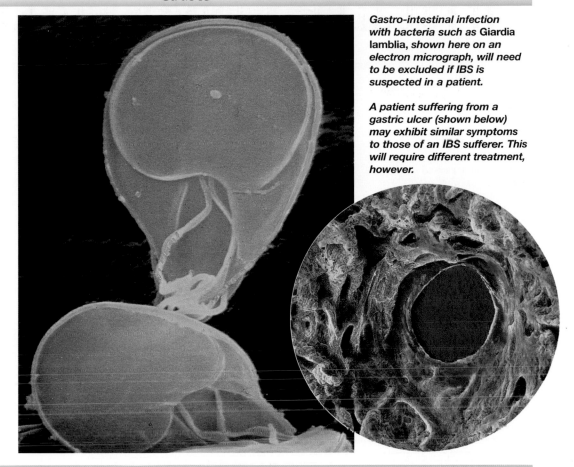

Gastro-intestinal infection with bacteria such as Giardia lamblia, *shown here on an electron micrograph, will need to be excluded if IBS is suspected in a patient.*

A patient suffering from a gastric ulcer (shown below) may exhibit similar symptoms to those of an IBS sufferer. This will require different treatment, however.

Treatment

It is of paramount importance that the IBS patient is reassured about their condition, and that they understand that no serious disease exists. The patient should also be made aware that pain and altered bowel habits are due to spasms in the muscles of the bowel or to increased perception of normal gut activity.

Dietary factors identified by the patient as causing the symptoms of the condition should be avoided. A high-fibre diet for constipation and bulking agents will help.

The patient should avoid drugs because their use is likely to become long-term with no obvious benefits, but the following are sometimes prescribed:

■ Drugs to reduce spasms, such as mebeverine and cyclomine
■ Antidiarrhoeals such as loperamide
■ Antidepressants.

Psychiatric referral is occasionally necessary, and hypnosis may help IBS that is otherwise unresponsive to treatment.

IBS may be a stress-related disorder, and psychotherapy can be very helpful in alleviating a patient's anxieties. However, this does not suit every sufferer.

Incidence and prognosis

Irritable bowel syndrome affects about 20 per cent of the population and is most common in Caucasian women, aged between 20 and 30. It is more common in women than men, and occurs mainly in developed countries.

Most patients' symptoms

A diet lacking in high-fibre foods, such as pasta, bran, fruit and vegtables, may contribute to the onset of IBS.

cease within about five years. However, symptoms may persist for longer in spite of a course of treatment.

Although the condition is particularly associated with stress and anxiety, and may well occur after severe infection of the intestine, the cause of IBS is not thoroughly understood. Therefore, although treatment can be effective, prevention of the condition is not possible at the moment.

Coeliac disease

Symptoms

Coeliac disease is also known as nontropical sprue, coeliac sprue, gluten enteropathy, and gluten intolerance. It is a life-long inflammatory condition of the gastrointestinal tract, involving damage to the lining of the small intestine caused by an intolerance to gluten.

This damage causes a type of malabsorption syndrome and nutrients cannot be properly absorbed by the intestines.

Symptoms can immediately follow consumption of gluten, or they can be delayed by days, weeks, or even longer. Typical symptoms, many caused by nutritional deficiencies, include:
■ General fatigue and a feeling of undefined ill health
■ Weight loss, despite a normal diet
■ Diarrhoea, with loose, soft, foul-smelling stools characteristic of fat malabsorption leading to high levels of fat in the stool
■ Abdominal discomfort, bloating and excessive flatulence
■ Iron and/or folate deficiency
■ Low blood levels of protein, potassium, calcium and sodium
■ Low levels of the clotting factor prothrombin, causing easy bruising and prolonged bleeding after injuries.

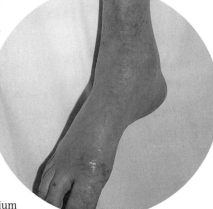

Dermatitis herpetiformis is a blistering skin condition commonly associated with coeliac disease. The condition clears with a gluten-free diet.

Symptoms in children

Coeliac disease in children can be extremely mild, causing only stomach upset; or more severe, causing symptoms similar to those in adults. Nutritional deficiencies can particularly affect children, stunting growth and resulting in other problems such as:
■ Anaemia and amenorrhoea (absence of menstrual periods) in previously menstruating girls
■ Calcium deficiency, causing long bones, such as the femur, to become bowed
■ Protein deficiency, leading to fluid-retention and oedema.

Coeliac disease causes a low uptake of nutrients, including calcium, which is necessary for strong bones. As a result, rickets may develop.

ASSOCIATED CONDITION

Coeliac disease is associated with an itchy, blistering skin condition called dermatitis herpetiformis, which affects the elbows, knees, buttocks and back. While only around 10 per cent of people with coeliac disease suffer from dermatitis herpetiformis, around 90 per cent of people with this skin condition demonstrate gluten-sensitive enteropathy (intestinal damage).

Causes

Coeliac disease is a genetically determined disease that develops when the affected individual is exposed to dietary gluten. This is a protein found in cereals such as wheat, barley and rye, and to a lesser extent, oats. It is

The lining of a healthy small intestine is covered in circular glands. The finger-like projections of villi surround each gland to absorb nutrients.

a cohesive, elastic protein that gives milled cereals their dough-making properties. When people with coeliac disease are exposed to gluten, the protein causes changes in the lining of the upper part of the intestine (small intestine).

These changes mainly involve the destruction of villi within the small bowel. Villi are the finger-like projections that normally line the walls of the small

intestine, giving it a brush-like appearance.

THE ROLE OF VILLI

Villi increase the surface area of the intestinal lining available for absorbing nutrients. In coeliac disease, the lining becomes flattened, smooth, and less able to absorb nutrients, leading to nutritional deficiencies. These in turn cause related problems, such as anaemia.

This micrograph shows the lining of the small intestine when affected by coeliac disease. The surface is flattened, with no villi in evidence.

Incidence

Coeliac disease is the most common genetic disease in Europe, with more children affected than adults. There are two incidence peaks for age of onset: 1–5 years and 30–40 years. It is most commonly found in people from north-west Europe, but prevalence varies with area. In the UK the figure is thought to be around 1:1,000, but may be as high as 1:100, as many coeliacs remain undiagnosed. People with Celtic ancestry seem to have a higher susceptibility.

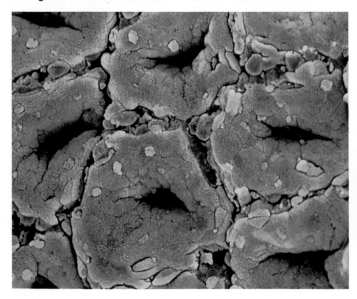

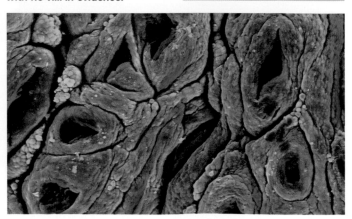

Diagnosis

Doctors may suspect coeliac disease in someone suffering from weight loss despite a normal diet who also shows symptoms of gastrointestinal discomfort. Characteristic warning signs in children include failure to thrive, diarrhoea and irritability.

INVESTIGATIONS
Further investigations include:
■ Laboratory tests to measure absorption of a simple sugar, such as xylose. Absorption will be impaired in coeliac patients
■ Biopsy of the lining of the small intestine (jejunal biopsy) using an endoscope to examine the small intestine via fibre optic visual relays. A tiny cutting implement can then be used to cut out a piece of the intestinal lining. This can be examined under a microscope to check whether the villi are missing and the lining looks flattened and atrophied
■ Blood tests – anaemia due to iron and/or folate deficiency is nearly always present.

Diagnosis is confirmed by taking a biopsy of the small intestine. This is carried out by passing an endoscope through the mouth to the small intestine.

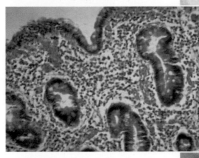

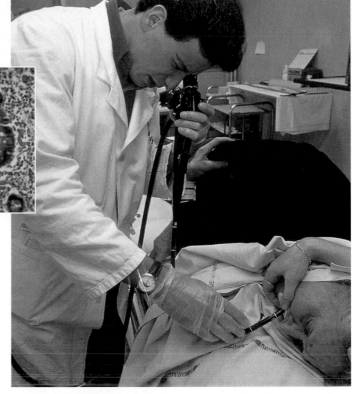

This sample of tissue shows the flattened intestinal lining typical of coeliac disease. When healthy, the lining would be covered in long finger-like villi.

The most convincing diagnosis is retrospective: a recovery from symptoms after following a gluten-free diet.

Recovery is checked by taking a biopsy following six months on this diet.

Treatment

These gluten-free foods are safe for people with coeliac disease to eat. They include rice noodles, corn spaghetti, corn and vegetable pasta and soya.

Exclusion of gluten from the diet is the primary treatment for coeliac disease. This involves cutting out all wheat, rye, barley and oats from the diet, which can be difficult because these cereals and their derivatives are present in a very wide range of foods. They are especially prevalent in processed foods and as additives in everything from sauces to sweets.

SUBSTITUTES
People are usually given a list of acceptable, gluten-free foods by their doctor. Substitutes are available for most of the relevant cereals, such as rice noodles or buckwheat pasta for durum wheat pasta. Rice and maize are frequently used as substitutes.

Supplements may be given to make up deficiencies of folic acid, iron, vitamin B_{12}, calcium and vitamin D. If dermatitis herpetiformis is present, this should be relieved by the change in diet.

TREATMENT FOR SEVERE CASES
Children suffering from severe forms of coeliac disease may initially require intravenous feeding to help them overcome nutritional deficiencies, especially if the diagnosis has been delayed and anaemia and rickets have developed.

Children will also need more frequent follow-up checks to monitor growth and development while following a gluten-free diet.

Prognosis

Although there is no cure for coeliac disease, most coeliacs recover completely by following a gluten-free diet:
■ The intestinal lining is restored to its normal condition as villi grow back
■ Absorption of nutrients is no longer impaired.

In adult patients there is a very small chance that severe coeliac disease can lead to the development of lymphomas (malignant tumours) or leiomyomas (benign tumours) of the intestine. Coeliacs are at twice the risk of these intestinal tumours developing.

Bone density must also be monitored, as coeliac disease is strongly associated with osteoporosis.

Prevention

As coeliac disease is due to a genetic susceptibility, it cannot be prevented.

However, it is possible to prevent the onset of symptoms by following a strictly gluten-free diet. As coeliac disease is a life-long condition, compliance with this diet is necessarily long-term.

Crohn's disease

Symptoms

Crohn's disease is a condition affecting the gastro-intestinal tract which results in inflammation and scarring of the intestine wall. It is a persistent condition characterized by periods of active disease and remission.

Crohn's disease is one of the family of diseases termed inflammatory bowel disease, although the condition can affect any part of the tract from the mouth to the anus. The small bowel is the major site of involvement (80 per cent of cases), and there is large bowel (colonic) disease in 50 per cent of cases.

The symptoms of Crohn's disease are often similar to those of ulcerative colitis, the other major inflammatory bowel disease. Symptoms vary according to site, severity and extent of disease. The small bowel is the main site for the absorption of digested food nutrients, and disease in this area may result in

malabsorption. Disease affecting the colon may lead to the passage of blood in faeces, and incontinence may occur in rectal disease. Oral Crohn's disease often causes persistent mouth ulcers.

The following general symptoms are typical when the disease is active:
■ Pain
■ Urgent diarrhoea
■ Weight loss
■ Mild fever.

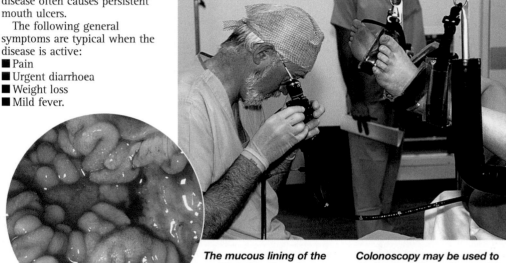

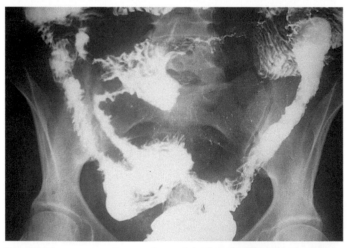

The mucous lining of the small intestine has a distinctive 'cobblestone' appearance in Crohn's disease. This is a result of ulceration.

Colonoscopy may be used to diagnose Crohn's disease. The colonoscope may be fitted with surgical instruments to retrieve tissue samples.

Diagnosis

Blood tests may reveal anaemia caused by malabsorption of iron, and laboratory tests of faeces should be performed to ensure that the symptoms are not due to infection.

Barium X-rays may reveal areas of ulceration, gut wall thickening or stricture. In the majority of patients, the diagnosis is confirmed by tissue biopsy with demonstration of tissue changes characteristic of Crohn's disease.

Rectal biopsy is undertaken using a sigmoidoscope, a telescopic device inserted via the anus. The large bowel is

A barium contrast X-ray of the abdomen and pelvis may confirm a diagnosis of Crohn's disease. The affected gut is thickened and pitted with fissured ulcers.

investigated using colonoscopy, in which a flexible fibre-optic camera tube, inserted via the anus, is manipulated round the large bowel loops.

The small bowel is imaged and biopsied using endoscopy: a fibre-optic camera inserted via the mouth and into the stomach.

These procedures require mild sedation, but are undertaken as day cases in most hospitals.

Causes

No single cause of Crohn's disease has yet been identified. It is probable that genetic factors place a predisposed individual at greater risk of developing the disease when exposed to 'trigger' environmental factors.
■ Genetic factors – there is an increased incidence of the disease in relatives of patients with Crohn's disease

Granulomas (growths of inflammatory tissue) are visible on this micrograph of the intestinal wall as the multiple areas of blue staining.

■ Environmental factors – several infectious agents, including the measles virus and an organism called *Mycobacterium tuberculosis* have been implicated as possible causative agents for Crohn's disease, but studies have failed to prove a definitive link
■ Diet – high intake of refined sugars and a low intake of fibre have been suggested as possible causes, but evidence is weak
■ Smoking – this is more common in Crohn's sufferers disease than in unaffected people, and is associated with more frequent relapse of the disease.

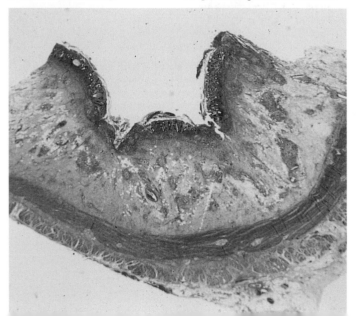

Treatment

In the majority of instances, treatment of Crohn's disease is by drug therapy, although surgical intervention may be required.

■ **General and supportive care**
Patients should be encouraged to maintain a balanced diet with adequate fibre. During periods of active disease, it is important to prevent dehydration and the depletion of blood electrolytes. Vitamin and mineral supplements should be given to correct deficiencies resulting from malabsorption.

■ **Surgical therapy**
Surgery is reserved for attacks resistant to drugs and other forms of treatment. Surgery is commonly employed for treatment of perforation, fistulae (abnormal openings between bowel loops), and abscesses and, in most cases, damaged areas of the gut will be removed.

This false-colour X-ray shows a colonoscope passing through the colon. The progression of Crohn's disease may be monitored using this technique.

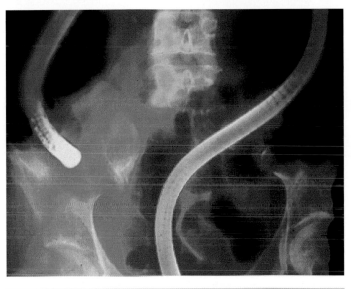

Drug treatment

Drug treatment includes:
■ Corticosteroids (most commonly prednisolone) are drugs that reduce inflammation and are the treatment of choice for active Crohn's disease
■ Aminosalicylates – such as sulphasalazine and mesalazine – may be used to treat colonic disease; these drugs may include coatings which are dissolved by differing levels of acidity present in the gut
■ Non-steroidal immunosuppressive therapy with drugs such as azathioprine may also be used when side effects of steroid drugs become unacceptable; these drugs are termed 'steroid sparing' drugs

Prednisolone is widely used in the treatment of Crohn's disease. It is taken orally and acts to suppress the symptoms and inflammation.

■ Antibiotics – most commonly metronidazole – may be used for treatment of fistulae and anal disease
■ An elemental diet – comprising a solution of essential amino acids, carbohydrate, fat, vitamins and trace elements – may be of use in the treatment of active disease of the ileum.
  Antimotility drugs, such as loperamide, may be given to reduce the diarrhoea.

Prognosis

Crohn's disease can be a painful and debilitating condition. The symptoms are unpleasant and can be embarrassing and this fact may lead to additional stress for patients. Accordingly, counselling and support should be offered in dealing with the associated problems; referral to self-help groups may be useful.

In the future, improvements in drug preparations will hopefully improve the medical management of Crohn's disease. At present, more than 50 per cent of patients will require surgery for the condition at some point in their life.

Surgery for Crohn's disease usually involves the removal of a section of gut. Many patients will need such an operation.

It is not just the intestines that can be affected in Crohn's disease. The mouth may also become ulcerated and painful.

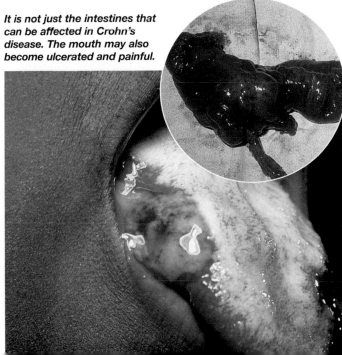

Incidence

Crohn's disease is most common in developed countries. Due to developments in diagnostic techniques, patients are diagnosed at a younger age.

There are approximately five new cases of Crohn's disease per 100,000 people each year, although this figure appears to be increasing slightly, especially among younger people. The disease affects all races, but is generally a disease of developed countries, with between 30,000 and 40,000 people affected in the UK alone.

The majority of patients first report symptoms between 15 and 35 years of age.

Ulcerative colitis

Symptoms

Ulcerative colitis is a non-infectious disease of the mucous membrane (mucosa) lining the gut, which becomes inflamed and ulcerated.

It always affects the rectum and often spreads back up the large intestine to involve part or all of the colon. In severe cases, inflammatory polyps can form.

CLINICAL FEATURES

The symptoms of an acute attack of ulcerative colitis include:
- Frequent bloody diarrhoea
- Fever
- Malaise
- Loss of appetite/weight loss
- Abdominal cramps
- Pain on the left side of the abdomen on opening the bowels
- Rectal pain, bleeding and mucous discharge
- Tenesmus (continuous or recurrent desire to open the bowels, despite passing small amounts of blood and mucus)
- Anaemia – due to blood loss
- Oedema (swelling in tissues) –

due to protein loss
- Mouth ulcers
- Rapid heartbeat (tachycardia).

Some people also develop:
- Rashes
- Inflammatory eye conditions
- Joint problems
- Liver, kidney and gall bladder disorders
- Blood clots (thromboses).

COMPLICATIONS

In an acute attack, life-threatening complications can occur. These include:
- Toxic dilatation – the large intestine becomes dilated, its walls stretching and thinning
- Perforation of the large intestine – the abdomen becomes rigid and extremely tender and the patient may suffer severe shock
- Massive haemorrhage.

Sufferers of ulcerative colitis often feel extremely unwell. The patient may need to be hospitalized and connected to a drip to replace lost fluids.

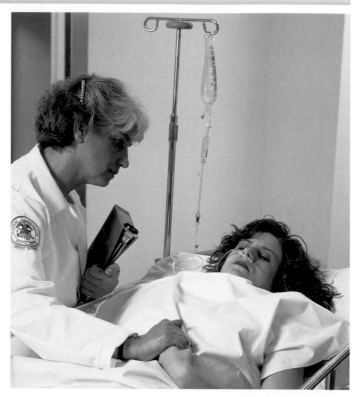

Causes

Although the primary cause of ulcerative colitis is unknown, a number of theories about its causes currently exist. These include:

ENVIRONMENTAL FACTORS

It is thought that ulcerative colitis may result from a genetically determined reaction to a dietary or microbiological factor in the environment, yet to be identified.

FAMILY HISTORY

The theory that ulcerative colitis may be genetically determined is supported by the fact that 10–15 per cent of patients have a first-degree relative (for example, parent or sibling) with ulcerative colitis or Crohn's disease. The latter is an

Inflammation of the bowel can bring about symptoms of the disease. Here, mucous glands (orange) are abnormally raised above the mucosal lining (pink).

inflammatory disease that can affect the gastro-intestinal tract from the mouth to the anus, and appears to have similar origins to ulcerative colitis.

Another indication of a genetic predisposition to ulcerative colitis is that sufferers often have a history of other diseases that can also run in families. These conditions include:
- Allergic diseases, such as asthma or eczema
- Auto-immune diseases, such as systemic lupus erythematosus or chronic active hepatitis.

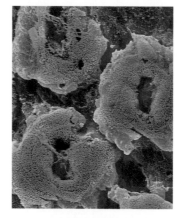

VIRAL LINK

Viruses have been isolated in tissue taken from people suffering from ulcerative colitis, suggesting that there may be a link between the two, although no definite evidence exists.

INFLUENCE OF SMOKING

The risk of developing ulcerative colitis appears to be increased in non-smokers and ex-smokers, but the reasons for this are not fully understood.

About one in 10 people with ulcerative colitis have a close relative with the disease. This confirms that there is a genetic predisposition to the condition.

Incidence

Ulcerative colitis occurs more often in the West than in less developed countries and its incidence appears to be increasing. Each year in Europe and the USA, about 10 per 100,000 of the population develop ulcerative colitis and about 150 per 100,000 suffer from it at any one time.

There are no major differences in incidence between men and women. The disease often first occurs in early adult life, but all ages can be affected.

Ulcerative colitis is more prevalent in the Western world than in less developed countries. The reasons for this are unclear.

Diagnosis

The diagnosis of ulcerative colitis can be delayed as patients are often reluctant to talk about their symptoms for fear that they have developed bowel cancer.

There are no specific clinical signs of ulcerative colitis, but the abdomen may be slightly distended and tender.

INVESTIGATIONS
Investigations include:
■ Laboratory stool examination to exclude infection
■ Plain abdominal X-ray
■ Barium enema – barium sulphate, which is opaque to X-rays, is used as a contrast medium during X-ray of the intestines
■ Rectal examination – this may reveal the presence of blood
■ Colonoscopy
■ Ultrasound and/or CT scans
■ Blood tests for anaemia and liver function.

Diseases to be excluded

before diagnosing ulcerative colitis include:
■ Infectious colitis, caused by bacteria, viruses, parasites or protozoa such as amoebae
■ Pseudomembranous colitis, which may follow some courses of antibiotics
■ Crohn's disease, which is

sometimes impossible to distinguish from ulcerative colitis
■ Diverticulitis – inflammation of pouches that form at weakened areas in the wall of the lower intestine
■ Tumours in the colon and rectum.

A colonoscopy involves the use of a flexible fibre-optic viewing instrument. This is inserted via the anus and then guided through the colon.

Colonoscopy enables a view of the lining of the rectum and colon to be obtained. Areas of inflammation and haemorrhage may be seen.

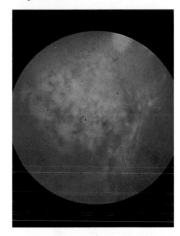

Treatment

Ulcerative colitis is treated either by drugs or surgery.

DRUG TREATMENT
The mainstays of treatment, which can be given by mouth or rectally, are:
■ Derivatives of 5-aminosalicylic acid
■ Corticosteroids (in a severe

In severe cases of ulcerative colitis, the entire colon may be removed. The cut end of the ileum is brought out onto the abdominal surface (stoma), the faeces draining into a bag.

attack, high doses may be life-saving).

In some cases, the dose of steroids may be reduced with the use of azathioprine, an immunosuppressant drug. Cyclosporin has also helped some very ill patients.

Patients with frequent relapses – which can be brought on by stress, antibiotics or non-steroidal anti-inflammatory drugs (NSAIDs) – often receive maintenance therapy with sulphasalazine, or a 5-aminosalicylic acid preparation.

SURGERY
In very severe ulcerative colitis, it may be necessary to remove part or all of the colon (a procedure called a colectomy), or most of the rectum and the colon. Surgery is also necessary if the disease is not responding to treatment or if the treatment causes unacceptable side effects.

Post-operatively, some patients will need a permanent ileostomy. In this operation the ileum is brought through the abdominal wall, and an artificial opening (known as a stoma) created, allowing the contents of the large intestine to drain through into a bag.

Alternatively, an ileorectal anastomosis can be formed, which avoids the need for an ileostomy. In this operation a pouch of small bowel is sewn onto the rectum and acts as a reservoir for liquid faeces. The faeces are then passed in the usual way several times a day.

Large intestine (colon)
Removed in surgery

Small intestine (ileum)

Stoma
Artificial opening of the ileum to the surface

Ileostomy bag

Rectum

Cancer risks

Patients with long-standing, extensive ulcerative colitis (eight years or more), liver complications and a family history of colon cancer are at increased risk of developing colon cancer. Ulcerative colitis sufferers should have regular follow-up and colonoscopies to detect disease and allow early treatment.

Prognosis

The prognosis is variable. Some people have only one attack of the disease, while others develop chronic symptoms or have intermittent relapses. The severity of a relapse is related to the extent to which the large intestine is affected and how deeply the ulcers have penetrated into the wall of the large intestine. It is during the first year that patients are most likely to need a colectomy.

LONG-TERM OUTLOOK
Long periods of complete remission are common, but after two years, only 20 per cent of patients will have had no relapses and less than five per cent after 10 years. Eventually, surgery is needed in 30 per cent of patients.

Colorectal cancer

Symptoms

Colorectal cancer (cancer of the colon or rectum) is the most common gastro-intestinal cancer in the UK. With early diagnosis the outlook is good, but early disease is often symptomless and many cases are not diagnosed until the cancer has spread to other parts of the body (metastasized).

Symptoms and signs of colorectal cancer, which may be related to the primary disease or its secondary effects, include:
■ A change in bowel habit, such as diarrhoea or constipation
■ A feeling of incomplete bowel emptying
■ A continuous or repeated desire to open the bowels (tenesmus), even if only small amounts of faeces (or of blood or mucus) are passed
■ Rectal bleeding – either fresh or dark blood
■ Lower abdominal pain
■ Iron-deficiency anaemia – caused by tumour bleeding
■ Weight loss, loss of appetite and fatigue.

Cases of severe colic, pain or rectal bleeding are often seen as emergencies, and account for 25 per cent of colorectal cancers.

WHO IS AFFECTED?
More than 750,000 cases of colorectal cancer are diagnosed worldwide each year.
■ Most colorectal cancer occurs in developed countries. In Europe and North America, colorectal cancer is the most common cause of cancer death in non-smokers
■ People aged 60 or over are at most risk
■ Colon cancer affects both sexes equally, but rectal cancer is more common in men.

In Britain, the lifetime risk for colorectal cancer is one in 25, but a family history of this type of cancer can double the risk.

In the early stages, colorectal cancer often has no symptoms. The disease may be picked up during regular screening of the colon and rectum.

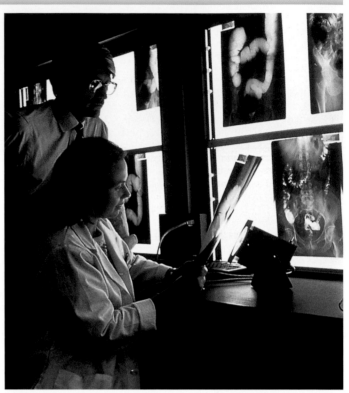

Diagnosis

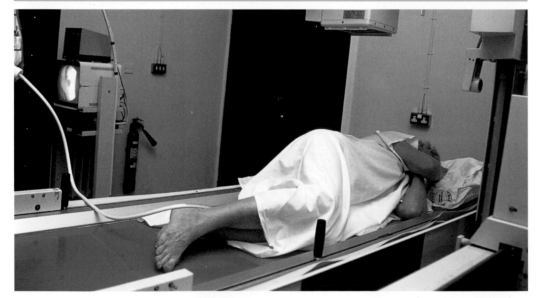

Untreated, colorectal cancer eventually spreads through the bowel wall and invades nearby organs such as the bladder and the prostate.

Cancer cells also spread to lymph nodes and through the bloodstream to form secondary growths (metastases), especially in the liver and lungs.

Usual investigations include:
■ A rectal examination – can detect 75 per cent of rectal tumours

■ Sigmoidoscopy – a sigmoidoscope provides a view of the rectum and the lower colon (the sigmoid colon)
■ Colonoscopy – the colon and rectum are viewed through a fibre-optic or video camera instrument. Tissue samples can be collected, and polyps can often be removed during the colonoscopy, avoiding the need for an abdominal operation
■ Barium enema – radio-opaque barium sulphate is

A barium contrast X-ray can help to diagnose colorectal cancer. Since barium is opaque to X-rays, the procedure detects any abnormalities in the bowel.

given rectally. A double contrast barium enema using air can be carried out for a clearer picture
■ Ultrasound and/or computed tomography (CT) scans
■ Blood tests to assess anaemia and liver function.

Causes

The risk factors for colorectal cancer include:
■ Diet – with high animal fat, low-fibre diets, the bowel contents stagnate and substances that may cause cancer (carcinogens) remain in contact with the bowel wall
■ Genetic factors – a family history doubles or trebles the risk. Cancer may result from the rare inherited condition called familial adenomatous polyposis
■ Inflammatory bowel disease (ulcerative colitis and Crohn's disease) – extensive colitis for more than 10 years increases the risk of colon cancer
■ Lifestyle – it is thought that increased alcohol intake, being overweight and lack of exercise may contribute to the risk.

TUMOUR ORIGIN
Most colorectal cancers develop from benign tumours or polyps arising from the glandular bowel lining. The malignant changes in the tissue can take up to 5–10 years to develop.

A series of genetic alterations such as mutations within oncogenes (genes that regulate processes such as cell division) and tumour suppressor genes on specific chromosomes occur in the tumour.

Treatment

Treatment depends on how far the cancer has spread:

■ Surgery
Most patients are treated surgically with the hope of curing the disease if it is localized to the intestinal wall, or relieving symptoms in advanced cancer. It is often necessary to remove a length of intestine with the tumour. The ends of the intestines can usually be rejoined, but this may be impossible with cancer that is low in the rectum. A colostomy (an opening in the abdominal wall through which intestinal contents are evacuated) may then be necessary.

■ Chemotherapy
Chemotherapy is increasingly used to prevent recurrences and improve survival after surgery. 5-fluorouracil (5-FU) with folinic acid 7 is a well-established therapy, but many new developments are taking place in this field.

■ Liver metastases
If the tumour has only metastasized to the liver, the surgical removal of one or more metastases is possible. With inoperable liver metastases, a pump may be implanted for continuous chemotherapy.

■ Gene therapy
Several approaches are under investigation, but there are practical difficulties; for example, replacing a single gene is unlikely to be effective and people at high risk would need therapy for many decades.

■ Immunotherapy
Immunotherapy with monoclonal antibodies may increase survival when used in addition to surgery.

Chemotherapy is used to treat patients suffering from advanced colorectal cancer. Suitable drugs are injected intravenously and destroy the cancerous cells.

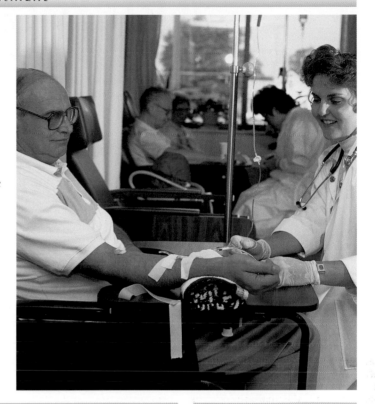

Prognosis

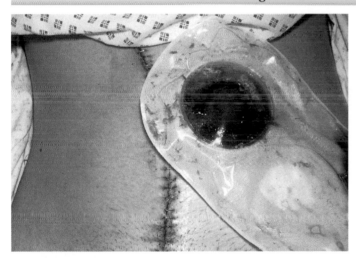

Survival is directly related to the extent of the disease at the time of an operation.

Overall, 40 per cent of people with colorectal cancer survive for five years from the time of the diagnosis; the figure rises to 70 per cent in people treated with surgery for localized disease. Under three per cent of people with distant metastases survive for five years.

During a bowel resection for colon cancer, a colostomy may be created. The cut end of bowel is brought out to the surface of the abdomen and a bag applied to collect faeces.

Incidence

Incidence data include:
■ About 30,000 people develop colorectal cancer every year in the UK
■ Colon cancer is 2.5 times more common than rectal cancer
■ Colon tumours are slightly more frequent in women than in men, whereas rectal carcinomas are more common in men than in women
■ The risk of developing colorectal tumours increases after the age of 40; the peak mean age is 60–65 years
■ The incidence of colorectal cancer is higher in industrialized regions.

Screening

■ Tests for blood in the stools (faecal occult blood tests) – detect bleeding before it is visible to the naked eye, but may give false positive results or miss tumours that bleed only intermittently
■ Regular colonoscopy – targeted at patients with high risk of colorectal cancer; reduces cancer deaths
■ Stool DNA tests – abnormal DNA from cancer cells in the stool is detectable with modern techniques
■ Genetic testing – in the future, genetic testing will identify people at risk so that they can be screened.

Prevention

Preventive measures include:
■ Regular screening for high-risk groups
■ Removal of polyps before they become cancerous
■ A low-fat, high-fibre diet
■ Hormone replacement therapy (HRT) – lowers the incidence of colorectal cancer in women
■ Non-steroidal anti-inflammatories – reduce polyp counts in familial adenomatous polyposis and lower death rates from colorectal cancer.

A low-fat, high-fibre diet is believed to protect against colorectal cancer. Dietary discipline is vital for people in high-risk groups.

Haemorrhoids

Symptoms

Haemorrhoids (commonly known as piles) are varicose veins of the anal canal. They appear as abnormally swollen cushions of tissue in the walls of the anal canal and may protrude through the anus.

The most common and earliest symptom of haemorrhoids is bright red bleeding when the bowels open (defecation). This is often slight, but may increase and persist for months.

Less common symptoms include anal itching, discomfort and pain, particularly if the haemorrhoids become inflamed, a heavy feeling in the rectum, and a mucous discharge from the anus.

TYPES OF HAEMORRHOID
Haemorrhoids are classed as:
■ First-degree – these stay inside the anus, but bleed during defecation
■ Second-degree – these bulge down (prolapse) through the anus during bowel opening, but return inside afterwards
■ Third-degree – these stay outside the anal canal unless pushed back by hand
■ Fourth-degree – these stay outside the anus all the time.

Haemorrhoids are varicose veins of the anal canal, which may involve veins at the upper or lower margins of the canal.

Haemorrhoids may occur outside the anal canal, when they are sometimes known as prolapsing haemorrhoids. They may need surgical removal.

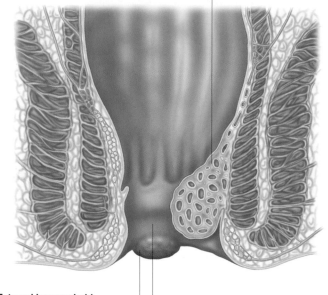

Internal haemorrhoid
Cross-section shows the multiple channels of varicosed vein inside the swelling

External haemorrhoid
A skin-covered varicosed anal vein that cannot be pushed back into the anal canal

Anus

Diagnosis

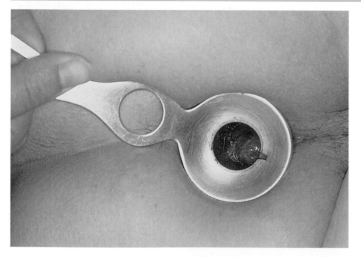

It is vitally important that anyone who passes blood with a motion sees a doctor as soon as possible in order to determine the cause of the bleeding. Conditions that cause symptoms similar to those of haemorrhoids include prolapse of the rectum, inflammatory bowel disease, anal polyps and fissures (splits in the lining of the anal canal) and even some forms of bowel cancer.

A proctoscope is an instrument that allows a doctor to visualize the anal canal. This is useful in the investigation of conditions such as haemorrhoids.

The doctor will need to examine the patient's abdomen, groin and genitals and then inspect the anus, rectum and lower bowel with a proctoscope and sigmoidoscope. These are metal instruments that give a view of the inner lining of the anal canal and lower bowel.

If the diagnosis is in doubt, the removal of a small piece of tissue for examination under the microscope (biopsy) may be necessary. A blood test to check for anaemia may also be necessary, as persistently bleeding haemorrhoids can cause anaemia because of the loss of iron in the blood.

Causes

Chronic constipation is the most common cause of haemorrhoids. This is often due to insufficient fibre in the diet. Prolonged straining to pass hard motions increases the pressure in the abdomen and the blood vessels in the anal region become congested.

Other risk factors include:
■ Pregnancy and delivery
■ Straining to pass urine –

as may happen with men with an enlarged prostate gland
■ Obesity
■ Jobs involving heavy lifting or sitting for long periods
■ A bad attack of diarrhoea.

Pregnancy is a well-known risk factor for developing haemorrhoids. This is because the pregnant uterus can compress the rectal veins.

Treatment

Many patients with mild symptoms can often treat themselves or will only need advice on diet and laxatives. Washing round the anus with tepid water and cotton wool and drying the area gently may help avoid irritation.

SYMPTOMATIC TREATMENT
Itching and soreness usually respond to ointments and suppositories and steroid creams may be soothing. Local anaesthetics can be used for acute pain, but not for more than a few days as they may irritate the anal skin.

If symptoms persist, surgical help may be needed. The aim is to remove the haemorrhoids completely or to thrombose (clot) the blood vessels in the haemorrhoids so that they wither away. There is a wide choice of methods including sclerotherapy, which involves injecting the haemorrhoids to block the blood flow, coagulation (by various means) and scalpel or laser surgery.

Patients with large prolapsing haemorrhoids associated with skin tags may need haemorrhoidectomy, an operation in which the haemorrhoids are tied off and removed. Post-operatively, non-steroidal anti-inflammatory drugs (NSAIDs) may relieve any discomfort.

Haemorrhoids may be treated with a number of over-the-counter preparations. Soothing creams, such as Anusol, help to relieve pain and itching.

Operating to remove haemorrhoids is not without possible complications. The wound shown here has ruptured and become infected.

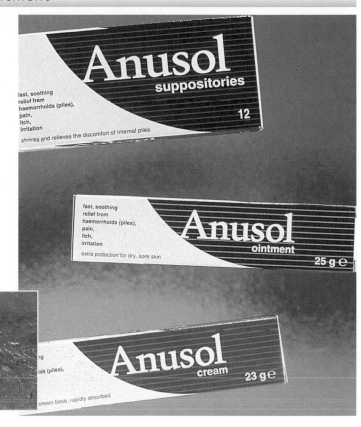

Prognosis

Once a definite diagnosis of haemorrhoids is made, patients can be reassured that they are not suffering from a serious disease. Many patients have minor haemorrhoids for years with little or nothing in the way of symptoms; others have short episodes of bleeding and pain that soon settles spontaneously.

Patients with more severe symptoms usually respond well

Maintaining a healthy lifestyle is important in reducing the risk of haemorrhoids. Drinking plenty of fluids will help to prevent the development of hard faeces.

to treatment but, to avoid a relapse, they must avoid constipation in the future by keeping their faeces soft with a high-fibre diet and lots of fluids.

Patients with haemorrhoids may develop itchy tags of skin around the anal margin. These can usually be removed under a local anaesthetic.

THROMBOTIC PILE
Patients with external haemorrhoids sometimes develop a small but extremely painful swelling beside the anus, known as an acute perianal haematoma or 'thrombotic pile'. This results from the rupture of a small vein in the anus during a bout of straining or coughing. Usually the swelling settles after about five days. If seen early on, it can be drained under a local anaesthetic.

Incidence

Haemorrhoids are very common. At least 40 per cent – and probably more – of the population of the developed world will suffer from haemorrhoids at some time in their lives.

Haemorrhoids are rare in children and tend to develop only after the age of 20. They occur equally in both men and women.

Prevention

To reduce the risk of developing haemorrhoids, patients are advised:
■ To eat a high-fibre diet containing plenty of fresh fruit and vegetables and whole-grain cereals
■ To drink plenty of fluids
■ To keep weight within normal limits
■ To avoid prolonged straining
■ Not to delay emptying the bowels.

Foods with a high dietary fibre content aid digestion, helping to prevent constipation and therefore haemorrhoids.

Cirrhosis

Causes

Cirrhosis is not strictly a disease but rather a syndrome which results from damage of the liver. The liver can regenerate damaged cells, provided the basic structure of the liver remains intact. If disease or alcoholism cause a constant loss of liver cells, the tissue heals by scarring, causing damage to the liver structure. When there is more scarring than healthy liver tissue, cirrhosis results. The blood supply within the liver is altered and the organ becomes inefficient.

Although frequently the result of alcoholism, cirrhosis is also the result of a variety of other pathological processes, which include:
■ Chronic active hepatitis – hepatitis B and C

■ Auto-immune diseases – primary biliary cirrhosis, lupoid hepatitis
■ Haemochromatosis – a hereditary condition where the body absorbs too much iron
■ Wilson's disease – a condition affecting copper metabolism
■ Veno-occlusive disease – may occur in those who drink medicinal teas containing the alkaloid pyrolozidine
■ Obstruction of hepatic veins
■ The effect of certain drugs
■ Cystic fibrosis
■ Glycogen storage diseases
■ Long-standing heart failure (cardiac cirrhosis).

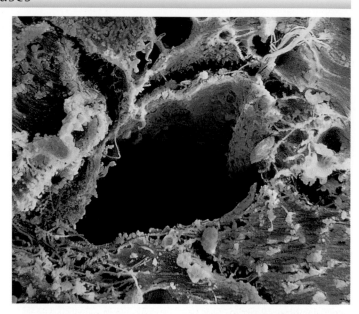

A false-colour image of a lobe of the liver shows cells affected by cirrhosis. Fibrous scar tissue is light brown.

Symptoms and signs

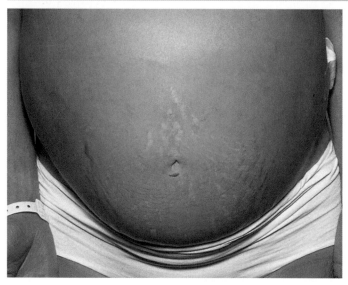

The clinical features of cirrhosis are largely the result of portal hypertension (increased pressure within in the portal vein) and liver cell failure. Portal hypertension causes the enlargement of the spleen, dilated veins in the oesophagus and fluid to collect in the peritoneal cavity

Blood clotting factors are produced by the liver. If the liver fails, the lack of these factors causes spontaneous bruising.

This patient has ascites, an accumulation of fluid in the abdomen leading to swelling. This is a typical sign of cirrhosis.

(ascites). Initially the liver may be enlarged, but as the disease progresses it usually shrinks and becomes contracted.

Liver failure results in lower levels of proteins and clotting factors in the blood and waste products not being excreted efficiently.

Jaundice and itching may be accompanied by destruction of the skin's surface layer and pigmentation changes. Lack of clotting factors results in spontaneous bruising. Spider naevi (small, red areas of skin caused by dilated superficial veins) may be apparent on the upper body, and fat deposits may occur in the eyelids.

Swollen abdomen (ascites) with characteristic distended veins may also be evident. Patients may suffer abdominal pain with loss of appetite, nausea and vomiting (with blood if oesophageal veins rupture).

Feminization may occur in men due to hormonal

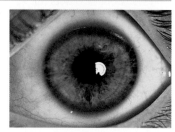

Kayser-Fleischer rings – a brown outer ring in the eye – are caused by deposits of copper in the cornea. This is diagnostic of Wilson's disease.

imbalances, and in cirrhosis due to Wilson's disease, brown rings may be seen in the cornea (Kayser-Fleischer rings).

Diagnosis

A diagnosis of cirrhosis can be confirmed by the following investigations:
■ Haematology. A full blood count may reveal anaemia (due to bleeding), increased size of red blood cells and clotting abnormalities
■ Microbiology. Hepatitis B, C, or D viral studies are done
■ Immunology. Immunoglobulin and antibodies may suggest an auto-immune cause
■ Diagnostic imaging. Ultrasound, CT scan or MR imaging may reveal abnormalities
■ Biochemistry. Albumen (a protein in blood) levels will be decreased
■ Raised liver enzymes and

bilirubin (breakdown products of haemoglobin). Serum iron and copper may reveal haemo-chromatosis (raised iron) or Wilson's disease (raised copper).

This micrograph shows liver tissue affected by chronic hepatitis. Darker inflammatory cells group around enlarged portal tracts (white holes).

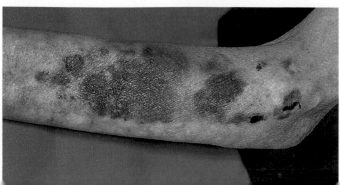

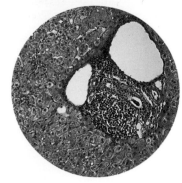

Treatment

Treatment of cirrhosis must be directed to the particular cause:
■ Chronic viral hepatitis B and C can be controlled with the drug interferon alpha, which is effective in reducing the activity of the virus
■ Auto-immune hepatitis is treated with immunosuppressant drugs, such as corticosteroids prednisone and azathioprine
■ Bleeding from distended veins in the oesophagus (bleeding varices), due to high blood pressure in the liver, is treated with the drugs octreotide, vasopressin and propranolol.

TREATING OTHER CAUSES
In cholestatic liver disease, caused by gall stones in the bile duct, for example, bile acids such as ursodeoxycholic acid are used along with surgery to remove the blockage.

Haemochromatosis, in which excessive amounts of iron are stored, damaging the liver, may require repeated blood letting or chelating drugs, which bind with iron to enable its safe excretion.

Effectively treating cirrhosis caused by alcohol requires the patient to abstain from alcohol. Psychological treatment for alcohol abuse is often necessary. Vitamin supplements are required to correct any deficiencies.

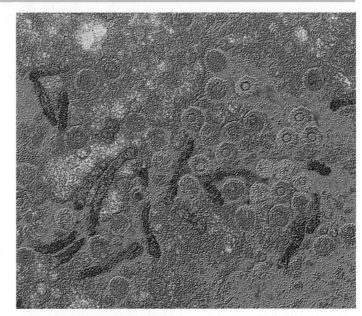

Infection with hepatitis B virus (pictured) is recognized as being a risk factor in developing cirrhosis. The virus cannot be destroyed, but it can be controlled with antiviral drugs.

Complications and prognosis

The most important complications of cirrhosis are:
■ Portal hypertension. This causes bleeding varices (in the oesophagus), swollen abdomen and haemorrhoids

■ Liver cancer. Cirrhosis is implicated in cancers of the liver, which typically arise from multiple sites
■ Liver failure. Causes symptoms resulting from inadequate production of some proteins and clotting factors.

Other complications occur due to the liver failing to break down and excrete various toxins. Prognosis depends on the cause but many patients can be very satisfactorily treated.

TRANSPLANTATION
Liver transplantation is a procedure that has continued since its introduction in 1963. The procedure may be indicated if the estimated survival of the patient is less than one year, or if patient's quality of life is intolerable.

Transplantation is not recommended under certain circumstances. These include patients with primary or secondary liver cancer, continued alcohol abuse, AIDS, hepatitis B infection or significant psychiatric disease.

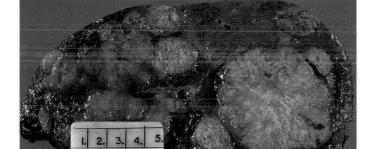

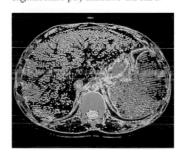

The commonest cancers in the liver spread from other organs – from the bowel, in this case. In cirrhosis, a tumour may develop in the liver cells directly.

This CT scan shows an enlarged spleen (green) due to portal hypertension. The enlarged liver appears as the yellow mass.

Incidence

Cirrhosis occurs in all age groups but particularly affects people over 30 years old. It affects men and women of all racial groups, and it can be caused by hereditary conditions. Geographically, the condition is found worldwide.

Hepatitis infection is an important factor in developing cirrhosis, particularly if combined with alcohol abuse. Many patients who are chronic carriers of hepatitis C will develop cirrhosis. About 10–20 per cent of patients infected with hepatitis B become chronic carriers of the virus, and about 20 per cent of these chronic carriers develop cirrhosis.

Prevention

Cirrhosis may be prevented in cases of alcohol abuse when the abuse is recognized early and by the treatment of any of the curable or controllable conditions. However, some conditions, such as primary biliary cirrhosis and some inherited causes, are not preventable.

Tattooing has been a common route for the transmission of viral hepatitis, so extreme caution is advised when considering this form of body adornment.

If chronic alcohol abuse is treated early enough, long-term complications, including cirrhosis, may be avoided.

Gallstones

Symptoms

The gall bladder is a pear-shaped sac that acts as a reservoir and concentrator of bile; it lies under the right lobe of the liver. Gallstones are hard masses composed of cholesterol, bile pigment and calcium in varying proportions that form in the gall bladder. Gallstones may be solitary or multiple, and as large as a golf ball or as small as a grain of sand. In developed countries, 80 per cent of gallstones consist predominantly of cholesterol.

Only about 20 per cent of gallstones ever cause symptoms. The remainder are discovered incidentally during investigations for other problems.

■ Acute cholecystitis
Acute inflammation of the gall bladder may cause mild or severe pain under the right ribs, which may radiate to the back and shoulder. Vomiting, fever and mild jaundice may occur. Gallstones are found in the gall bladder in over 90 per cent of cases of acute cholecystitis. Serious complications include perforation of the gall bladder, abscesses and peritonitis (inflammation of the membrane surrounding the abdominal cavity).

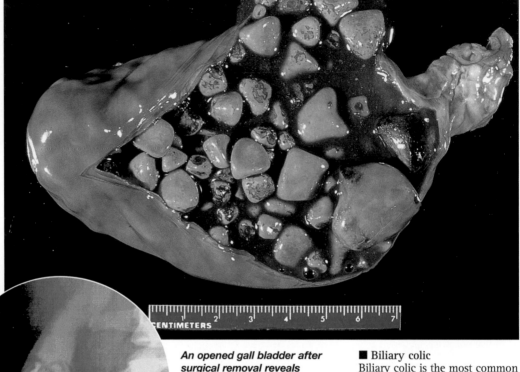

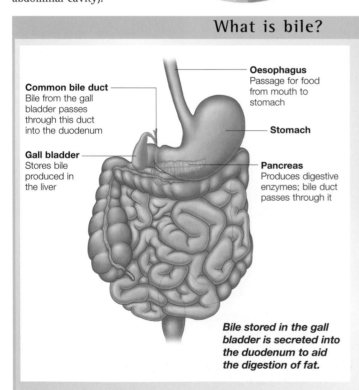

An opened gall bladder after surgical removal reveals gallstones of varying sizes. Symptoms range from mild discomfort to severe pain.

Gallstones can be seen within a gall bladder on this coloured X-ray. The gallstones are highlighted with iodine which the patient takes orally.

■ Biliary colic
Biliary colic is the most common symptom of gallstones. It occurs when a gallstone obstructs the flow of bile from the gall bladder or through the common bile duct. The pain is intermittent and felt under the right ribs. It may be mild or severe and may last for several hours, often after a meal.

■ Chronic cholecystitis
Gallstones increase the risk of chronic cholecystitis (chronic inflammation of the gall bladder). The gall bladder becomes scarred and cannot contract normally. Patients may develop chronic pain beneath the right ribs.

■ Stones in common bile duct
These may cause recurrent pain to the centre and right of the upper abdomen, fever and jaundice with dark urine and light-coloured stools.

■ Cholangitis
Inflammation of the bile ducts is a serious complication of gallstones. Patients may be very ill, often with high fever.

■ Pancreatitis
Inflammation of the pancreas is a possible complication of gallstones. Symptoms include pain in the upper abdomen and back; nausea and vomiting are also common.

What is bile?

Common bile duct
Bile from the gall bladder passes through this duct into the duodenum

Gall bladder
Stores bile produced in the liver

Oesophagus
Passage for food from mouth to stomach

Stomach

Pancreas
Produces digestive enzymes; bile duct passes through it

Bile stored in the gall bladder is secreted into the duodenum to aid the digestion of fat.

Bile is a thick, bitter, yellow or greenish fluid that aids the digestion of fats. It is secreted by the liver and stored in the gall bladder until it is needed. After a meal, the gall bladder secretes bile into the duodenum via a tube called the common bile duct. This shares its opening into the duodenum with a duct from the pancreas called the pancreatic duct. Bile contains:

■ Water
■ Cholesterol
   A fat-like substance mostly formed in the liver but also obtained from the diet
■ Fats and fatty acids
■ Lecithin
■ Bile salts
   Necessary for the emulsification of fats
■ Inorganic salts
■ Bile pigments
   Break down products of blood haemoglobin.

Diagnosis

The clinical history and examination of a patient often suggest the presence of gallstones. A distended and/or tender gall bladder on abdominal examination indicates gall bladder disease and the probable presence of gallstones.

Other investigations include:
■ Ultrasound scan – detects gallstones in the gall bladder
■ Scintiscan – a radioactive tracer can be used to diagnose gallstones in the bile duct
■ Endoscopic retrograde cholangeopancreatography (ERCP) – a radio-opaque dye is injected directly into the bile duct to confirm the diagnosis of stones in the common bile duct and also when removing them endoscopically
■ Intravenous cholecystography – injection of a radio-opaque medium may outline gallstones on X-ray
■ Abdominal X-ray – calcified gallstones (10 per cent of cases) also show on plain X-ray.

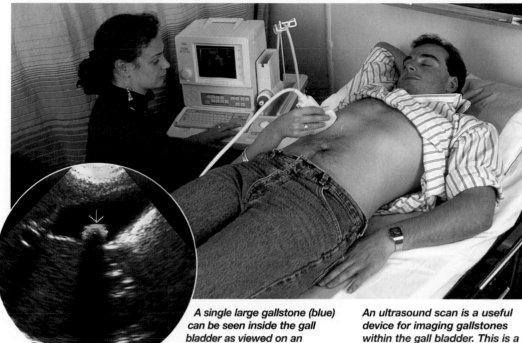

A single large gallstone (blue) can be seen inside the gall bladder as viewed on an ultrasound scan. The patient may have no symptoms of gallstones.

An ultrasound scan is a useful device for imaging gallstones within the gall bladder. This is a painless and reliable method of investigation.

Causes

Cholesterol gallstones form when the bile contains too much cholesterol and the gall bladder fails to empty efficiently.

Risk factors include:
■ Being female. Gallstones are more common in young women than in men
■ Diet. Fasting decreases gall bladder movement, and fat breakdown during rapid weight loss increases cholesterol excretion; a diet high in animal fats also increases risk
■ Ethnic origin. Native and Mexican Americans are genetically predisposed
■ Drugs. Excess cholesterol

passes into the bile when drugs are taken to lower blood cholesterol levels
■ Pregnancy, the contraceptive pill and hormone replacement therapy increase the risk
■ Obesity
■ Diabetes.

PIGMENT STONES
Pigment stones form when bile becomes saturated with bilirubin. They occur in the common bile duct after gall bladder removal, with infections of the biliary tract, and with blood disorders in which red blood cells are excessively broken down, such as sickle-cell anaemia.

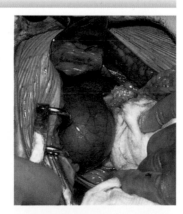

Prognosis

About 10 per cent of patients with symptomless gallstones develop symptoms within five years of diagnosis. With gallstones in the bile duct, 20 per cent of asymptomatic patients develop complications, such as cholecystitis or jaundice.

Incidence

Gallstones occur in people of all ages and races. In developed countries, about 10–20 per cent of the population have gallstones, and they are the most common digestive cause of hospital admission. Gallstones are rare in Asia and Africa.

Treatment

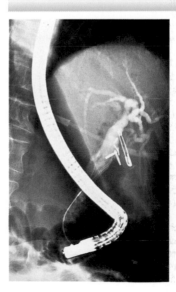

This X-ray shows an operation to remove gallstones. An endoscope, visible within the bile duct (white tube), provides a clear view of the gallstones.

Symptomless gallstones in the gall bladder are left untreated. Symptomatic gallstones are often treated by removal of the gall bladder (cholecystectomy). Laparoscopic (keyhole) or open surgery is usually the treatment of first choice.

Stones in the common bile duct may be removed using an endoscope. If too large to be removed whole, they can be crushed mechanically or fragmented by extracorporeal shockwave lithotripsy (ESWL).

If surgery is not used, attempts may be made to dissolve the gallstones with oral doses of bile acid preparations, but this is only suitable for patients with mild symptoms and small, non-calcified stones. Stones re-form in five per cent of patients.

Patients with acute cholecystitis may need antibiotics and intravenous fluids, and cholecystectomy is performed later. Antibiotics and decompression of the bile duct may be needed in cases of acute cholangitis.

Treatment for chronic cholecystitis is often unsatisfactory. Removing the gall bladder does not always relieve the symptoms.

The surgical removal of the gall bladder is the first choice of treatment for cholecystitis. Keyhole or open surgery (above) techniques can be used.

Hernia

Symptoms

Hernias are swellings formed by organs or tissues protruding through weak spots in the wall of a body cavity, such as the abdomen. Abdominal hernias are the most common types of hernias.

EXTERNAL HERNIAS
External abdominal hernias are visible on the surface of the body and consist of a membranous sac, usually containing fat and often a small length of gut. These include:
■ Inguinal hernias – appear in the groin and sometimes pass down to the scrotum in men
■ Femoral hernias – appear at the top of the thigh
■ Umbilical hernias – these protrude at the umbilicus (navel)
■ Epigastric hernias – appear in the midline above the umbilicus.

This X-ray shows an example of hiatus hernia. In this condition, stomach acid may reflux (flow back) into the oesophagus (circled).

An inguinal hernia, seen as a lump in this man's groin, is due to fat or part of the gut protruding through the abdominal wall.

INTERNAL HERNIAS
■ Diaphragmatic hernias – abdominal contents protrude through a defect in the diaphragm into the thorax; they may press on the lungs and cause asphyxia. In hiatus hernia, the stomach protrudes through the oesophageal opening in the diaphragm.

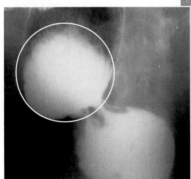

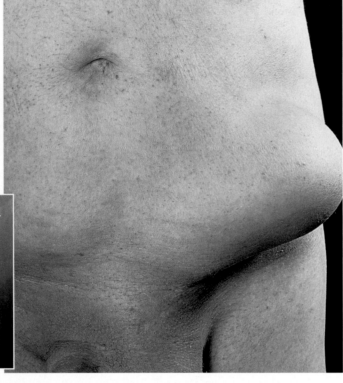

Causes

The repeated strain on the abdominal muscles during coughing may lead to a hernia. This is a particular problem in people who also have congenital weakness of the abdominal muscles.

Stress on the abdominal wall, such as occurs during pregnancy, may cause a hernia. Women may also be at risk of hernia through the incision made for a Caesarean section.

■ Inguinal, umbilical and diaphragmatic hernias are often due to congenital weaknesses in the abdominal wall
■ Indirect inguinal hernias are due to the abnormal persistence of the canals through which testes pass to the scrotum during fetal development
■ Femoral hernias protrude though a weakness where the femoral artery, the main artery to the leg, passes to the thigh.
  Many abdominal hernias are

due to factors that increase pressure in the abdomen, such as:
■ Obesity
■ Coughing or straining
■ Lifting heavy weights
■ Pregnancy.

DIAGNOSIS
Inguinal, femoral, umbilical, epigastric and incisional hernias are usually diagnosed by clinical examination. Hiatus and diaphragmatic hernias are diagnosed by X-ray examination.

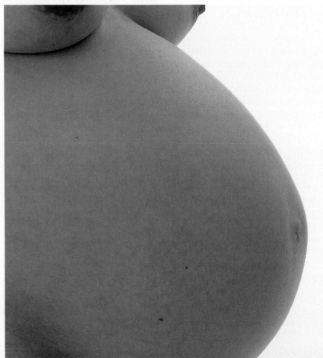

Strangulated hernia

Strangulation occurs when a loop of intestine becomes trapped in a hernia and its blood supply is blocked. Following this:
■ The bowel contents cannot pass through the gut
■ The hernia becomes very painful, and the patient vomits and has severe colic
■ Without treatment, the loop of bowel becomes gangrenous within 5–6 hours and may perforate
■ Generalized abdominal pain develops
■ The bowel becomes paralysed and pain lessens – this is a dangerous sign.

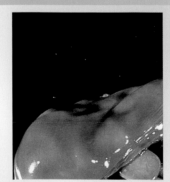

A strangulated hernia is a medical emergency, as blood supply to the affected area is cut. Without surgery, the loop of bowel may burst.

Treatment

With the exception of umbilical hernias in infancy, surgical repair is recommended for almost all external abdominal hernias. The chances of a successful repair are increased if patients:
■ Lose excess weight
■ Avoid constipation
■ Stop smoking to minimize the risk of coughing bouts.

SURGICAL TECHNIQUES
Various stitching and patching techniques have been devised over the years to repair defects in the abdominal wall. Many surgeons now successfully incorporate a fine mesh into their repair. Non-emergency inguinal and femoral hernia repairs are now often performed in day surgery units, sometimes under a local anaesthetic.

Men with hernias were often provided with trusses, but they were uncomfortable and inconvenient and needed very skilled fitting. They are now rarely recommended.

Most patients with hiatus hernias can be treated by controlling acid reflux by:
■ Raising the head of their bed

■ Taking antacids or other drugs which inhibit stomach acid production
■ Losing weight.

Small and moderately sized umbilical hernias in children often disappear without treatment. Infants with large hernias need immediate surgery.

Acid reflux caused by hiatus hernia can be relieved by taking antacid drugs. These inhibit the production of stomach acid.

Surgery is usually the most effective treatment for hernia. Femoral hernias may be treated surgically as day cases.

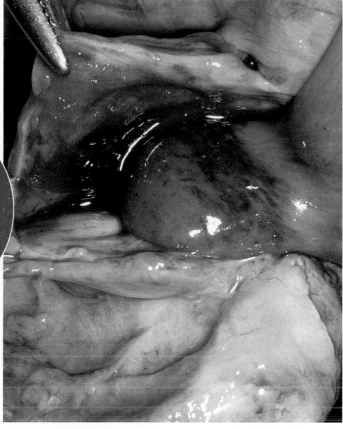

Prognosis

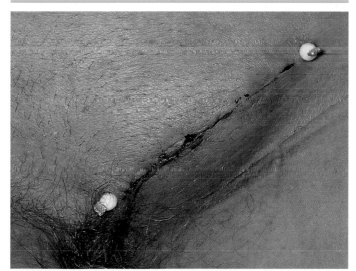

Most external abdominal hernias can be successfully repaired. If untreated, most will increase in size. Indirect inguinal hernias left untreated for years may become extremely large and may grossly distend the scrotum. Direct inguinal hernias do not become so large.

External abdominal hernias do not need to be large to be at risk of strangulation, which can be fatal without prompt surgical treatment. Femoral hernias are more likely to strangulate than inguinal hernias.

The prognosis is good for hernias which have been surgically corrected. Without treatment, strangulated hernias may be fatal.

Hiatus hernias may never cause any symptoms. If acid regurgitation is a problem, medical treatment is usually effective. Prolonged untreated acid reflux may scar the base of the gullet, making swallowing difficult, and pre-cancerous changes may appear in the lining of the oesophagus. These can be reversed with treatment.

Incidence

At least one in 100 people has a hernia at some time. Of these, 70 per cent are inguinal, 20 per cent femoral and 10 per cent umbilical.
■ Indirect inguinal hernias occur most often from infancy to early adult life; they are bilateral in nearly 30 per cent of cases, and men are affected 20 times more often than women
■ 10–20 per cent of inguinal hernias probably originate from muscle damage due to physical strain or trauma (direct inguinal hernias); they usually occur in older men with weak muscles, but occasionally in younger men
■ Femoral hernias are rare before the age of 15, and they affect women twice as often as men; women who have had children are at most risk
■ About 30 per cent of people over the age of 50 suffer a hiatus hernia.

People who regularly lift heavy weights are more prone to abdominal hernias. Using safe lifting techniques can reduce the strain on abdominal muscles.

Appendicitis

Symptoms

Acute appendicitis is the most common cause of severe abdominal pain requiring surgery in the UK. The condition can affect all ages, but is commonest under 40 and is rare before the age of two.

PRESENTATION
The vast majority (95 per cent) of patients will experience:
■ Pain – vague, then localized
■ Lack of appetite.
However, less than 50 per cent of cases exhibit 'typical' signs as appendicitis is a great mimic of other abdominal conditions.

Very young children and older adults often have non-specific symptoms and tend to present later in the disease process, increasing the risk of complication.

The appendix normally lies in the lower right quadrant of the abdomen, and its position determines the location of the pain of appendicitis. An appendix lying behind the large bowel, or down in the pelvis, causes tenderness that may only be found on rectal or pelvic internal examination, whereas pregnancy may displace the appendix, and therefore the pain, upward.

Initially, the pain of appendicitis is felt around the navel and slowly migrates to the right lower part of the abdomen. Nausea and vomiting occur shortly after.

Acute appendicitis

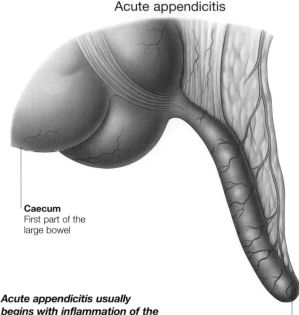

Caecum
First part of the large bowel

Inflamed appendix
Thickened, red and swollen mucosa due to inflammation

Acute appendicitis usually begins with inflammation of the lining of the appendix, which spreads through the wall to involve the covering peritoneum (abdominal lining).

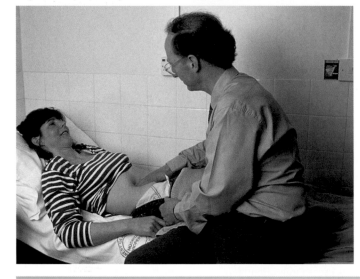

Classic signs of appendicitis

■ Gradual onset of pain in the upper abdomen or around the umbilicus (navel), accompanied by nausea, vomiting and lack of appetite
■ After a few hours, the pain shifts to the lower right quadrant (McBurney's point), with tenderness on direct pressure and on release of the pressure (rebound tenderness)
■ Patient shows 'guarding' – the abdominal muscles contract on palpation or coughing
■ Low grade fever: temperature 37.7–38.3 °C (100–101 °F)
■ Low-grade raised white blood cell count (leucocytosis).

Diagnosis

Diagnosis is usually based on the patient's history and their clinical picture. The typical picture of acute appendicitis develops very quickly, usually in less than 24 hours. If symptoms have been present for more than 48 hours, appendicitis is less likely.

There are no specific diagnostic tests for appendicitis and investigations other than physical examination are only used when the diagnosis is in doubt.

DIAGNOSTIC OPTIONS
■ Laboratory tests and imaging techniques are more helpful for excluding other causes of the pain, rather than helping make a positive appendicitis diagnosis
■ Laparoscopy – internal examination of the abdomen using an instrument that incorporates a camera

■ Ultrasonography (using sound waves to generate an image) is sometimes helpful, especially when diagnosis is in doubt or a gynaecological cause (such as pelvic inflammatory disease) is considered possible.

Experienced doctors are good at diagnosing appendicitis on the history and clinical picture alone, but some 15 per cent of operations performed for acute appendicitis find a different cause, or sometimes none at all.

The risk of missing acute appendicitis is so dangerous that surgeons have a low threshold for operating on a suspected case.

Laparoscopy may be used to confirm a doubtful diagnosis of appendicitis. The technique enables the surgeon to view the interior of the abdomen.

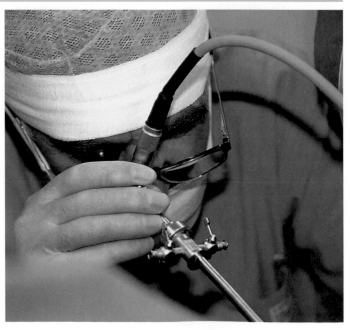

Causes

Obstruction causes raised pressure within the lumen (interior) of the appendix and damages the inner mucous lining. This allows the bacteria that normally live in the bowel to invade the wall of the appendix, causing infection. Continued secretion of mucus into the lumen further increases the pressure, ultimately cutting off the blood supply. Gangrene then sets in and the wall may rupture.

COMMON CAUSES

There is some (unproven) evidence that the initial causative event is ulceration of the mucosa, possibly due to infection with *Yersinia* bacteria.

The commonest cause of obstruction is a faecalith (a collection of faecal matter around undigested vegetable fibres) stuck in the appendix. Other causes are:
■ Intestinal worms
■ Tumours
■ Swollen glandular tissue in the walls due to viral infection.

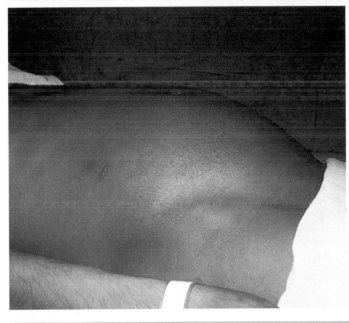

Sometimes, if appendicitis is not recognized early enough, the inflamed appendix becomes gangrenous (circled). Rapid treatment is vital at this stage.

While the precise causes of appendicitis may be uncertain, the characteristic pain of the condition is usually easily recognized.

Prognosis

Acute appendicitis progresses quickly. A missed diagnosis will lead to the wall of the inflamed appendix rupturing and bowel contents spilling into the abdomen (perforation).

CONSEQUENCES

■ When rupture happens rapidly, generalized inflammation and infection of the abdomen (peritonitis) occurs, which is potentially fatal
■ Occasionally, slower progression allows the nearby omentum (specialized periosteum) to wall off the perforation and an abscess is formed.

Peritonitis – acute abdominal inflammation – is a very serious complication. It occurs when the appendix ruptures.

Incidence

■ Acute appendicitis is most common in childhood and early adulthood, especially between puberty and 25 years of age, males being more often affected (3·2 ratio compared to females)
■ Although occurring at any age, the increased risk of complications in the very young and very old make it fortunate that these age groups are affected relatively rarely by appendicitis
■ The overall incidence of appendicitis is reducing across the world. The exact reason for this is not known, but a much lower incidence in developing countries (especially parts of Africa) suggests that dietary factors and nutrition play a part.

Treatment

The only safe treatment for acute appendicitis is removal (appendicectomy), usually by open operation. However, laparoscopic appendicectomy (keyhole surgery) is becoming more common.

RAPID RECOVERY

Recovery is usually quick and chances of infection spreading at operation are reduced by giving intravenous antibiotics before and during surgery.

Abscesses must be drained. If large, or involving the caecum and small bowel, the whole mass must be removed, requiring an ileostomy (whereby the small bowel is brought to the surface of the skin and empties into a removable bag).

PRECAUTIONS

During the operation, the abdomen and bowel are closely inspected in order to rule out any other diseases.

One possible but very rare reason for this is the presence of an inflamed Meckel's diverticulum (a small sac protruding from the small bowel). Even if there is no inflammation present, the removal of this sac will prevent problems arising later.

After removal at surgery, this appendix is seen to be very inflamed. The operation is known as an appendicectomy.

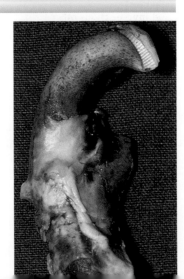

Acute pancreatitis

Symptoms

Acute pancreatitis is severe, sometimes fatal and always requires admission to hospital. Patients are very ill, often in shock, with severe abdominal pain, profuse sweating, fever and shortness of breath.

Pain is steady and 'boring' in nature, often radiating through to the back and is worse when lying flat. The sufferer may find that sitting up and leaning forward may help. This unrelenting pain persists for several days.

CLINICAL FEATURES
■ The upper abdomen is always tender, may be swollen and is sometimes rigid
■ Most patients are nauseous and vomit; some experience dry retching
■ There may be a faint blue discoloration around the navel (Cullen's sign), or a bruise-like discoloration of the flanks (Grey Turner's sign). Either is evidence of bleeding occurring within the abdomen.

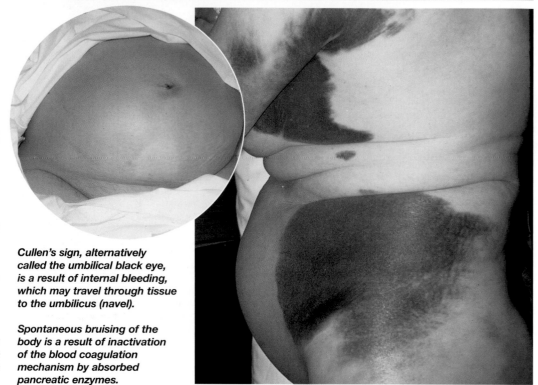

Cullen's sign, alternatively called the umbilical black eye, is a result of internal bleeding, which may travel through tissue to the umbilicus (navel).

Spontaneous bruising of the body is a result of inactivation of the blood coagulation mechanism by absorbed pancreatic enzymes.

Function of the pancreas

The pancreas is a gland lying at the back of the abdomen behind the lower part of the stomach. Its head lies in the bend formed by the first part of the small bowel (duodenum).

The pancreas secretes:
■ Insulin and glucagon – hormones (secreted directly into the bloodstream) that control blood sugar levels
■ Pancreatic juice – a powerful mixture of four enzymes which digest protein (trypsin, chymotrypsin) and break up fats (lipase) and starch (amylase).

The gland's duct joins with the common bile duct just before opening into the side of the duodenum. Pancreatic juice, along with bile, mixes with partially digested food as it leaves the stomach, becomes activated and completes the process of digestion.

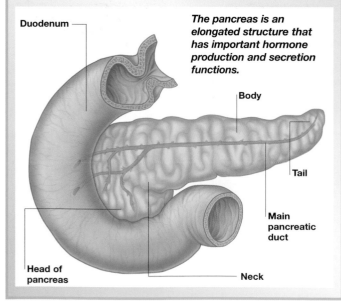

Duodenum

Body

Tail

Main pancreatic duct

Neck

Head of pancreas

The pancreas is an elongated structure that has important hormone production and secretion functions.

Causes

The two commonest causes are:
■ Disease of the biliary tract (45 per cent); for example when a gallstone gets stuck before it can pass into the bowel
■ Alcoholism (35 per cent).
Other causes are:
■ Blunt or penetrating trauma to the abdomen following surgery; perforating duodenal ulcer
■ Metabolic disease: for example high levels of calcium in the blood (disease of the parathyroid glands, drug-induced); hypertriglyceridaemia (too high a level of fatty acids in the blood); renal failure
■ Reactions to certain drugs, such as those contained in some oral contraceptive pills
■ Infection, such as mumps, hepatitis, HIV
■ Structural: pancreatic cancer, for example
■ Idiopathic (unknown cause).

How these factors trigger the inflammation of the gland is unknown, but 'autodigestion' – when the pancreatic enzymes are activated within the gland – is one theory. These destroy the gland and activate other enzymes such as elastase (which dissolves elastic fibres in blood vessels) and phospholipase.

FORMS OF THE DISEASE
Active pancreatic enzymes can result in cell destruction and tissue damage, causing bleeding (haemorrhage), swelling (oedema) and tissue destruction (necrosis) of the pancreas. In cases of extensive haemorrhage, nearby tissues can also be damaged, thus increasing the chances of shock and other complications.

In milder forms of acute pancreatitis, the inflammation is confined to the gland itself.

Most cases of chronic pancreatitis are associated with alcoholism. This X-ray shows calcified debris (circled) within the pancreas.

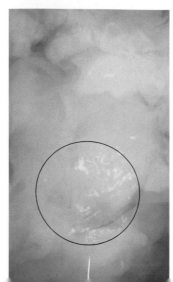

Diagnosis

Symptoms and signs can suggest several other severe conditions of the chest (heart attack, pneumonia) and abdomen (perforated or obstructed intestine, acutely inflamed gall bladder).

BLOOD TESTING

Blood tests are not specific to pancreatitis, but can support the clinical picture. Levels of pancreatic enzymes (amylase and lipase) in the blood are high in the majority of cases. These tests are more sensitive early in the condition, as levels usually return to normal within a week.

High levels of free fatty acids generated by the enzyme lipase, cause saponification ('soap' formation) and a low calcium concentration in the blood.

The white blood cell count is usually raised (leucocytosis) and fluid loss from vessels increases the haematocrit (volume of red blood cells).

IMAGING

The only investigations giving a definitive diagnosis in acute pancreatitis are imaging techniques: ultrasonography and CT scanning. CT should always be performed in severe pancreatitis or if a complication arises. These tests can also help identify the cause of the pancreatitis in some cases.

It is important that the underlying cause is found, when possible, as treatment of this could prevent future bouts of pancreatitis.

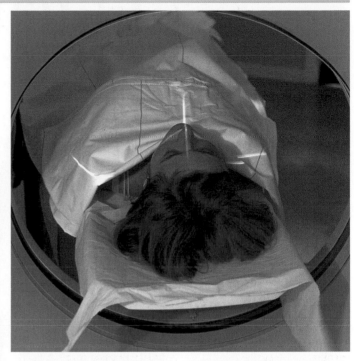

The yellow spheres in this false-colour SEM are lymphocytes, the smallest type of white blood cells. The white blood cell count is usually raised in pancreatitis.

Definitive diagnosis of acute pancreatitis can only be made by imaging – in this case CT scanning. This allows very clear visualization of the abdomen.

Treatment

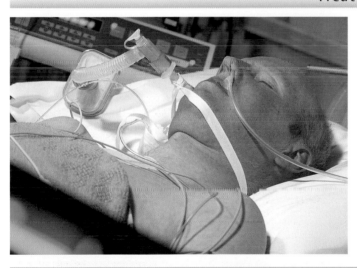

The inflammation in mild oedematous pancreatitis can resolve spontaneously. The patient is placed on an intravenous drip and kept nil-by-mouth (given no fluids or food).

A nasogastric tube keeps the stomach empty, relieving nausea and vomiting. The drip helps prevent shock by replacing fluids. It is also used to administer pain relief by means

When a patient is in intensive care for pancreatitis, a nasogastric tube is used to aspirate fluid from the stomach, thereby reducing nausea.

of a patient-controlled device. This allows the patient to self-administer small doses depending on the level of pain. In order to prevent an overdose, there is a limit set for the number of doses within a certain time.

CLOSE MONITORING

Severe necrotic pancreatitis requires admission to a specialist intensive care unit, where the patient can be closely monitored for danger signs, as the risk of death is high in these cases. Treatment is designed to prevent complications of the condition.

Prognosis and complications

Prognosis is estimated by a scoring system of 11 factors:
- Age over 55 years on admission
- Ten laboratory tests (four on admission and six after 48 hours).

The presence of three or more of these criteria on admission carries a one in five risk of death; seven or more and the risk of death is higher.

Death in the first few days is from multi-system organ failure. Most deaths (80 per cent) occur after the first week, usually from infection (abscess) or pseudocyst problems.

Infection of the dead pancreatic tissue should be suspected when treatment fails, or there is sudden deterioration. CT scan-guided aspiration can aid diagnosis. Unless the infection is drained promptly, the death rate is almost 100 per cent.

The collection of debris and fluid within necrotic (dead) pancreatic tissue is called a pseudocyst as there is no definitive cyst 'wall'.

Carcinoma of the pancreas

Symptoms

Cancer, or carcinoma, of the pancreas is common in the Western world, but it is very difficult to diagnose and treat, as the pancreas lies deep in the upper abdomen, behind the stomach. The pancreas has several important functions including the production of pancreatic juice and several important hormones.

Pancreatic juice contains enzymes involved in food digestion. It collects in a duct that runs through the pancreas and joins the common bile duct, which opens into the upper part of the small intestine (the duodenum) and drains both bile from the liver and gall bladder, as well as pancreatic juice.

Hormones produced by the pancreas include insulin and glucagon. These pass directly into the bloodstream and control blood sugar levels.

SIGNS OF PANCREATIC CANCER
■ Abdominal pain
■ Back pain that is often worse at night
■ Jaundice
■ Itching (common in jaundiced patients)
■ Loss of appetite
■ Weight loss
■ Feeling generally unwell
■ Vomiting
■ Fatty stools (steatorrhoea –

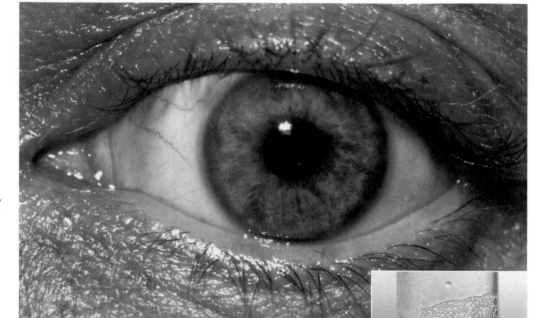

Jaundice is often a symptom of pancreatic cancer. It is caused by the accumulation of the bile pigment bilirubin and leads to yellowing of the skin and eyes.

stools are pale, bulky and smell offensive)
■ Indigestion
■ Diabetic symptoms, such as thirst and passing a lot of urine.

The diagnosis of pancreatic cancer is often delayed until late in the illness as the symptoms

Bile pigments in the urine may be indicative of a pancreatic cancer. A tumour may restrict the flow of bile from the liver, leading to jaundice.

are often vague and may be attributed to other conditions, such as irritable bowel syndrome. By the time it is diagnosed, the cancer has often invaded other tissues such as the liver, stomach, intestine, lungs and lymph nodes.

Causes

Long-term exposure to industrial pollutants is a known risk factor for pancreatic cancer. Smoking increases the risk further.

A portion of stomach is shown here, surgically removed due to ulceration. This type of surgery is a risk factor for pancreatic cancer.

The exact cause of pancreatic cancer is unknown, but there are several known risk factors:
■ Smoking doubles the risk
■ Chronic inflammation of the pancreas (chronic pancreatitis) is important
■ Diabetes mellitus, particularly in overweight people
■ Contact with industrial pollutants and DDT (an insecticide)
■ Partial removal of the stomach (partial gastrectomy) some years previously also increases the risk.

Incidence

Pancreatic cancer ranks fifth among the most common cancers in developed countries and rates are increasing world-wide. It accounts for 5.5 per cent of all cancer deaths in the UK and is the fourth most common cause of cancer deaths in men.

Pancreatic cancer is more common in young men than young women, but the difference lessens with age. Each year, about 10 people in every 100,000 of the general population in the UK develop pancreatic cancer, with the incidence rising to 100 per 100,000 in people over 65 years of age.

Diagnosis

Doctors examining patients with suspected pancreatic cancer may find that they are jaundiced and have an enlarged liver and distended gall bladder (found under the right rib margin). This is sometimes a sign that a tumour is obstructing the outflow of bile from the liver, but gallstones may have a similar effect. Possible investigations include:

■ A blood test to check how well the liver is functioning (liver function tests)
■ Ultrasound scanning – this may detect the tumour and can be used to guide a needle in order to collect a biopsy

■ CT (computed tomography) scanning and/or MR (magnetic resonance) imaging – these produce a computerized picture of the inside of the abdomen
■ Endoscopy – this provides a direct view of the interior of the small intestine
■ ERCP (endoscopic retrograde cholangiopancreatography) – a flexible tube is passed down the throat, through the stomach and into the small intestine, and a radiopaque medium is injected into the common bile duct to demonstrate any obstruction
■ Laparoscopy – a laparoscope is inserted through an incision in the abdominal wall, allowing a biopsy to be taken.

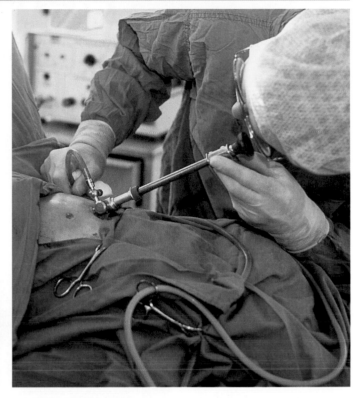

A test to measure specific blood chemicals will be performed to assess liver function. The results may suggest a blockage of bile from the liver.

Laparoscopy is one of the techniques used for diagnosing pancreatic cancer. A tube is inserted into the abdomen, allowing biopsies to be taken.

Treatment

Treatment for pancreatic cancer will depend on the patient's age and overall health, the size of the tumour and whether it has spread to other organs.

SURGERY
Small tumours confined to the pancreas can be treated surgically by removing part or all of the

pancreas. Part of the small intestine and stomach, the bile duct, the gall bladder, spleen and lymph nodes in the area may also be removed. These are major operations but, in recent years, the death rate from surgery has fallen dramatically as anaesthetic and surgical techniques have improved.

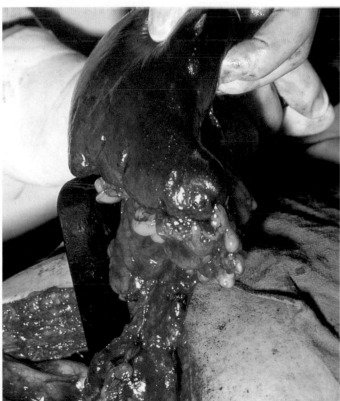

Surgical removal of the pancreas is often the best option. The success of such operations has improved over recent years.

If the bile duct is obstructed but the tumour is inoperable, a stent may be surgically implanted to allow the passage of bile. This will only ease symptoms.

With inoperable tumours, treatment is aimed at symptom relief rather than a cure. If the tumour obstructs the common bile duct, it may be possible to bypass it to free the flow of bile, using a metal device (stent) to keep the passage open. This may be inserted during ERCP with the relief of itching and jaundice.

DRUG THERAPY
Radiotherapy or chemotherapy may be used to kill cancer cells and shrink tumours in some cases, but their effect is usually palliative rather than curative. Strong analgesic drugs (painkillers), such as long-acting oral preparations of morphia, and injection techniques to block pain impulses, may also play a part in treatment.

Prognosis

The outlook for patients with pancreatic cancer is very poor, as the disease has already spread to the lymph nodes in 80 per cent of cases by the time of diagnosis.

SURVIVAL RATES
Overall, only two per cent of patients with pancreatic cancer survive for five years and patients with inoperable tumours survive only for an average of nine weeks from the time of diagnosis. If the tumour is operable, this figure improves to about 10 per cent.

Hepatitis

Symptoms

Hepatitis is a diffuse inflammation of the liver caused by alcohol, drugs (toxic reactions and overdoses) or viral infection. Viruses causing hepatitis are numerous and include glandular fever and HIV.

The term 'viral hepatitis' refers traditionally to infection with one of the so-called hepatitis viruses, of which there are at least six known at present: A, B, C, D, E and F. The most clinically significant of these are hepatitis A, B and C.

CLINICAL FEATURES

Acute hepatitis follows a similar clinical picture regardless of the virus involved. Patients experience a mild flu-like illness with nausea, vomiting and loss of appetite, and can sometimes feel very unwell. Other symptoms include:
■ Fever
■ Fatigue
■ Abdominal pain
■ Diarrhoea.
As the virus damages liver cells, jaundice (yellowing of the skin) and dark urine commonly occur.

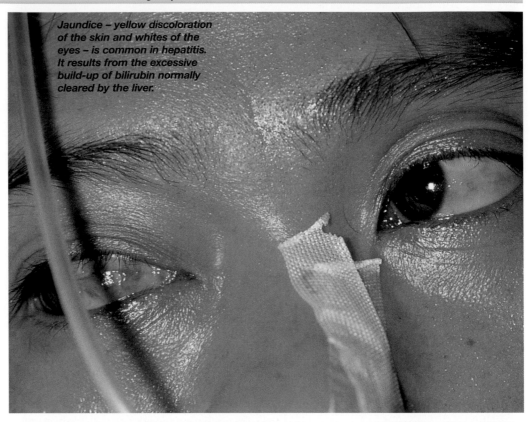

Jaundice – yellow discoloration of the skin and whites of the eyes – is common in hepatitis. It results from the excessive build-up of bilirubin normally cleared by the liver.

Types of hepatitis

■ **Hepatitis A virus (HAV)**
Infectious hepatitis is spread by ingesting contaminated water or food. The virus thrives where food preparation and sanitation conditions are poor.

During the incubation period of about four weeks, HAV proliferates in the gut and is found in the faeces.

Virus shedding stops once symptoms begin, so the infectious phase has already

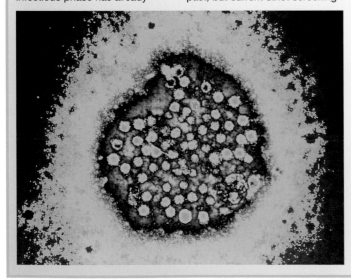

passed when diagnosis is made.

The disease goes unnoticed in most people and most recover completely without any special treatment, although bed rest is usually advised.

■ **Hepatitis B virus (HBV)**
Serum hepatitis is spread by contaminated blood or body fluids. Infection following transfusion was common in the past, but current strict screening

programmes checking donated blood have reduced the risk. The commonest mode of transmission is among drug users who share needles. Other 'at risk' groups include people who are sexually promiscuous and healthcare workers.

Onset is usually gradual after an incubation period of one to six months. Ninety per cent of patients recover. However, five to 10 per cent go on to develop chronic hepatitis. The rare fulminant hepatitis develops rapidly and survival is unusual.

■ **Hepatitis C virus (HCV)**
HCV is transmitted in a similar fashion to HBV, though contraction via sexual activity seems less easy. It is responsible for up to 80 per cent of post-transfusion hepatitis cases. Incubation is six to nine weeks and most cases are unaware they have become infected.

The majority of HCV cases

Hepatitis A virus does not usually cause severe disease. After an incubation period of up to 40 days, the patient develops a fever, followed by jaundice.

The hepatitis A virus spreads easily in overcrowded conditions where there is poor sanitation. Epidemics often occur in developing countries.

have been identified through blood tests in apparently well patients. HCV carries the highest risk of developing chronic hepatitis – up to 75 per cent of cases – which is asymptomatic. Only 50 per cent of infected people ever recover.

Diagnosis

IgM (immunoglobulin) antibody is produced during the acute phase of hepatitis A, and is then replaced by protective IgG antibody. Detection of IgM is therefore diagnostic of active hepatitis, whereas detection of IgG merely indicates the person has had hepatitis A in the past and is now immune.

HEPATITIS B ANTIGENS

Hepatitis B has at least three distinct antigen–antibody systems, which have been utilized to distinguish the presence of active disease as opposed to immunity and enabled the production of effective vaccines.
■ Surface antigen – HBsAg – is usually the first evidence of infection and disappears during convalescence. Anti-HBs antibody appears after recovery and persists for life, indicating past infection. Persistent HBsAg and lack of anti-HBs leads to chronic hepatitis or carrier status. HBsAg is the diagnostic marker of hepatitis B.
■ Core antigen – HBcAg – is found in infected liver cells but not blood. Anti-HBc generally appears at the onset of clinical illness and then diminishes. It can sometimes be the only sign of recent infection.
■ HbeAg is only found in HBsAg positive blood and implies greater risk of infection and a higher possibility of chronic disease.

VACCINES

The multiple subtypes of hepatitis C vary geographically and also over time in individuals. Anti-HCV is diagnostic of active disease as it is not protective.

Vaccines have been developed for HAV and HBV, which can be administered singly or as a combined injection to confer active immunity. However, the antigenic multiplicity of HCV has so far precluded the development of a vaccine.

Blood samples are analysed for the presence of IgM antibody; this reveals that the patient is suffering from acute hepatitis.

Treatment

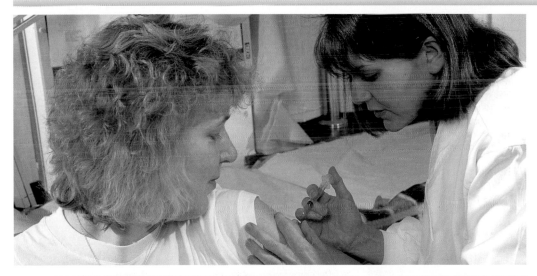

Passive immunization (immunoglobulin injections to prevent infection) can decrease the risk of disease in immediate contacts of HAV and HBV. Use of active immunization (HAV, HBV) prevents acute hepatitis and therefore some of the associated chronic disease.

The only treatment for HCV is interferon (antiviral protein substance), which is of limited effectiveness and not without risk of serious side effects.

An immunoglobulin injection gives temporary immunity against hepatitis A or B in a patient exposed to the virus. This provides passive immunity.

Prognosis

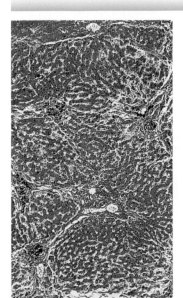

Hepatitis persisting for more than six months is defined as chronic and ranges from mild inflammation to cirrhosis – a condition in which damaged liver cells are replaced by non-functioning fibrous scar tissue.

A third of cases develop following acute hepatitis (HBV, HCV), but most are insidious with non-specific symptoms –

Cirrhosis of the liver is evident on this micrograph. Bands of fibrous tissue (stained blue) appear to disrupt the liver cells (pink), which are damaged.

such as tiredness, lack of appetite and a general feeling of being unwell – which appear to arise without any obvious acute phase.

CHRONIC HEPATITIS

Many patients are unaware they have chronic hepatitis and often continue to suffer from the condition without realizing for years, sometimes even decades.

However, there is increasing evidence that cirrhosis and hepatocellular carcinoma (primary liver cancer) will eventually develop in all cases.

Jaundice

Symptoms

Jaundice is a sign of several different diseases. It is a condition in which the skin and the eyes acquire a distinct yellow colour. This is due to the presence of abnormally high blood levels of a bile pigment called bilirubin. Bilirubin is a normal breakdown product of haem, the iron-based compound that is found in the haemoglobin of red blood cells.

There are two main kinds of jaundice: haemolytic and obstructive. The symptoms produced by the two are quite different from each other, and need to be explored in detail for clues to the final diagnosis.

HAEMOLYTIC JAUNDICE
Haemolytic jaundice is a result of red cell destruction. Patients with haemolytic jaundice will have a normal urine colour as the bilirubin is not water-soluble. This is because urobilinogen is still present in the faeces (the liver is still functioning), which are of a normal colour.

OBSTRUCTIVE JAUNDICE
Obstructive jaundice is caused by liver cell damage. Patients have brown-coloured urine due to the presence of water-soluble bilirubin, and the faeces are pale because bile pigments do not get into the faeces. The increased blood levels of soluble bilirubin cause significant itching and, rarely, high fevers with rigor are indicators of extrahepatic bile duct obstruction.

Patients with jaundice have distinct symptoms. The skin and sclerae (whites of the eyes) acquire a distinct yellow colour, which is due to the presence of high blood levels of bilirubin.

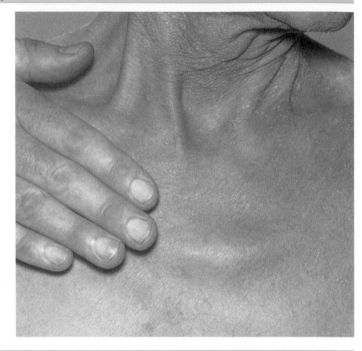

Causes

High bilirubin levels, and thus jaundice, can have three distinct causes:
■ Increased destruction (haemolysis) of red cells with rapid release of insoluble bilirubin into the blood
■ Liver cell damage, such that less of the water-soluble form of bilirubin is processed
■ Obstruction of the excretion of water-soluble bilirubin through the biliary system into the bowel. The result is that even the usual amounts of bilirubin cannot be excreted through the faeces and the kidneys.

HAEMOLYTIC JAUNDICE
Increased red cell destruction in haemolytic jaundice occurs in:
■ Newborn babies who have more red blood cells than they need
■ Patients with malaria
■ People with disorders such as sickle-cell disease
■ People with hereditary spherocytosis (the presence of abnormally shaped red cells in the blood).

OBSTRUCTIVE JAUNDICE
Obstructive jaundice can occur in viral infections. Hepatitis can be caused by hepatitis viruses A, B, C, D and E. Liver cirrhosis and therapeutic drugs can also cause this form of jaundice.

Hepatitis A virus, shown on this micrograph, is a common cause of jaundice. The yellow skin discoloration normally persists for up to three weeks.

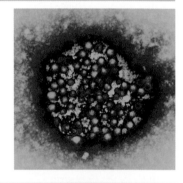

Jaundice is often a result of hepatitis infection. Certain forms of hepatitis can, in turn, be transmitted through food contaminated by a carrier.

How bile pigments are produced

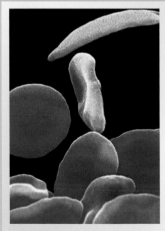

Haemolytic jaundice can be caused by sickle-cell disease. In this condition, abnormal forms of red cells are present which include those with a sickle shape.

Red blood cells normally function for about 120 days and are then broken down in the spleen. The bilirubin that is released in this process is insoluble and therefore cannot be excreted by the kidneys.

Instead, it is carried in the bloodstream to the liver where it is altered to become water-soluble. The liver excretes most of the soluble bilirubin from where it passes through the bile duct into the gall bladder and into the bowel.

Within the bowel, the soluble bilirubin is further converted by normal bacteria into substances that colour the stools. Urobilinogen, a reduced form of bilirubin, is partially reabsorbed into the bloodstream and excreted through the kidneys and the liver.

Diagnosis

It is important to clarify the diagnosis of jaundice:
■ The presence of episodes of pain and intermittent jaundice suggest gallstones
■ Steadily increasing severe jaundice associated with weight loss suggests cancer (specific signs for cancer of the pancreas)
■ A history of alcohol or drug abuse suggests liver cell damage.

DIAGNOSTIC TESTS
■ Blood tests help to confirm the type of jaundice as well as its severity. In obstructive jaundice, levels of a liver enzyme called alkaline phosphatase are markedly raised. In liver cell damage, liver enzymes called transaminases are raised. In anaemia, a full-blood count will reveal excess red cell breakdown, sickle cells and spherocytes
■ Ultrasound and other scans will clarify the type of obstruction
■ Liver biopsies may be needed when chronic hepatitis is diagnosed.

Blood tests help to confirm the type of jaundice as well as its severity. These tests also diagnose conditions such as anaemia and liver cell damage.

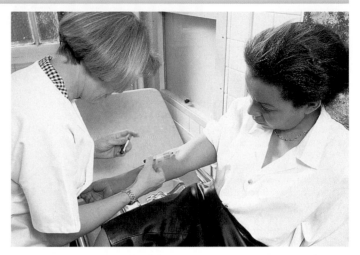

Treatment

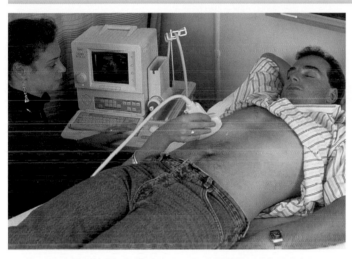

Treatment will depend on the type of jaundice and its cause.
■ Viral hepatitis usually settles down without any active treatment. Patients are advised to avoid alcohol
■ Chronic hepatitis is more difficult to treat but antiviral agents are available.
   Surgical jaundice may require the removal of gallstones, depending on the cause of the obstruction and its site.

If gallstones are suspected as the cause of a patient's intermittent jaundice, ultrasound scanning will confirm their presence.

Prognosis

The outlook for most types of jaundice is very good. Chronic hepatitis is more likely when:
■ Symptoms do not resolve
■ The liver remains enlarged
■ There is tissue death found at liver biopsy
■ Liver function tests remain high for 6-12 months.
Chronic hepatitis and especially cirrhosis are dangerous. They can both lead to:
■ Liver failure
■ Haemorrhage from tiny veins in the oesophagus.

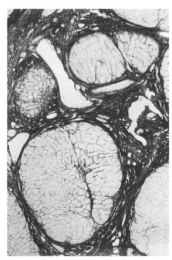

Liver cirrhosis can be due to chronic hepatitis which, in turn, can lead to jaundice. Liver cirrhosis is dangerous as it can lead to liver failure.

Prevention

Jaundice, which is a symptom of many liver disorders, is a preventable disease.
   With regard to obstructive jaundice, the same precautions need to be taken as those employed to counter hepatitis when in high-risk areas. Travellers are advised to:
■ Drink only boiled or bottled water even for cleaning teeth
■ If using water-sterilization tablets, ensure that the instructions are followed carefully
■ Avoid food stored or prepared in unhygienic conditions
■ Avoid ice in drinks and avoid salads and poorly cooked foods
■ Always peel fruit before eating
■ Wash hands before meals and after going to the toilet
■ Avoid casual sexual contact
■ Always use condoms.

Travellers in high-risk areas need to take precautions against hepatitis. These include steps such as drinking only boiled or bottled water.

VACCINATION
Since liver cell damage in obstructive jaundice is caused by hepatitis, vaccination is the best long-term preventive measure.
   Vaccines against hepatitis A and B are vital for frequent travellers to high-risk areas, people with haemophilia, members of the armed forces, diplomatic staff and sewage workers, as well as certain medical staff.

Incidence

Jaundice is not a common condition. In a general practice of 2,500 patients, a doctor will see two or three cases each year. The average district general hospital will admit perhaps 200 cases every year.

Diabetes mellitus

Symptoms and incidence

Diabetes mellitus is a chronic disorder in which glucose accumulates in the blood, rather than being stored or used for energy. Diabetes mellitus is classified as Type I or Type II (see box below).

Common to both types are associated disturbances of protein and fat breakdown. In addition, minute blood vessels that nourish the heart, kidney, retina and nervous system often deteriorate.

People with diabetes are at increased risk of heart disease, kidney failure, foot ulcers and blindness, and severe infections are common; up to 40 per cent of diabetic men become impotent.

Typical symptoms include:
■ Polyuria – the production of a large volume of dilute urine during the day and at night
■ Thirst – which may be intense
■ Tiredness
■ Weight loss.

The onset of Type II diabetes is often less clear-cut than that of Type I but, when initially diagnosed, some patients report suffering from frequent urination and thirst for months or even years. Women may first experience vulval itching.

In severe cases, patients with very high blood glucose levels may develop life-threatening ketoacidosis due to the excessive breakdown of fat. The patient's breath smells of acetone and they may suffer from nausea, vomiting, abdominal pains and confusion. If untreated, they become comatose.

INCIDENCE
About 75 per cent of diabetic patients in Britain have Type II, and 10 per cent of Britons over the age of 70 are affected. Most patients are over 40 at the time of diagnosis and men are more often affected than women.

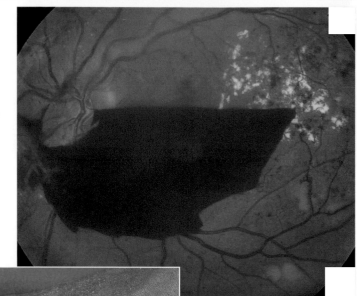

Diabetic retinopathy is prevalent among non-insulin dependent diabetic patients. It occurs when the blood vessels of the retina become damaged.

People with diabetes are susceptible to ulcers, especially on the feet. Such ulcers are due to neuropathy, a disease of the peripheral nerves.

Classifying diabetes

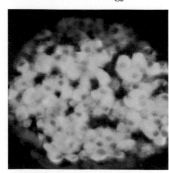

There are two main types of diabetes mellitus: insulin dependent diabetes mellitus (also known as Type I or juvenile) and non-insulin dependent diabetes (Type II).

Type I diabetes mellitus
This is an autoimmune condition resulting from the interaction of genetic and environmental factors. T-lymphocytes from the body's immune system destroy

Type I diabetes mellitus can cause considerable disability and can even be life-threatening. Regular medical checks are essential, and life-long administration of insulin is necessary.

the beta cells in the pancreas over several years and insulin production eventually fails. The HLA gene is involved in the immune damage and other markers, such as antibodies, indicating a risk of diabetes, have also been found in the blood.

Viral infections may trigger Type I, which often develops when seasonal infections are common. Those possibly implicated include the mumps, rubella and coxsackie viruses, cytomegaloviruses and retroviruses, such as HIV.

Type II diabetes mellitus
This mostly affects middle-aged, obese people. People with Type II diabetes produce some insulin but, in some cases for an unknown reason, the tissues

become insensitive to its action. In other cases, insulin production is reduced or abnormal.

Some people appear to be genetically predisposed to developing Type II. Poor nutrition in the womb may be a risk factor and may also increase a tendency to become obese.

Obesity – defined as when body weight is 20 per cent or more over the desirable maximum – is a major risk factor for diabetes.

Causes

Diabetes mellitus is due to a failure in the production of the hormone insulin or a reduction in its activity. Insulin is produced by beta cells in the pancreas. It normally controls carbohydrate metabolism and regulates glucose levels in the blood, and the cells in the body all depend on insulin to obtain glucose from the blood for nourishment and energy.

The groups of cells in the pancreas known as the islets of Langerhans secrete insulin from central beta cells (green). In diabetes mellitus, there are difficulties producing insulin.

Diagnosis

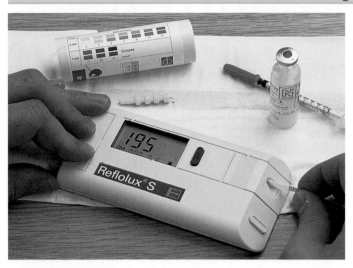

A definite diagnosis of diabetes should be made only on the basis of laboratory blood tests. Finding a fasting plasma glucose level of 7.9 mmol/l is diagnostic. Finding glucose in the urine suggests the need for further checks as none should be present, but does not make the diagnosis definite.

About three per cent of the UK population over the age of 19 years have diabetes. Type I diabetes mellitus affects about one in 400 people, about 25 per cent of all diabetic patients. In the UK, it is most common in Scotland, where the incidence has doubled in the last 10 years. Type I occurs at any age but typically under the age of 20. The diagnosis is usually made on the basis of typical symptoms (polyuria, thirst and weight loss) developing over the previous 2–4 weeks, but some patients are first seen in diabetic coma.

INCIDENTAL DIAGNOSIS
Many patients are diagnosed by screening tests; others are first diagnosed when they develop complications of diabetes such as a myocardial infarct (heart attack), eye disease or a foot ulcer.

Blood glucose testing is very important in monitoring diabetes. A drop of blood is placed on a strip and inserted into the electronic meter.

Treatment

The aim of treatment is to relieve symptoms and prevent long-term complications by keeping blood glucose and blood pressure within normal limits. A healthy diet, losing excess weight, stopping smoking and regular exercise are all important. In Type II diabetes, these measures may control the disorder without the need for insulin.

INSULIN THERAPY
Life-long treatment with regular insulin injections is essential for Type I diabetes; some people with Type II also need insulin. Insulin cannot be given by mouth, but the injections are relatively painless and most patients learn to self-inject; many patients use disposable

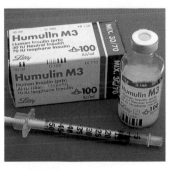

Most people with Type I diabetes administer insulin injections themselves. Pen injectors make this simpler.

plastic syringes or pre-filled multidose pen injectors. The dose depends on diet, activity and general state of health and may need adjustment, for example if the patient suffers an infection or becomes pregnant. Many patients also check their own blood glucose levels and adjust their own doses.

In Type II diabetes, oral drugs may be needed: sulphonyl urea stimulates insulin secretion; metformin stimulates the uptake of glucose into the tissues; and acarbose acts to prevent the breakdown of complex sugars.

RECENT ADVANCES
Pancreatic transplants are as yet in their early stages; the aim is to reduce or remove the need for insulin injections in some patients – long-term immuno-suppressive therapy is essential.

Insulin can be of human or animal origin. Human insulin is synthesized by a process that involves a cloned synthetic gene.

Sugar treatment

Hypoglycaemia develops if the blood glucose level falls dangerously low. It is a common side effect of insulin therapy and needs immediate treatment:
■ Patients are at risk of brain damage or even death
■ Patients may feel cold, sweaty and shaky and their heart pounds
■ Later they may become

clumsy, irritable or aggressive, develop convulsions or lapse into a coma, and may appear to be drunk
■ Treatment with any form of easily absorbed carbohydrate (sugar, sweets, glucose drinks) rapidly relieves symptoms
■ Unconscious patients need urgent hospital treatment with intravenous glucose.

Prognosis

In the last 20 years, the outlook for diabetics has considerably improved but the death rate from Type I diabetes is still about five times that of the general population. People diagnosed under the age of 30 can expect to live for at least another 35 years, and 60 per cent will reach the age of 60. Kidney damage will probably occur in 25 per cent of people – renal failure is a major cause of death.

The outlook for Type II is more difficult to assess, as many cases remain undiagnosed. However, death rates are increased by 40 per cent or more. Myocardial infarction and kidney failure are the commonest causes of death.

Regular monitoring of blood glucose assists in control of the condition. In the future, healthy lifestyles may lower the incidence of Type II diabetes.

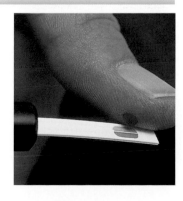

Cushing's syndrome

Symptoms

Cushing's syndrome is an endocrine condition that can result from a number of possible causes, all of which lead to excess production of cortisol, the major hormone in the group known as glucocorticoids.

Glucocorticoids are hormones essential for the processing of carbohydrate, fat and protein. If cortisol is present in excessive amounts, it has many harmful effects (detailed below). These include excessive weight gain and excessive growth of facial and body hair, as well as more subtle physiological changes.

Common features of Cushing's disease include obesity, hirsuteness in women and reddening of the face and neck.

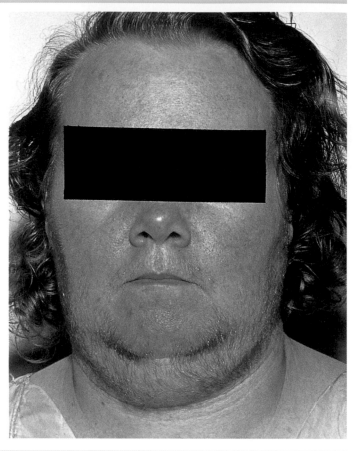

Physical changes

■ Weight gain, with abnormal fat deposition – particularly around the face ('moon face'), abdomen, neck and upper back ('buffalo hump')
■ Wasting of the muscles of the legs and upper arms
■ Skin is easily bruised and is characteristically thin and marked with striae (pink/purple stretch marks) on the abdomen, thighs, breasts and shoulders
■ In women, there is an increased tendency for acne, hair growth on the face and loss of hair from the scalp
■ Neck and face may appear ruddy, with darker skin on the neck (acanthosis)

■ Children may become obese and show poor growth in height – excess cortisol suppresses the secretion of pituitary growth hormone.

Associated symptoms
■ Back pain resulting from osteoporosis (bone thinning) and vertebral collapse
■ Glucose intolerance
■ Polydipsia (excessive thirst) and polyuria (increased urination)
■ Hypertension (high blood pressure)
■ Polyphagia (increased appetite)
■ Kidney stones.

Causes

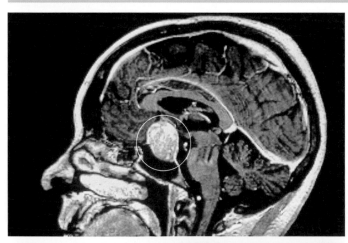

A tumour of the pituitary gland (circled) is apparent on this MR scan. Such a tumour may stimulate the adrenal glands to overproduce cortisol.

Cushing's syndrome is most often the result of tumours of the pituitary gland or the adrenal glands (one is situated above each kidney). The various symptoms are due to the overproduction of hormones.

CUSHING'S DISEASE
Cushing's disease (distinct from Cushing's syndrome) is caused by overproduction of adrenocorticotrophic hormone (ACTH), resulting from a tumour of the pituitary gland. ACTH controls how much cortisol the adrenal glands produce. Pituitary tumours in turn cause the adrenal glands to enlarge and secrete excessive cortisol.

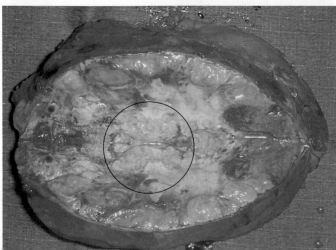

A tumour of the adrenal gland (shown here dissected) often causes overproduction of cortisol. Excessive amounts may cause Cushing's disease.

Adrenal Cushing's is caused by excessive cortisol as a result of a tumour of the adrenal gland. The simultaneous overproduction of adrenal androgens – male sex hormones – also causes virilization (in which women develop masculine characteristics).

Ectopic ACTH production (that is, ACTH from a location other than the pituitary) may arise from tumours of the lung, thymus gland or pancreas, for example. The reason for the ectopic ACTH production in such cases is unknown, but the result is that cortisol levels rise, and the patient develops the typical symptoms.

IATROGENIC CUSHING'S
Iatrogenic Cushing's syndrome is a possible side effect of certain forms of medical treatment. In such cases, excessive cortisol production is the result of high-dose steroid treatment for disorders such as asthma, rheumatoid arthritis, inflammatory bowel disease and certain allergies.

Diagnosis

Diagnosis is based on the clinical symptoms shown by the patient and laboratory investigations. However, many of the symptoms are apparent in other conditions, such as polycystic ovary syndrome, congenital adrenal hyperplasia – increase in kidney size – and chronic alcoholism. Therefore, the doctor will be careful to exclude these possibilities before confirming in a patient a diagnosis of Cushing's syndrome or a related disorder.

Two of the most obvious visible signs of Cushing's syndrome are evident here. These are abnormal deposition of fat, resulting in a pendulous abdomen, and Cushing's striae.

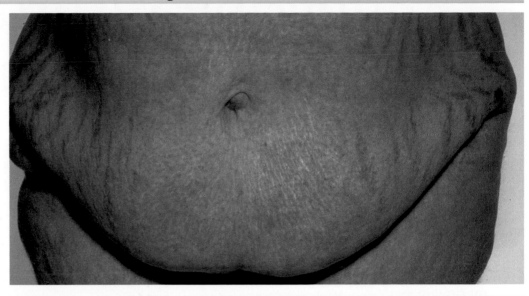

Clinical findings

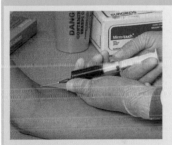

When Cushing's is suspected, a blood sample will be taken for laboratory analysis.

Diagnosis of Cushing's is aided by a number of investigations:
■ Blood tests may reveal a high white blood cell count, high blood sugar and low blood potassium
■ Urine testing will show concentrations of cortisol to be higher than normal
■ Cortisol is normally secreted in daily rhythms; these levels peak twice a day. Loss of this rhythm is symptomatic of Cushing's syndrome. A supervised stay in

hospital will be necessary to measure this
■ Administering the drug dexamethasone, another glucocorticoid hormone, normally depresses production of cortisol (dexamethasone suppression test). However, most patients with Cushing's syndrome will continue to produce high levels of cortisol
■ Measuring the level of ACTH will distinguish ectopic Cushing's (ACTH levels will be high) from

adrenal Cushing's (levels of ACTH will be too low to measure)
■ Bilateral inferior petrosal sinus sampling (BIPSS) involves passing catheters into sinuses of the skull where the pituitary gland drains. In cases of Cushing's disease, the levels of ACTH are found to be high
■ MR and CT scans may be carried out to locate ACTH-producing tumours. For pituitary and non-pituitary tumours, CT imaging is the method of choice.

Incidence and prognosis

In spite of its dramatic nature, Cushing's syndrome is a relatively rare condition, with a prevalence of approximately one in 100,000 of the population. It occurs most often after puberty, and patients usually fall into the 25–45 age group. Cushing's disease is more prevalent in women by a ratio of 10:1, whereas ectopic Cushing's is more common in men.

Left untreated, Cushing's syndrome leads to increasingly severe symptoms. These can

include diabetes, cardiovascular disease, liver and kidney failure, hyperthyroidism and chronic infections.

Cushing's disease has a poorer prognosis. Impaired pituitary function may result if the condition is not recognized.

If Cushing's syndrome is suspected, a CT brain scan may be performed. This allows detailed imaging of the pituitary gland, and will clearly show the presence of any tumour.

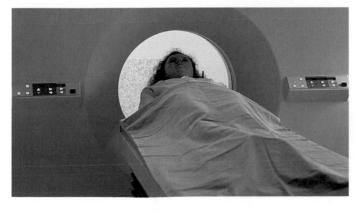

Treatment

The clinical treatment of Cushing's syndrome is dependent largely on the severity of the symptoms and the variety of Cushing's affecting the patient.
■ Cushing's disease used to be treated by surgical removal of the entire pituitary gland. However, advances in imaging techniques now mean that removal of the tumour, leaving much of the pituitary intact, is now a feasible alternative to removing the entire gland. If the gland is removed, lifelong pituitary hormone replacement therapy is required
■ The drug metyrapone reduces cortisol levels in blood plasma, and is useful in treating the condition before the exact cause is determined. Radiotherapy may also be beneficial
■ Adrenal Cushing's is treated by removal of the tumour responsible, after a course of pre-treatment with metyrapone. A single, well-defined adrenal tumour can be removed by laparoscopy (minimally invasive surgery). With a large tumour,

Surgical removal of the adrenal gland is often necessary when a large tumour has been located.

the whole gland will be removed
■ Ectopic Cushing's is often due to a rapidly growing cancer of the lung, and treatment for Cushing's syndrome only relieves the symptoms, without treating the underlying condition. Again, removal of the tumour will often effect a cure
■ Iatrogenic Cushing's usually resolves after withdrawal of the steroid hormone treatment which produced the symptoms.

Endocrine disorders: Addison's disease

Symptoms

Important endocrine glands in the body include the pituitary, thyroid, parathyroid, adrenal glands, pancreas, ovaries and testes. These glands are responsible for the production of hormones and their secretion into the bloodstream. Endocrine disorders, such as Addison's disease, result from the under- or overproduction of hormones.

ADRENAL GLAND
The affected gland in Addison's disease is the adrenal gland, which becomes underactive (primary hypoadrenalism). Symptoms include:
■ Loss of appetite and general weakness
■ Increased skin pigmentation
■ Low blood pressure

■ Abdominal pain, vomiting, diarrhoea or constipation
■ Joint and muscle pains
■ Confusion.

OTHER SIGNS
People with Addison's disease may become severely ill (Addisonian crisis) if they are unwell with an unrelated disorder. They may develop:
■ Very low blood pressure
■ Rapid heartbeat and fever
■ Severe abdominal pain
■ Low blood sugar
■ Signs of kidney failure.

Increased skin pigmentation, for example in the mouth, is a symptom of Addison's disease. Symptoms often go unnoticed for a long period of time.

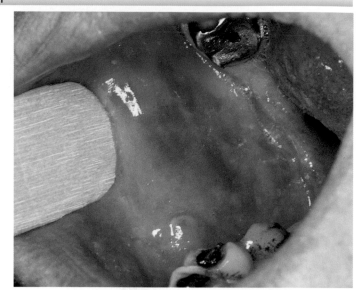

Causes

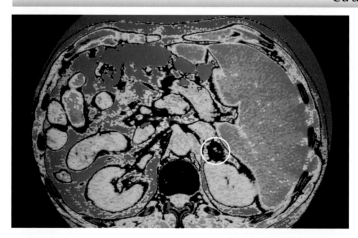

Addison's disease is usually caused by damage to the adrenal gland as a result of autoimmune disease, in which the body starts to attack its own tissues.

LOW HORMONE LEVELS
As a result, production of the three main types of hormones falls beneath a critical level:

Addison's disease occurs when the adrenal glands become damaged. This CT scan shows the right adrenal gland (circle) above the kidney.

■ Glucocorticoids – such as cortisol – which regulate the metabolism of glucose, particularly in times of stress
■ Mineralocorticoids – such as aldosterone – which regulate blood sodium and potassium levels, blood pressure and blood volume
■ Sex steroids, mainly androgens (male hormones).
   The levels of these hormones also fall in secondary hypoadrenalism. This can occur when a patient is given high doses of corticosteroids for a prolonged period of time.

Diagnosis

Many endocrine disorders are diagnosed clinically, but confirmatory tests are needed. Diagnosis can be difficult as many disorders start gradually.
   In Addison's, as with most endocrine disorders, blood tests can confirm the diagnosis by detecting antibodies. Other investigations for this disease include abdominal X-rays and CT scans of the adrenals to exclude tuberculosis or an adrenal tumour.

Endocrine disorders such as Addison's disease can be diagnosed by a simple blood test. The blood is investigated for antibodies.

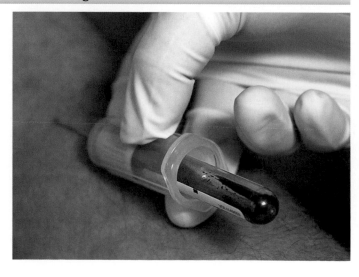

Incidence

Addison's disease affects nearly 1 per 100,000 of the population. Women and patients with other autoimmune diseases, such as pernicious anaemia, thyroiditis (inflammation of the thyroid gland), premature ovarian failure, and type 1 (insulin-dependent) diabetes, are most at risk.
   Other endocrine disorders are relatively common. For example, underactivity of the thyroid gland affects up to two per cent of women, and about 1 person in 300 in the UK receives insulin treatment for diabetes.

Treatment

Treatment usually aims to restore a patient's hormone levels to normal. Hormone deficiencies are treated with natural or synthetic hormones.

HORMONE REPLACEMENT
In Addison's disease, treatment involves long-term hormone replacement therapy with hydrocortisone (synthetic form of cortisol) and fludrocortisone. Fludrocortisone helps to restore the body's normal excretion of electrolytes (salt and potassium), mimicking the action of natural aldosterone.

An Addisonian crisis is a

Hormones to treat Addison's disease may be taken as tablets. The minimum effective dose is given to avoid hormonal side effects.

hospital emergency. Patients are often in a state of collapse and require intravenous dextrose (sugar solution) and saline to balance fluid levels. Hydrocortisone may be given intravenously first and by mouth as symptoms improve.

Prognosis

In Addison's disease, untreated patients sometimes struggle on undiagnosed for several years, feeling unwell in a non-specific way but always at risk of developing an Addisonian crisis. Early and accurate diagnosis is therefore essential.

With adequate hormone replacement therapy, the outlook for patients is good.

Prevention

Underactivity of the adrenal glands cannot be prevented. However, measures can be taken to prevent serious complications such as an Addisonian crisis. Those with Addison's disease or secondary hypoadrenalism should:
■ Always carry a steroid card (to notify medical staff that the patient is taking steroids)
■ Wear a warning bracelet
■ Carry an emergency ampoule of hydrocortisone for injection.

Doctors advise people with Addison's disease to carry a steroid card or wear a warning bracelet. If a crisis occurs, steroids can be administered.

Other endocrine disorders

Gland (hormone)	Overproduction	Underproduction
Pituitary gland – growth hormone	Gigantism (excessive height) before puberty. Acromegaly (abnormally large hands, feet) in adults	Abnormally short stature with normal proportions
Thyroid gland – thyroid hormone	Thyrotoxicosis (weight loss, shaky hands, anxiety, heat intolerance)	Myxoedema (appetite loss, weight gain, dry skin)
Parathyroid gland – parathyroid hormone	Transfers calcium from bones to blood. May cause weakness of the bones and kidney stones	Tetany (muscular spasms)
Adrenal glands – corticosteroid hormone	Weight gain, reddening of face, excess growth of facial and body hair, high blood sugar, mental disturbance, high blood pressure	Weakness, loss of energy, low blood pressure, dark pigmentation of the skin and mucous membranes
Ovaries – oestrogen and progesterone	Early sexual development, polycystic ovarian syndrome, irregular periods	Lack of sexual development, scanty or absent periods
Testes – androgen	Masculinization in women	Delayed puberty, impotence
Pancreas – insulin	Low blood sugar, leading to faintness/loss of consciousness	Rise in blood sugar level (diabetes mellitus)

Acromegaly occurs when there is an oversecretion of the growth hormone. This hormone (somatotrophin) is secreted by the pituitary gland.

Thyroid disease

Symptoms

Thyroid disease results from either under-production (hypothyroidism) or over-production (hyperthyroidism) of thyroid hormones. The thyroid gland lies just below the thyroid cartilage (Adam's apple) on the windpipe and is like a bow tie in position and shape. Its function is to secrete the thyroid hormones which control the body's metabolism.

HYPERTHYROIDISM

Hyperthyroidism is the most common hormonal disorder and leads to an over-stimulation of the body's metabolism. The symptoms include:
■ Anxiety and insomnia
■ Restlessness and irritability
■ Weight loss despite an increased appetite
■ Excessive sweating
■ Tremor
■ Palpitations
■ Diarrhoea
■ Less frequent, or absent, menstruation
■ Decreased sex drive

■ Worsening or onset of angina (if heart disease is present)
■ Eyes that appear to protrude (exophthalmos)
■ Swelling in the neck (goitre) – due to enlarged thyroid.

HYPOTHYROIDISM

A deficiency in thyroid hormones results in the mechanisms of the body slowing down, and may cause:
■ Tiredness
■ Depression
■ Intolerance to cold
■ Dry skin with coarse hair
■ A hoarse voice
■ Weight gain
■ Constipation
■ Heavy or irregular periods
■ Pale, waxy skin and easy bruising
■ Pins and needles in the hands (carpal tunnel syndrome).

In people with high levels of thyroid hormones there are certain characteristic features. This woman has exophthalmos, protrusion of the eyes.

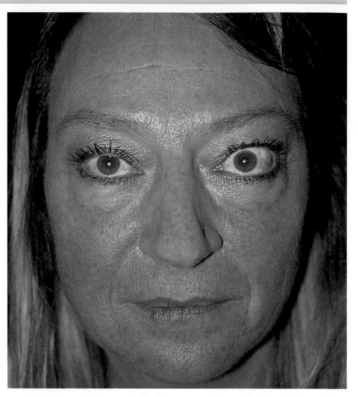

Causes

There are various causes of thyroid disease.

OVER-PRODUCTION

Over-production of thyroid hormones may be caused by:
■ Graves' disease – this is the commonest cause. It is an autoimmune disorder in which abnormal antibodies affect hormone production
■ Thyroid nodules – growths may produce excess hormone

This thyroid specimen contains typical nodules (growths). The nodules are non-cancerous, but they can cause excess production of thyroid hormone.

■ De Quervain's thyroiditis – this is an acute inflammation, probably viral in origin.

UNDER-PRODUCTION

Under-production of thyroid hormones may be a result of:
■ Autoimmune hypothyroidism – this is the commonest cause and is due to antibodies attacking the thyroid tissue
■ Hashimoto's thyroiditis – this is an autoimmune disorder
■ Iodine deficiency – a lack of iodine in the diet, although this no longer occurs in the UK
■ Treatment for an overactive thyroid gland – may destroy hormone-producing tissue.

Diagnosis

If hyperthyroidism is suspected the doctor will feel the patient's neck to check for lumps within the thyroid. A scan of the thyroid can be helpful to visualize inflammation or growths. Sometimes a biopsy of the thyroid tissue is performed.

BLOOD TESTS

Diagnosis of both conditions is always confirmed by blood tests to measure thyroid hormone levels and detect the presence of abnormal antibodies that are

affecting the gland:
■ In hyperthyroidism, levels of the hormones triiodothyronine (T_3) or thyroxine (T_4) are high and those of thyroid stimulating hormone (TSH) levels are low
■ In hypothyroidism, there is a raised TSH level and T_4 levels are abnormally low.

Sometimes, an enlarged thyroid gland is unmistakable, as is the one shown here. The doctor will, however, feel the neck for specific abnormal masses.

Incidence

Thyroid disease occurs in about six per cent of the population in the UK
■ Hypothyroidism is more common in women than men
■ Hypothyroidism affects less than one per cent of men and two per cent of women
■ Hyperthyroidism is most common between 20 and 40 years but affects any age
■ One out of every 4,000 infants is born without a working thyroid gland.

Treatment

There are several treatment options for thyroid disease.

HYPERTHYROIDISM
Over-production of thyroid hormones can be treated using:

■ Drugs – such as carbimazole interfere with thyroid hormone production. Side effects include rashes, alopecia, gastro-intestinal upsets and bone marrow depression. Tablets may be given for six to 24 months.

■ Radioactive iodine – this is given orally and usually only once. It destroys thyroid tissue and suppresses the production of hormones. Patients may become hypothyroid.

■ Surgery – this is not often recommended. If too much gland is removed the patient may become hypothyroid. There is also a risk to the vocal cords, and the nearby parathyroid glands may be accidentally removed.

■ Beta blockers – given for symptoms of anxiety or tremor.

If the eyes are affected, a specialist opinion is important.

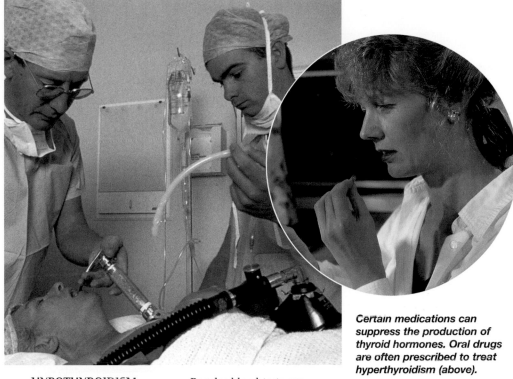

HYPOTHYROIDISM
Hypothyroidism is treated with thyroxine tablets (synthetic thyroid hormone). The usual dose is between 100 and 150 micrograms daily.

Regular blood tests are performed to ensure correct dosage. In older patients the thyroxine dose is increased slowly in order to avoid heart problems.

Certain medications can suppress the production of thyroid hormones. Oral drugs are often prescribed to treat hyperthyroidism (above).

Surgery to remove all or part of the thyroid gland is sometimes necessary. This may be recommended if a tumour or nodules are present (left).

Prognosis

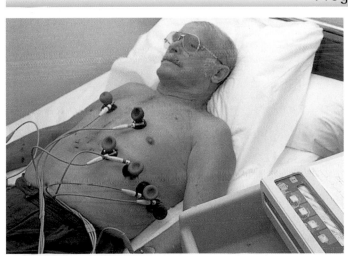

If an over-active thyroid gland is left untreated, complications can develop, such as:
■ Osteoporosis
■ Heart failure
■ Myocardial infarction (heart attack) and stroke.

RELIEVING SYMPTOMS
Symptoms of hyperthyroidism are usually relieved with treatment, and complications can be avoided. However

Untreated hyperthyroidism may cause serious complications. In particular, patients are at risk of developing heart problems; they can be monitored by ECG.

symptoms may recur, especially in those who have been diagnosed with Graves' disease.
When hypothyroidism is treated with the hormone thyroxine, symptoms resolve within a few weeks.

MONITORING PROGRESS
People with thyroid disorders are regularly followed-up in outpatient clinics. Progress is monitored using blood tests to check the levels of thyroid hormones.
Once the disorder is under control, these blood tests can be organized on a less regular basis.

Prevention

It is important that women who have thyroid disorders and who are pregnant are properly monitored.

PREGNANCY CHECKS
Pregnancy checks are performed to prevent damage to the growth and mental development in children that results from thyroid deficiency in fetal or early neonatal life. If a problem is detected, the mother's T_3 and T_4 levels may need adjustment.

SCREENING
Screening of the whole population for hyperthyroidism and hypothyroidism is not justifiable. However, there is some medical evidence to suggest that screening for thyroid disorders in diabetics may be useful.

Pregnant women with thyroid problems need specialist care. Regular blood tests will help to monitor hormone levels.

Breast lumps

Symptoms

Breast lumps are very common; most are non-cancerous (benign), but it is vitally important that persistent lumps are promptly investigated.

BENIGN BREAST LUMPS

Benign breast lumps include fibroadenomas, cysts and abscesses.

■ Fibroadenomas are overgrowths of the glandular and fibrous tissue of the breast. They may be painless or painful, particularly before a period when extra fluid collects in the breast tissue. They may be single or multiple. They feel smooth and rubbery and move freely in the breast tissue

■ Breast cysts may be single, but are often multiple; they may be hard or soft and symptomless or painful

■ Breast abscesses form red, tender, pus-filled lumps that are acutely painful.

BREAST CANCER

Lumps caused by breast cancer tend to be harder, more irregular and less mobile than fibroadenomas. Sometimes they are painless. The skin may become puckered and ulcerate. The glands in the armpit (axilla) may feel large and there may be a discharge from the nipple.

If the cancer metastasizes (spreads) to other parts of the body, symptoms such as backache, headache, breathlessness and abdominal swelling may occur.

Women often detect the presence of breast lumps during self-examination. Any lump found should be investigated by a medical practitioner.

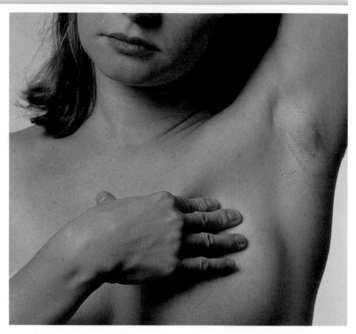

Causes

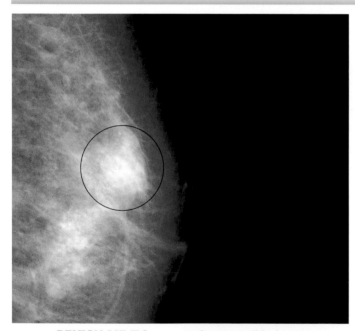

This mammogram shows a breast cyst, which appears as a white mass. Fibrocystic breast disease is common in mature pre-menopausal women.

BENIGN LUMPS

The development of breast cysts and fibroadenomas may be related to hormonal factors. Cysts are more common in childless women and women whose periods are irregular. Breast abscesses are mostly caused by the bacterium *Staphylococcus aureus*.

BREAST CANCER

The factors associated with increased risk of developing breast cancer include:

■ Inherited susceptibility to breast cancer. Genes are thought to be responsible for up to 10 per cent of breast cancers. Many genes are currently being identified: BRCA 1, for example, is responsible for 30 per cent of breast cancer in women under the age of 45

■ Previous personal history of primary cancer of the ovary, uterus or breast

■ Starting periods at an early age

Staphylococcus aureus is a species of bacteria often associated with the formation of abscesses, including those of the breast.

■ First full-term pregnancy after the age of 35

■ Taking the contraceptive pill – may lead to a small increase in risk, but this reverts to normal in the years after ceasing medication

■ Hormone replacement therapy (HRT), which involves taking oestrogen after the menopause for more than 10 years – this may increase the breast cancer risk by 50 per cent

■ Obesity doubles the risk in postmenopausal women

■ Cigarette smoking for more than 30 years

■ Radiation therapy for Hodgkin's disease – women remain at high risk.

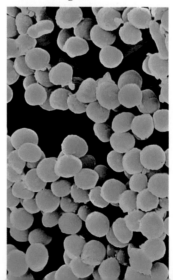

Incidence

■ **Benign lumps**

About one in two women in the UK have symptoms of benign breast disease during their child-bearing years. Fibroadenomas are common between the ages of 15 and 30. Breast cysts are more common in women aged 40–50 years. Breast abscesses occur occasionally in breast-feeding women.

■ **Breast cancer**

In the UK, breast cancer is the commonest cancer in women, affecting 1 in 10 women at some time in their lives. It is rare in young women but progressively increases in incidence from about the age of 45.

Blocked milk ducts in lactating women may become infected, forming an abscess. Breast-feeding can continue during treatment.

Diagnosis

If a woman has a lump in her breast, she should be examined to check the characteristics of the lump and assess her general health. Further investigations may include an ultrasound scan, mammography and aspiration cytology; the latter is an out-patient procedure in which a small portion of the lump is removed with a special needle for examination under the microscope.

BREAST CYST

Fluid aspirated from a breast cyst can be examined in the same way. A biopsy (surgical removal of tissue for analysis) may be needed to make the final diagnosis.

Mammography involves low-dose X-ray examination of the breast tissue. The image produced is then assessed by a radiologist.

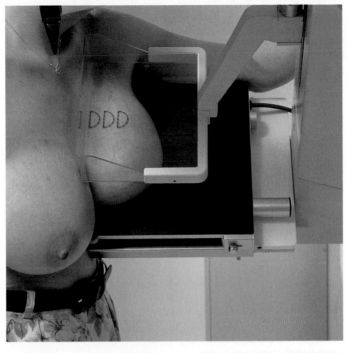

Screening

Early breast cancer can often be diagnosed by mammography (low-dose X-ray of the breast).
■ It detects lumps from 1 mm (0.03 in) in diameter, before they can be felt by hand (tumours must be at least 1 cm /⅓ inch in diameter to be palpable)
■ Mammography is more accurate in older women than younger women as they have less-dense breast tissue
■ In the UK, the government has decided to offer all women from the age of 50 a mammogram every three years. All patients with an abnormal mammogram are asked to attend an assessment clinic to undergo further tests.
   Women with a strong family history of breast cancer may have a mammogram in their 30s or 40s.

Treatment

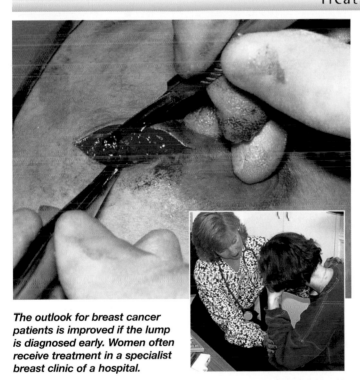

The outlook for breast cancer patients is improved if the lump is diagnosed early. Women often receive treatment in a specialist breast clinic of a hospital.

If a breast abscess is found to be the cause of a lump, surgical drainage may be required. Abscesses are usually caused by Staphylococcus aureus.

Depending on the cause of the breast lump, the treatment may involve surgery, radiotherapy or chemotherapy.

BENIGN BREAST LUMPS

There are different treatments for the three types of benign breast lumps:
■ **Fibroadenomas**
If the lump grows or causes worry, it can be surgically removed.
■ **Breast cysts**
These can often be drained with a syringe. If they reform, they can be removed surgically.
■ **Breast abscesses**
Antibiotic treatment, for example with flucloxacillin, may be successful, but abscesses may need surgical drainage.

BREAST CANCER

The aim is to remove the lump and to prevent recurrences and metastases. Lowering oestrogen levels with drugs or surgery is often important, as breast cancer appears to be dependent on oestrogen.
■ **Surgery**
Options include removal of the lump or part or all of the breast (mastectomy). Glands may be removed from the axilla to see if they contain malignant cells (node positive). Removal of the ovaries (oophorectomy) may be advised to reduce oestrogen levels.
■ **Radiotherapy and chemotherapy**
Increasingly successful regimes of therapy are now available to prolong disease-free survival; for example, chemotherapy with cyclophosphamide, methotrexate and 5-fluorouracil reduces the death rate in pre-menopausal women by 25 per cent.

Prognosis

■ **Benign tumours.** About one in five fibroadenomas disappear without treatment and few enlarge. Most persist until the menopause when they become less obvious. About one in 10 breast cysts refill after drainage, and about 50 per cent of women with one cyst develop another.
■ **Breast cancers.** Treatment regimes have reduced breast cancer death rates by 30 per cent in the last decade. Early treatment is vital as the smaller

the lump, the better the outlook.
   Up to 90 per cent of women with a lump of less than 2 cm (¾ in) in diameter are alive five years later, but this figure drops to 60 per cent for women who have a lump that is 2–5 cm (¾–2 in) in size.

Radiotherapy is used to destroy cancer cells. Ionizing radiation passes through the diseased tissue and destroys the abnormal cells.

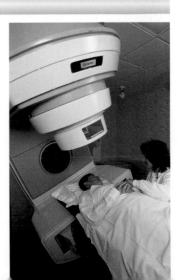

Menorrhagia

Causes and symptoms

Menorrhagia is the medical term for recurrent, excessively heavy periods, whether regular or irregular. Periods occur as part of the menstrual cycle and the average blood loss is about 30 ml. With menorrhagia, this increases to 80 ml or more and may be associated with the passage of large blood clots. Excessive blood loss often leads to anaemia (a reduction in the amount of oxygen-carrying haemoglobin in the blood), making women feel tired and fatigued.

UTERINE ABNORMALITIES
In about 50 per cent of women with menorrhagia, there is no sign of disease in the pelvic organs and the condition is classified as dysfunctional uterine bleeding. In some women, dysfunctional uterine bleeding is associated with failure of ovulation, and their hormone levels are abnormal.

In women who ovulate regularly, excessive bleeding may be due to abnormalities in local factors in the uterus. Fibrinolytic activity in the endometrium (the lining of the uterus), which prevents blood clotting, may be increased, or prostaglandin (a hormone-like substance) synthesis may be abnormal.

Other possible causes include hypothyroidism, congenital abnormalities of the uterus leading to a larger internal bleeding area than normal, the presence of an intrauterine contraceptive device (IUD), chronic pelvic infection, fibroids, blood disorders, endometriosis, hormonal disturbances and medically prescribed anti-clotting drugs.

Psychological factors, such as anorexia, can also affect menstrual bleeding by disturbing hormone production.

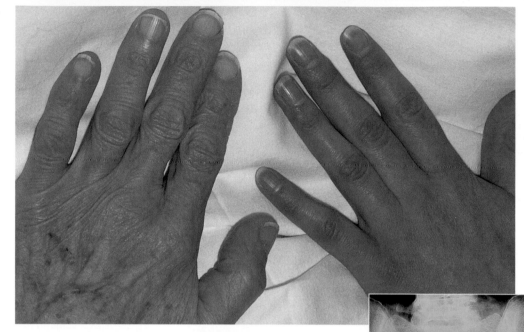

The hand on the left is exhibiting signs of iron deficiency (anaemia), as a result of reduced haemoglobin in the blood; this can be caused by menorrhagia. In comparison, the hand on the right is a normal, healthy colour.

A calcified fibroid (circled) is visible within the uterus in this coloured X-ray. The presence of uterine fibroids may cause menorrhagia.

Diagnosis

A full blood count will be taken once a woman has contacted her GP to complain of excessively heavy periods.

This blood sample indicates that the patient is suffering from anaemia. The large, spherical structures are red blood cells, many of which are smaller than normal and irregularly shaped.

Diagnosis is usually based on a woman's report of heavy periods. A GP may ask a woman to keep a diary recording her pad and/or tampon use throughout a period to gauge the extent of bleeding.

Investigations include a general physical examination, a pelvic examination, a full blood count and possibly thyroid function tests. Swabs may be taken from inside the cervix to exclude pelvic infection.

In women aged 40 or over, a specimen of the endometrium should be taken for laboratory examination (endometrial biopsy). A specimen may be obtained during an out-patient visit or admission to hospital may be required for a 'D and C' (dilatation and curettage); general anaesthetic may be recommended for this.

Menstrual cycle

The ovaries release an egg about once a month (ovulation). About two weeks before ovulation, rising levels of the female hormones oestrogen and progesterone prepare the lining of the uterus – the endometrium – to receive and nourish a fertilized egg. The lining thickens as its blood supply increases.

If no pregnancy occurs, the hormone levels fall and the endometrium degenerates and the inner surface of the uterus bleeds for about three to seven days – this is known as a period. The endometrium then regenerates and the cycle is repeated. Periods may still occur without ovulation, but tend to be irregular.

The menstrual cycle is controlled by the hypothalamus and hormones released by the pituitary gland in the brain.

Treatment

If any abnormality is found in the uterus, such as a fibroid, infection or hormonal disturbance, the appropriate treatment must be given.

REDUCING BLOOD LOSS

With dysfunctional bleeding, several drugs are effective. Mefenamic acid, naproxen, ibuprofen and diclofenac reduce period pain (dysmenorrhoea) by inhibiting prostaglandin production and may reduce blood loss. They can be very effective but can cause gastro-intestinal side effects.

Tranexamic acid is also often very effective and may reduce blood loss by half. It reduces fibrinolytic activity in the endometrium but should not be taken by women with a history of thrombosis (blood clots).

Treatment with mefenamic acid and its related drugs as well as tranexamic acid should be started on the first day of each period and continued for three or four days. If successful, it can be continued indefinitely. Patients with heavy bleeding with a non-hormonal intra-uterine device (IUD) may also benefit from these drugs.

Oral progestogens have been

used to control heavy blood loss. They have not proved very effective, but they can delay the onset of periods.

CONTRACEPTIVES

The combined oral contraceptive pill (containing oestrogen and a progestogen) may markedly reduce menstrual blood loss and cramps. It can also lead to regular periods. Mefenamic acid can be added if necessary.

The progestogen-releasing IUD may provide good control

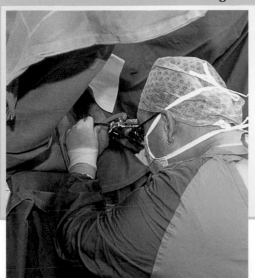

The contraceptive pill regulates the menstrual cycle and prevents pregnancy. It is sometimes used to treat menorrhagia as it helps reduce blood loss.

Treatment will depend on the patient's age and the severity of symptoms. Some women can be treated with drugs, while surgical intervention may be needed in other patients.

for menorrhagia in the long term. Some light bleeding may occur in the first few months but many women then cease to have periods (amenorrhoea), which many consider to be a major advantage. The device releases a small amount of levonorgestrel daily for at least five years and is a highly effective contraceptive.

Long-acting progesterone injections have similar benefits. As with the IUDs, bleeding is irregular at first, and then ceases. Injections are repeated after 8–12 weeks.

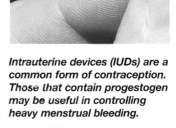

Intrauterine devices (IUDs) are a common form of contraception. Those that contain progestogen may be useful in controlling heavy menstrual bleeding.

Surgical options

In the few patients whose problems cannot be controlled by one of the above means, surgery may be considered. Removal of the uterus (hysterectomy) is one possibility in women who have finished child bearing, but a possible modern alternative is endometrial ablation. This is a more minor procedure that involves the destruction of the endometrium, often with the use of a laser, while the inside of the uterus is visualized through a fibre-optic instrument (hysteroscope). The short-term results are often good, but the long-term results are less certain.

Surgery can be used to treat severe cases of menorrhagia. Options include hysterectomy, hysteroscopy and endometrial ablation.

Incidence

Menorrhagia is very common, with about 20 per cent of women losing 80 ml of blood or more during each period. In 1993 in the UK, about 822,000 prescriptions were written for the treatment of menorrhagia.

Prognosis

The outlook for menorrhagia will depend on its cause. For most women, medical treatment is possible and the need for surgery is becoming infrequent. Reaching the menopause is the natural cure for heavy periods.

Cervical cancer

Symptoms

Cancer of the cervix (also known as cervical cancer) is one of the most common female cancers worldwide. However, it is usually slow-growing and, if detected early enough, it can be effectively treated. In developed countries, advanced cervical cancer has become a decreasing problem as a result of widespread cervical screening but, in many developing countries, screening is not generally available and cervical cancer remains the most common cause of cancer death.

CELL ABNORMALITIES
The cervix (the neck of the womb) is the lower third of the uterus. It projects into the vagina and surrounds the cervical canal which links the vagina to the inside of the womb. Cells on the outer surface of the cervix sometimes develop abnormalities but often return to normal without treatment.

Occasionally, however, the abnormalities persist and after several years the cells may become cancerous. Abnormalities that are

recognized as pre-cancerous can usually be simply treated with a laser, freezing or diathermy during an out-patient appointment.

CLINICAL SYMPTOMS
Pre-cancerous changes in the cervix and early cervical cancer cause no symptoms, so cervical screening is vital to detect early disease. At a later stage, cervical cancer may cause abnormal vaginal bleeding between periods, a vaginal discharge and discomfort may occur after intercourse. Women who have reached their menopause and who no longer have periods may develop new bleeding.

Pain is a late symptom of cervical cancer and a sign that the cancer has spread widely in the pelvis. Persistent mild fever, weight loss, anaemia and urinary and bowel problems may also occur in advanced disease.

Cervical screening involves a smear of cells being taken from the cervix. This is then analysed in a laboratory for cell changes.

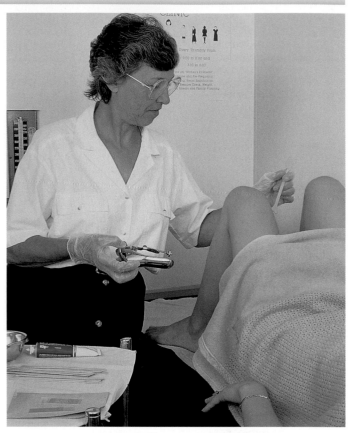

Diagnosis

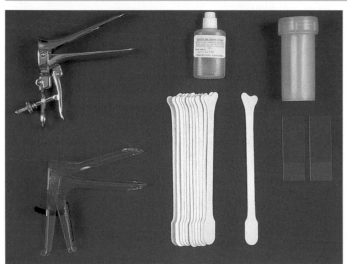

CERVICAL SMEAR TEST
In its very early stages, cervical cancer is diagnosed by the examination of cells taken from the surface of the cervix (a cervical smear). During a smear test, the doctor inserts an instrument called a speculum into the vagina in order to hold the vaginal walls apart and obtain a clear view of the cervix. A wooden spatula and/or a small brush is then used to

take a sample of cells from the cervix. These samples are spread on a microscope slide and sent to a laboratory.

If the laboratory finds persistently abnormal cells or pre-cancerous (dyskaryotic) or cancerous cells, the woman will be asked to attend hospital for a colposcopy, an out-patient procedure involving the use of a magnifying instrument to view the cervix. Small

The equipment used for a smear test consists of a speculum, spatulas, a fixative and slides and containers for preserving samples for testing.

biopsies of cervical tissue may be taken and sent for laboratory examination.

CONFIRMING THE DIAGNOSIS
More advanced cancer of the cervix is not diagnosed reliably by a smear test, but the diagnosis may be suspected when the cervix is viewed through a speculum. Colposcopy

and biopsy may therefore be needed to confirm the diagnosis and determine the extent of the disease.

Further tests may be conducted, including: blood tests, X-rays, an ultrasound examination and CT (computed tomography) or MR (magnetic resonance) imaging scans. In some cases, a pelvic examination under anaesthetic (EUA) may also be required.

A photograph may be taken of the cervix (cervicography). This enables the image to be examined by a specialist.

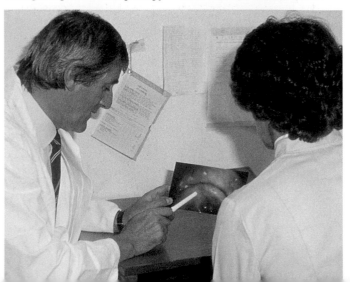

Causes and prognosis

Risk factors for cervical cancer include having sexual intercourse, having sexual intercourse at an early age and having several sexual partners. These all expose the cervix to the risk of infection with the human papilloma (wart) virus (HPV). HPV infection does not always lead to cervical cancer but infection with a type 16 strain of HPV is an important risk factor. Some women appear to have an increased genetic susceptibility to cervical cancer. Smoking and conditions that affect the immune system also increase the risk.

The outlook for women with cervical cancer depends on the stage of their disease. Cervical cancer can often be very successfully treated in its early stages, before it has spread to the lymph system. If the cancer has spread, the outlook is less favourable.

Only about 65 per cent of women treated for advanced cervical cancer will survive for five years.

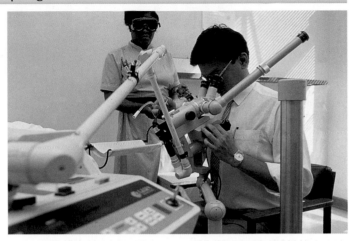

A gynaecologist uses a laser to treat cervical cancer. This can be effective in the very early stages of the disease.

Stages of cancer of the cervix

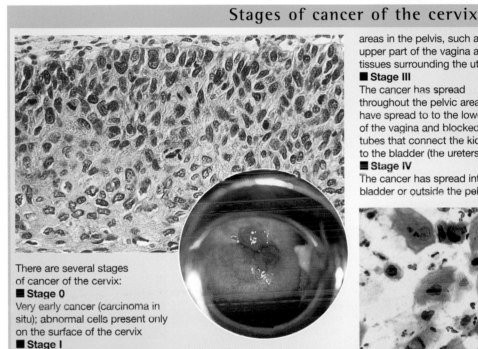

There are several stages of cancer of the cervix:
■ **Stage 0**
Very early cancer (carcinoma in situ); abnormal cells present only on the surface of the cervix
■ **Stage I**
Cancer cells have penetrated the cervix but remain confined to the uterus
■ **Stage II**
The cancer has spread to nearby

This cervical smear slide shows abnormal growth of cells. First stage pre-cancerous cells are visible as a discoloured area of the cervix (insert).

areas in the pelvis, such as the upper part of the vagina and the tissues surrounding the uterus
■ **Stage III**
The cancer has spread throughout the pelvic area; it may have spread to to the lower part of the vagina and blocked the tubes that connect the kidneys to the bladder (the ureters)
■ **Stage IV**
The cancer has spread into the bladder or outside the pelvis.

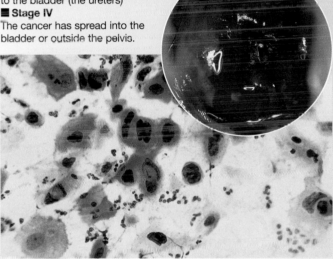

An abnormal cervix as seen on colposcopy (insert). Pre-cancerous epithelial cells are seen on the slide below as pink-stained cells with abnormally large nuclei.

Incidence

Cancer of the cervix is rare below the age of 25 but the incidence rises until the age of about 54, when it peaks and then levels off. The disease kills about 7,500 women in the European Union each year, and is responsible for two per cent of all cancer deaths.

The effectiveness of cervical screening in reducing the incidence of cervical cancer has been shown in several countries. In the UK, it is estimated that screening for cervical cancer has reduced deaths due to the disease by over 60 per cent in women under the age of 55. In Sweden, where cancer of the cervix was once the third most common cancer in women in their early 60s, it has now fallen to 14th place.

A nurse places a specimen of cells, taken during a smear test on a slide. Screening for abnormal cells has reduced the incidence of cervical cancer.

Treatment

The treatment of cervical cancer will vary according to the stage at which the disease is diagnosed. Surgical removal of the womb (hysterectomy) and radiotherapy may be necessary if the cancer has progressed beyond its very earliest stage.

Recent research suggests that the effectiveness of radiotherapy may be increased if the patient is also treated with the effective anti-cancer drug, cisplatin. Antibiotics may also be needed to improve the patient's general condition, and treating underlying or associated problems, such as anaemia, may help to improve response to treatment.

Menstrual disorders

Symptoms

Menstrual blood loss results from a series of hormonal changes controlled by the ovaries and the brain. A cyclical rise and fall in the levels of oestrogen and progesterone leads to the release of an egg from the ovaries (ovulation) every 21–35 days. If no pregnancy occurs, the uterus sheds its endometrium (inner lining) and menstrual bleeding results. Menstruation usually starts between the ages of 10 and 16 and finishes at the age of around 50.

UNUSUAL PATTERNS
The following unusual conditions do not constitute a disorder:
■ Anovulatory cycles – periods may occur without ovulation. This is common in young girls and older women, due to irregular hormone production
■ Irregular periods – cycles may vary from the normal range,

Many women are affected by some form of menstrual disorder. The resulting problems can range from severe pain or anaemia to infertility.

especially as women progress towards the menopause
■ Heavy blood loss – monthly blood loss is usually around 30 ml, but may be higher or lower. Blood loss of more than 80 ml can lead to anaemia.

MENSTRUAL DISORDERS
Menstrual disorders include:
■ Menorrhagia – unusually heavy and/or prolonged periods
■ Polymenorrhoea – abnormally frequent periods
■ Oligomenorrhoea – infrequent periods
■ Amenorrhoea – an absence of periods
■ Dysmenorrhoea – excessively painful periods.

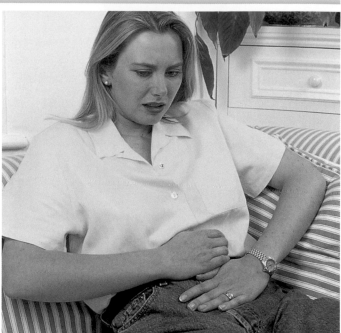

Causes

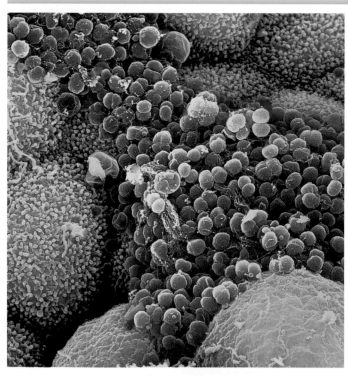

Risk factors for menstrual problems include the following:
■ Endocrine abnormalities – disturbances in hormone production in the ovaries, hypothalamus and pituitary gland may lead to menorrhagia, amenorrhoea or irregular periods. These disturbances may be related to factors such as stress, obesity, anorexia or excessive physical training

■ Excess prolactin production – this may be caused by stress, a pituitary tumour (usually non-cancerous) or medication (such as certain indigestion drugs)
■ Hormonal disturbances in other organs, such as the thyroid gland. Short-term amenorrhoea often occurs when women stop taking the contraceptive pill
■ Polycystic ovarian syndrome

▶ *Polycystic ovary syndrome is characterized by the growth of cysts within the ovary, greatly enlarging it (right). This causes infrequent or heavy periods.*

◀ *This electron micrograph shows Neisseria gonorrhoeae bacteria (red) infecting body cells (green). Pelvic infections can cause dysmenorrhoea.*

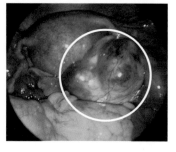

– the abnormally high levels of oestrogen produced are related to obesity and excessive hair development, while periods may be infrequent, absent or heavy
■ Excess production of prostaglandins (hormone-like substances) – this may cause dysmenorrhoea in the presence of an intrauterine contraceptive device (IUCD) or a disorder such as endometriosis (abnormal tissue growth), pelvic inflammatory disease, uterine polyps or fibroids (benign tumours of the uterine wall)
■ Congenital abnormalities, such as bicornuate uterus (in which the upper part of the uterus is divided in two). The increase in internal surface area causes heavy periods
■ IUCDs – some types may lead to heavier, longer periods
■ Chronic pelvic infection by bacteria such as *Neisseria gonorrhoeae* and *Chlamydia* may cause dysmenorrhoea
■ Fibroids (benign) and polyps

on the endometrium – these may cause heavy bleeding
■ Endometriosis – in this condition, endometrium-like tissue grows at sites in the pelvis remote from the uterus, causing pelvic inflammation and prolonged, painful periods
■ Blood clotting defects – the use of long-term anticoagulant therapy can cause heavy periods, as can disorders that affect the clotting mechanisms.

Incidence

Menstrual disorders are very common. About 20 per cent of women have menorrhagia, which is the eighth most common cause of all referrals to hospital in the UK. About 50 per cent of cases are due to endocrine disturbances.

Around 15 per cent of women suffer dysmenorrhoea that is severe enough to prevent normal activities.

Diagnosis

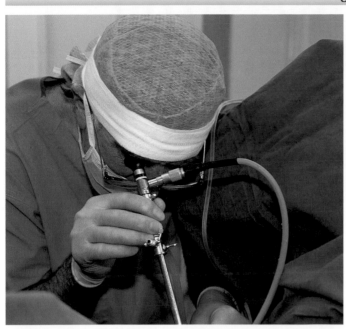

Diagnosis of menstrual disorders would involve the following tests as appropriate:
■ Careful history taking
■ A physical examination – including an internal pelvic examination except in the case of very young women
■ Blood tests for anaemia and hormone levels
■ Urine tests
■ Tests for pelvic infection
■ Endometrial biopsy – removal of a small sample of tissue from the endometrium for examination
■ Hysteroscopy (using a telescopic instrument to view the inside of the uterus)
■ Transvaginal ultrasound –

If detailed investigations are necessary, a laparoscopy may be performed. This enables the surgeon to view abnormalities of the uterus or ovaries.

this allows an assessment of the thickness of the endometrium and detects polyps
■ Laparoscopy (examination of the abdominal organs via an illuminated telescope)
■ Pituitary scan – this is only necessary in the presence of persistently raised prolactin levels.

In women under 40 with regular but heavy periods, biopsy and hysteroscopy are not usually necessary as the risk of cancer is low.

Prevention

Some menstrual disorders may be prevented by avoiding factors which disrupt the hormonal balance, such as stress, obesity, anorexia and over-exercise.

Treatment

If there is no evidence of a tumour or infection, reassurance that periods will return to normal with time may be the only treatment needed. However, where heavy bleeding has caused anaemia, iron tablets may prove beneficial. Any existing weight problem will need to be addressed, as many menstrual disorders, such as polycystic ovarian syndrome, may be caused by obesity.

DRUGS AND IUCDs
Common medical treatments include the following:
■ Mefenamic acid (a non-steroidal anti-inflammatory drug) – often used to relieve severe dysmenorrhoea
■ Tranexamic acid – is able to almost halve menstrual loss
■ The contraceptive pill – may be used to lighten periods and is often able to relieve symptoms of polycystic ovarian syndrome or mild endometriosis
■ Norethisterone (a hormonal, non-contraceptive pill) – may be taken orally to reduce bleeding. Danazol and GnRH analogues are more powerful hormonal preparations that are used to treat conditions such as severe endometriosis
■ Insertion of a progestogen-bearing IUCD – often effectively relieves menorrhagia within a few months.

SURGICAL INTERVENTION
Surgery may be indicated for menorrhagia that remains uncontrolled by medical means. Women whose families are complete may be offered a

hysterectomy, while more minor surgery will be attempted for women wishing to remain fertile.
Minor procedures might include:
■ Endometrial ablation – a relatively new technique in which the full thickness of the endometrium is destroyed by laser or other means
■ Myomectomy (the surgical removal of fibroids) – this may be carried out where fibroids are responsible for menstrual disorders. A hysterectomy may be necessary for severe fibroids.

A hysterectomy involves the removal of the uterus (centre). It may be performed in cases of severe menstrual disorders that fail to respond to drug treatment.

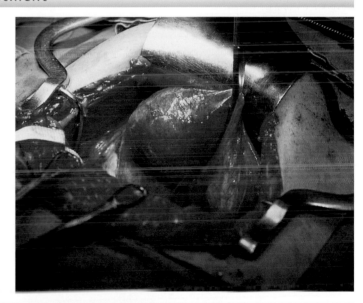

Prognosis

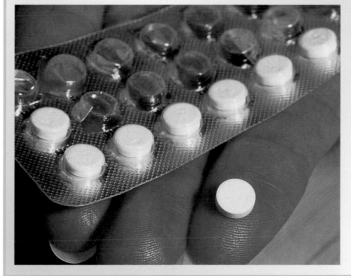

Most menstrual disturbances resolve naturally or can be relieved with treatment. Heavy periods in girls and young women are unlikely to be due to disease of the pelvic organs and in most cases the disorder will eventually cure itself. In rare cases, persistent heavy bleeding in older women may be related to changes in the endometrium, including the development of cancer, so follow-up is needed.

Post-pill amenorrhoea usually resolves within six months.

Many menstrual disorders resolve naturally over time. Any caused by contraceptive pills disappear a few months after cessation of the Pill.

Vaginal discharge

Symptoms

All women of child-bearing age have some vaginal discharge between periods. The amount varies during the menstrual cycle and between individuals.

Normal discharge has the following characteristics:
■ It is white when fresh and yellow or pale brown when dry
■ It lubricates and moisturizes the vagina, protecting it against infection.

Discharge usually increases:
■ At ovulation
■ Before a period (pre-menstrually)
■ When taking certain oral contraceptives
■ When using an intrauterine contraceptive device (IUCD)
■ With sexual excitement.

MEDICAL ADVICE
It is important to seek medical advice if the normal discharge:
■ Suddenly increases in volume
■ Becomes yellow or greenish
■ Contains fresh red blood or old brown or blackish blood
■ Smells unpleasant
■ Causes itching, soreness, burning or ulceration in or around the vagina.
Or if a patient experiences:
■ Pain during sexual intercourse (dyspareunia)
■ Painful urination (dysuria).

A certain amount of vaginal discharge in women is normal. However, medical advice should be sought if the appearance, volume or smell changes.

Causes

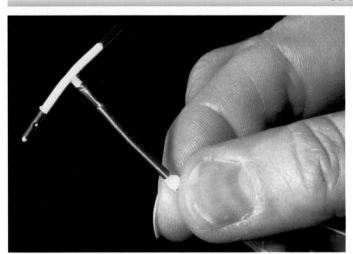

There are numerous causes for an abnormal vaginal discharge:
■ Infection – the most common cause (see box below)
■ Abnormalities of the cervix – such as a polyp or cancer
■ Foreign bodies in the vagina – for example a 'lost' tampon, contraceptive devices, or rings for uterine prolapse
■ Chemical vaginitis – due to the use of antiseptic douches or perfumed bath additives

Abnormal vaginal discharge may be caused by a foreign body in the vagina, such as an intrauterine contraceptive device.

■ Uterine prolapse – the uterus may become infected if it drops low in or protrudes from the vagina
■ Oestrogen-containing drugs – such as hormone replacement therapy
■ Atrophic vaginitis – this develops in older women. Oestrogen deficiency after the menopause or following surgical removal of the ovaries (known as an oophorectomy), makes the vagina less resistant to infection
■ Vaginal fistulae – disease of other pelvic organs may lead to the discharge of bowel contents or urine through false openings in the vaginal wall.

Infectious organisms

Micro-organisms causing vaginal infections include:
■ *Candida albicans* (thrush) – a yeast-like fungus that may cause itching, dysuria and a thick yellow or white discharge
■ *Gardnerella vaginalis* – an overgrowth of this bacterium causes a condition known as bacterial vaginosis. This can cause a watery grey discharge with a fishy smell
■ *Trichomonas* – this single-celled organism (protozoan) may cause no symptoms or severe inflammation (vaginitis) with a purulent bubbly discharge.
■ *Chlamydia* – infection of the cervix with *Chlamydia trachomatis* is initially symptomless but later may cause a mild discharge
■ Neisseria gonorrhoeae –

gonorrhoeal infections with this bacterium are sexually transmitted. The symptoms and problems following infection are similar to those caused by chlamydia
■ Human papilloma virus (HPV) – this agent causes genital warts. They may cause itching and discharge
■ *Herpes genitalis* – the herpes virus may cause severe burning, itching and pain; vaginal discharge usually occurs
■ Multiple agents – several transmitted infections can occur in the vagina at the same time.

This micrograph shows the fungus Candida albicans, which is the cause of thrush. It is commonly present in the vagina, mouth and gut.

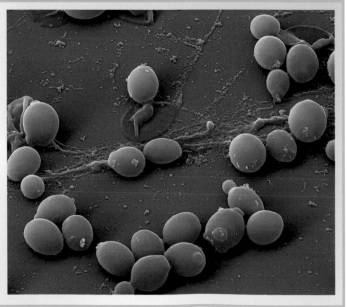

Diagnosis

A woman concerned about a vaginal discharge should seek medical advice. If there is any possibility that the infection has been sexually transmitted, it is advisable for her to visit a genitourinary medicine (GUM) clinic or sexually transmitted disease (STD) clinic, as these clinics have diagnostic facilities that are often not available in GP surgeries. No referral letter is needed to visit a GUM clinic and the visit is confidential.

MEDICAL QUESTIONS
The doctor is likely to ask:
■ How long the discharge has been abnormal
■ How it differs from normal in appearance, volume and smell
■ Whether passing urine is painful
■ Whether the woman has had sexual intercourse and whether she has recently been with a new sexual partner
■ Details of previous illnesses, medical treatment or self-medication.

PHYSICAL EXAMINATION
The doctor will then:
■ Examine the woman's external genital region
■ Use a speculum (a metal instrument that holds the walls of the vagina apart) to inspect the cervix and inside walls of the vagina
■ Assess whether the pelvic organs are inflamed by inserting two fingers into the vagina while pressing down on the lower abdomen with the other hand (a bimanual examination).

FURTHER TESTS
Other possible tests include:
■ Taking vaginal and cervical swabs for laboratory culture
■ Examining a specimen of discharge under a microscope
■ Taking a blood sample to test for viral or bacterial antibodies.

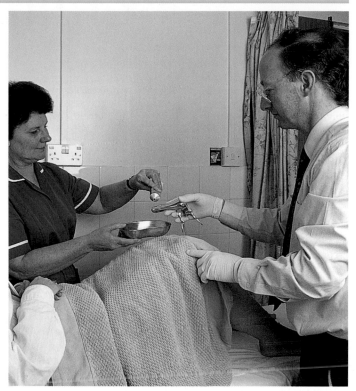

To make a diagnosis a GP will carry out a physical examination. A speculum is used to view the inside of the cervix and vagina.

Treatment

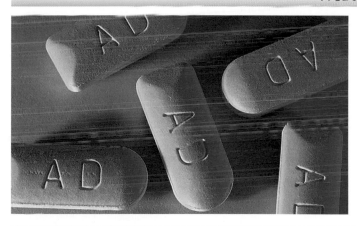

Treatment will vary according to the cause of the discharge. For some women, changing to a different brand of contraceptive pill or the removal of an IUCD may lessen their vaginal discharge. Other vaginal foreign bodies must be removed.

Atrophic vaginitis may be helped with hormone

Vaginal infections may be treated using pessaries. These are inserted into the vagina and therefore act directly on the infective organisms.

replacement therapy. Women with uterine prolapse or disease of the cervix will need to be referred to a gynaecologist.

TREATMENT OPTIONS
Some vaginal infections can be satisfactorily treated with vaginal pessaries or creams, but oral antibiotic, antiviral or antifungal drugs are sometimes needed. The prescribed course of treatment should always be completed. Self-treatment is inadvisable, except occasionally for recurrent candida.

Prognosis and prevention

Most abnormal vaginal discharge can be effectively relieved. In order to help protect against sexually transmitted disease and bacterial infections, condoms should be used and tampons should be changed regularly.

COPING WITH CANDIDA
Candida is usually treated only if it causes symptoms. It responds well to clotrimazole vaginal preparations or oral fluconazole. Self-medication is sometimes possible for recurrent candida, if the diagnosis has been recently confirmed.

The following measures may prevent recurrence:
■ Keeping the genital area clean and dry, but not washed excessively
■ Avoiding use of perfumed,

deodorant or disinfectant preparations
■ Not wearing tight-fitting underpants, tights and jeans
■ Using emollients (moisturizers) may be soothing
■ Advice about treatment should be sought by women who are pregnant or breast-feeding, and those who are diabetic or have decreased immunity.

Sexually transmitted diseases are frequently responsible for abnormal vaginal discharge. Using condoms will reduce the risk of transmission.

Women who suffer from candida should avoid using perfumed substances, such as bath oils. These may further irritate infected areas of skin.

Incidence

Vaginal discharge is common: one in 10 women seeing their GP mention the symptom and almost one in five attending gynaecological clinics have an abnormal vaginal discharge of a type that suggests infection.

Chlamydia

Causes

Chlamydia is the most common sexually transmitted bacterial infection in England and Wales. Its increasing prevalence has worrying implications for sexual health and fertility.

THE CAUSE
The bacterium responsible, *Chlamydia trachomatis*, targets the cells that line the urethra, cervix, rectum and eye. The organism is a major cause of lower genital tract infection, being responsible for about 40 per cent of all cases of non-gonococcal urethritis. If left untreated, chlamydia can lead to complications such as epididymitis and pelvic inflammatory disease (PID).

Chlamydia is eminently treatable. However, 80 per cent of women and 50 per cent of men are initially asymptomatic. Consequently, there is a permanent reservoir of undiagnosed and unrecognized infection in the community, enabling increased transmission.

TRANSMISSION
Chlamydia is transmitted by:
■ Sexual intercourse, either vaginal or rectal, without the use of condoms
■ Non-penetrative genital to genital contact and oral sex
■ Transferral from a pregnant woman to her baby's eyes, if chlamydia in the pregnant woman is untreated.

Risk factors include:
■ Being less than 25 years of age and sexually active
■ Having more than one sexual partner, or changing partners within the last 12 months.

Some sufferers of chlamydia experience lower abdominal pain. The spherical bacteria that cause chlamydia (inset) are among the smallest bacteria.

Symptoms

Symptoms, if they are present, usually appear 1–3 weeks after infection. It is possible to pass on the infection even when there are no obvious symptoms.

MEN
Symptoms would include the following:
■ A clear discharge from the urethra

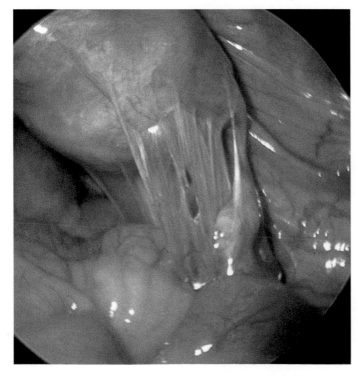

This laparoscopic view of a woman's pelvis shows the reproductive organs in an inflamed state, with pyosalpinx (pus in the uterine tube).

■ Some discomfort when passing urine.

WOMEN
Women are often asymptomatic (have no symptoms) even when infected. Symptoms that may manifest include:
■ A slight bleed from the vagina, directly after sex or between menstrual cycles
■ Contact bleeding from the cervix following a smear test
■ Purulent vaginal discharge
■ Lower abdominal pain.

COMPLICATIONS
If left untreated, many complications occur:
■ At least 10 per cent of women with chlamydia will develop pelvic inflammatory disease (PID). PID is associated with the formation of scar tissue, adhesions and blockages within the uterine tubes.

PID can cause chronic pain and even tubal infertility. Around eight per cent of women with PID who become pregnant will have an ectopic pregnancy
■ 10–20 per cent of women with PID may develop Fitz-Hugh–Curtis syndrome. This is caused by inflammation of the membrane surrounding the liver and the formation of adhesions. Pain in the upper right abdomen is a characteristic symptom
■ Pregnant women with untreated chlamydia may pass the infection to their baby during a vaginal delivery. As a result, affected neonates may

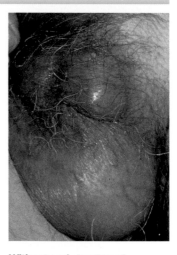

Without early treatment, chlamydia in men can result in epididymitis. This chronic inflammation of the ejaculatory ducts can cause infertility.

suffer from a kind of conjunctivitis known as ophthalmia neonatorum. This can look quite dramatic but it is relatively mild and usually responds well to treatment
■ Men with untreated chlamydia may develop epididymitis which, if bilateral, may lead to the formation of adhesions in the ejaculatory ducts and resultant infertility
■ The condition may trigger reactive arthritis, especially in men.

Diagnosis

Genital chlamydia is usually diagnosed by a technique known as enzyme immunoassay. This involves analysis of swabs taken from the urethra, vagina and cervix. Obtaining these specimens can be uncomfortable.

In recent months there has been a gradual shift towards more sophisticated molecular technologies such as DNA probes. The new techniques allow non-invasive screening methods, for example, through urine testing. Although expensive, the new tests are more specific and accurate.

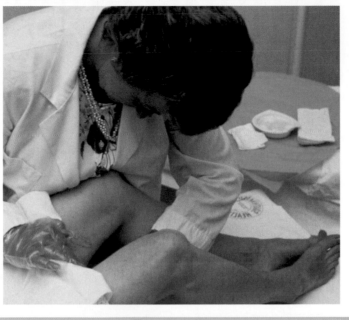

Chlamydia can be diagnosed by analysing swabs taken from the vagina. These are then tested using a technique known as enzyme immunoassay.

Prevention

If used correctly, condoms help in cutting chlamydia transmission. Limiting the number of sexual partners also reduces the risk as does having remained with the same partner for the last 12 months.

People with chlamydia should avoid intercourse until they and their sexual partners have completed their treatment. Otherwise, the cycle of infection and re-infection is likely to continue.

Widespread screening programmes, with the active tracing and treatment of sexual contacts, offer most hope for controlling the infection. Sweden has carried out such a policy and reduced the incidence of chlamydia.

Treatment

There are three antibiotic treatments available for chlamydia:
■ Uncomplicated infections are usually treated with doxycycline tablets, taken twice a day for a week
■ A single dose of azithromycin taken by mouth provides an effective alternative. Although more expensive, azithromycin is useful when patient compliance with treatment is likely to be poor or erratic
■ If the patient is pregnant, erythromycin four times a day for seven days is usually prescribed.

People with chlamydia should not have intercourse until they and their sexual partners have

Chlamydia may be present without manifesting any symptoms. In these cases all sexual partners from the previous six months must be notified.

successfully completed their course of treatment.

PARTNER NOTIFICATION
It is not certain for how long a patient can have chlamydia without showing symptoms, and this has implications in terms of notifying sexual partners:
■ Men displaying symptoms are advised to notify all sexual partners for the previous month
■ Asymptomatic men and all women are advised to notify all sexual partners within the previous six months. Where they have not had intercourse for six months, they should notify their last sexual partner.

GENITOURINARY CLINIC
A patient with chlamydia should attend a genitourinary medicine clinic. These clinics will perform a full screen for concurrent infections and assist in partner notification.

Incidence

The impact of chlamydia has increased dramatically:
■ Diagnoses of genital chlamydia almost doubled during the 1990s
■ In 1999 there were over 56,000 cases of uncomplicated chlamydia infection diagnosed in UK genitourinary medicine clinics. Of these, around 25,000 cases involved men and over 32,000, women. Diagnostic rates were highest in women from the ages of 16–19 and, in the case of males, between the ages of 20 and 24. Around 3–5 per cent of sexually active women attending GP practices in the UK are found to be chlamydia positive. Since women tested for chlamydia by their GPs are usually symptomatic, this understates the actual size of the problem
■ The incidence of chlamydial infection in men in the general population is uncertain. One study suggests a figure of 1.9 per cent
■ People of Afro-Caribbean origin appear to be at higher risk of chlamydial infection than Caucasians. The reasons for this are unclear.

Prognosis

Chlamydia responds well to early treatment. Problems do not tend to arise unless the patient remains untreated or has been re-infected. In such cases, certain complications may arise, most of which can prove difficult to treat.

If the condition is not treated early enough, chlamydia can cause pelvic inflammatory disease in women. This can lead to extensive scarring and the formation of abscesses.

In some susceptible individuals, usually men, chlamydia can trigger reactive arthritis.

Gonorrhoea

Causes

Gonorrhoea is a serious sexually transmitted infection. The infection is caused by the bacterium *Neisseria gonorrhoeae.* This organism, which does not survive long outside the human body, is transmitted through sexual activity, including vaginal, oral and anal contact.

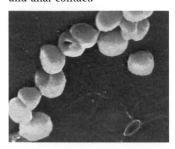

TRANSMISSION
As well as being transmitted during sexual contact, gonorrhoea can be passed by a woman to her baby during its passage down the birth canal. As a result, the baby may develop a serious eye infection, ophthalmia neonatorum.

Gonorrhoea is a sexually transmitted infection that is becoming more common. Any symptoms should be discussed with a doctor immediately.

Neisseria gonorrhoeae is the species of bacteria that causes gonorrhoea. It infects the lining of the genital tract, including the cervix in women.

Symptoms

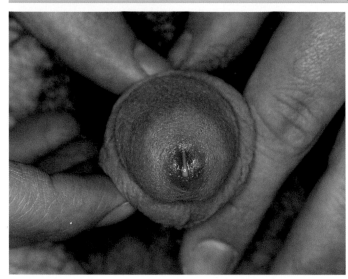

Both men and women can have gonorrhoea without showing symptoms. Indeed, as many as half of all infected women may not be aware that they have the condition.

SYMPTOMS IN MEN
Men are more likely to be aware of a problem. Symptoms include:
■ A creamy or green, thick, purulent discharge from the penis
■ Pain on passing urine

Around 10 per cent of men have no symptoms. However, many may experience inflammation of the urethra and penile discharge.

■ Irritation around the urethral opening (meatus)
■ Testicular pain.

SYMPTOMS IN WOMEN
Women's symptoms are usually less obvious. However, there may be:
■ Vaginal discharge
■ A burning sensation when passing urine
■ Irregular vaginal bleeding
■ Lower abdominal pain or pain during sexual intercourse.
  Both sexes may also have the infection in the throat and the rectum. This is usually symptomless but there may be rectal irritation or a discharge from the rectum. Patients may complain of a slight malaise.

Incidence

In 1999, 15,572 cases of uncomplicated gonorrhoea were diagnosed in England, nearly half of them in London.

Age group at risk
Young people between the ages of 16 and 25 are most at risk of becoming infected with gonorrhoea. The problem is common and infection rates are increasing despite the availability of effective treatment.

Men and women
Infection may be found in heterosexual and homosexual men as well as in women. The risk of infection for men who have unprotected sex with an

infected partner is between 20 and 50 per cent after a single exposure. Transmission risk from men to women can be as high as 80 per cent.

Transmission
Oral to genital contact is more common from the penis to the mouth but can also occur from vagina to mouth. Anal intercourse transmits infection at rates similar to vaginal intercourse.

Incubation period
The incubation period (which is the time between exposure and the onset of symptoms) may be as short as two days but it can be as long as 10 days.

Diagnosis

The diagnosis is confirmed in the laboratory. Swabs are taken from the infected areas, such as the lining of the cervix in women and the urethra in men.
  The smears are examined under the microscope after staining. Culture by incubation is also undertaken. During microbiological assessment, a

search is made for the causative agents of other sexually transmitted infections in addition to gonorrhoea.

To diagnose gonorrhoea, swabs are taken from the areas of likely infection. The specimens are then placed on a slide and viewed under a microscope.

Treatment

Uncomplicated gonorrhoea is effectively treated with a single injection of a large dose of penicillin or a related antibiotic.

Treatment may be given before the results of tests are available because the earlier the infection is treated, the more certain the cure.

HOSPITAL ADMISSION
If the infection has spread, prolonged treatment may be for necessary and hospital admission may be required. All patients should be tested for bacteriological cure 5-10 days after treatment. A person is considered to be infectious until treatment is successful.

Antibiotics are given by injection to treat gonorrhoea. After treatment, patients should be followed up to ensure the bacterium has been eradicated.

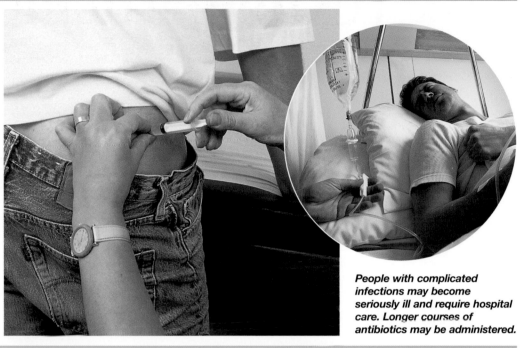

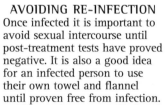

People with complicated infections may become seriously ill and require hospital care. Longer courses of antibiotics may be administered.

Prognosis

If the patient is treated promptly, there are usually no problems and symptoms start to settle within 24 hours.

COMPLICATIONS
If treatment is delayed in men, the main complication is epididymitis, an inflammation of the testicles which can lead to infertility.

If the condition is untreated in women, it is possible for the infection to spread to the reproductive organs including the uterine (fallopian) tubes. This is known as pelvic inflammatory disease (PID) and when the tubes become blocked, infertility will result. Pelvic inflammatory disease can be a very painful condition. The bacterium *Chlamydia* is the cause of PID in about 50 per cent of cases; gonorrhoea is the cause in about 25 per cent. The risk of ascending infection in women with gonorrhoea is about 10 per cent.

There is a possibility that the organism may enter the blood supply and produce a gonococcal septicaemia. Rarely the condition may spread to the heart, the liver or the brain and death may ensue.

Prevention

Sexually active people are potentially at risk of sexually transmitted infections.

The only certain way to avoid gonorrhoea and other such infections is to abstain from sexual intercourse or to restrict having intimate contact to someone who is known to be free of infection.

CONTRACEPTION
Sexually transmitted infections, such as gonorrhoea, can be prevented by always using condoms during vaginal, anal and oral sex.

GENITOURINARY CLINIC
Once infection has occurred it is important to seek treatment as soon as possible. People with symptoms should either visit their GP or attend a genitourinary (GU) clinic.

In the majority of these specialized clinics, no appointment is necessary. Confidentiality is absolute and staff do not send letters back to the family doctor unless this is requested by the patient. The staff of these clinics have special training and a consultant physician is usually in charge.

AVOIDING RE-INFECTION
Once infected it is important to avoid sexual intercourse until post-treatment tests have proved negative. It is also a good idea for an infected person to use their own towel and flannel until proven free from infection.

All sexual partners of infected people should be tested as soon as possible. Contact tracing is a vital part of disease control and confidentiality is assured.

Sexually active people can best protect themselves against gonorrhoea by using barrier contraception. Condoms can be purchased at a pharmacy.

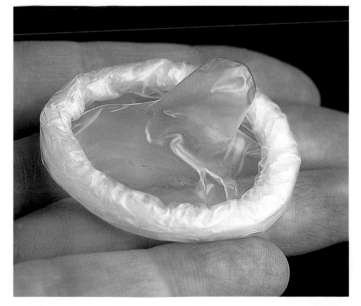

Testicular cancer

Symptoms

Testicular cancer occurs mostly in young men, but recent advances in treatment mean that they only rarely die from the disease, particularly if it is diagnosed early and treated promptly.

The first symptoms of testicular cancer may be related to the testicle or to other sites in the body.

TESTICULAR SYMPTOMS
■ Swelling – most men first notice a painless swelling in the testicle. The swelling is usually smooth, but may be irregular.

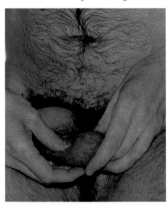

The scrotum may feel heavy
■ Pain – a few men initially notice pain in their testicle, rather than swelling.

GENERAL SYMPTOMS
In about 1 in 10 men, symptoms related to the spread of the tumour may be the first sign of testicular cancer. The malignancy sometimes spreads to other parts of the body while the primary testicular tumour is still too small to feel.

Possible symptoms of advanced disease include:
■ Abdominal pain
■ Backache
■ Swollen glands
■ Difficulty in breathing
■ Coughing up blood.

Some men believe that a recent testicular injury may be to blame for the cancer, but the injury probably only draws attention to a pre-existing tumour.

Regular self-examination is important for detecting testicular cancer. Early detection ensures a better chance of an effective cure.

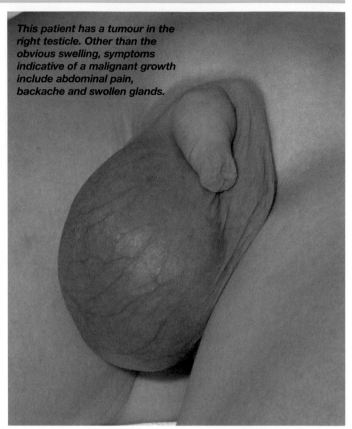

This patient has a tumour in the right testicle. Other than the obvious swelling, symptoms indicative of a malignant growth include abdominal pain, backache and swollen glands.

Causes

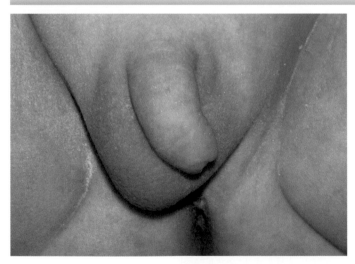

The risk of developing testicular cancer is increased by:
■ **Testicular maldescent**
The testicles normally descend to the scrotum by birth or soon after. In about two per cent of boys, one or both testicles remain in the abdomen or descend only as far as the groin region. Cancer is about 30 times more likely to develop in testicles that remain in the abdomen or are surgically brought down to the scrotum than in testicles

that have descended normally
■ **Prenatal events**
Fetal exposure to some hormones or radiation increases the risk of testicular cancer
■ **Testicular atrophy**
Tumours are more likely in testicles that have become wasted, such as after injury, twisting, infection or surgery
■ **Diet**
A diet high in saturated fat and low in fruit and vegetables appears to increase the risk.

An undescended testicle is a major risk factor; a male with this condition is 30 times more likely to develop testicular cancer in the future.

Seminomas – malignant testicular tumours – often appear as a swelling. In this case, an undescended testicle is affected.

TUMOUR ORIGIN
Most testicular tumours arise from germ cells, which are cells involved in sperm production. They are classified as seminomas and nonseminomas, with some tumours being a combination of the two.

The remaining 2–5 per cent of testicular cancers include Leydig cell tumours, Sertoli cell tumours and malignant lymphomas. Sertoli cells nourish the germ cells, while Leydig cells secrete androgens (male sex hormones).

Many testicular cancers produce protein substances that can be identified in blood samples and used to monitor tumour size and the effect of treatment.

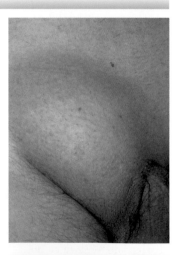

Incidence

Each year in the UK, about 600 men develop testicular cancer. Men between the ages of 25 and 34 are most affected. There are marked racial differences in incidence. Testicular cancer is rare in men of African descent, with 0.9 per 100,000 black Africans being affected, compared with four per 100,000 Caucasians.

Diagnosis

A firm or hard swelling in the testicle suggests testicular cancer, but this must be differentiated from a swelling due to infection or twisting of the testicle (testicular torsion), which cuts off the blood supply to the testicle and causes severe pain.

INVESTIGATIONS
Tests to confirm the diagnosis and assess whether the cancer has spread include:
- Biopsy – the removal of a small portion of the tumour for examination under the microscope; samples may also be taken from nearby lymph nodes
- Blood tests for tumour markers
- Chest X-ray to look for secondary tumour in the lungs
- Ultrasound scan to determine whether the tumour has spread to the abdomen or spine.

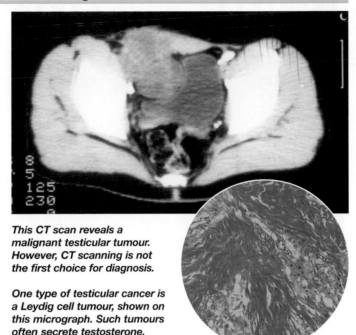

This CT scan reveals a malignant testicular tumour. However, CT scanning is not the first choice for diagnosis.

One type of testicular cancer is a Leydig cell tumour, shown on this micrograph. Such tumours often secrete testosterone, a male sex hormone.

Prevention

Maldescended testicles are unlikely to produce sperm normally and are at much increased risk of becoming cancerous. Doctors therefore usually recommended that they should be removed.

Eating a diet rich in fresh fruit and vegetables and low in animal fat may also help prevent testicular cancer.

A healthy, low-fat diet rich in vitamins can help in lowering the incidence of testicular cancer.

Treatment

Treatment depends on the tumour type and on the stage it has reached at diagnosis. It involves a combination of surgery, radiotherapy and/or chemotherapy.

THERAPY OPTIONS
Early seminomas can be very successfully treated with radiotherapy alone, with a very low risk of recurrence. In more advanced cases, the radiotherapy is combined with chemotherapy. Secondary (metastatic) seminoma tumours respond very well to chemotherapy.

Early nonseminomas may be

Cryopreservation techniques enable sperm taken before treatment to be conserved if radical surgery for testicular cancer is necessary.

cured by the surgical removal of the testicle (orchidectomy) alone, but relapse occurs in just over a quarter of patients. Chemotherapy is therefore often used in such circumstances. In more advanced disease, some surgeons advise more extensive surgery, which includes removal of the lymph nodes, as well as chemotherapy.

SIDE EFFECTS
Possible side effects of some treatments include loss of the ability to ejaculate and infertility related to chemotherapy. These effects are sometimes only temporary.

The cryopreservation of semen obtained before treatment has enabled some men to father children by means of artificial insemination.

Prognosis

Most men with testicular cancer can now be cured, and this is a tremendous advance on the situation 20 years ago when many would have died. It is now estimated that more than 95 per cent of patients will survive with appropriate treatment. The improved outlook is largely due to the development of effective chemotherapy for advanced disease.

EARLY DIAGNOSIS
Early diagnosis improves the patient's outlook, but even with advanced tumours, a combination of surgery

and chemotherapy gives hope of a cure. The effectiveness of treatment is related to the size of the tumour and levels of tumour markers when the patient is first seen.

A few men with cancer in one testicle also already have cancer in their other testicle or go on to develop it later. It is therefore very important that they report any change in their remaining testicle without delay.

Chemotherapy is often used to treat patients with advanced testicular cancer. It may be used in conjunction with radiotherapy.

Prostate disorders

Symptoms

The prostate gland is part of the male reproductive system. The gland surrounds the upper part of the urethra (tube conducting urine from the bladder to the exterior) and is responsible for producing some of the secretions that form semen. Common prostate disorders include:
■ Benign enlargement (benign prostate hyperplasia or BPH)
■ Prostate cancer
■ Prostatitis (inflammation of the prostate).

URINARY PROBLEMS
Prostate disorders usually cause urinary symptoms such as:
■ Frequency (frequent urination)
■ Nocturia (need to pass urine at night)
■ Urgency (need to pass urine urgently, even if the bladder is not full)
■ Difficulty in starting urination
■ Poor urine stream
■ Dysuria (pain on passing urine)

■ Haematuria (blood in the urine)
■ Retention (complete or partial inability to pass urine)
■ Incontinence (leaking urine)
Other symptoms include:
■ Bone pain, for example sudden low back pain – often the first symptom of prostate cancer. Unfortunately, it is also

a sign of metastasis (spread of the cancer from the prostate to other parts of the body)
■ Fever, and pain in the region of the prostate – may occur with prostatitis.
   The onset of symptoms of prostate disease varies according to the condition. For example, acute prostatitis may develop

Prostate problems commonly affect men over age 50. Often, symptoms are part of the natural process of ageing but they may indicate a problem.

suddenly, whereas enlargement only causes symptoms once the prostate is so large that it is obstructing the urethra.

Causes

The causes of prostate problems vary according to the disorder.

BENIGN PROSTATE HYPERPLASIA (BPH)
In BPH, the part of the prostate surrounding the urethra enlarges and may eventually impede urine flow. The process usually starts in middle age and is due to the action of male hormones

on the prostate. Genetic factors may also be important.

PROSTATE CANCER
Prostate cancer develops in the glandular cells of the prostate. Risk factors include:

■ Age – most men with prostate cancer are over 65
■ Genetic factors – about nine

Prostate cancer cells can be seen here, magnified under a microscope. This type of cancer occurs most frequently in men over age 65.

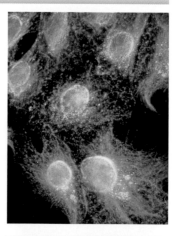

per cent of prostate cancer cases have a genetic basis
■ Race – black males are more at risk than white males
■ Diet – a diet high in red meat, fat and dairy products may increase the risk. Fresh fruit and vegetables can protect against the disease
■ Environment – those working with certain industrial chemicals, and nuclear power workers are at increased risk.
   Men whose testicles fail to function or are removed before puberty are at low risk.

PROSTATITIS
■ Acute prostatitis – usually results from a bacterial infection, for example, *Escherichia coli* or *Chlamydia*
■ Chronic prostatitis – the cause is sometimes bacterial, but often unknown.

Environmental factors have an impact on the development of prostate cancer. Men working in the nuclear power industry are at increased risk.

Incidence

About 43 per cent of men over the age of 65 years have symptoms of BPH.
   Prostate cancer is second only to lung cancer as a cause of cancer death in males; in the UK, almost 10,000 men die from the condition each year. By the age of 80, 80 per cent of men have cancer cells in their prostate, but many of these men never have any symptoms.
   Prostatitis is a common condition in young and middle-aged men.

Diagnosis

The clinical history is important. Physical examination usually includes a rectal examination, in which the doctor passes a gloved finger through the anus to feel the prostate through the rectal wall. Smooth enlargement of the prostate suggests BPH; hard, irregular nodules suggest prostate cancer; tenderness suggests prostatitis.

INVESTIGATIONS
Possible investigations include:
■ Blood test for prostatic specific antigen (PSA) and kidney function
■ Urine culture and microscopy
■ Intravenous urogram (IVU) – a contrast X-ray that outlines the urinary tract
■ Urodynamic studies to check urine flow
■ Examination of the bladder

■ Transrectal ultrasound – a small probe passed into the rectum produces an image on a screen, which is used to measure prostate size. A sample of tissue for examination under the microscope may be collected (biopsy) at the same time – in BPH cases, this can reveal unsuspected prostate cancer
■ Isotope bone scan – this detects secondary bone deposits of prostate cancer cells before they show on X-ray
■ Chest X-ray – to check for secondary deposits in the lungs
■ Magnetic resonance imaging (MRI) and CT scans.

An intravenous urogram may reveal an enlarged prostate gland. This appears as the pale yellow shadow (circled) on the dark-red, contrast-filled bladder.

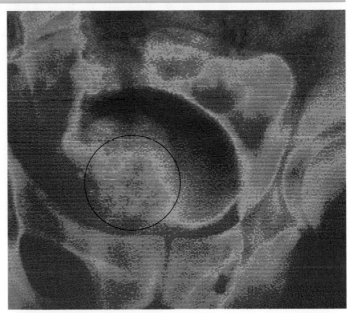

Treatment

Acute prostatitis usually responds to antibiotics. Chronic prostatitis sometimes runs a prolonged course and can be difficult to treat.

Treatments for BPH include:

■ Drugs – recently, drug treatment to reduce the size of the prostate is an alternative to surgery in some cases
■ Transurethral resection of the prostate (TURP) – an endoscopic

instrument is passed up the urethra to shave away prostate tissue; however, there may be side effects and a repeat operation may be necessary after five years. Radiofrequency ablation (TURAPY) of tissue causes fewer side effects than TURP
■ Insertion of a small stent (tube) to hold the urethra open
■ Ablating (cutting away) tissue with microwaves or laser therapy.

PROSTATE CANCER
Treatment of prostate cancer depends on whether the cancer is localized to the prostate or has already spread. The following may be considered:
■ Radical prostatectomy (removal of the prostate, the seminal vesicles and the vas deferens ducts)

An enlarged prostate can be reduced in size by TURP. An endoscope is passed up the urethra and the excess gland tissue 'shaved' away.

■ Radiotherapy – delivered by an external beam or radioactive implant (brachytherapy).

METASTATIC DISEASE
If cancer has spread (metastasized) from the prostate, the disease can often be controlled by treatment that deprives the cancer cells of the stimulus to their growth provided by male hormones. This can be achieved by a variety of means:
■ Surgical removal of both testes (bilateral orchidectomy)
■ Long-acting injections of goserlin or leuprolide. These drugs interfere with the production of testosterone by the testes
■ Anti-androgen therapy – drugs such as cyproterone, flutamide and bicalutamide block male hormone receptors.

New drugs that give increasing hope for the control of advanced prostate cancer are under development.

Prevention

The avoidance of risk factors may help in the prevention of prostate disease. A change in diet may also be protective.

It is advisable that men with a strong family history of prostate problems are regularly screened by their doctor.

Men with a family history of prostate cancer are at increased risk of developing the disease. Screening involves a simple blood test to reveal PSA levels.

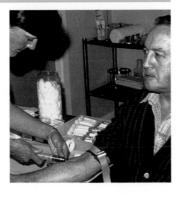

Prognosis

Medical treatment for BPH often helps, but many men still require TURP at some stage. Post-operatively, retrograde ejaculation (when semen passes back into the bladder) is common, and impotence occasionally develops.

For cancer confined to the prostate gland, radical prostatectomy or radiotherapy may provide a cure, but there is a risk of impotence and incontinence.

Infertility in men

Causes

In men, infertility is caused either by a problem with sperm production or quality, or by a structural barrier to its release. The shape of some of the spermatozoa or their capacity for movement may be impaired, or sufficient effective sperm may not be present in the ejaculate.

There are various predisposing factors for the above scenario – although sometimes infertility cannot be accounted for.

■ Environmental and lifestyle factors

Concerns about the effects of lifestyle and the environment on fertility have been increasing in recent years. Pesticides are suspected of leading to the production of antibodies that attack sperm, while it is thought that increasing levels of oestrogen and detergent derivatives in drinking water may affect sperm production. It is definitely known, however, that abuse of alcohol and drugs can decrease fertility.

■ Hormonal imbalance

Sperm production depends on the production of hormones, primarily by the pituitary gland but also by the thyroid and adrenal glands. If these hormone levels are reduced, insufficient sperm may be produced, resulting in infertility.

During the course of investigations into male infertility, an ultrasound scan may be undertaken to assess the health of the man's testes.

■ Varicocele

A varicocele is a widening of the veins of the scrotum and testes that prevents cooler venous blood from reducing the temperature of the warmer arterial blood; sperm production depends on the temperature in the scrotum being lower than that inside the body. It is estimated that a varicocele is responsible in 40–70 per cent of cases of male infertility.

■ Antisperm antibodies

Normally, antibodies – part of the body's natural defences against disease – cannot come

When a couple attend a fertility clinic, both partners will be questioned to determine the underlying cause. In most cases, treatment is possible.

in contact with sperm. However, in about 10 per cent of infertile men, antibodies to sperm are found in semen samples. They attach to the wall of sperm, treating them as foreign bodies. The effect is that motility is impaired and sperm tend to clump together; antibodies may also make it more difficult for a spermatozoa to penetrate an egg.

Large numbers of deformed sperm – such as this one with multiple tails – may be a cause of infertility. Such sperm are unable to swim effectively.

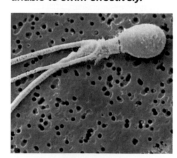

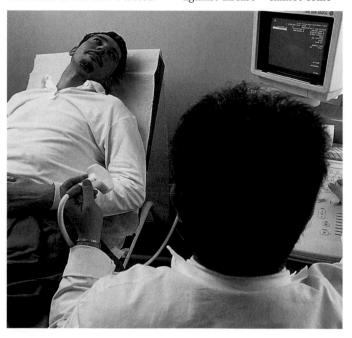

Medical causes

A number of medical conditions can reduce male fertility, such as:
- ■ Sexually transmitted diseases
- ■ Prostatitis
- ■ Cystic fibrosis
- ■ Orchitis (inflammation of the testicles caused by post-pubescent mumps)
- ■ 'Retrograde ejaculation', when sperm are ejaculated into the bladder as a result of a failure of a valve at the base of the bladder
- ■ Damage to the testes as a result of trauma or radiation
- ■ Undescended testes (cryptorchidism).

Prescription drugs, such as cimetidine and anabolic steroids, can also affect sperm production.

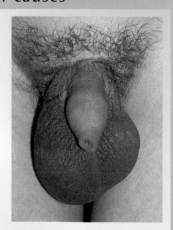

Orchitis – inflammation of the testis – occurs in some men who contract mumps after puberty. If both testicles are affected, infertility can result.

Diagnosis

A number of tests are used to determine whether the male partner is infertile when a couple cannot conceive. These follow the taking of a full medical and sexual history, and include:

■ **Physical examination**
The scrotum and testes are examined and a digital rectal examination is performed to check the prostate gland.

■ **Semen analysis**
A sample of ejaculate is examined under a microscope to check for any irregularities in spermatozoal shape or motility; a sperm count is also performed – each millilitre of ejaculate should contain about 30 million spermatozoa.

■ **Post-coital test (PCT)**
The ability of sperm to pass through the woman's cervical mucus may be tested. The couple is asked to have sex several hours before a pre-arranged visit to the fertility clinic, where a sample of the cervical mucus is taken during an internal examination. This is examined under a microscope to see how many spermatozoa are

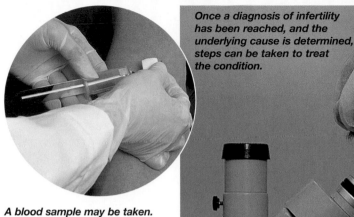

A blood sample may be taken. This can be tested to check for the presence of antibodies that might interfere with sperm production or quality.

present, and how sperm and mucus interact (an 'invasion test'). To check whether the spermatozoa are abnormal or the mucus is hostile to them, a 'crossover test' is then performed: the interaction between the sperm and mucus that is known to be normal is monitored. Finally, the sperms' ability to penetrate and fertilize the partner's egg is tested.

■ **Acrosome test**
This uses fluorescent chemicals to reveal the presence or absence of enzymes in the cap (acrosome) of individual

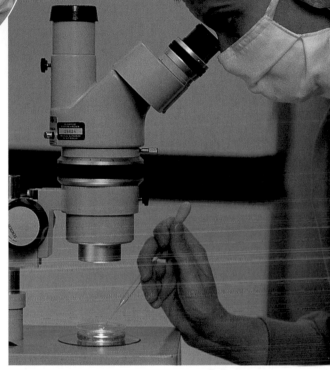

Once a diagnosis of infertility has been reached, and the underlying cause is determined, steps can be taken to treat the condition.

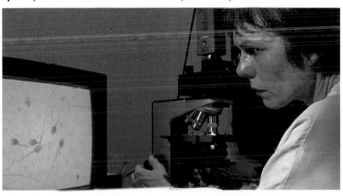

A semen sample can be examined to assess the health and motility of the sperm. Any abnormalities, such as deformed sperm, will be identified.

spermatozoa that help the spermatozoa to break through the egg wall. An 'egg penetration test' is also used for the same purpose: spermatozoa are introduced to hamster eggs to see whether it can penetrate the egg wall.

■ **Antisperm antibody assay**
Two tests are used to detect the presence of antibodies on the spermatozoa membranes: the immunobead assay and the mixed agglutination reaction

(MAR). In both cases, antibodies bound to a marker, such as red blood cells, are introduced to the sperm and these attach to any antibodies already present.

■ **Hormone level tests**
A blood sample is analysed to check the levels of the hormones that stimulate sperm production. They operate on a feedback system, so high levels are as significant as low ones, since high levels indicate a response to very low sperm levels.

Assisted fertility treatment

If the cause of male infertility cannot be addressed by other treatment, and the sperm count or quality are still low, assisted fertility techniques may be necessary. These are:

■ **Intrauterine insemination (IUI)**
This technique is used when the sperm count is low but motility is reasonably good. The sperm is injected directly into the uterus when the woman is ovulating, so that only a short distance must be covered by spermatozoa before the egg is reached.

■ **In vitro fertilization (IVF)**
This technique is used when

sperm count and motility are poor. The sperm is placed with the woman's eggs in a test tube in the laboratory.

■ **Intracytoplasmic sperm injection (ICSI)**
A single, healthy spermatozoon is harvested, either from the ejaculate or, by surgery, from the testis, and injected directly into the egg.

A range of different techniques is available to assist fertility. These include incubating sperm and egg together to maximize the chances of fertilization.

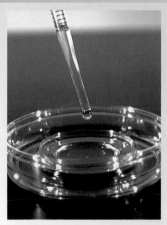

Infertility in women

Causes

The inability to conceive is something that profoundly affects some women's lives. However, advances in fertility medicine over the last 30 years, both in terms of pinpointing the cause of problems and treating them, have given these women new hope.

There are a number of reasons why a woman may be infertile:
■ An inability to ovulate (release an egg)
■ A problem with the egg's progress down the uterine (Fallopian) tube, with the result that it cannot be reached by sperm
■ An environment in the cervix that is hostile to her partner's sperm
■ A problem with implantation of the egg in the wall of the uterus once it has been fertilized.

HORMONE IMBALANCES

Failure to ovulate accounts for about a third of cases of female infertility. Most commonly, this is due to an imbalance in the level of hormones – follicle stimulating hormone (FSH) and luteinizing hormone (LH) – that control ovulation. This may

There are many causes of infertility in women. Even if the egg is released normally, as seen in this micrograph, an obstruction may block its path.

itself result from a malfunction of the hypothalamus, which controls the hormones' release, or of the pituitary gland, which actually releases them.

Hormonal imbalances are treated by replacement hormone therapy and by fertility drugs, such as clomiphene. Human chorionic gonadotrophin (hCG) may also be given to ensure the release of an egg. Treatment causes ovulation in about 90 per cent of cases, but, for reasons that are not fully understood, conception takes place in only about two-thirds of cases.

PROBLEMS WITH OVULATION

There are a number of other reasons why a woman may not ovulate. These include:
■ Prolonged stress
■ Excessive weight loss, as in anorexia
■ Obesity
■ Alcohol or drug abuse.

In addition, a woman's supply of eggs may have run out as a result of damage to the ovaries following surgery (to remove ovarian cysts, for example), or

Abnormalities of the woman's cervical mucus (seen here) may prevent sperm from passing into the uterus. It may also contain antisperm antibodies.

A uterine fibroid, seen as a red mass behind the uterus (blue), can cause infertility if it interferes with the egg's passage down the ovarian tube.

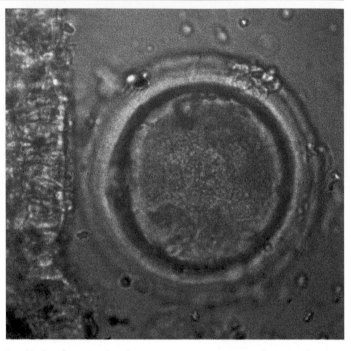

irradiation (as a result of radiotherapy), or following the menopause, whether of normal or premature onset. If there are no more eggs, assisted fertility may be the only solution.

UTERINE AND CERVICAL PROBLEMS

Fibroids – benign tumours in the muscular wall of the uterus – can, depending on their site,

prevent an egg from implanting in the lining of the uterus.

Abnormalities of the cervical mucus may affect fertility. There may be too little mucus to provide a medium in which spermatozoa can move; in other cases the mucus may be too thick to allow their passage.

Some women's cervical mucus contains antisperm antibodies, affecting the sperm's motility.

Damaged uterine tubes

It is essential that the egg is able to move freely down the uterine (Fallopian) tube if fertilization is to occur. A tube can become damaged or blocked as a result of a number of problems. These include:
■ Birth defects
■ Adhesions and scar tissue following surgery
■ Infections, such as salpingitis and postpartum infections
■ Sexually transmitted diseases
■ A previous ectopic pregnancy
■ Endometriosis
■ Pelvic inflammatory disease (PID).

The most common cause of uterine tube damage is PID. This is an infection of the

ovaries, uterine tubes or uterus that may be acute or chronic. The most common cause of PID is an infection by the parasite *Chlamydia trachomatis*. Damage to the uterine tubes can usually be repaired successfully by microsurgery or laser surgery.

Infections of the ovaries and uterine tubes may prevent normal ovulation. Chlamydia infections, in particular, can cause serious scarring.

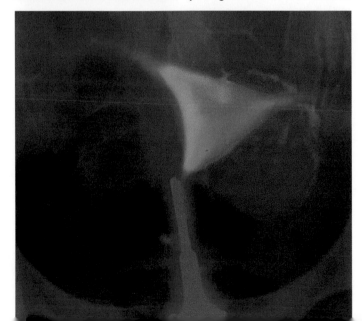

Diagnosis

If a woman fails to conceive after a set period of time, tests will be carried out to determine the cause of infertility. These tests include:

■ **Ovulation test**
The easiest and most precise way of confirming ovulation is to use an ovulation testing kit, available from a chemist. This is a urine test that identifies the rise in luteinizing hormone (LH) levels that occurs just before ovulation.

The test is performed daily on the two or three days prior to the midpoint of the menstrual cycle.

■ **Ultrasound**
The condition of the ovaries may be established by an ultrasound examination, which is also used to monitor changes in the ovarian follicle as it prepares to shed the egg.

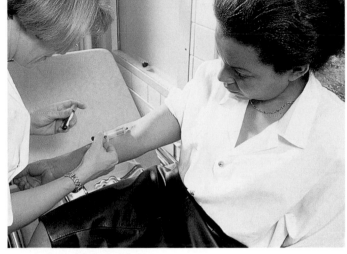

■ **Hormone analysis and biopsy**
Blood tests to check hormone levels are carried out not only if ovulation does not occur, but routinely to check that the

uterine lining – the endometrium – has been prepared correctly, by the hormone progesterone, to receive the fertilized egg. An endometrial biopsy may also be performed to check on the condition of the blood vessels.

■ **Post-coital test (PCT)**
This test is used to detect any abnormalities of the cervical mucus (and also to evaluate the quality of the male sperm). The couple is asked to have sex a few hours before a pre-arranged clinic appointment, several days

Ultrasound scanning can show the reproductive structures clearly. This is helpful in determining the health of the woman's ovaries.

Blood samples will be taken for testing hormone levels. If low levels of hormones prevent ovulation from occurring, hormone replacement may help.

before ovulation. A sample of cervical mucus is taken and tests are performed to see whether it is hostile to sperm – too acidic, for example, or contains antisperm antibodies.

■ **Hysterosalpingogram (HSG)**
This test is used to check that there are no blockages in the uterine tubes. Contrast medium is injected into the uterus and its progress through the tubes monitored on X-ray.

■ **Laparoscopy**
A fibre-optic tube is inserted into the woman's abdomen through a small surgical incision. The surgeon can then view the exterior the reproductive tract and check for adhesions, endometriosis and other abnormalities.

A hysterosalpingogram (HSG) is an X-ray technique using a contrast medium to outline the uterine tubes. The tube on the right is blocked in this patient.

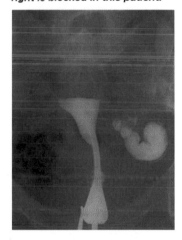

Options for treatment

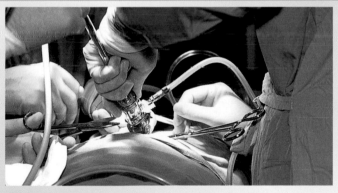

If treatment for the underlying cause of female infertility is unsuccessful or impossible, a number of assisted fertility techniques can be used to achieve conception:
■ Intrauterine insemination (IUI) – the man's sperm is injected into the woman's uterus at the time of ovulation
■ In vitro fertilization – an egg is removed from the woman's

ovary during laparoscopy and placed in a test tube with the man's sperm; the embryo is transferred to the uterus
■ Gamete intra-Fallopian transfer (GIFT) – eggs and sperm

An egg is about to be injected with a spermatozoon in an in vitro fertilization procedure. The embryo will then be placed in the uterus.

Laparoscopy is employed to harvest eggs for in vitro fertilization techniques. For some women, assisted fertility is the only option.

are placed together in a uterine tube
■ Zygote intra-Fallopian transfer (ZIFT) – the eggs are fertilized in a test tube and placed in a uterine tube just after they have started to divide
■ Donor eggs – when a woman does not produce any eggs of her own, those of a donor may be fertilized by her partner's sperm.

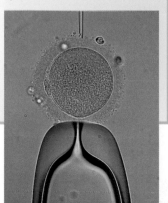

Urinary tract infections

Symptoms

The urinary tract is normally sterile, and does not house any infectious organisms. Bacterial urinary infections are, however, common, particularly in women.

Urinary tract infections are particularly common in women. A GP uses a urine dipstick which changes colour if an infection is present.

DRAINAGE SYSTEM
A urinary tract infection may involve all or part of the urinary drainage system, which includes:
■ The kidneys
■ The ureters – a pair of tubes, 25–30 cm long, that connect the two renal pelves to the bladder. The junction between the ureters and bladder (vesicoureteric junction) acts as a one-way valve, allowing urine to enter the bladder, but shutting the ureters off when the bladder contracts
■ The bladder – a sac-shaped muscular organ. Urination occurs when the bladder contracts
■ The urethra – drains the bladder. It is about 3.5–4 cm long in women and 20 cm long in men. In women, the opening to the urethra is fairly close to the anal area.

CLINICAL FEATURES
Symptoms of infection in the lower part of the urinary tract involving the bladder and urethra include:
■ Pain when passing urine (dysuria), often described as 'passing razor blades'
■ The urge to pass urine very frequently, only small amounts being passed each time
■ Pain and tenderness in the lower abdomen
■ Blood in the urine (haematuria)
■ Offensive-smelling urine
■ Fever.

PYELONEPHRITIS
Acute infection of the urinary tract involving the kidney and its pelvis is known as pyelonephritis.
Typically, this more severe

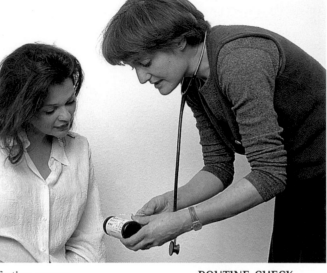

infection causes:
■ High fevers
■ Attacks of shivering (rigors) due to the high temperature
■ Pain in the lower back
■ Nausea and vomiting.

ROUTINE CHECK
In some people, however, symptoms of infection in the urinary tract are mild or non-existent and the infection is only detected by a routine urine examination.

Causes

Bacteria entering the urinary tract via the urethra cause most urinary infections. Infection via the blood or lymph circulations is less common. Once in the bladder, the infection often travels up to the kidney. Any abnormality that impedes the flow of urine increases the risk of infection.

Escherichia coli, which normally inhabits the bowel, causes about 80 per cent of urinary tract infections in the community and about 50 per cent in hospital patients. A variety of other bacteria cause the remainder.

The presence of more than 1,000,000 of the same species of

bacteria per millilitre of urine indicates the presence of a urinary tract infection.

PREDISPOSING FACTORS
There are certain groups who are at increased risk of severe urinary tract infections:
■ Females – women have short urethras. Infection often occurs during sexual intercourse
■ Older men with enlarged prostate glands – incomplete bladder emptying can occur
■ Children with anatomical defects – a congenital abnormality of the implantation of the ureters into the bladder wall often causes recurrent upper urinary tract infections by allowing the urine to pass back into the upper urinary tract during urination (vesicoureteric reflux). The reflux improves or resolves with growth
■ Pregnant women – the ureters and renal pelves dilate, disturbing the flow of urine
■ Patients with diabetes and immunosuppressed patients
■ People with a tumour in the

urinary tract, abdomen or pelvis may develop a urinary tract infection. Stones in the urinary tract also increase the risk of infections
■ People with long-term urinary catheters (drainage tubes) left in place to drain the bladder.

Incidence
At least eight per cent of girls and two per cent of boys have a urinary tract infection in childhood. Boys have more infections before the age of three months as they have more congenital malformations of the urinary tract than girls.

Adult women, particularly if sexually active, are at higher risk than men. At least 50 per cent of women have at least one urinary tract infection at some time. After the age of 60, urinary infection in men increases as the incidence of prostate enlargement increases. Up to six per cent of pregnant women have bacteria in their urine. If untreated, 20 per cent of these women will go on to develop pyelonephritis (kidney infection).

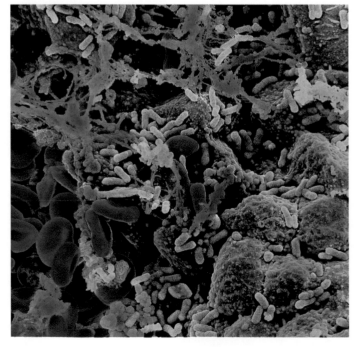

Urinary tract infections are often caused by the rod-shaped bacterium, E.coli. Here, it is shown magnified on the cells of the bladder (blue area).

Diagnosis

A definite diagnosis of urinary tract infection can be made only by culturing a sample of urine for bacteria as some patients with symptoms of a bladder or urethral infection (cystitis or urethritis) have no evidence of infection in their urine.

Urine culture should be done if a baby, child or man is suspected of having a urinary tract infection, but it is not always necessary if a sexually active woman has mild cystitis.

SPECIMENS

A urine specimen is collected in a sterile bottle, using a clean technique so bacteria from the skin do not contaminate the specimen, and sent to the laboratory or refrigerated.

Examination of the urine provides information about the likelihood of infection by detecting white blood cells and products of inflammation.

Other investigations include:
■ Ultrasound scanning
■ Intravenous urogram or pyelogram (IVU or IVP) – X-rays of the urinary tract are taken after an intravenous injection of a contrast medium that is concentrated and excreted by the kidneys
■ Cystourethroscopy – an illuminated endoscopic instrument is passed through the urethra into the bladder
■ Micturating cystourethrogram – a contrast medium is introduced; then an X-ray is taken while the patient urinates, to show bladder emptying.

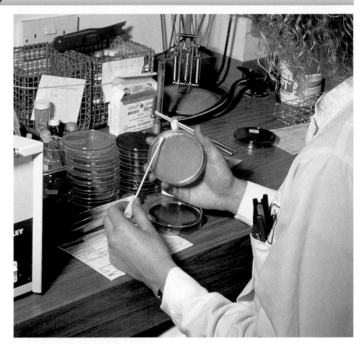

Infections are often diagnosed by sending a urine sample to a laboratory. Drops of urine are spread on an agar plate to encourage bacterial growth.

Treatment

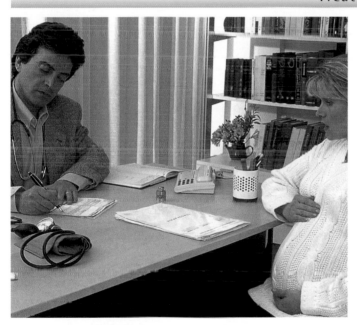

In general, treatment aims to eliminate bacteria from the urine and correct abnormalities of the urinary tract. Treatment includes:
■ Antibiotics – a short course of an antibacterial drug, for example trimethoprim or amoxicillin, is often sufficient for cystitis (bladder infection). Acute pyelonephritis (kidney infection) requires a longer course of antibiotics and may need hospital admission
■ Fluid therapy – increasing fluid intake flushes the urinary tract and reduces the pain
■ Analgesics.

Pregnant women with urine infections should always be prescribed antibiotics. These drugs do not harm the developing fetus.

RISK GROUPS

Management of specific patient groups includes the following:
■ Pregnant women with infected urine should be treated with antibiotics, even if they have no symptoms
■ Elderly women often have bacteria in their urine but, unless they develop symptoms, are best left untreated
■ Sexually active women with recurrent infections are helped by long-term, low-dose antibacterial treatment taken last thing at night or after intercourse. In older women, hormone replacement therapy (HRT) may help
■ Children should be treated with antibiotics until the urine is sterile. Long-term antibiotics may be needed to prevent recurrences.

Prognosis

Urinary infections are usually mild and easily treated. Some groups, however, such as young children, pregnant women and people with diabetes, are at high risk of a serious illness that may affect kidney function.

The prognosis is much improved if each episode of infection is treated with antibiotics. In some cases, the long-term preventive use of antibiotics is also necessary. Surgery involving re-implantation of the ureters into the bladder may be considered in severe cases.

Prevention

The following measures can be taken to prevent infection of the urinary tract:
■ Empty the bladder completely when urine is passed
■ Drink plenty of fluids regularly throughout the day to flush out the urinary tract. Water is ideal, but avoid very sweet drinks
■ Wipe only from front to back after going to the lavatory. This will prevent *Escherichia coli* bacterium (which lives in the bowel) from entering the urinary tract – this bacteria is the main cause of urinary tract infection
■ Use a vaginal lubricant during intercourse

■ Always empty the bladder immediately after intercourse
■ Avoid the use of deodorants or scented soaps in the genital area
■ Wear loose-fitting underwear made out of cotton instead of man-made fibres
■ If a diaphragm is used as a contraceptive device, it is important to check the fit with a doctor. If this method is causing infections, it may be worth considering a different form of contraception
■ Antibiotics may occasionally be used as a long-term preventive measure if the infection keeps recurring.

Drinking plenty of water will help to prevent the recurrence of bladder infections. Keeping fluid intake high is particularly important during pregnancy.

Cystitis

Symptoms

Cystitis is an inflammation of the bladder, and bacterial infection is the commonest cause of this. When cystitis has an infective cause, it is referred to as a urinary tract infection (UTI). The condition is very common and accounts for 1–2 per cent of GP consultations. It usually affects females, and is most prevalent from adolescence to middle age.

The main symptoms are:
■ Frequency of urination
■ Dysuria (pain on passing urine)
■ Haematuria (passage of blood in the urine)
■ Cloudy urine.

Patients may also complain of low abdominal pain, and many will have foul-smelling urine.

CYSTITIS IN CHILDREN
In babies and children, the symptoms are less well defined, and include:
■ Crying on urination
■ Vague abdominal pain
■ Failure to thrive
■ Fever
■ Vomiting.

Cystitis should always be considered in the differential

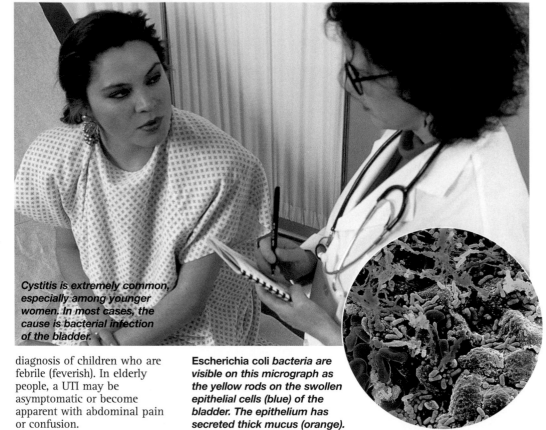

Cystitis is extremely common, especially among younger women. In most cases, the cause is bacterial infection of the bladder.

diagnosis of children who are febrile (feverish). In elderly people, a UTI may be asymptomatic or become apparent with abdominal pain or confusion.

Escherichia coli bacteria are visible on this micrograph as the yellow rods on the swollen epithelial cells (blue) of the bladder. The epithelium has secreted thick mucus (orange).

Diagnosis

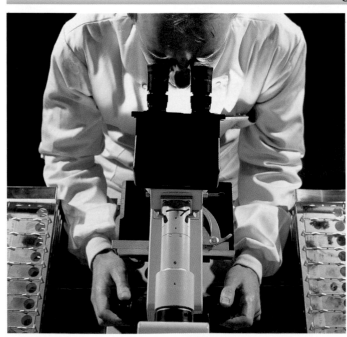

Diagnosis of cystitis depends on the clinical findings and the results of urine microscopy and bacterial culture. Often a UTI in a woman may have no predisposing cause, and adult women with a single attack of a

lower urinary tract infection, which will usually respond to antibiotics, need no further investigation.

A second attack of cystitis in an adult woman, or a first attack of UTI in a child or a

Diagnostic microscopy may be used to examine a urine specimen in an attack of cystitis. The presence of pus in the urine is a sign of bladder inflammation.

man warrants investigation, as these are likely to have a predisposing cause.

SPECIMEN EXAMINATION
Microscopy may reveal pus in the urine (pyuria), and the causative organism can usually be identified.

A mid-stream specimen of urine (MSU) is collected into a sterile container. The MSU is then examined under the microscope, and cell counts will provide evidence of inflammation in the urinary tract. Bacterial counts higher than 100,000 colonies/ml of a single organism are usually considered to be significant.

Skill is required to exclude contaminants in the urine and low counts as causes of UTI. Suprapubic aspiration (inserting a needle directly into the bladder) may, rarely, be necessary in cases of doubt.

FURTHER INVESTIGATION
Further investigations to discover other possible causes of cystitis, such as intravenous urography (IVU) or micturating cystograms, may be necessary. The latter may be necessary in children under four years of age who have an abnormal IVU to exclude reflux of urine into the ureters.

Once the causative bacteria have been identified, antibiotic sensitivity tests may be performed to determine the most effective drug treatment.

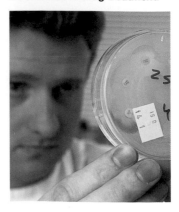

Causes

Most cases of cystitis result from the introduction of bowel organisms via the urethra into the bladder.

Various factors facilitating infection in females include sexual intercourse, atrophic (post-menopausal) vaginitis and pregnancy. In men, such factors as incomplete bladder emptying (as in prostatic enlargement) or structural abnormalities of the urinary tract may be the cause of urinary tract infection or cystitis.

The common causative organisms of cystitis are:
- *Escherichia coli* – 68 per cent

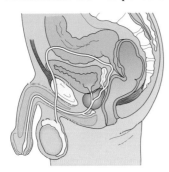

of infections
- *Proteus mirabilis* – 12 per cent
- *Staphylococcus epidermidis* – 10 per cent
- *Streptococcus faecalis* – six per cent
- *Klebsiella aerogenes* – four per cent.

INTERSTITIAL CYSTITIS
This is the name given to chronic bladder inflammation that is not believed to be caused by bacterial infection, and does not respond to antibiotic therapy. Symptoms, which are often debilitating for sufferers, include frequency, urgency and pain. The cause is unknown.

Men are protected by their longer urethra from urinary tract infection, and also by the fact that the prostatic fluid has bactericidal properties.

Women have a short urethra, and are therefore more prone to bladder infection, especially by organisms that normally reside in the bowel.

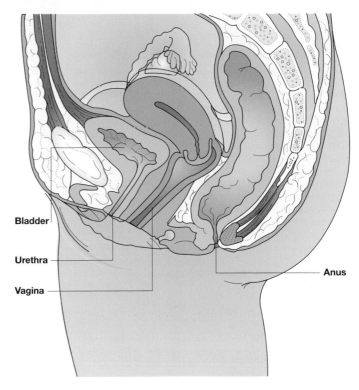

Bladder

Urethra

Vagina

Anus

Treatment

Often the severity of symptoms requires immediate therapy with appropriate antibiotics. It is preferable, if possible, to obtain a clean-catch mid-stream specimen of urine (MSU) for microscopic and microbiological detection of the offending organisms. Culture

and antibiotic sensitivities performed in the laboratory will determine the most appropriate treatment.

It is sometimes necessary to prescribe medication before the results of urine culture are available, or in a first attack.

Simple lifestyle measures, such as a high daily fluid intake, can help control the symptoms of cystitis. Good hygiene measures are also important.

DRUG THERAPY
The following antibiotics are usually prescribed: trimethoprim, co-trimoxazole, amoxcillin, nitrofurantoin and nalidixic acid. Sometimes a single-loading dose of amoxcillin (3 g in adults) is adequate to ensure cure.

It is always best to follow up treatment with a further examination of an MSU to ensure resolution of the infection. A high fluid intake (at least three litres a day) is necessary in all UTIs to prevent urinary stasis and to limit bacterial replication.

When antibiotic drugs have been prescribed for cystitis, the doctor will usually take further urine samples to assess the effectiveness of the treatment.

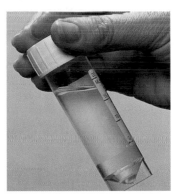

Prognosis and prevention

Most attacks of bacterial cystitis respond promptly to antibiotics. In women with frequent attacks, or in children or men, investigations to discover a possible underlying cause are essential in order to exclude or prevent more serious kidney complications.

Most lower urinary tract infections can be successfully treated by antibiotics, such as trimethoprim, shown here.

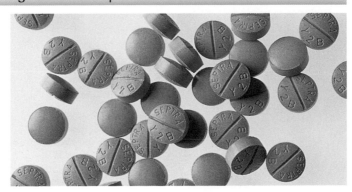

Bladder cancer

Symptoms and causes

By far the commonest symptom that brings people with bladder cancer to their GP is blood in the urine. There are usually no other symptoms, although if small clots are being passed there may be some pain and difficulty in passing urine. Large tumours can block the urethral orifice, causing urine to stagnate; some people develop a urinary infection (cystitis).

CAUSES

The causes of bladder cancer are not fully understood. There are certain risk factors which render people more likely to develop the disease although not all people with these factors develop bladder cancer.

Risk factors include:
■ Smoking – there is a consistent, but relatively low, risk among smokers who are probably two to five times more likely to develop bladder cancer than non-smokers
■ Occupation – may be relevant in up to 20 per cent of cases. There is an increased risk to workers in the chemical dye, solvents or rubber industries
■ Chronic inflammation – an infection such as the tropical parasitic infection schistosomiasis can cause long-term inflammation and a resulting risk of malignancy.

CARCINOGENS

The risks to industrial workers arise because they handle potentially cancer-causing substances called carcinogens. These substances are absorbed during a working lifetime and excreted in the urine, and so have contact with the bladder lining. In developed countries, workers are offered regular urine screening tests.

The presence of blood in the urine is often the first sign of bladder cancer. GPs will then refer patients for further specialist investigation.

Diagnosis

GPs will not be able to make a diagnosis of bladder cancer themselves – they can only suspect that the disease is present so referral is usually made to a urologist.

CYSTOSCOPY

The diagnosis is made by a urological surgeon, who will arrange to look inside the bladder with an instrument called a cystoscope. This is a hollow viewing tube which is inserted into the bladder under local or general anaesthesia.

A small sample (biopsy) of any suspicious tissue is sent to the pathologist for examination under a microscope.

On this X-ray of the bladder, the cancer is evident as the large, dark mass on the right-hand side. A cancer of this size is likely to be quite advanced.

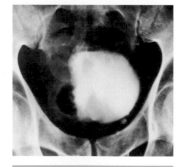

DIAGNOSTIC IMAGING

Special X-rays called cystograms and excretion urograms may be employed, as well as CT scans, MRI scans, bone scans and chest X-rays to look for spread of the cancer.

STAGING THE CANCER

Once bladder cancer has been confirmed, it is important to establish the grade of the disease and the stage or extent it has reached. Low-grade cancers (where the tissue removed at biopsy is nearly normal) spread more slowly than high-grade cancers.

The staging is important as a guide to how far the cancer has spread to nearby tissues or to other parts of the body. Treatment therefore depends on the size and stage of the tumour.

If doctors suspect a bladder tumour, cystoscopy is usually carried out. In this procedure, a flexible fibre-optic tube is passed up the urethra into the bladder to allow direct viewing.

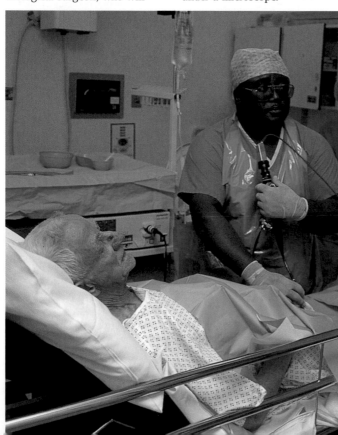

Incidence

Incidence data includes:
■ Bladder tumours are second only to prostate tumours as sites for cancers within the urinary tract
■ Three-quarters of all cases occur in men, usually after the age of 50
■ In England and Wales bladder tumours account for about seven per cent of all cancer in men and 2.5 per cent in women
■ Bladder tumours are 50 times more common than those of the ureter or renal pelvis.

Bladder cancers have a tendency to recur and regular follow-up checks on all patients are therefore important.

Treatment

The treatment of bladder cancer depends on whether the tumour has infiltrated the muscle of the bladder wall and the type of cell of which the tumour consists.

TREATMENT OPTIONS
In the case of an early superficial tumour, the following treatments may be used:
■ Diathermy (or burning away of the tissue) – there are few post-operative problems. Patients may have some blood in their urine and there may be slight discomfort for a few days
■ Insertion of radioactive material – into the bladder to destroy the tumour.

For more extensive tumours, surgery is the most common form of treatment:
■ Partial cystectomy – the part of the bladder containing the tumour is removed and the remainder left in place
■ Total cystectomy – complete removal of the bladder, may be carried out when tumours recur after megavoltage irradiation or when multiple tumours are too extensive for diathermy.

AFTER SURGERY
After total cystectomy patients need an alternative storage reservoir for urine. One such alternative is to bring the ends of both ureters out through an opening in the abdominal wall, (an ileal conduit) so that urine can be drained into a bag.

RADIATION
Radiation therapy is the use of high-energy X-rays to kill cancer cells. External megavoltage irradiation is reserved for tumours that invade bladder muscle and those that are more malignant. Patients often become very tired after

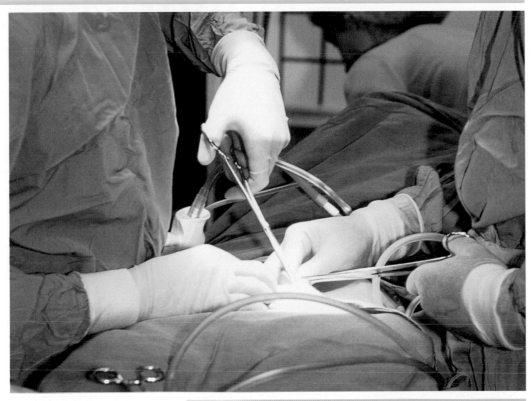

In some cases of bladder cancer, the removal of the whole bladder may be appropriate. This operation is called a total cystectomy.

radiotherapy and there may be permanent darkening of the skin in the treated area. It is also common to lose hair and the skin may become dry, tender and itchy. There may also be nausea, vomiting and some urinary discomfort.

CHEMOTHERAPY
Chemotherapy is the use of drugs to destroy cancer cells. The drugs are usually given orally or intravenously and absorbed through the body.

Prevention

Stopping smoking reduces the risk of bladder cancer, lung cancer and several other types of cancer as well as other problems such as heart disease. People who work in industries that are associated with an excess risk of developing the disease should avail themselves of all the screening tests on offer through their employers.

People whose work involves regular contact with potentially carcinogenic substances should take suitable precautions.

Prognosis

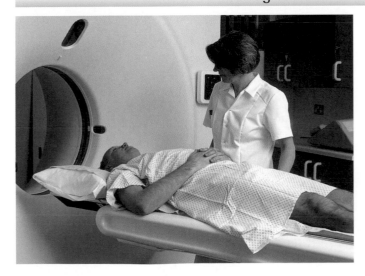

Once bladder cancer has been diagnosed, cystoscopic follow-up, usually at six-month intervals, must continue for life. Tumours may recur 13 years or so after first diagnosis.

Approximately 80 per cent of patients with superficial tumours and 60 per cent of those having had interstitial irradiation are still alive after five years, and around 30 per cent of those who have had a total cystectomy are still alive after three years.

Patients who have been treated for bladder cancer may need regular follow-up scans. These will reveal whether the cancer has spread.

Nephritis

Symptoms

Nephritis is the general term for inflammation of the kidneys. Each kidney contains about a million microscopic filtration units, called nephrons, and each nephron contains a network of tiny blood vessels (a glomerulus) and a tubule that connects with the ureter, which drains urine from the kidney to the bladder.

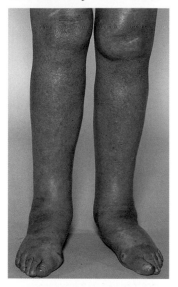

A glomerulus is the site of filtration of fluid and waste products from the blood; the tubule reabsorbs most of the fluid and substances still needed by the body. Normally, about 180 litres of filtrate are formed each day, but only about 1.5 litres of urine are excreted.

Types of nephritis include:
■ **Glomerulonephritis**
The glomeruli become inflamed and filter less efficiently. Waste products build up in the body, and protein and red blood cells leak into the urine.

Severely ill patients pass less urine than normal, which may be smoky or red in colour, and develop oedema (swelling) of the lower legs and/or back, puffy eyes and high blood pressure. Severe glomerulonephritis may cause lethargy, nausea and vomiting, due to nitrogenous waste in the blood (uraemia).

Nephrotic syndrome is characterized by large amounts of protein in the urine, low serum protein and severe oedema (fluid-filled tissues).

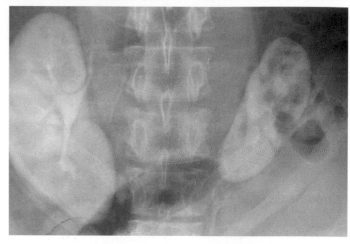

Chronic pyelonephritis results from untreated pyelonephritis. The kidney on the right of this X-ray is shrunken and scarred.

■ **Nephrotic syndrome**
The urine contains a large amount of protein and patients develop severe oedema.
■ **Pyelonephritis**
This is a bacterial infection affecting one or both kidneys. Pain occurs with high fever and

shivering fits. Urine may contain blood, and the kidneys shrink, scar and may fail.
■ **Kidney (renal) failure**
Early renal failure is often symptomless. Later symptoms may include malaise, loss of appetite, frequent urination, itching, nausea/vomiting, pins and needles, spasms and breathlessness, mental slowing and coma. When advanced, the kidneys stop producing urine.

Causes

Acute glomerular nephritis has many possible causes, but many cases are due to an abnormal immune reaction, damaging the glomeruli. In many types of nephritis, the antigen is unknown. Known antigens, however, include bacteria, parasites and viruses:
■ **Bacteria**
A common cause of glomerular nephritis, particularly in

children, is infection with one type of streptococcal bacteria (Lancefield group A beta haemolytic *Streptococcus*). This causes tonsillitis, middle ear infection or cellulitis (skin infection), which may be followed by glomerulonephritis. Other bacteria such as *Salmonella*, *Staphylococcus* or *Gonococcus* may also cause kidney damage.

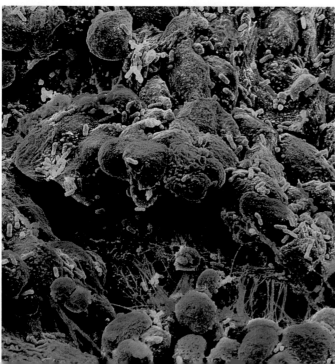

Escherichia coli (yellow) bacterium, seen within a bladder, may infect the kidneys if the flow of urine is obstructed.

This patient's face has the typical scaly rash of systemic lupus erythematosus. This auto-immune disease is sometimes associated with nephritis.

■ **Parasites**
Parasites such as *Plasmodium malariae*, *Schistosoma* blood flukes and filariasis worms may cause nephritis.
■ **Viruses**
Viral infections, including mumps, measles, chickenpox, glandular fever, coxsackie, hepatitis A and B, and HIV may all be associated with cases of nephritis.

In addition to these causative factors, obstruction of urine flow by an enlarged prostate gland, an enlarged uterus or a ureteral valve (in children) predisposes a patient to urinary infection which is associated with the development of acute pyelonephritis.

Diseases which cause abnormal immune reactions (autoimmune diseases) such as

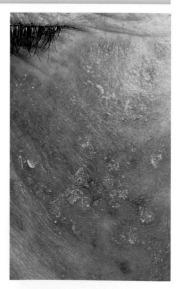

systemic lupus erythematosus (SLE) and polyarteritis nodosa, are associated with nephritic disease. SLE damages the glomeruli of the kidneys in both adults and children, and polyarteritis nodosa (a connective tissue disease of the arteries) particularly affects middle-aged and elderly men. Biopsies of the kidneys may reveal cell damage and death of cells in the walls of medium-sized arteries.

Diagnosis and investigations

As with other renal diseases, nephritis will be investigated to establish the precise diagnosis. Investigations into kidney function may include:

■ Urine tests – for protein, red blood cells and casts (microscopic masses of dead

Urine can be tested using a gas chromatograph. This enables the quantities of constituents in the samples, such as protein or casts, to be measured.

cells or fatty material)
■ Urine output measurement
■ Blood tests – to gauge levels of proteins and waste products, such as urea and creatinine in the blood
■ Throat, skin or ear swabs for bacterial infection
■ Chest X–ray – this may show fluid in the lungs and an enlarged heart secondary to fluid overload
■ Renal imaging – with X–rays and CT scans (necessary for women with repeated urinary tract infections and men and children after just one attack)
■ Renal biopsy – a needle is used to obtain small pieces of kidney tissue for microscopic examination
■ Micturating cystogram – an imaging technique that illustrates the efficiency of bladder emptying.

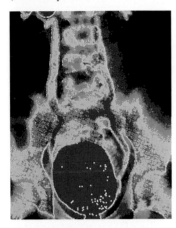

This coloured urogram shows urinary reflux from the bladder (bottom, red) to the kidney at the top. A urogram may be undertaken during diagnosis.

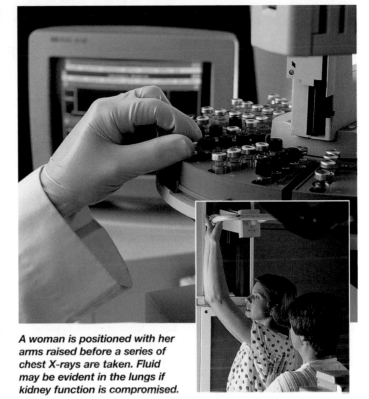

A woman is positioned with her arms raised before a series of chest X-rays are taken. Fluid may be evident in the lungs if kidney function is compromised.

Treatment

Patients with acute glomerulonephritis should be carefully observed, with daily recordings of fluid intake and output and weight. Blood pressure should be taken regularly, and drugs will be needed if blood pressure is high. Antibiotics are used to treat infection, and a low-salt diet is also important; protein restriction may be necessary in very ill patients.

Some patients need urgent treatment with corticosteroids and cyclophosphamide (an anticancer drug which can be used where a tumour has caused nephritis). Patients with renal failure associated with glomerulonephritis may need dialysis treatment.

Patients with nephrotic

syndrome are given a low-salt diet, and may need high-dose corticosteroid therapy to stop the leak of protein in the urine. Diuretics may be used to increase urine flow if there is serious oedema.

Patients with acute pyelonephritis are treated with antibiotics. Early treatment of urine infections in children is important to prevent high blood pressure and renal failure in later life. Surgery to correct urine flow may prevent the onset of chronic pyelonephritis.

Patients with severe renal failure require dialysis to filter the blood. Normally the kidneys eliminate waste from the blood being excreted in urine.

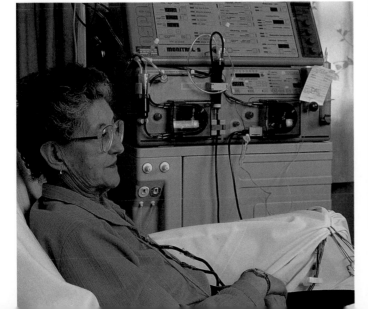

Prognosis

About 70 people per million develop life-threatening renal failure each year and need renal replacement therapy involving dialysis or a kidney transplant.

■ Post-streptococcal glomerulonephritis
Most children recover well, but some adults fail to recover completely and develop kidney failure and/or hypertension
■ Glomerulonephritis of unknown cause
The outlook is not good and careful follow-up is needed. Some patients develop renal failure within weeks or months
■ Nephrotic syndrome
Children recover well with corticosteroid treatment but the results are poorer in adults
■ Acute pyelonephritis
Patients usually respond well to antibiotics. Surgery to correct any obstruction to the urine flow or vesicoureteric reflux may be needed
■ Chronic pyelonephritis
Patients may need treatment for hypertension and renal failure.

Incidence

About 10–15 per cent of the 70 people per million who develop acute renal failure each year have glomerulonephritis. In 1994, about 23,000 people in the UK received dialysis or transplant treatment for kidney failure. Patients with glomerular nephritis were the largest group. Pyelonephritis was another common cause.

Alport's syndrome is an

inherited disorder that affects about one person in 5,000. Incidence data include:
■ Men are more often affected than women
■ Patients develop progressive renal impairment and deafness
■ The kidney damage is mostly to the glomeruli
■ Blood in the urine is often the first sign.

Renal calculi

Symptoms

Renal calculi, more commonly known as kidney stones, can cause extreme pain, obstruction of the urinary system and kidney problems. They can sometimes be treated without surgery.

Kidney stones usually form in the kidney itself – in the renal pelvis or calyces – but can pass into the ureter. Many are tiny and pass out in the urine without being noticed or causing problems, but larger ones can become lodged along the urinary tract, causing obstruction and pain.

INITIAL SYMPTOMS
The most common, and usually the first, symptom of kidney stones is excruciating pain:
■ Typically originating in the flank or back, the pain is usually intermittent and can be felt on one or both sides. It can move along the course of the ureter to the pelvis and groin and radiate to the inner thigh (and the testicles in men)
■ If the stone passes into the bladder, it can cause pain just above the pubis. This may come in spasms, get progressively worse, and be accompanied by nausea and vomiting.

OTHER SYMPTOMS
Other symptoms of kidney stones can include:
■ Distension of the abdomen and abdominal pain
■ Haematuria (blood in urine)

Staghorn calculi are branched stones that form a cast of the collecting system of the kidney. This type of stone can cause the kidney to stop functioning.

■ Persistent urge to urinate, with increased frequency
■ Painful urination, with a burning sensation
■ Fever and chills, which can be signs of an infection that requires urgent treatment
■ A build-up of urine with accompanying temporary failure of kidney function.

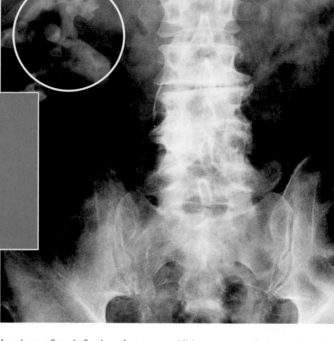

Kidney stones show up clearly on X-rays. This X-ray shows the most serious form of stone – a large staghorn calculus – in the right kidney (circled).

Causes

A renal calculus forms from a build-up of salt crystals that are normally dissolved in the urine. If urine becomes saturated with salts, they begin to crystallize from the solution. It is thought that a substance in the urine normally acts to prevent this, and that a failure of this system might be involved in the formation of kidney stones.

TYPES OF STONES
The majority of kidney stones (around 80 per cent) are made of calcium, most commonly combined with oxalate, but sometimes combined with phosphate or carbonate. Calcium stones are more common in men, and generally appear between the ages of 20 and 30.

Other substances that can form stones include uric acid and the amino acid, cystine. Urinary tract infections can cause struvite stones consisting of magnesium, ammonium and phosphate; these are more common in women. Stones can also be named according to their location in the urinary tract; for example, ureteric stones (found in the ureter).

METABOLIC DISORDERS
Excess salts in the urine can be caused by metabolic disorders, such as hyperparathyroidism (overactivity of the parathyroid glands) or hyperoxaluria (high urinary levels of oxalic acid).

Some of these problems are hereditary, and a family history of kidney stones increases the risk of incidence. More than 70 per cent of people with the rare hereditary disorder renal tubular acidosis develop kidney stones.

Stone formation is also promoted by hypocituria, a disorder in which levels of citrates (which bind to calcium in the urine helping to keep it in solution) are depressed.

Urinary tract infections are a common cause of kidney stones. Bladder infections may be due to E. coli (yellow) invading the bladder cells (blue).

OTHER CAUSES
Factors such as hydration levels and diet can contribute to the development of kidney stones, but only in susceptible people.

Other problems that increase the risk of stones include kidney disorders, bowel inflammation, intestinal bypass surgery, urinary tract infections, chemotherapy, high vitamin D intake, urinary tract obstruction, some diuretics and calcium-based antacids.

Incidence

Kidney stones are known to have affected people as far back as ancient Egypt, 7000 years ago, but the incidence seems to be increasing. It now stands at 1:1000 adults in the US. In the developed world, about five per cent of women and 10 per cent of men will have at least one episode by age 70, and stones are found in about one per cent of autopsies. White men aged 20–40 are the group most at risk.

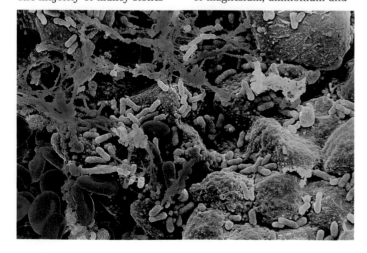

Diagnosis

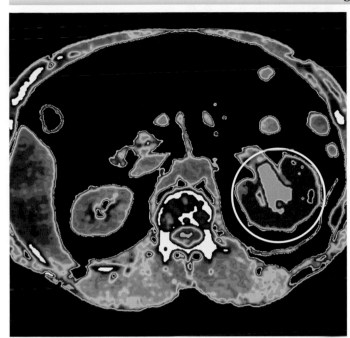

Complaints of blood in the urine and sudden flank or abdominal pain strong enough to require narcotic analgesics are obvious signs of renal calculi.

'Silent' or asymptomatic stones are sometimes found when a patient is X-rayed or when their urine is sampled for some other reason.

IMAGING
The presence of a renal calculus can be confirmed using:
■ Ultrasound of the kidney
■ Intravenous urogram – an X-ray taken with radio-opaque contrast medium. This will show radiolucent stones
■ X-rays, MRI or CT scans.

CT scans may be used in the diagnosis of kidney stones. In this case, the right kidney (circled) has become enlarged due to the presence of a stone.

SAMPLE ANALYSIS
Urine samples will be investigated for the presence of:
■ Blood
■ Bacteria
■ Stones or crystals
■ High levels of urine salts that may give a clue as to the underlying cause of the stones.

Stones or crystals will be sent to a laboratory for crystallography, to determine their chemical composition. Blood samples may also be tested for abnormal levels of substances such as calcium.

HISTORY
The patient's medical history may reveal a family history of kidney stone or metabolic problems, or medication that could be responsible. A dietary history may reveal contributory factors (such as high levels of protein consumption).

Treatment

Most kidney stones are small enough to be passed naturally, without special intervention. In these cases, the following steps may be taken:
■ The administration of strong painkillers
■ The person is told to drink large quantities of water. If treatment is carried out in hospital, fluids may be given intravenously
■ Once the stone is passed, the person is asked to retain it for further examination.

SHOCK-WAVES
If the stone is very large, or causing a build-up of urine or infection, it may be necessary to break it up or remove it. The preferred method is non-invasive, shockwave lithotripsy in which ultrasonic waves are focused on the stone to shatter

it into pieces small enough to pass out in the urine.

SURGERY
Large renal stones may be removed by:
■ Cystoscopy – a viewing tube is passed up to the kidney via the urethra and forceps are used to crush or remove the stone
■ Percutaneous nephrolithotomy – the affected kidney is accessed through the person's back via an endoscope (viewing tube) and the stone is removed along this track.

Open surgery may be carried out in the case of very large stones, such as staghorn calculi.

Large renal calculi may be broken up using lithotripsy. This is a non-invasive, shock-wave treatment that focuses ultrasonic waves on the stone.

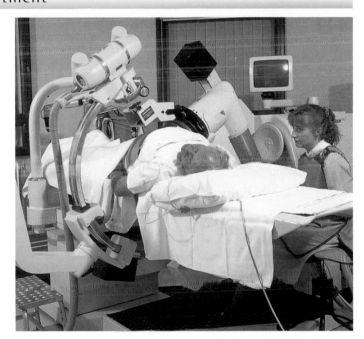

Prevention

If known, any underlying causes of renal calculi can be treated in the following ways:
■ Some metabolic disorders can be treated with drugs, for example, thiazide diuretics for hypercalciuria or allopurinol for uric acid stones
■ Dietary modification can also help in some cases. For example, people who have

The main preventative measure is to increase water intake. After forming a calcium stone, people should also avoid oxalate-rich foods such as spinach.

developed calcium stones should avoid eating too many oxalate-rich foods such as tea, chocolate, coffee, nuts, spinach and rhubarb.

General prevention
In general, the most important but simple step to take in preventing kidney stones is to increase the intake of fluids by drinking at least two litres of water a day. This is particularly important during warm weather, following exercise or after a fever, as these conditions may cause a rise in the concentration of urine.

Prognosis

Kidney stones rarely cause lasting damage to the kidneys. Most stones are either removed or passed without complications. The risk of recurrence, however, is high: 15 per cent at one year after diagnosis, and 40 per cent at five years. Preventative measures are therefore very important to avoid a recurrence.

Where a metabolic or other form of underlying disorder has caused stone formation, the risk of developing further stones is increased.

Renal tumours

Symptoms

Renal (kidney) tumours may be non-cancerous (benign) or cancerous (malignant).

Benign tumours seldom cause any symptoms and are usually only discovered incidentally when the kidneys are investigated for some other reason.

Malignant tumours that arise in the kidney include renal cell cancers (previously known as hypernephromas or Grawitz tumours) and nephroblastomas (Wilms' tumours).

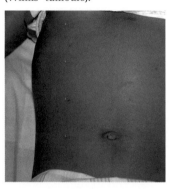

Nephroblastomas mostly occur in young children. Swelling of the abdomen, due to malignant growth, is often the first clear indication of a tumour.

RENAL CELL CANCERS
Renal cell cancers mainly affect older adults and cause:
■ Blood in the urine (haematuria) – a common symptom
■ Pain and swelling in the loins
■ Fever – in about 20 per cent of patients
■ Anaemia
■ Weight loss
■ Polycythaemia – raised haemoglobin and red blood cell levels due to the overproduction of erythropoietin, a hormone produced by the kidney
■ Swollen veins in the testicle – due to tumours on the kidney obstructing the neighbouring renal vein.

In addition, about 25 per cent of patients with renal cell cancer first consult their doctors about symptoms such as swollen glands, cough or bone pain. This is a result of secondary cancers (metastases) in the lungs, bones or liver due to spread via the lymphatic system (to the lymph nodes) or the blood.

NEPHROBLASTOMAS
Nephroblastomas, also known as Wilms' tumours, usually occur in children up to the age of

three; they are rare over the age of eight. In a few cases, tumours develop in both kidneys. Children with nephroblastomas develop:
■ A large mass in the abdomen – this is usually the first and principal symptom. The mass is usually painless but may bleed internally, causing some pain
■ Blood in the urine – this is

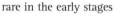

If doctors suspect that a patient has a renal tumour from the symptoms, they feel (palpate) the kidney area. The presence of a lump can indicate cancer.

rare in the early stages
■ Loss of appetite
■ Nausea and vomiting
■ A feverish illness
■ Raised blood pressure – due to kidney damage.

Causes

The cause of renal tumours varies according to the nature of the disorder.

SMOKING
Little is known about the cause of renal cell cancer, except that current cigarette smokers are at approximately double the risk of developing the disease compared to those who have never smoked.

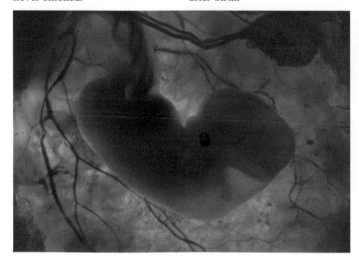

GENETIC ABNORMALITIES
The underlying cause of nephroblastomas is unknown. However, genetic abnormalities, particularly of chromosome 11, have been found in children with nephroblastomas. The tumours develop from cells involved in the development of the kidneys before birth, which usually disappear after birth.

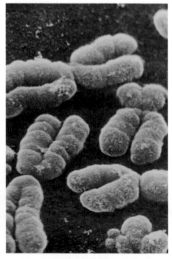

Genetic disorders, usually of chromosome 11, have been linked to nephroblastomas. About two per cent of cases have a relative with the disease.

Nephroblastomas are tumours arising from the embryonic tissue that develops into the kidneys during gestation (seven-week-old embryo shown).

Incidence

Renal cell cancer is about twice as common in men as in women. This type of cancer is rare under the age of 40, and usually occurs over the age of 50 years. The average age for first seeking medical advice is 55 years.

The number of cases occurring each year has increased in recent years, particularly among people of Afro-Caribbean origin in the USA.

Childhood malignancy
Nephroblastomas are the most common abdominal tumours in childhood, affecting about 75 children in Britain each year. About 10 per cent of cases occur in children born with other abnormalities, such as absence of the iris (the coloured part of the eye), abnormalities of the genito-urinary tract or learning disabilities. Around 1–2 per cent of patients have a family history of nephroblastoma.

Diagnosis

Renal cell cancer may be diagnosed by an X-ray of the urinary tract using a radiopaque medium (excretion urography). This is effective at visualizing large masses, although small tumours may not show clearly. An ultrasound or CT scan may confirm the diagnosis. Secondary deposits in the lungs from a renal cell cancer have a characteristic 'cannon-ball'-like appearance on a chest X-ray.

NEPHROBLASTOMA TESTS
Nephroblastomas are often first diagnosed clinically when a child develops a large smooth abdominal tumour or, in a few cases, large tumours on each side. Investigations include blood and urine tests, chest X-rays to see if the disease has spread to the lungs, ultrasound and CT scans.

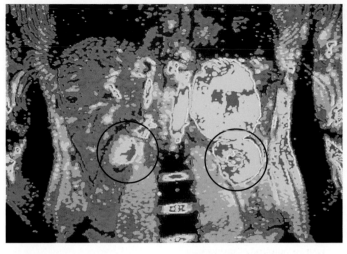

This MR image shows the kidneys (circled) on either side of the spine. A large malignant tumour can be seen above the right kidney.

MR imaging produces cross-sectional images through a person's body. These images can reveal diseased internal organs, such as the kidneys.

Treatment

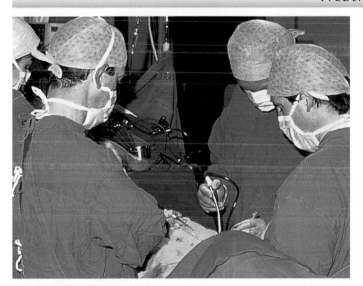

Surgery to remove a renal cell tumour gives the only chance of a complete cure. Unfortunately, by the time of diagnosis, many tumours are too advanced to be totally removed or have already metastasized. However, surgery may still be indicated as the metastases sometimes shrink if the primary tumour in the kidney is removed.

Chemotherapy and radiotherapy have little effect in renal cell cancer. Some tumours respond to hormones, for

Surgical removal of a renal cell tumour is often the only option. A cure may not be possible, however, if the cancer has spread beyond the kidney.

example progesterone. Treatment with interferon-alpha (a substance produced by the body which is able to inhibit viral growth) sometimes produces a short-term response.

NEPHROBLASTOMA
Treatment involves surgery, chemotherapy, which may be given before surgery to shrink the tumour or after to help prevent recurrences, and sometimes radiotherapy.

Prevention

Since renal cell cancer is more common in people who smoke, it is likely to be prevented by not taking up smoking or by ceasing to smoke.

There is at present no known method of preventing a nephroblastoma.

Prognosis

The outlook for those with renal cell cancer depends on how closely the cancer cells resemble normal kidney cells and whether the disease has already spread from the kidney. If the cancer cells are very dissimilar to normal cells (poorly differentiated), the outlook is worse than if they are similar (well differentiated).

If the tumour is confined to the kidney at the time of diagnosis, about 60–70 per cent of patients survive for at least five years and 50 per cent are alive 10 years later. The outlook is less optimistic for people whose lymph nodes contain cancer cells or who have metastases in distant organs, such as the lungs, when the disease is first diagnosed.

HIGH CURE RATE
The outlook for most children with a nephroblastoma is good. A combination of surgery, chemotherapy and radiotherapy cures about 90 per cent of children, including those who have metastases at the time of diagnosis. A few children do, however, develop recurrences or a second tumour so careful follow-up treatment is needed.

The presence of a particular genetic abnormality, loss of heterozygosity of 16q, appears to be more common in children with a poor outlook than in children who do well. The abnormality is more common in children who develop a nephroblastoma when over the age of two.

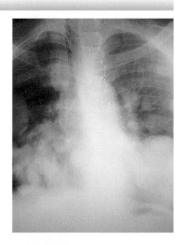

The outlook for patients with renal tumours worsens if the cancer spreads. In this case, secondary tumours have developed in the patient's lungs.

Conjunctivitis

Symptoms

Conjunctivitis is the most common eye problem encountered by general practitioners. The sore and bloodshot eyes that characterize the condition are due to inflammation of the clear mucous lining of the front of the eyeballs and the inner eyelids, the conjunctiva.

There are several types and different causes of the condition and all ages may be affected. Although conjunctivitis is the most common cause of red and/or sticky eyes, vision is not normally affected.

The symptoms associated with conjunctivitis include:
■ Sore and gritty eyes
■ Red and congested eyes
■ Sticky discharge from the eyes; the eyelids may feel crusted on waking in the mornings
■ Swollen eyelids in severe cases
■ Itchy eyelids in allergic conjunctivitis

In cases where conjunctivitis results from trauma rather than infection, there may be a history of exposure to toxic chemicals, fumes or excessive ultraviolet light.

Conjunctivitis typically results in redness and inflammation of the eyes around the iris, where normally the sclera is white. Vision is not usually affected, however.

INITIAL SIGNS
The typical signs that indicate conjunctivitis include:
■ Red, congested (hyperaemic) conjunctivae
■ Mucus discharge on the eyelids with crusting around the edges
■ Swelling of the eyelid and oedema (fluid accumulation) of the conjunctivae
■ A lymph node in front of the ear may be palpable
■ Papillae (small bumps) occur on the tarsal (eyelid) conjunctivae in cases of allergic conjunctivitis
■ Watering (lacrimation) and light sensitivity in chronic allergic conjunctivitis

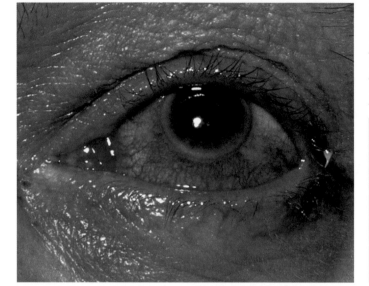

Conjunctivitis sicca

Dry, gritty eyes – termed conjunctivitis sicca – are relatively common in women after middle age. This may be due to Sjögren's syndrome, a condition affecting the lacrimal (tear-producing) glands, which itself may be associated with rheumatoid disease.

A test for measuring the extent of this condition involves placing strips of filter paper in the corner of the eyes for approximately five minutes to measure the tear production and the subsequent absorption by the paper. The test, known as Schirmer's test, is used to determine treatment, usually with artificial tears.

Causes

Conjunctivitis may be primary when there is no associated cause, or it may be secondary to a toxic effect or a local spread of inflammation. When associated with corneal inflammation, it is known as kerato-conjunctivitis; when associated with eyelid inflammation it is known as blepharo-conjunctivitis.

COMMON CAUSES
■ Bacterial – purulent discharge due to bacteria, such as staphylococci, streptococci, gonorrhoea or chlamydia
■ Viral – herpes simplex, herpes zoster (shingles), measles or mumps. A pre-auricular (in front of the ear) gland may be present in these cases
■ Allergic – vernal or spring catarrh. May be confirmed using blood tests on serum and tears looking at the IgE levels (immunoglobulin associated with allergic reaction)
■ Fungal
■ Chemical or toxic – such as cosmetics or fumes
■ Mechanical irritation – such as a foreign body in the eye
■ Contact lenses – poor lens hygiene is another cause of conjunctivitis.

People who wear contact lenses are particularly susceptible to conjunctivitis. Inadequate cleaning of the lenses increases the danger of infection.

It is important to exclude herpes simplex virus, shown on this electron micrograph, when diagnosing a red eye that does not respond to antibiotics.

Rarer causes of conjunctivitis

Newborn conjunctivitis
Acute conjunctivitis of the newborn infant (ophthalmia neonatorum) may be due to infection from the birth canal, often by chlamydia, or by staphylococci or pneumococci.

Trachoma
A chronic and severe form of conjunctivitis is trachoma, a disease which occurs mainly in developing countries; it is a very common cause of blindness. Trachoma is caused by the bacteria *Chlamydia trachomatis*, which is prevalent in tropical countries. In extreme cases, the infection leads to severe scarring of the conjunctiva.

Diagnosis

Diagnosis of conjunctivitis depends on ascertaining the cause in each case, such as a foreign body, viral infection or allergy. Neonatal cases may be due to obstruction of the flow of tears by blocked tear ducts.

Gonorrhoea, chlamydia and bacterial causes can be confirmed in the laboratory. Trachoma is diagnosed clinically by the rough appearance of the upper tarsal conjunctivae. The chlamydial inclusion bodies inside the cell can be demonstrated by specific immunofluorescence and staining methods.

Trachoma causes the inside of the eyelids to become inflamed and scarred. In later stages, the lids can turn inwards so that the lashes scratch the cornea.

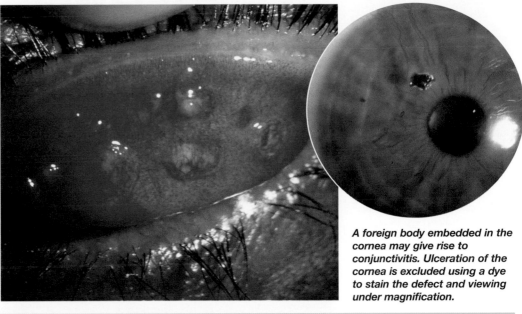

A foreign body embedded in the cornea may give rise to conjunctivitis. Ulceration of the cornea is excluded using a dye to stain the defect and viewing under magnification.

Treatment

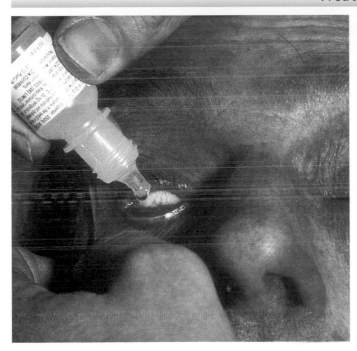

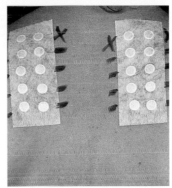

When an allergic cause of conjunctivitis is suspected, skin patch testing may be necessary. This determines the specific agent resulting in the reaction.

Topical antibiotics resolve surface eye infections quickly, often within a week. Antibiotic eyedrops are effective and simple to administer.

■ Specific antibiotics will readily clear the infective types of conjunctivitis
■ Non-steroidal anti-inflammatories, such as cromoglycate, are effective against seasonal allergic conjunctivitis
■ Antihistamines and corticosteroids may occasionally be used
■ Vasoconstrictor eye drops may reduce the chemosis (swelling) and hyperaemia (congestion).

Acute allergic or toxic reactions may occur with many topical agents in contact with the eyes, such as cosmetics. Patch testing to determine the cause of the allergy may be necessary to determine the cause of the inflammation. Once this has been discovered, avoiding the responsible agent will usually resolve the condition.

Prevention

Preventing conjunctivitis relies on identifying the likely causes and reducing the risk of being affected by them. Further recurrences can also be reduced in this way. Prevention includes:
■ Well-defined measures at the delivery of a baby will usually prevent serious neonatal infection occurring
■ Advice on lens hygiene for contact lens wearers is essential
■ It is important to recognize irritant or toxic causes so that they may be eliminated before causing conjunctivitis
■ Trachoma requires community health measures to be implemented.

Incidence and prognosis

Conjunctivitis in its various forms is the commonest eye disease in the UK. Fortunately, recognizing the condition is straightforward and – providing the patient seeks early medical help – serious outcomes can be avoided.

Conjunctivitis of bacterial or viral origin is highly contagious and can be transmitted directly from eye to eye. Poor hygiene will exacerbate the spread of infection.

The outcome in most cases of conjunctivitis depends on diagnosing the true cause of the condition and eliminating the causative factor. If the symptoms are caused by an allergy, then treating the allergic reaction with antihistamines, for example, should resolve the problem. Newborn conjunctivitis will resolve within a week or so with specific diagnosis and treatment.

Trachoma is still a major cause of blindness in developing countries, affecting up to 400 million people. However, when the condition is diagnosed and treated it responds well to antibiotics. Preventative measures taken within the affected community should be then be taken to minimize further spread.

Glaucoma

Symptoms

Glaucoma is a condition in which the pressure inside the eye (intra-ocular pressure) becomes abnormally high, leading to visual impairment and sometimes blindness.

PRIMARY GLAUCOMA
In most cases, there is no other associated eye disorder, and the condition is termed primary glaucoma. There are two main classifications:

■ **Angle-closure glaucoma** (acute or congestive glaucoma). In this medical emergency, the angle where the aqueous humour (fluid in the front chamber of the eye) drains closes, leading to a rapid increase in intra-ocular pressure. This results in pain and blurring of vision. Nausea and vomiting may occur if the pain is severe.

■ **Open-angle glaucoma** (chronic simple glaucoma). This is a common cause of blindness and affects both eyes. The drainage of aqueous

Parts of the eye affected by glaucoma

Angle between cornea and iris
Contains drainage channel for aqueous humour; in glaucoma, the fluid cannot drain away, leading to a build-up of pressure within the eye

Anterior (front) chamber
Filled with aqueous humour; this fluid normally drains at the angle, but cannot in glaucoma

Iris
Coloured part of the eye

Cornea
Transparent cover of eye; often has an abnormal appearance in glaucoma and may be hazy or swollen

Optic disc
Where blood vessels and the optic nerve pass into and out of the eye; becomes 'cupped' in congenital glaucoma and open-angle glaucoma due to atrophy of the nerve fibres

Vitreous body
Largest chamber of the eye; pressure here rises in glaucoma – raised intra-ocular pressure

humour is blocked, although the angle remains open. Raised intra-ocular pressure leads to 'cupping' of the optic disc (dipping of the centre of the

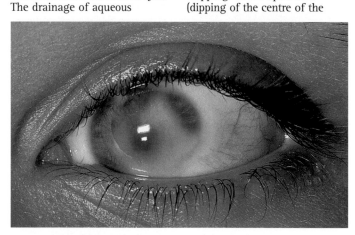

optic disc) due to thinning of the nerve fibre layer. This causes abnormalities in the visual field and often blindness.

SECONDARY GLAUCOMA
Glaucoma can also arise as a result of other conditions and diseases affecting the eye. In common with primary glaucoma, secondary glaucoma occurs when the drainage of aqueous humour is impaired, resulting in raised intra-ocular pressure. Examples include:
■ Pigmentary glaucoma, when

In certain cases, glaucoma is congenital, as in this teenage girl. The clouding of the iris is a result of the abnormally high pressure within the eye.

pigment is present in the anterior chamber of the eye, deposited on the corneal surface
■ Exfoliation syndrome, in which white flakes are deposited on the surface of the lens and in the drainage angle.

Glaucoma may also be secondary to changes in the lens of the eye or the uveal tract, or following trauma or eye surgery; it may also be induced by steroid drops or ointment used around the eye for more than a week.

CONGENITAL GLAUCOMA
Otherwise known as buphthalmos, this condition is present at birth. The baby's eyes are watery, red and painful, with an enlarged cornea and cupping of the optic disc.

Incidence

Glaucoma is the leading cause of preventable blindness, and the third commonest form of blindness after cataract and age-related macular degeneration.

Primary open-angle glaucoma is the commonest form, affecting approximately two per cent of people over the age of 40. Angle-closure glaucoma is very rare, especially below the age of 60.

People with a family history and/or hypermetropia (long-sightedness) have a tendency to develop primary open-angle glaucoma.

Causes

In all forms of glaucoma, the outflow of aqueous humour from the eye is impaired as a result of abnormalities within the drainage system of the front chamber of the eye or impaired access of the aqueous humour to the drainage system. The reason for the defect depends on the type of glaucoma, but the pain and deterioration in vision arise from the abnormally high pressure within the eye.

Characteristic of glaucoma is 'cupping' of the optic disc (the central yellow circular area). Surrounding blood vessels are hooked over the disc's edge.

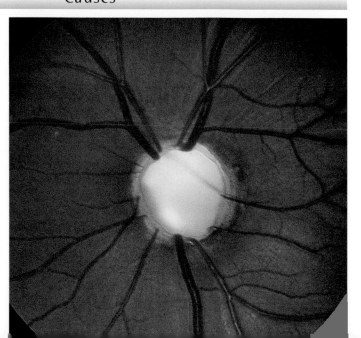

Diagnosis

Diagnosis is made when there is a typical history in the acute types of glaucoma; otherwise, routine examination of vision and visual fields determine a particular pattern of visual field loss. Tests include:

■ Measurement of the intra-ocular tension (tonometry) and examination of the back of the eye (fundus) using an ophthalmoscope are essential

■ Gonioscopy – an examining technique of the front chamber of the eye, utilizing a corneal contact lens magnifying device, allows direct visualization of the angle structures and the tissue at the junction of the cornea and sclera, where aqueous humour drains

■ Optic disc assessment is essential with the visual fields, as visual field defects cause tunnel vision and may progress to blindness; in the absence of symptoms until relatively late in the disease, screening is necessary for the detection of primary open-angle glaucoma.

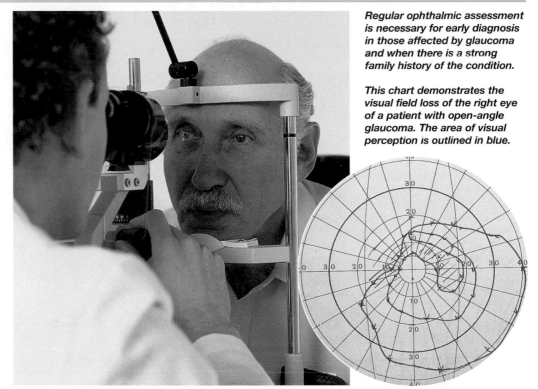

Regular ophthalmic assessment is necessary for early diagnosis in those affected by glaucoma and when there is a strong family history of the condition.

This chart demonstrates the visual field loss of the right eye of a patient with open-angle glaucoma. The area of visual perception is outlined in blue.

Treatment

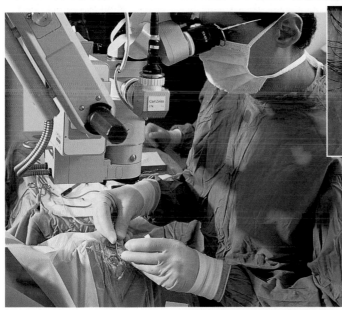

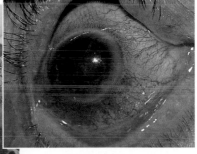

Acute glaucoma is a medical emergency, requiring immediate treatment to reduce the intra-ocular pressure. Laser surgery may be offered subsequently.

Chronic, open-angle glaucoma may be treated by an operation known as a trabeculectomy. This is designed to improve the drainage of fluid within the eye.

Treatment of chronic, open-angle glaucoma is aimed at reducing the intra-ocular pressure:

■ By suppressing production of aqueous humour; for example, with drugs such as beta-blockers applied topically

■ By increasing the outflow of aqueous humour with parasympathomimetic agents such as pilocarpine

■ By reducing aqueous volume with hyperosmotic agents.

Pupil constriction is important in angle-closure glaucoma; for instance, by using a mydriatic drug for pupil dilation.

Surgical treatments include laser iridotomy and surgical peripheral iridectomy for chronic glaucoma; laser trabeculoplasty removes a small segment of the eye to facilitate aqueous outflow.

Prevention

Regular eye tests, especially in those with a family history of chronic open-angle glaucoma, are essential to ensure the early recognition of the onset of the disease. This also ensures regular supervision and should help to avoid what is a very common form of blindness.

Early diagnosis offers the best chance of successful treatment. The identification of other risk factors for chronic glaucoma, such as ischaemic heart disease, may also aid prevention.

Prognosis

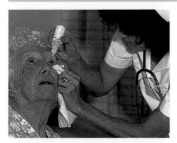

In at-risk patients, preventative medication (eye-drops) may help delay the progression of open-angle glaucoma.

Without treatment, open-angle glaucoma may progress to complete blindness. If anti-glaucoma eye-drops are used, and the eye has not suffered extensive damage, the prognosis is good. When the condition is detected early, medical management is most successful. It is imperative that patients receiving topical or systemic steroid therapy undergo periodic tonometry and ophthalmoscopy, particularly if there is a family history of glaucoma.

Cataracts

Symptoms

A cataract is an opacity of the lens of the eye that causes blurred vision. The normally transparent lens lies immediately behind the pupil and focuses light on the retina. It has a transparent capsule that is attached to the ciliary muscle, which contracts to make the lens more convex, and thus focus the eye on near objects.

SIGNS OF CATARACTS
Cataracts interfere with the passage of light through the eye. Small cataracts may not cause any noticeable problem to sufferers, but larger cataracts can be the cause of:
■ Reduced visual acuity (blunted vision) – interferes with everyday activities such as reading or driving; eyesight is often worse-affected in a bright light, and distant and central vision are affected first
■ Spots – these may appear in a fixed place in front of the eyes
■ Diplopia (double vision) – this may affect only one eye and remains when the other eye is covered

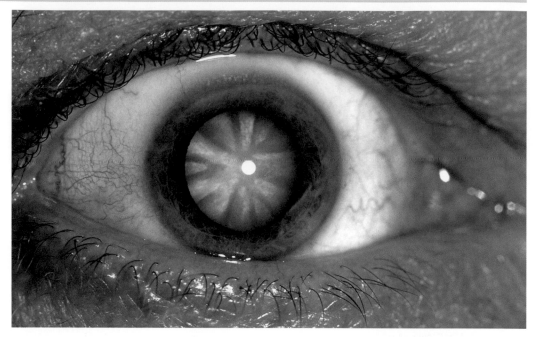

■ Halos – orange halos may seem to appear around lights or any bright areas, and everything in the patient's general environment may look as if it has a slightly orange glow

■ Easier reading – people who previously needed reading glasses sometimes no longer need them; a cataract-related change in the shape of the lens makes them more short-sighted.

A close-up of the eye shows a cataract with its distinctive milky glaze. The term 'cataract' derives from the original idea that the condition was like a little waterfall that fell inside the eye.

Causes

Diabetes sufferers, such as this man self-injecting insulin, can be affected by cataracts due to under-nourishment of the lens of the eye.

Opacities of the lens may be:
■ Age-related – the lens degenerates with age
■ Congenital – they may result from intrauterine viral infections, such as rubella (German measles), or metabolic disorders such as galactosaemia, in which the sugar galactose accumulates in the blood
■ Inherited – a genetic tendency to develop cataracts at an early age occurs in some families
■ Traumatic – secondary to bruising of the eye, penetrating injuries from windscreen glass or metal fragments, or previous eye surgery
■ Inflammatory – patients with persistent inflammation of the iris (iritis) are at increased risk
■ Diabetic – high blood sugar levels may affect the nourishment of the lens
■ Radiational – from prolonged exposure to sunlight or other ionizing radiation
■ Corticosteroid-induced – prolonged courses of corticosteroids can cause cataracts
■ Associated with skin disorders, such as atopic dermatitis.

Diagnosis

Cataracts are diagnosed by a full eye examination – this will also check for other problems, such as glaucoma or retinal disease.

Patients with cataracts should be able to point to the position of a light and their pupils should react normally. In advanced cases, the lens may appear brown or white.

USING AN OPHTHALMOSCOPE
The use of an ophthalmoscope, (a specialized instrument for examining the interior of the eye) will confirm the presence of a cataract. When the light beam is shone through the pupil from about two feet away, the back of the eye normally appears red (the 'red eye' that appears in some photographs); cataracts will show as dark patches.

CONGENITAL CATARACTS
All babies should be examined at birth and at six to eight weeks for cataract and other eye conditions. Congenital cataracts must be treated within the first three months of a baby's life. If treatment is delayed, normal vision may not develop, even if the cataracts are removed at a later stage.

Opticians use specialized ophthalmoscopes to examine the interior of the eye. This can be used to confirm a diagnosis of cataracts.

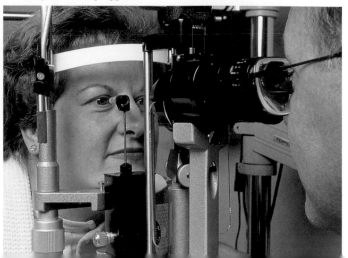

Treatment

There is no medical cure for cataracts. In the early stages, tinted glasses may prevent the dazzle from bright light. Good illumination from above and behind will help reading.

SURGERY

Surgery to remove the cataracts (cataract extraction) is safe and very effective. It is the most common non-emergency operation performed on older people: 105,000 cataract extractions are performed in the UK each year on the NHS.

Patients used to be told that surgery was inadvisable until the cataract had become very advanced and sight was very poor. With modern operating techniques, this delay is no longer necessary. The operation is usually performed as a day case under a local anaesthetic.

SURGICAL TECHNIQUES

■ Extracapsular extraction is the most commonly used procedure – using microsurgery techniques, the surgeon removes the lens through a small incision in its capsule

In an extracapsular cataract extraction, the central, more solid part of the lens (the nucleus) may be liquefied before removal by ultrasonic probe.

Following a cataract operation, most patients will notice a substantial improvement in their vision. Glasses may still be needed for reading, however.

■ Intracapsular extraction involves the removal of the entire lens within its capsule, usually with a cryoprobe; this technique is not now commonly used.

Patients recover rapidly, but may need to use anti-inflammatory and antibiotic eye drops for several weeks.

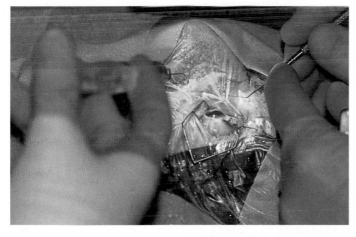

Optical correction after surgery

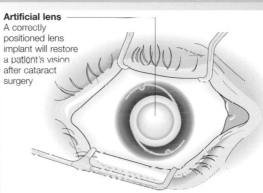

Artificial lens
A correctly positioned lens implant will restore a patient's vision after cataract surgery

Without a lens, the eye has distant vision but cannot focus on near objects. Spectacles or lens implants will correct vision:
■ Spectacles – the spectacles needed after cataract surgery are cumbersome and restrict the field of vision while magnifying near objects; intraocular lens implants means that they are now rarely needed
■ Intraocular implants – the development of intraocular lens implants followed on from the

There are various types of lens implant, including rigid polymethylmethacrylate (pMMA) lenses and foldable silicone lenses, inserted through a minute incision.

Second World War discovery that fragments of Perspex from aircraft windscreens remained safely in the eye, unlike many other foreign bodies; most lens implants are now placed in the empty lens capsule.

Prognosis and incidence

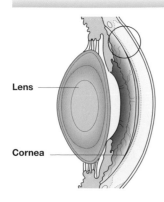

Lens

Cornea

Cataracts tend to grow in size over time and may eventually cause blindness. By blocking the view of the inside of the eye to medical examination, they may also prevent the diagnosis of other treatable eye conditions. Surgery restores good vision if

During corrective surgery for cataract, an incision is made near the edge of the cornea (area circled). This allows the wound to heal without sutures.

the eye is otherwise healthy.

After a lens implant, the capsule sometimes thickens, causing a progressive deterioration in vision. This may respond to laser treatment. Cataracts are a very common cause of impaired sight among the elderly. Between the ages of 50 and 59, 65 per cent of people have lens opacities, not necessarily causing them any trouble. Over the age of 80, 100 per cent of people are affected.

Deafness

Causes and symptoms

Deafness, which may be congenital or acquired, is a partial or total loss of hearing in one or both ears; it may result from disorders of any part of the complex mechanism by which we hear. There are two main types of deafness: conductive and sensorineural.

CONDUCTIVE DEAFNESS
Conductive deafness arises from a defect in the transmission of sound waves from the outer ear to the inner ear. Causes include:
■ Obstruction – by wax, inflammation of the lining of the ear or accumulation of discharge (as in otitis externa)
■ Perforation of the eardrum – from infective damage, trauma, or rarely from pressure changes
■ Disorders in the small bones of the middle ear (the ossicles)

■ Effusions ('glue ear') in children; in adults, respiratory infections or trauma to the ear.

SENSORINEURAL DEAFNESS
Sensorineural deafness is caused by damage to the structures of the ear, and can result in poor transmission of nerve impulses from the inner ear to the brain. It may take one of three patterns:
■ Bilateral (on both sides) and progressive – usually a result of degeneration due to old age
■ Unilateral (one-sided) and progressive – this occurs in acoustic neuroma, Ménière's disease and syphilis
■ Sudden.

Drugs or exposure to noise or pressure are also causes of sensorineural deafness. A full examination will determine the cause and subsequent treatment.

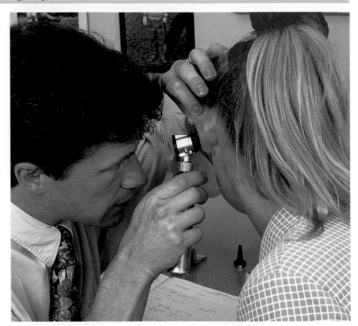

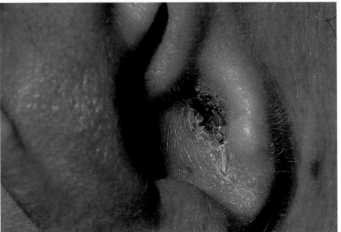

This patient has an ear infection (otitis externa), affecting the outer ear and the ear canal. Otitis externa is one cause of conductive deafness.

A doctor examines a patient's ear using an auriscope. This device can be used to detect conditions that may cause transient (temporary) deafness.

Diagnosis

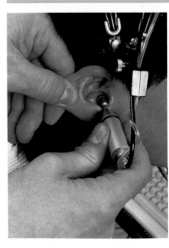

One device used to detect hearing problems emits sounds of varying pitch and loudness. The patient indicates when a sound is detected.

There are a number of tests used in the diagnosis of deafness:
■ Whisper test – whispering into an ear from a fixed distance can help detect gross hearing loss
■ Two tuning fork tests – used to distinguish between conductive and sensorineural deafness in reduced hearing on one side
■ Pure-tone audiometry – noises are introduced into each ear via headphones at different volumes and frequencies; this permits accurate measurement of sound conduction on each side
■ Tympanometry – measures movement of the eardrum at variable air pressure and helps indicate the presence of auditory (Eustachian) tube dysfunction
■ MR scanning – must be performed to exclude acoustic neuroma in a patient with one-sided sensorineural hearing loss.

Testing for conductive deafness

When investigating a patient with unilateral (one-sided) deafness, the specialist will use a vibrating tuning fork to determine whether hearing is better through bone or through air.

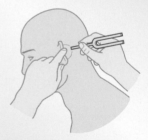

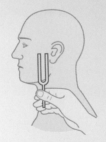

The mast of the tuning fork is placed behind the ear (on the mastoid process). This is a test for conduction of sound through bone.

The tuning fork is then placed adjacent to the outer ear to test conduction of sound through air. The patient is asked which appears loudest.

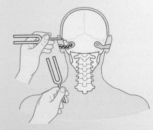

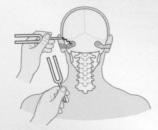

In normal hearing, sound conducted through air is perceived by the patient as being louder than that conducted through bone.

When hearing is reduced on one side, conductive deafness may be indicated by the perception of sound being louder through bone than air.

Treatment and management

Conductive deafness can be treated by:
■ Removal of wax
■ Stapedectomy surgery to correct otosclerosis
■ Myringoplasty to repair a perforated eardrum
■ Ossiculoplasty – may mend breaks in the ossicular chain
■ Myringotomy to drain a secretory otitis media or for the insertion of a grommet.

HEARING AIDS

A wide variety of hearing aids is available, including those worn either in or behind the ear. Ongoing technological advances mean that modern hearing devices are smaller, more efficient and more acceptable cosmetically. For an aid to be useful for speech discrimination, the patient needs to distinguish at least half of the speech content.

In some patients, cochlear defects make amplified sounds intolerable; this may assist in the choice of aid. In bilateral deafness, it is usually preferable to fit an aid in the better ear.

Bone conduction aids may be useful in some patients, especially bone-anchored hearing aids, secured surgically into the temporal bone.

Cochlear implants, electronic devices that stimulate the surviving auditory nerve in those patients with profound bilateral deafness, are being used in both adults and children. Lip-reading should be taught when the level of hearing is still useful in the severely deaf.

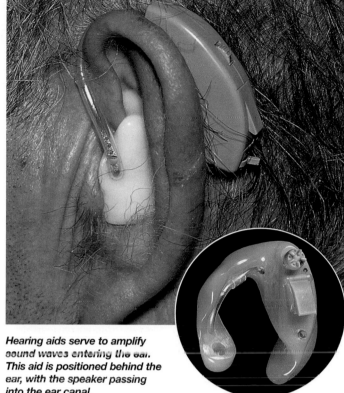

Hearing aids serve to amplify sound waves entering the ear. This aid is positioned behind the ear, with the speaker passing into the ear canal.

A cochlear implant consists of a receiver and an electrode. The electrode is inserted into the inner ear, enabling impulses to reach the brain.

With a high-loss helix hearing aid, the volume of incoming sound and the range of frequencies can be altered to maximize hearing capability.

Deafness in children

In children, deafness may be congenital or acquired. Congenital deafness is usually sensorineural. It may be due to genetic factors, maternal infection or drugs, or may follow events such as birth trauma, anoxia or haemolytic disease of the newborn. Glue ear is the most common cause of conductive deafness in children.

Screening

Recognizing deafness before the age of six months is the aim, before time for learning speech is lost. If deafness is suspected, various diagnostic methods are used, depending on age:
■ Up to six months – assessment of the infant's response to short bursts of high-intensity sound; later, distraction techniques such as spoken voice or rattles
■ At one to two years of age – quiet speech is the best test

The oto-acoustic emission test may be used in newborns. It analyses the response of the inner ear to sound emissions.

It is preferable for hearing-impaired children to attend normal schools, where possible. A number of technological devices can assist this.

■ By three years – any severe hearing loss should have been discovered; special clinics will use specialized techniques.

Once deafness is diagnosed, referral to an ENT clinic should be made. Auditory training, fitting hearing aids and educational planning may be necessary.

Education in a normal school, a special unit for deaf children or a deaf school are all options. About half of all deaf children are able to attend normal schools.

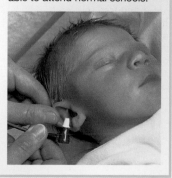

Incidence

Over three million adults (six in every 100 in the UK) have impaired hearing, and over 10,000 children need special education. About 45 per cent of deaf people are over 80 years of age, and 84 per cent are over 60 years of age. There are probably 900,000 people with severe impairment and 150,000 who are profoundly deaf, of whom only 10 per cent may have been affected since childhood.

Otitis media

Symptoms

In this common childhood condition, a bacterial or viral infection causes inflammation of the middle ear (the part of the ear located between the eardrum and the inner ear).

COMMON SYMPTOMS
The symptoms of the condition may include:
- Fever
- Earache
- Hearing loss
- Dizziness.

Small children cannot express their symptoms clearly and often appear generally unwell rather than having any specific symptoms. Children with otitis media may have a loss of appetite, sometimes with vomiting and diarrhoea.

COMPLICATIONS
Otitis media sometimes leads to perforation of the eardrum. If this happens, there may be a discharge from the affected ear; earache is then likely to subside due to the decrease in pressure.

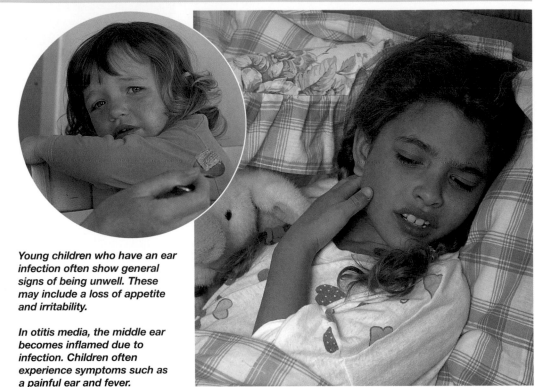

Young children who have an ear infection often show general signs of being unwell. These may include a loss of appetite and irritability.

In otitis media, the middle ear becomes inflamed due to infection. Children often experience symptoms such as a painful ear and fever.

Causes

Otitis media develops as a result of an upper respiratory tract infection passing along the eustachian tube, which runs from the back of the throat to the middle ear. This tends to take place when the tube is blocked, and often occurs as a result of a cold but may also be due to the pressure of enlarged adenoids, located above the tonsils at the back of the nose.

INFECTED FLUID
The blockage of the tube prevents the secretions produced in the middle ear from flowing to the back of the throat as they normally would. As a result, the collection of fluid in the middle ear becomes infected with bacteria.

In some cases, otitis media is caused by a viral infection, which usually affects both ears and is often accompanied by a throat infection. The infections are often passed on from child to child at nursery or school.

Exposure to cigarette smoke in the home can also put children at increased risk of developing otitis media.

Otitis media often occurs when a child has a cold. This is because the eustachian tube between the throat and ear becomes blocked.

Otitis media is caused by viral and bacterial infections. These infections can pass between children in close proximity, such as in the classroom.

Incidence

Otitis media occurs most commonly in the first seven years of life and can affect small babies. One fifth of children under the age of four are affected at least once a year.

The condition develops because children have immature eustachian tubes that are easily blocked, often by the adenoids. Enlarged adenoids can also affect breathing through the nose, and if this is the case, removal may be considered.

For reasons unknown, there is a higher incidence of otitis media in boys than girls.

Diagnosis

The diagnosis of otitis media is made during an examination of the eardrums.

EXAMINING THE EAR
The examination requires use of an otoscope, which illuminates the eardrum and provides a clear view. The affected eardrum may be red and bulging or there may be tiny red blood vessels visible on its surface. If there is discharge from the ear, a swab of the fluid is often taken to look for a bacterial cause.

Children who have recurrent episodes require assessments to monitor their hearing, as they are at risk of impairment.

An examination of a child's ear should be performed if otitis media is suspected. An otoscope is used to illuminate and magnify the eardrum.

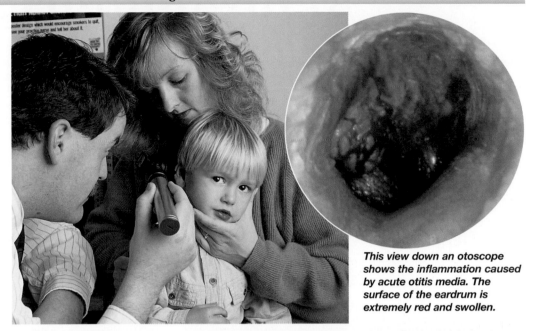

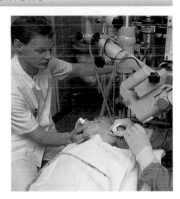

This view down an otoscope shows the inflammation caused by acute otitis media. The surface of the eardrum is extremely red and swollen.

Prognosis

For most children, otitis media is a mild and benign condition. Any hearing problems associated with otitis media tend to be short-lived and perforations usually heal within a few weeks.

'GLUE EAR'
In some cases, there is a build-up of fluid in the middle ear cavity, known as persistent middle ear effusion or 'glue ear'. This complication can cause prolonged hearing impairment, speech problems and learning difficulties.

Often, this fluid clears without treatment within a few weeks or months and hearing is restored.

A test may be performed to check if hearing loss has occurred. A noise is made behind the child, who should turn in response to the sound.

Treatment

Painkillers, such as paracetamol, may help to relieve the earache and bring down a fever. The doctor may also prescribe antibiotics. In many cases, however, antibiotics are not necessary – many middle ear infections clear without antibiotic treatment.

SURGERY
If the fluid collection persists, surgery may be carried out to drain the fluid from the middle ear. Under anaesthetic, a small incision is made in the eardrum and then a tiny tube (grommet) is inserted to allow air to circulate normally, preventing fluid accumulating. Some children require reinsertion if a grommet falls out.

A much rarer complication of otitis media is mastoiditis, in which a bacterial infection spreads from the middle ear to

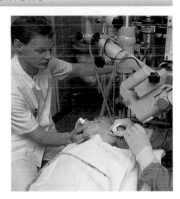

Treatment for otitis media may involve implanting a small tube called a grommet into the eardrum. This drains fluid from the ear and restores hearing.

the bone behind the ear. This is a serious condition requiring urgent treatment, usually with antibiotics, but sometimes surgery is also required.

Prevention

It is not possible to prevent a child having an ear infection. However, if a child appears unwell and complains of earache it is important to seek medical advice.

Prompt diagnosis of otitis media and treatment where necessary can prevent the condition becoming worse or leading to complications.

HEARING LOSS
Hearing loss associated with otitis media should be dealt with early, as late diagnosis can have a damaging effect on a child's ability to communicate.

Otitis externa

Otitis externa is a bacterial or viral infection of the ear canal. The causes of infection include:
■ An injury to the skin lining the outer ear, such as scratching it with a cotton bud
■ A skin condition affecting the outer ear.
Getting water in the ears when swimming can also predispose to otitis externa.

Symptoms
The outer ear is often itchy and the skin reddened. The skin may also be dry and flaky with discharge. There may be pain in the ear and the outer ear can become swollen, narrowing the ear canal. Without treatment the condition may persist for several weeks or months.

Treatment
The measures taken by the doctor may include:
■ Cleaning the outer ear
■ Regular ear drops – these may contain steroids, antibiotics or antifungal treatments
■ Strong painkillers
■ Antibiotic tablets
■ Minor surgery if an abscess (a collection of pus) develops.

Acne vulgaris

Symptoms

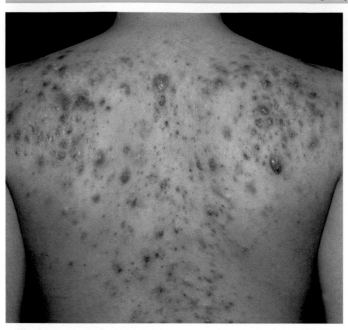

Acne vulgaris (or common acne) is a chronic inflammatory skin condition that particularly affects adolescents. It is a disorder of the sebaceous glands in the skin that produce sebum (a fatty secretion that lubricates hair and skin). The lesions (spots) are most numerous on the face and neck (in 99 per cent of sufferers), back (60 per cent) and chest (15 per cent).

Acne usually occurs at puberty and clears by the mid-20s. A more persistent form may continue up to about 40 years of age, especially in women who have premenstrual exacerbations (flare-ups).

The characteristic signs of an

In over half of all cases of acne, the typical spots and pustules (pus-containing blisters) will be found on the sufferer's back.

outbreak of acne may include:

■ Seborrhoea – excessive production of sebum, leading to greasiness of the skin predisposes to acne, but is not a cause in itself
■ Comedones – tiny nodules on the skin which first appear as whiteheads above pores and follicles (see diagram below) and develop into blackheads
■ Papules (raised red spots) – appear after blackheads rupture, causing skin irritation
■ Skin scarring (excoriated acne) – a result of picking and squeezing the lesions
■ Skin lesions which suppurate pus – young males in particular may develop these highly inflamed pustules
■ Skin cysts (cystic acne) – may arise from pustules after they rupture; scarring of the skin is also common

Causes

Acne results from a combination of factors. Overactive sebaceous glands produce large amounts of sebum, which is unable to escape and becomes infected by bacteria. Fatty acids are broken down in the glands, leading to inflammation. Sebaceous activity is dependent on androgen (male-type) hormones and the balance of these is found to be disturbed in 50–60 per cent of female acne patients.

Cosmetics, skin preparations and shampoos can all cause acne, especially in young women. Acne is a side effect of treatment with certain drugs, such as bromides, steroids, androgenic hormones, oral contraceptives and barbiturates.

Very rarely, neonatal acne occurs in infants, because of maternal hormone imbalance.

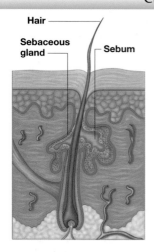

Normal hair follicles contain sebaceous glands. The glands release lubricating sebum into the follicle, or sometimes into a pore on the surface of the skin.

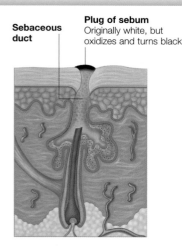

Sebum can accumulate and block the duct, forming a whitehead on the skin. Contact with air causes this to harden and darken into a blackhead.

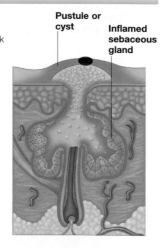

Beneath the blackhead, sebum continues to collect, forming a pustule or cyst on the skin. The gland is infected by bacteria and becomes further inflamed.

Diagnosis and incidence

Acne is rarely misdiagnosed, as the signs easily recognized owing to the characteristic lesions. The patient is usually aware of their condition before visiting the doctor.

Acne vulgaris typically appears at puberty, normally a year or two earlier in girls than in boys. At the age of 16, some degree of acne affects 95 per cent of boys and 83 per cent of girls. Peak incidence is 14–17 in girls and 16–19 in boys.

Although the condition is not infectious and cannot be transmitted, the bacterium *Propionibacterium acnes* is often present in the sebaceous glands. Staphylococcus bacteria are also believed to contribute towards the inflammatory effect of acne.

A close-up photograph shows papules, pustules, inflamed skin and the scars of earlier acne lesions. Developing white- and blackheads are also present.

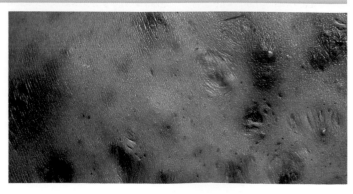

Treatment

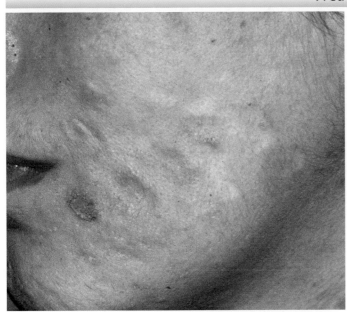

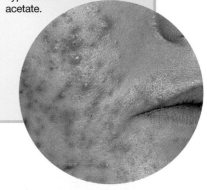

Medication

The severity of the acne dictates the most suitable treatment:

- **Mild acne:** topical (directly applied) therapy
- **Moderate acne:** oral and topical therapy
- **Severe acne:** oral isotretinoin

- **Topical therapy:** includes benzoyl peroxide, antibiotic creams or lotions containing tetracycline, erythromycin and clindamycin, azaleic acid, retinoids such as isotretinion, adapalene (anti-inflammatory)
- **Oral (systemic) therapy:** antibiotics such as tetracycline, doxycycline, minocycline, erythromycin, clindamycin and trimethoprim

- **Oral contraceptives** containing oestrogen (which works against male hormones) can be effective in female sufferers unresponsive to antibiotics. Alternatively, hormonal treatments may be given alongside topical drugs. These are usually anti-androgens which suppress sebum production, such as cyproterone acetate.

Many patients, especially, adolescents, are quite distressed by the disfiguring appearance of acne. In mild cases, the lesions persist for four to six years but severe cases may last in excess of 12 years.

Oral antibiotics and topical preparations (applied to the skin) are usually effective against acne. If not, isotretinoin is very successful, although it is an

Excoriated acne results from scratching the lesions, further damaging the surrounding skin.

expensive treatment and may be teratogenic (causing defects in the unborn fetus). It is therefore essential to counsel the patient before commencing therapy, and for women to take contraceptive measures when this treatment is prescribed. It is also necessary to

monitor blood, urine and liver function tests during this therapy.

Isotretinoin is effective against severe acne because it reduces sebum production and acts against bacteria within the pores. By peeling away the very top layers of skin, it helps to prevent excessive scarring. Usually this treatment will last for 16–20 weeks.

The GP or dermatologist will recommend the best course of treatment when a patient with acne requires medication. The side effects of certain drugs on an individual may necessitate a reduced dose or an alternative.

Prognosis and prevention

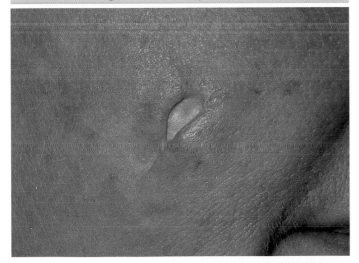

Although it is mainly an adolescent condition, acne can occur at any age, depending on the causative factors. However, the prognosis tends to be very good, as the majority of sufferers respond well to drug therapy, which helps markedly in lessening the unpleasant features, such as subsequent formation of scars. In the most severe cases, the patient may require psychological counselling.

Acne is not preventable and the vast majority of people will

In severe acne, lesions can take the form of sebum-filled cysts in the skin. These can rupture and leave an obvious scar.

suffer to a degree during their teenage years. However, only a small proportion will have anything more than a mild or moderate form of the condition.

Certain measures may lessen some of the effects of acne. Good hygiene and a healthy diet are both factors that can help to control the unpleasant appearance of the condition.

Further treatment

- **Acne surgery:** such as removal of comedones and needling abscesses. Dermabrasion (skin layer removal) is rarely used nowadays.
- **Corticosteroid injections:** triamcinolone hexacetonide injected directly into a lesion is sometimes prescribed.
- **Cryosurgery** (using extreme cold to remove unwanted tissues): occasionally used to remove skin blemishes.
- **Ultraviolet light:** direct sunlight is believed to be beneficial but sun lamps will only result in peeling of the epidermis.

- **X-ray therapy:** rarely used now as it may cause skin cancer in the long term.
- **Diet:** it is thought by some that certain foods may aggravate acne, such as chocolate, dairy products and nuts. Avoiding these may help.
- **Hygiene:** experts recommend washing with soap and water at least twice a day. Although acne develops beneath the skin, washing helps prevent the lesions from becoming infected.

Acne is not caused by dirt, but regular cleansing of the skin will help to minimize its effects and reduce infection.

Dermatitis and eczema

Symptoms

Dermatitis and eczema are common inflammatory skin conditions. They may be acute when the onset of a reddish rash is rapid and accompanied by blistering, swelling and weeping.

Chronic dermatitis refers to a long-standing irritable area, which may be:
■ Darker than surrounding skin
■ Thickened, dry and scaly, with evidence of scratch marks
■ Cracked.

Itching is a major symptom of all forms of dermatitis and eczema. In response to itching, people often scratch themselves, introducing infection into the deeper skin, which then causes further damage.

This patient with severe eczema on the hand has typical signs: the skin has become inflamed, scaly and cracked.

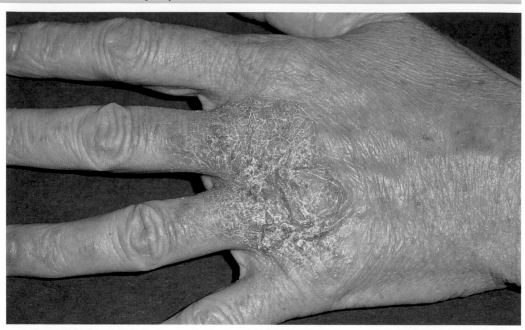

Diagnosis

A diagnosis of dermatitis or eczema is normally made by the characteristics of the inflammation. There are several different types of manifestation:

■ **Atopic eczema**
This is commonest in infants and young toddlers but often clears up over time. There is often an inherited family history of allergic disorders, such as eczema, hay fever or asthma.

■ **Nummular eczema**
These are circular patches in adults, which appear scaly and itch intensely. They can be confused with ringworm.

■ **Hand eczema**
In many cases the palms of the hand are involved and the condition is itchy. The soles of the feet may also be involved due to a reaction to shoe dyes or the shoe lining.

■ **Contact dermatitis**
This can occur anywhere on the body. The skin becomes irritated and inflamed as a result of

contact with some irritant or allergen, such as cosmetics, nickel in jewellery, brassiere straps or washing powder.

■ **Seborrhoeic dermatitis**
Some parts of the skin (the scalp, face, back and chest) are greasy as they contain a lot of sebaceous oil. A red, scaly, itchy rash can occur in these areas. Dandruff is associated with this type of eczema. It affects babies under three months of age and adults between 30 and 60.

■ **Varicose eczema**
People who have varicose veins have a less efficient system for returning venous blood in the legs to the heart. The skin on the legs becomes reddened, itchy and easily damaged. There may be associated oedema (fluid) in the ankles and legs.

PATCH TESTING
Patch testing may be helpful if contact dermatitis is suspected. The process takes five days. The

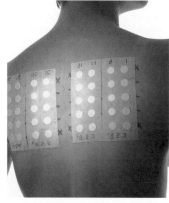

Patch testing involves a small amount of an allergen, such as pet hair, being stuck onto the skin. Sensitivity is denoted if the skin is inflamed around a patch.

standard European test contains 30 common allergens, which are applied to the back. However, it is not helpful in children with atopic eczema.
The patient returns two days later to have the patch test removed and a first reading carried out. The final reading is taken two days after that.

Allergy testing is not helpful in children with atopic eczema. Elimination of certain foods from the diet may be helpful.

Atopic eczema is usually associated with other allergic reactions, and a tendency to suffer from the condition may be inherited.

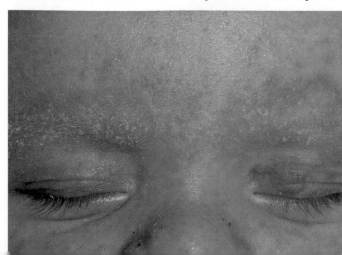

Incidence

Dermatitis and eczema affect about one in every five children and one in every 10 adults.

DEFINING TERMS
Although dermatitis is, in fact, a form of eczema, the two terms are used by doctors to distinguish between different causes:

■ Dermatitis should be used medically to describe the reaction following external contact irritation, such as in allergic or industrial dermatitis. Industrial dermatitis was first described in 1895 when contact with mercury was the cause. Before 1982 the DHSS kept statistics which showed that occupational dermatitis was the most common industrial disease, accounting for over 50 per cent of working days lost.

■ Eczema should be used to describe a case when there is no obvious cause but there may be an allergy to something ingested. Atopic eczema runs in families and is associated with other allergic disorders, such as hay fever and asthma.

WHO IS AFFECTED?
Allergies are common and appear to be increasing. About 15–20 per cent of children of school age may have atopic eczema, but three out of four cases will resolve over time.

Causes

About 80 per cent of contact dermatitis is caused by irritants and 20 per cent by allergens.

Important irritants include:
- Water
- Detergents
- Solvents
- Harsh chemicals
- Friction.

Common allergens include:
- Nickel, chrome and mercury
- Perfumes, rubber and some plants
- Some medications have also been implicated.

Dry skin and skin injuries contribute to dermatitis as does stress and infection.

DIET
Some, but not all, children improve if they are put onto a diet free from dairy products. These substances can be eliminated from the diet to see what happens and then be reintroduced as a challenge.

However, any changes to a child's diet should only be undertaken following advice from a qualified dietitian.

Contact dermatitis is an allergic reaction triggered by particular compounds. In this case, the skin on the abdomen has reacted to a nickel belt buckle.

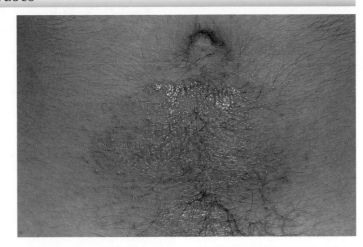

Treatment

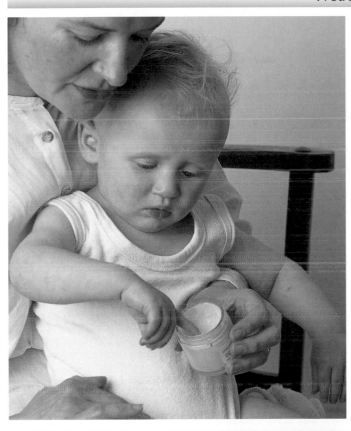

People with dermatitis and eczema are advised to protect their skin, using topical creams and lotions as appropriate.

Skin disorders can have a huge psychological impact upon sufferers and doctors should provide reassurance and explanations of treatment.

PROTECTING THE SKIN
There are several measures which help protect the skin:
- Use of soap substitutes and lukewarm water are preferable
- Clothing should be soft, smooth and cool; wool is best avoided
- The skin should be protected from dust, water, solvents and injury
- Emollients which moisturize the skin and special bath oils should be used liberally, especially when the skin is itchy
- A mild topical steroid can be bought over the counter to treat mild eczema
- Creams are best for weeping eczema, and ointments for dry, scaly eczema.

OTHER MEASURES
If the problem does not settle, a family doctor may recommend:
- Topical steroids
- Topical antibiotic if there is secondary infection
- Antihistamine at night to prevent scratching and promote sleep
- Dietary intervention.

When the problem is severe, a potent topical steroid may be needed along with occlusive bandages and oral antibiotics. Oral steroids and phototherapy (using ultraviolet light) may be used, but only under the guidance of a qualified dermatologist.

FURTHER MEASURES
Referral to a specialist may be needed if the eczema is resistant to conventional treatments in order to exclude alternative diagnoses, such as fungal infection or scabies.

A specialist will also be required if there is severe secondary infection or for exclusion of allergic contact dermatitis by patch testing.

Prevention

As all cases of dermatitis are triggered by a particular substance, the only way to prevent the condition is to avoid it. Hairdressers and car mechanics are particularly at risk of dermatitis due to exposure to chemicals. People who are prone to dermatitis should avoid these occupations.

Frequent application of emollients can protect skin against irritant substances.

People whose work brings them into contact with irritant substances should take adequate protective measures.

Prognosis

The purpose of treatment is to control rather than cure the condition, to allow sufferers, and children especially, to lead a normal life. The condition often resolves spontaneously.

Skin cancer

Symptoms

Skin cancer is the most common cancer in the UK but most cases, if treated early, can be cured. It is important to seek medical advice if a skin abnormality persists for more than two weeks.

SKIN CHANGES
Changes to watch for are:
■ A spot, lump or scaly area that bleeds or becomes crusted
■ An ulcer that fails to heal
■ A mole that grows, becomes raised, crusted or itchy, starts to bleed, changes colour unevenly or loses its well-defined edge.

Common skin cancers include squamous cell and basal cell cancers and malignant melanomas, all of which originate in the epidermis.

Skin cancer can take a number of forms. Squamous cell carcinomas are scaley lesions that tend to develop in areas that are exposed to the sun.

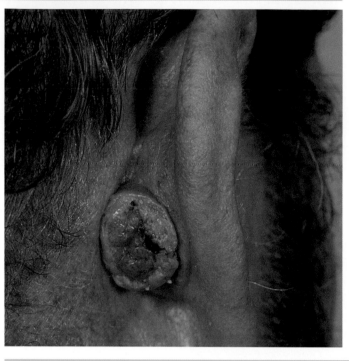

Incidence

Anyone can develop skin cancer, but fair-skinned people are most at risk. Basal cell cancer is the most common form, followed by squamous cell cancer. Malignant melanoma is becoming increasingly common.

In 1998 in Britain, there were 40,000 cases of skin cancer; 467 deaths occurred from squamous or basal cell cancers (sometimes known as non-melanoma skin cancers) and 1,640 deaths from melanomas.

In the US, it has been predicted that up to 50 per cent of Americans who live to the age of 65 years will develop skin cancer. Worldwide, the highest rates of skin cancer are found in South Africa and Australia, areas that have high levels of UV radiation.

The skin

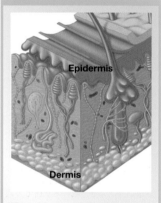

The skin consists of two layers: the epidermis and the dermis. Skin cancer occurs when epidermal cells undergo abnormal changes.

The skin is formed of two layers:
■ The epidermis – this is very thin and mostly consists of layers of squamous cells. The inner layers divide, rise to the surface and are eventually shed as scales. The deepest layer of the epidermis contains melanocytes, which produce melanin (a brown pigment) in response to sunlight
■ The dermis – this contains hair follicles, sweat glands, blood vessels and nerves, and is held together by collagen fibres.

Causes

Most skin cancers are caused by prolonged exposure of the skin to ultraviolet radiation (UVA and UVB) from the sun.

Statistics show that people who regularly use sunbeds are at an increased risk of skin cancer, as are those who are immunosuppressed.

TYPES OF SKIN CANCER
The three most common forms of skin cancer are:
■ Basal cell cancer – this develops from small round cells in the epidermis. It rarely occurs before middle age and is more common in men. Most basal cell cancers occur on the face, and usually start as a pearly spot that develops a characteristic rolled edge, while the centre disintegrates. Basal cell cancer grows slowly and rarely spreads to other parts of the body
■ Squamous cell cancer – this mainly occurs in areas of maximum sun exposure, but sometimes arises in an area previously damaged by sun. A few squamous cell cancers develop in patients previously exposed to arsenic or radiation or who have lupus vulgaris

Kaposi's sarcoma is a rare but serious skin cancer that often affects people with AIDS. The lesions are pinkish-brown and are often prolific.

(tuberculous infection of the skin) or burn scars. Squamous cell cancers are scaley at first, become crusted and may bleed. They grow faster than basal cell cancers, and may spread
■ Malignant melanomas – these are most common in men. People with a large number of moles or freckles are most at risk. One third of malignant melanomas develop from pre-existing moles, while the rest develop from previously normal skin.

Malignant moles itch, increase in diameter, develop an irregular edge and become red and inflamed. The primary growth may remain quite small, but large secondary tumours may develop elsewhere.
■ Kaposi's sarcoma – once a rare condition, this form of skin cancer is seen increasingly in people with AIDS and is associated with herpes infection. It appears as a pinkish-brown patch that develops on the skin.

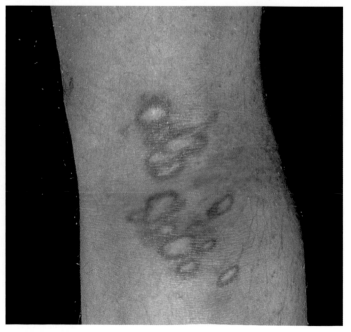

Diagnosis

The diagnosis of skin cancer is often made clinically (by physical examination of the patient). If a lesion appears suspicious, all or part of the abnormal area must be removed (biopsy) and examined under a microscope to confirm the diagnosis.

DETERMINING SPREAD
Other tests, such as X-rays and CT scans, determine whether or not the cancer has spread to other parts of the body (metastasized), except in the case of basal cell tumours, which rarely metastasize.

If an area of skin appears suspicious, a biopsy will need to be taken. This will be studied beneath a microscope for signs of abnormal cellular changes.

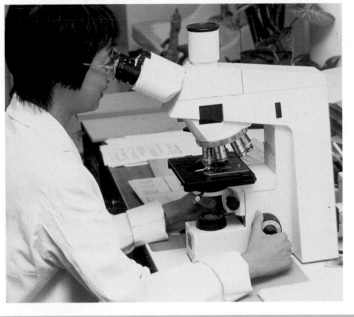

Prognosis

The outlook for individuals with skin cancer is usually good. Skin cancer causes less than one per cent of cancer deaths, and 85 per cent or more cases are cured.

The overall cure rate of basal cell and squamous cell carcinomas is directly related to the stage of the disease when treatment starts.

Malignant melanoma
In malignant melanoma, the prognosis depends on how deeply the tumour has penetrated the skin. If it has penetrated 0.76 mm (0.029 in), 80 per cent of patients survive for five years, but if it has penetrated more than 3.5 mm (⅛ in), only 40 per cent survive this long.

Treatment

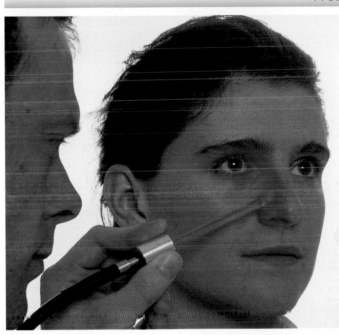

Treatment of skin cancer may involve the following therapies:
■ Surgery
■ Electrodessication– drying the tissue with a high-frequency electric current
■ Curettage – scooping out the cancer with a spoon-like instrument
■ Freezing with liquid nitrogen (cryosurgery)
■ Laser therapy
■ Radiotherapy or chemotherapy
■ Creams or lotions containing anticancer drugs
■ Photodynamic therapy – using a specialized lamp to kill cancer cells.

In photodynamic therapy, cream is applied to the lesion and is taken up by the cancer cells. A special lamp activates the drug in the cream and kills the cells.

NEW TREATMENTS
New treatments include the use of interferon (a substance produced by cells) and retinoids (drugs derived from vitamin A). The use of the drug tamoxifen is also being investigated in the treatment of malignant melanoma.

MICROGRAPHIC SURGERY
Mohs' micrographic surgery is a specialized technique sometimes used to treat squamous and basal cell cancers.

Under a local anaesthetic, the cancer is gradually shaved off and each layer is examined microscopically until all the cancer cells are removed. This treatment can be very successful at preventing recurrences.

If a large cancer is removed, skin grafting may be necessary to aid healing and reduce scars.

Prevention

There are a number of measures that can be taken to prevent skin cancer:
■ Use a strong suncream with a sun protection factor (SPF) of 15 or more
■ Stay out of the sun when it is at its strongest
■ Wear long-sleeved shirts and full-length trousers of tightly-woven cloth
■ Wear a wide-brimmed hat that covers the ears.

Skin cancer can be prevented by minimizing exposure of the skin to solar radiation. Sun creams and hats both provide protection from the sun.

Melanoma

Symptoms

Melanoma, or malignant melanoma, is a rare type of skin cancer. It can spread rapidly and become fatal if not treated promptly.

MELANOCYTES

Malignant melanoma is caused by an abnormal proliferation of melanocytes – specialized cells which produce a dark pigment called melanin, designed to protect the skin from the effects of ultraviolet irradiation.

Small clusters of melanocytes are simply 'moles', which appear in childhood and adolescence. Malignant melanoma may develop within an existing mole or in normal skin. A doctor should be consulted if a mole:
■ Changes in size
■ Develops an irregular edge
■ Changes in pigmentation
■ Oozes, bleeds or itches.

OTHER SITES

Less commonly, melanomas may also appear in the eye, either in the iris (the coloured part of the eye) or the choroid (lining of the eyeball).

Melanomas may also appear under the nailbed, in the nose or in the superficial lining of internal organs such as the oesophagus. Symptoms will be related to the organ involved, and include difficulty in swallowing, nose bleeds, or disturbances of vision.

FOUR TYPES

The four main types of malignant melanoma can be categorized as follows:

■ Superficial spreading: this accounts for about 70 per cent of the total. These melanomas occur particularly on the back in men and the legs in women. The cancer cells invade the deeper layers of the skin, but usually spread horizontally first. Early recognition allows prompt excision of the melanoma, hopefully before vertical spread has occurred, giving a better chance of cure
■ Nodular: this appears as a nodule on the skin which can bleed and is often seen on the chest and back. Spread occurs only vertically and there is a very high potential for spread to other organs (metastasis)
■ Acral: these appear on the palms, soles and near or under the nail, where they may appear as discoloration
■ Lentigo maligna: these flat, dark-brown spots often appear on the faces of sun-damaged elderly people. They may spread after many years in a dormant condition.

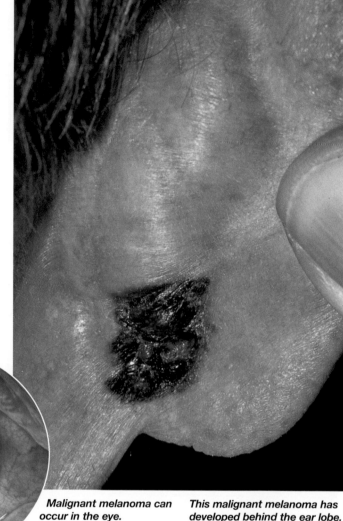

Malignant melanoma can occur in the eye. Symptoms of this rarer form of melanoma include disturbances of vision.

This malignant melanoma has developed behind the ear lobe. Melanomas may cause itching and the fragile surface may bleed or ooze, and crust over.

Causes

Malignant melanoma is caused by exposure to ultraviolet rays, emitted by:
■ Sunlight – over-exposure to the ultraviolet rays from the sun damages the skin and predisposes people to melanoma. Episodic sunburn is more likely to induce melanoma than chronic sun exposure
■ Sun-beds – like the sun, sun-beds also give off ultraviolet rays and may cause damage to the skin.

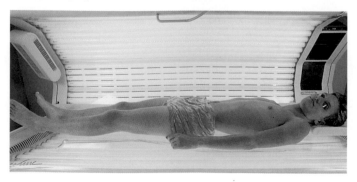

RISK FACTORS

Known risk factors for malignant melanoma include:
■ Light skin type – fair-skinned people are at highest risk of developing melanoma
■ Sunburn sustained in childhood – children who are over-exposed to the sun are at risk of developing melanoma later in life
■ High number of moles – people with a lot of moles (more than 100) seem to be at higher risk of developing melanoma.

The ultraviolet radiation emitted from sunbeds is believed to be harmful to the skin. Excessive sunbed use should therefore be avoided.

Incidence

In recent years, there has been a dramatic increase in the number of cases of skin cancer. There are now over 40,000 new cases every year in the UK, making it the second commonest form of cancer.

The two most common skin cancers are squamous cell carcinoma and basal cell carcinoma. Malignant melanoma accounts for the remaining 10 per cent of cases.

Malignant melanoma affects people of all ages, although it is most prevalent in those aged 40–60 and is more common in women. About 10 per cent of patients seem to have a family member who has been previously affected.

Diagnosis

Diagnosis of malignant melanoma may be confirmed by an excision biopsy. This involves the removal under local anaesthetic of any suspicious-looking mole and some surrounding normal skin and examining them under the microscope. A second (wider) excision may sometimes be required and, if a large area of skin is removed, a skin graft may be necessary.

CANCER SPREAD

There are a number of ways to ascertain whether the cancer has spread to other parts of the body. These include:
■ Examining lymph nodes – lymph nodes are the first site of cancer spread. If lumps (often in the armpit or groin) are felt,

they can be removed surgically.
A sample of six to 10 nodes may be removed, each one being examined under the microscope for evidence of spread. If any lymph nodes removed contain cancer cells, then node clearance is performed (surgery to remove all the lymph nodes in that area). The more nodes containing cancer, the higher the chances of spread elsewhere in the body
■ Performing chest X-rays, bone scans and CT scans to assess cancer spread to other organs.

This micrograph shows excess melanin (shown dark red) arising from a malignant melanoma. This melanoma has spread to a nearby lymph node.

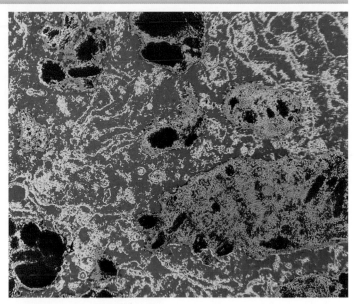

Treatment

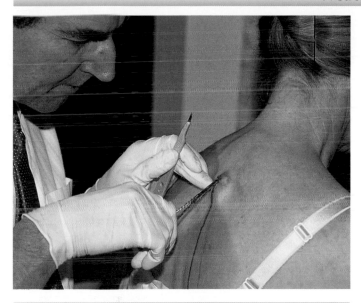

If, once the melanoma and any enlarged lymph nodes have been removed, no evidence of spread is found, no other treatment is required.

If the melanoma has spread beyond the lymph nodes to distant organs such as the lungs or liver, the cancer is incurable. Chemotherapy can be used, but does not offer a cure.

SELF-HELP MEASURES

Self-examination of lymph node areas and regular follow-up as an out-patient is recommended,

Malignant melanomas are usually removed under local anaesthetic. A wide area of skin may be excised to ensure the removal of all malignant cells.

as any further enlarged lymph nodes can potentially be removed surgically. It is still very important for the patient to continue to protect the skin from the sun.

NEW THERAPIES

Medical trials are currently taking place in the following areas:
■ Vaccine therapy – vaccines are being developed by altering melanoma cells so that they can be injected into the body to enhance its immune response against cancer cells
■ Immunotherapy – this involves the use of substances naturally occurring in the body's immune system, such as interferon.

Prevention

As malignant melanoma is thought to be caused by the damaging effects of ultraviolet rays, the most effective way of preventing melanoma is to reduce exposure to ultraviolet radiation. This involves:

■ Reducing the time spent in the sun, especially in the case of fair-skinned people. Ozone layer depletion allows increased ultraviolet radiation to penetrate the earth's atmosphere and so suncreams should be used when outdoors in the summer
■ Ensuring that children are not over-exposed to sunlight
■ Reducing exposure to the ultraviolet rays emitted by sun-beds
■ Seeking medical advice in the event of any changes in the condition of moles on the body, such as itching or bleeding.

Children in particular should be protected from the sun's rays. Sunburn as a child increases the chance of developing a melanoma later in life.

Prognosis

The most important prognostic factor in melanoma is the thickness of the tumour (the degree of invasion downwards through the different layers of skin).

This method, now referred to as Breslow's thickness, was established in 1970 by A. Breslow, an American pathologist.

It states that, if the tumour is less than 1.5 mm (0.05 in) thick, 90 per cent of patients will still be alive after five years (the five-year survival rate).

If the tumour is 1.5–3.5 mm (0.05–0.15 in) thick, this rate is reduced to 70 per cent.

A tumour any thicker than 3.5 mm (0.15 in) results in a five-year survival rate of only 40 per cent.

Alopecia

Symptoms

Alopecia is the medical term for baldness or hair loss. Alopecia may be classified as:
■ Primary – when the fault lies in the hair itself or its mechanism of production
■ Secondary – when disease destroys the hair follicles; this may also be associated with scarring of the skin.

Alopecia may also be defined in terms of the area affected:
■ Diffuse – when the hair loss is generalized, either over the whole scalp or even the whole body
■ Patchy – when only specific areas are involved, such as following trauma or infection.

Alopecia may be further classified as scarring and non-scarring, depending on whether the underlying skin is affected, or the hair follicles only.

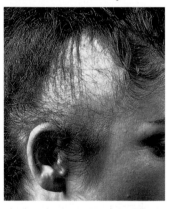

ALOPECIA AREATA
Alopecia areata is a condition of unknown cause with a sudden onset of either diffuse or patchy hair loss. Hairy skin anywhere on the body can be affected. Characteristically, the condition involves round or oval patches of hair loss.

Traction alopecia is often caused by tight hairstyles which break the hairs or pull them out of the follicles in the scalp.

Hair growth

Hair growth can be divided into stages. At any one time, 80 per cent of scalp hair is in anagen – the growing phase – and 20 per cent is in catagen – the resting phase. During the latter phase, hair is shed (telogen) and new hair grows from the same follicles due to cellular activity in those follicles.

Normally, hair replacement is distributed evenly over the scalp, but in alopecia areata, all the hair in one area is shed at the same time. This results in a bald patch.

This micrograph of a hair root in the scalp shows the tubular follicle, which consists of five layers of epithelial cells.

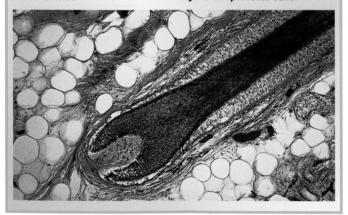

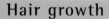

Generalized (diffuse) alopecia may have no discernible cause, in which case it is referred to as idiopathic diffuse hair loss.

There may be 'exclamation mark' hairs seen in the bald patches. These are short, broken hairs about 5 mm long. The underlying skin of the scalp may be erythematous (flushed) but there are no signs of scaling or scarring. The condition may also affect the eyebrows and the beard area of the face in men. Rarely, the baldness spreads to become alopecia totalis, when all scalp hair is lost; or alopecia universalis, when all body hair is lost as well.

Although alarming, in most cases of alopecia areata the hair loss usually slows and hair growth returns to normal, but sometimes the hair loss is recurrent. Alopecia areata is sometimes associated with nail dystrophy (pitting and ridging of the nail surfaces); this can occur in more severe cases.

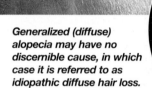

Alopecia areata may occur at any age and in either sex. It is possible that the condition is associated with shock or stress.

SCALP DISORDERS
Certain skin disorders, such as lichen planus (an itchy skin disease of unknown cause), scleroderma and discoid lupus erythematosus, may affect the scalp and produce what is known as scarring alopecia. In these cases, the skin of the scalp may feel tight, with thickening or flaking.

Alopecia areata often gives rise to regular round or oval bald patches. Hair loss can be sudden, and the cause may be unknown.

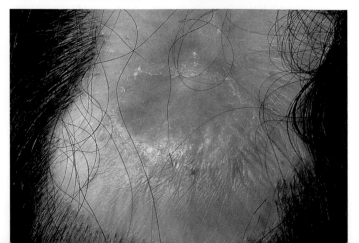

Causes and diagnosis

CAUSES OF DIFFUSE HAIR LOSS

There are many possible reasons for hair loss. These include:

■ Male pattern baldness – this is a normal inherited process; hair loss usually begins over the temples. Some women are affected by constitutional female alopecia
■ Endocrine disorders – such as thyroid disease, diabetes mellitus or hypopituitarism
■ Telogen effluvium – this is a condition in which hair follicles all enter the telogen (shedding) stage at the same time; it commonly occurs following pregnancy, or sometimes after severe illness or a major operation, or even as a result of stress
■ Drug-induced – as a side effect of cytotoxics used for cancer chemotherapy, anticoagulants or antithyroid drugs
■ Erythrodermic – as a result of certain skin conditions, such as psoriasis and eczema
■ Nutritional – such as iron or protein deficiency
■ Alopecia areata.

CAUSES OF PATCHY HAIR LOSS

The causes of patchy hair loss include:

■ Alopecia areata
■ Trauma – this may include trichotillomania, when the

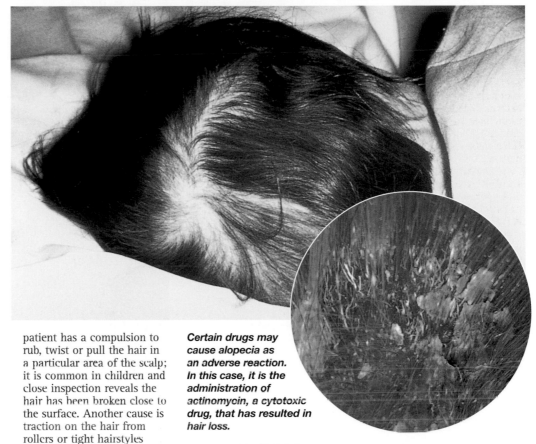

patient has a compulsion to rub, twist or pull the hair in a particular area of the scalp; it is common in children and close inspection reveals the hair has been broken close to the surface. Another cause is traction on the hair from rollers or tight hairstyles
■ Scarring alopecia can arise from physical trauma, such as burns or skin disease
■ Severe infection – bacterial, viral or fungal – can cause hair loss.

Certain drugs may cause alopecia as an adverse reaction. In this case, it is the administration of actinomycin, a cytotoxic drug, that has resulted in hair loss.

DIAGNOSIS

Diagnosis is usually evident on examination. Occasionally, microscopic examination of the hair or a skin biopsy may be necessary to determine the cause.

The presence of ringworm on the scalp may be revealed by a fluorescence photograph. The use of ultraviolet light can identify this fungal infection easily.

Treatment

There is no treatment for male pattern (androgenic) baldness. Minoxidil (Regaine) applied topically to the scalp may reduce the hair loss, but it is not a cure. Alopecia areata may respond to steroid tablets, but this is not advised as the hair may fall out again when the steroids are stopped.

Treatment must be directed towards the cause when it is known. Scarring alopecia is

usually associated with a concurrent skin disease, whereas in non-scarring alopecia the process affects the hair follicle. Advice to women regarding the avoidance of traction alopecia includes avoiding tight hair rollers and certain hairstyles.

When alopecia has arisen secondary to thyroid disorder or iron deficiency, correction of the disorder will usually bring

If alopecia is irreversible, one possible treatment is hair transplantation. Healthy hairs are taken from another part of the scalp and surgically implanted.

about a resolution. Endocrine disorders can be corrected with appropriate therapy, such as in thyroid disease, hypopituarism and diabetes mellitus.

Patchy hair loss may respond to intra-lesional corticosteroids by injections (which may stimulate hair follicles) or by dermo-jet, which is painless. Wigs are useful, especially in women with diffuse hair loss and in those with a total hair loss due to chemotherapy. After this therapy, the hair usually grows back. However, some forms of scarring alopecia may require plastic surgery, especially if only small areas are involved.

Other diffuse non-scarring alopecias will respond to appropriate therapy. Hair loss is usually reversible in eczema and psoriasis.

Prognosis

Alopecia will usually resolve as the underlying condition is treated. Many cases resolve spontaneously, but persistent alopecia areata does not have a good prognosis for hair regrowth.

In cases of telogen effluvium, there is no specific treatment, and the pattern of hair growth usually re-establishes after several months. However, male pattern baldness cannot be stopped or reversed.

Psoriasis

Symptoms

Psoriasis is a common, chronic, non-contagious skin disease which results in scaly, itchy patches (plaques) forming on the skin. The areas of the body that are particularly affected are the elbows, knees and scalp.

COMMON PSORIASIS
The more common types of psoriasis include:

■ **Plaque psoriasis**
This is the commonest form of psoriasis, also known as psoriasis vulgaris. The plaques are raised, red and scaly and there is a sharp demarcation line between the plaques and normal skin. They are often found on the extensor surfaces where straightening occurs at the knees and elbows. If the lesions are gently scraped the surface becomes whiter and more scaly.

■ **Guttate psoriasis**
This form of psoriasis is often seen in children and young adults. A sudden outbreak of small, red, scaly papules may appear on the trunk and back. Two thirds of these patients have had a recent bacterial throat infection.

■ **Seborrhoeic psoriasis**
Red, scaly lesions affect the scalp, shoulders, armpits, groin, face and skin behind the ears.

■ **Nail psoriasis**
Over 50 per cent of patients show abnormal nail changes, characteristically pitting ridges, and a separation of the nail plate from the nail base.

RARE PSORIASIS
The rarer forms of psoriasis include:

■ **Pustular psoriasis**
This form of psoriasis is often severe. Small blisters filled with non-infective pus develop on the hands or feet.

■ **Inverse psoriasis**
This mostly affects elderly people. Large, red areas appear in folds of the skin, affecting the groin and the skin under breasts and armpits.

■ **Erythrodermic psoriasis**
The whole body is affected, the entire skin surface being red and scaly. It can be triggered by drugs or withdrawal of steroids.

Psoriasis is characterized by red patches, or plaques, covered with a scaly, flaky surface. Skin on any part of the body may become red and inflamed.

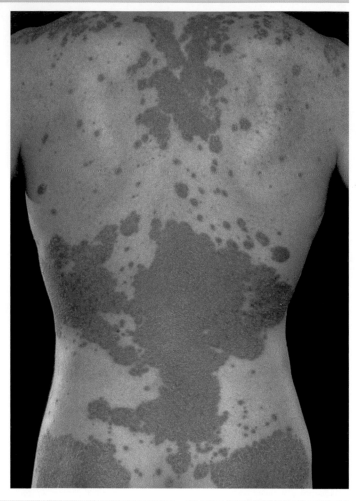

Causes

Psoriasis is caused by new skin cells being produced faster than dead skin cells are lost, resulting in excess thickened skin.

CAUSAL FACTORS
A number of factors are responsible for psoriasis:
■ Genetic predisposition – about

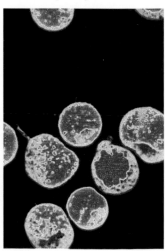

two thirds of cases are inherited
■ Autoimmune disorder – psoriasis may due to an abnormal immune reaction. Following exposure to a virus or bacterium, a sub-group of white blood cells (T cells) which normally protect the body from infection become activated against skin proteins. This leads to inflammation and excess skin cell multiplication.

AGGRAVATING FACTORS
Symptoms may be triggered by:
■ Trauma – including lacerations, insect bites, burns

These blood cells, known as T cells (orange), normally help the body fight infection. In psoriasis, T cells mistakenly attack skin protein, causing inflammation.

In someone who has psoriasis, skin injuries, such as cuts or burns, can trigger a flare-up in that area. Knees and elbows are prone to such injuries.

■ Medications – including drugs for hypertension, antimalarials, antidepressants
■ Viral and bacterial infections
■ Excess alcohol
■ Obesity
■ Stress
■ Cold climate
■ Sunburn or lack of sunlight.

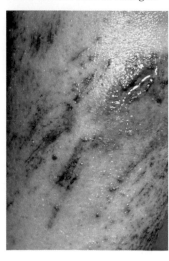

Diagnosis

Psoriasis is diagnosed by clinical examination of the skin. Diagnosis may be difficult as psoriasis can sometimes resemble other skin conditions.

The characteristic rash is dry and red with silvery scales. Scraping the surface of lesions produces white discoloration and more scaling.

DIAGNOSTIC TESTS
A skin biopsy (sample) may be taken for histological examination under a microscope. A blood test to look for the HLA antigen (protein) may be positive in psoriasis.

Incidence

Psoriasis affects about two per cent of the population. It occurs equally in men and women and usually develops between 15 and 35 years of age. The condition can affect any part of the body.

Treatment

All treatments for psoriasis aim to control symptoms rather than cure the disease. Treatment is determined by the type of psoriasis, its extent or severity, and the patient's medical history, age and sex.

TOPICAL TREATMENTS

Topical treatments, applied directly to the affected skin, can sometimes effectively clear psoriasis:
■ Corticosteroids – topical steroids are one of the most common therapies prescribed for mild or moderate psoriasis. There is a risk with potent steroids of skin thinning and the disease recurring, therefore long-term use should be avoided. Steroids should not be applied to the face
■ Topical vitamin D_3 analogue – calcipotriene ointment is used to treat mild to moderate psoriasis and is easy to apply
■ Coal tar – this can be messy but is very effective especially when applied in increasing concentrations in plaque psoriasis
■ Dithranol – applied as paste or cream in varying strengths
■ Bath solutions – help to descale the skin especially when followed by moisturizing medication
■ Coconut oils – can be rubbed into the scalp at night in association with a tar shampoo.

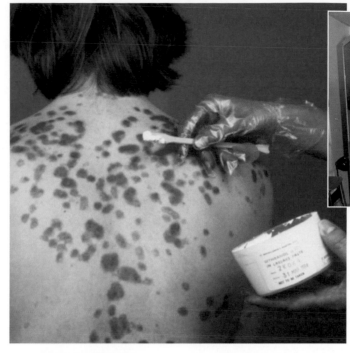

Phototherapy is an effective treatment for some forms of psoriasis. The patient receives UV light directly to the skin inside a special light box.

Plaque psoriasis is often treated using topical applications. Dithranol paste is messy and time-consuming to apply but often has excellent results.

PHOTOTHERAPY

Exposure to ultraviolet light may be recommended when psoriasis is resistant to other therapies. The options include:
■ UVB – ultraviolet light is administered using a light box. At least three treatments a week for several months are required
■ PUVA – this treatment is for people with severe or extensive psoriasis, and combines taking psoralen, a light-sensitive drug, with exposure to ultraviolet light using cabinets containing fluorescent tubes.

DRUG THERAPY

Severe psoriasis may require:
■ Oral retinoid drugs – which increase the rate at which the outer layers of skin are shed
■ Antibiotics – when an infection has triggered psoriasis
■ Cyclosporin – which is an immunosuppressant drug.

COUNSELLING

Embarrassment, frustration, fear and reduced self-esteem are common feelings among patients and may need to be addressed through counselling.

Doctors should explain the nature of the skin condition and what can be done to alleviate symptoms. It must be emphasized that psoriasis is not infectious.

Prognosis

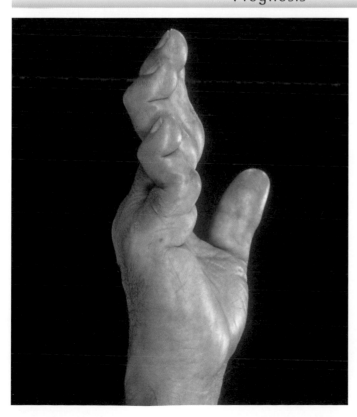

The course of chronic plaque psoriasis is variable. The condition may persist for several years with no apparent change, it may undergo spontaneous remission, or it may spread and become more extensive.

In the majority of patients with guttate psoriasis the condition resolves without specific treatment.

Some patients may develop a polyarthritis associated with their psoriasis (psoriatic arthropathy).

PSORIATIC ARTHRITIS

Psoriatic arthritis is an inflammatory joint condition which is associated with psoriasis but is considered to be a separate condition.

It affects between seven and 42 per cent of people with psoriasis, and of these 80 per cent have psoriatic nail changes.

In some patients with psoriasis, psoriatic arthritis may develop. This often affects the fingers, causing inflammation of joints.

Prevention

In view of the known effect of infection, stress and certain drugs it should be possible to minimize exacerbations by trying as far as is practicable to avoid these. Sore throats that are not obviously associated with colds may need to be treated with penicillin.

Index